COLONIAL SYSTEMS OF CONTROL
CRIMINAL JUSTICE IN NIGERIA

ALTERNATIVE PERSPECTIVES IN CRIMINOLOGY COLLECTION

Internationally, the search for solutions to social conflict has resulted in reconsideration of traditional approaches and the development of innovative harm reduction based analyses that extend beyond the narrow focus of conventional criminology. Contemporary alternative perspectives in criminology range from critical analyses of current punitive justice policies and practices to explorations of non-punitive approaches such as peacemaking, transformative justice, and penal abolition.

This collection welcomes a range of theoretical and practice-based contributions that challenge established notions of punitive justice: from pre-colonial approaches (e.g. Aboriginal Healing), ethnographic studies, and harm reduction models to radical critiques of contemporary models of social control.

The collection publishes works in both English and French.

Collection Editor
Robert Gaucher

COLONIAL SYSTEMS OF CONTROL
CRIMINAL JUSTICE IN NIGERIA

BY VIVIANE SALEH-HANNA

With contributions by
Chris Affor
Uju Agomoh
Biko Agozino
Clever Akporherhe
Sylvester Monday Anagaba
O. Oko Elechi
Osa Eribo
Mechthild Nagel
Igho Odibo
Julia Sudbury
Chukwuma Ume

UNIVERSITY OF OTTAWA PRESS
OTTAWA

© University of Ottawa Press 2008

All rights reserved. No parts of this publication may be reproduced, stored in a retrieval system or transmitted in any form or by any means, electronic or mechanical, including photocopy, recording, or otherwise, without permission in writing from the publisher.

LIBRARY AND ARCHIVES CANADA
CATALOGUING IN PUBLICATION

Colonial systems of control : criminal justice in Nigeria /
by Viviane Saleh-Hanna ; with contributions by Chris Affor ... [et al.].

Includes bibliographical references and index.
ISBN 978-0-7766-0666-8

1. Criminal justice, Administration of--Nigeria. 2. Imprisonment--Nigeria. 3. Prisoners--Civil rights--Nigeria. 4. Prisoners--Nigeria--Biography. 5. Alternatives to imprisonment--Nigeria. 6. Imperialism.
I. Saleh-Hanna, Viviane, 1976- II. Affor, Chris

KTA3800.C65 2008   365.9669   C2008-901473-1

Published by the University of Ottawa Press, 2008
542 King Edward Avenue
Ottawa, Ontario K1N 6N5
www.uopress.uottawa.ca

The University of Ottawa Press acknowledges with gratitude the support extended to its publishing list by Heritage Canada through its Book Publishing Industry Development Program, by the Canada Council for the Arts, by the Social Sciences and Humanities Research Council, and by the University of Ottawa.

In Loving Memory of

Sylvester Monday Anagaba – a.k.a. Motivating Monday -

and the many others who perish behind the violent walls of colonial prisons around the globe

CONTENTS

Acknowledgements xvii

Foreword
Julia Sudbury xxi

Chapter 1: Introduction: Colonial Systems of Control
Viviane Saleh-Hanna 1

SECTION I: CONTEXTUALIZING NIGERIA

Chapter 2: Penal Coloniality
Viviane Saleh-Hanna 17

Chapter 3: An Evolution of the Penal System:
***Criminal* Justice in Nigeria**
Viviane Saleh-Hanna and Chukwuma Ume 55

Chapter 4: The Militarization of Nigerian Society
Biko Agozino and Unyierie Idem 69

SECTION II: NIGERIAN PRISONS: VOICES FROM INSIDE

Chapter 5: Another Face of Slavery
Osadolor Eribo 121

Chapter 6: My Nigerian Prison Experience
Clever Akporherhe 127

Chapter 7: My Story
Chris Affor 131

Chapter 8: A Tribute to Solidarity: My Oasis
Chris Affor 141

Chapter 9: June 14, 2003
Igho Odibo 147

Chapter 10: The System I Have Come to Know
Sylvester Monday Anagaba 149

Chapter 11: Man's Inhumanity to Man
Sylvester Monday Anagaba 153

Chapter 12: Patriotism: Illusion or Reality?
Osadolor Eribo 157

SECTION III: COLONIAL SYSTEMS OF IMPRISONMENT: GENDER, POVERTY AND MENTAL HEALTH IN PRISON

Chapter 13: Nigerian Penal Interactions
Viviane Saleh-Hanna 173

Chapter 14: Women's Rights behind Walls
Mechthild Nagel 223

Chapter 15: Nigerian Women in Prison: Hostages in Law
Biko Agozino 245

Chapter 16: Protecting the Human Rights of People with Mental Health Disabilities in African Prisons
Uju Agomoh 267

SECTION IV: RESISTANCE

Chapter 17: Women, Law, and Resistance in Northern Nigeria: Understanding the Inadequacies of Western Scholarship
Viviane Saleh-Hanna 293

Chapter 18: Fela Kuti's Wahala Music: Political Resistance through Song
Viviane Saleh-Hanna 355

SECTION V: STEPPING BEYOND THE COLONIAL PENAL BOX: AFRICAN JUSTICE MODELS AND PENAL ABOLITIONISM

Chapter 19: Alternatives to Imprisonment: Community Service Orders in Africa
Chukwuma Ume 379

Chapter 20: The Igbo Indigenous Justice System
O. Oko Elechi 395

Chapter 21: Penal Abolitionist Theories and Ideologies
Viviane Saleh-Hanna 417

Chapter 22: The Tenth International Conference on Penal Abolition (ICOPA X)
Viviane Saleh-Hanna 457

Index 489

CONTRIBUTORS

Chris Affor wrote "My Story" and "A Tribute to Solidarity: My Oasis" while serving time in Kirikiri maximum security prison in Lagos State, Nigeria. He was a member of the PRAWA programme, which works to build solidarity among prisoners. Chris continues to serve time on awaiting-trial holding charges.

Uju Agomoh has a PhD in criminology and prison studies (University of Ibadan, Nigeria), an MPhil degree in Criminology from the University of Cambridge, England, and an LLB from the University of London (Queen Mary and Westfi eld College). She is involved in monitoring human rights violations within African penal systems. Her work includes training, research, documentation, and provision of support services to prisoners, ex-prisoners, torture survivors, and their families. She has undertaken prison assessment visits in over 100 prisons in Nigeria, South Africa, The Gambia, and Rwanda. Her work has facilitated training over 5,000 prison guards in good prison practice and international human rights standards for the treatment of prisoners in Ghana and Nigeria. She is the founder and executive director of a human rights non-governmental organization, Prisoners Rehabilitation and Welfare Action (PRAWA), with headquarters in Lagos, Nigeria. She was appointed in July 2000 as a federal commissioner and member of the Governing Council of the National Human Rights Commission in Nigeria. She is the special rapporteur on police, prison, and other centres of detention for the Nigerian Human Rights Commission and a member of the Nigerian Presidential Committee on the Prerogative of Mercy.

Biko Agozino is a professor of sociology, Coordinator of the Criminology Unit and the Acting Head of Behavioral Sciences at The Univerisity of the West Indies, St. Augustine, Trinidad and Tobago. His teaching and research interests include crime and social order, research methods, theoretical criminology, race-class-gender articulation, sociology, social statistics, law and popular culture, and comparative justice systems. His books include *Black Women and the Criminal Justice System* (1997); *Theoretical and Methodological Issues in Migration Research* (edited, 2000); *Nigeria: Democratising a Militarised Civil Society* (coauthored, 2001); *Counter-Colonial Criminology* (2003); and *Pan African Issues in Crime and Justice* (coedited, 2004). He was educated at the University of Edinburgh (PhD), the University of Cambridge (MPhil), and the University of Calabar (BSc). He is the series editor for the Ashgate Publishers Interdisciplinary Research Series in Ethnic, Gender, and Class Relations and the editor-in-chief of the *African Journal of Criminology and Justice Studies*.

Clever Akporherhe wrote "My Nigerian Prison Experience" after being released from Kirikiri medium security prison. These experiences describe his time as a convicted prisoner. Since then Clever has been arrested by the Nigerian Police Force and is currently serving time in Kirikiri medium security prison on awaiting-trial holding charges. He has orally communicated that prison conditions experienced by awaiting-trial prisoners are far worse than those he experienced as a convicted prisoner.

Sylvester Monday Anagaba wrote "The System I Have Come to Know" and "Man's Inhumanity to Man" while serving time on awaiting-trial holding charges in Kirikiri maximum security prison in Lagos State, Nigeria. He passed away in 2004 in the maximum security prison hospital. Prisoners have confirmed that he was told before he died that he had earlier been diagnosed with AIDS. Prison officials failed to inform him of that diagnosis until shortly before his death. He was never provided with any medication.

O. Oko Elechi is an associate professor of criminology and criminal justice at the Prairie View A&M University. He received his PhD from Simon Fraser University in Burnaby, Canada. He also holds two degrees from the University of Oslo, Norway. His writings on restorative justice, community policing, and African indigenous justice systems have been extensively published in international journals, book chapters, and anthologies. He is also the author of *Doing Justice without the State: The Afikpo (Ehugbo) Nigeria Model* (2006).

Osa Eribo wrote "Another Face of Slavery" while imprisoned in Kirikiri maximum security prison in Lagos State, Nigeria. He was a soldier in the Nigerian army, and upon demanding proper medical attention after sustaining injuries during peacekeeping missions in Sierra Leone and Liberia. About two years later, he was taken to Egypt for a supposedly medical treatment which never materialized due to Algeria's Army corrupt practices. He was brought back to Nigeria, charged with "mutiny," and imprisoned. He has since been released from prison due to interest in his case by several human rights activists and lawyers. He wrote "Patriotism: Illusion or Reality?" after being released from Kirikiri maximum security prison. He has orally communicated the difficulties he faces as a person carrying the ex-prisoner stigma. In addition, he has experienced hardships through "unpleasant" interactions with Nigerian military personnel, who took offence to his criticisms, actions, and triumphs. Eribo managed to land safely in Italy and now resides in Canada, where he has been granted protection as a conventional refugee who has survived a series of abuses and persecutions between 1999 and 2004. He is currently enrolled as a student of Woodsworth College, University of Toronto. Based on his convictions and philosophical concepts of a better world, he is very much involved in grassroots organizing in Toronto around prisoners' rights, immigrants' rights, and anti-poverty campaigns. Among the groups he works with are Global Importune, No One Is Illegal (NOII), and Ontario Coalition against Poverty (OCAP).

Unyierie Idem holds an award-winning Ph.D. in Applied Linguistics from Edinburgh University, Scotland; an MA in French from the University of Calabar, Nigeria; and a First Class Honours MA in French from the University of Calabar, Nigeria.

Mechthild Nagel is a professor of philosophy at the State University of New York, College at Cortland, and a senior visiting fellow at the Institute for African Development at Cornell University. She is the author of *Masking the Abject: A Genealogy of Play* (2002), coeditor of *Race, Class, and Community Identity* (2000), and coeditor of *Prisons and Punishment: Reconsidering Global Penality* (2007). Nagel is the editor-in-chief of the online journal *Wagadu: A Journal of Transnational Women's and Gender Studies*. Her current research focuses on African prison intellectuals and African approaches to restorative justice.

Igho Odibo wrote "June 14, 2003," while serving time in Kirikiri maximum security prison in Lagos State, Nigeria. He has not been convicted of any offence. He is currently living with HIV/AIDS and continues to struggle for access to medication and due process.

Viviane Saleh-Hanna is an activist scholar and an assistant professor in the Department of Sociology, Anthropology, and Crime and Justice Studies at the University of Massachusetts in Dartmouth. She lived and worked in Lagos, Nigeria, from 2000 to 2002. While in West Africa, she worked with prisoners in the Kirikiri prisons and ex-prisoners in Lagos State. She is currently an editorial board member for the *Journal of Prisoners on Prisons* and the *African Journal of Criminology and Justice Studies*.

Her research interests include historical and contemporary abolitionist movements; black musicianship and survival through the war on blackness; the interrelationships between European institutions of slavery and contemporary mass incarceration; and the deconstruction of Eurosupremacist academic accounts of history and their resulting constructions of gender, sexuality, ethnicity, and identity.

Julia Sudbury is a professor of ethnic studies at Mills College, a liberal arts women's college in Oakland, California. From 2004 to 2006 she was the Canada Research Chair in Social Justice, Equity, and Diversity at the University of Toronto. Julia is the author of *Other Kinds of Dreams: Black Women's Organizations and the Politics of Transformation* (1998), the editor of *Global Lockdown: Race, Gender, and the Prison-Industrial Complex* (2005), and the coeditor of *Color of Violence* (2006) and (under the name Oparah) *Outsiders Within: Writing on Transracial Adoption* (2006). Julia has been involved in anti-racism, anti-violence, global justice, and prison abolitionism work in the United Kingdom, the United States, and Canada. She is a founding member of Critical Resistance, a national abolitionist organization based in the United States, and the Prisoner Justice Action Committee in Toronto, and she has been a member of the Prison Activist Resource Center, Arizona Prison Moratorium Coalition, and Incite! Women of Color against Violence.

Chukwuma Ume is an ex-prison officer with the Nigerian Prison Service and now works as a consultant on penal reform. He has considerable years of experience working with civil society organizations, specifically working in the areas relating to penal reform, human rights, and peacebuilding in Africa, and specifically Nigeria. He currently lives and works in Lagos, Nigeria.

ACKNOWLEDGEMENTS

This book is the result of two years (2000-2002) spent working with prisoners in West Africa, and at the outset I extend deep solidarity to the people who have been kidnapped by the police and are involuntarily confined inside the Kirikiri medium and maximum security prisons. Weekly circles with prisoners in these prisons provided me with community, strength, and family in Nigeria. Each of you has incredible insight and foresight, and I thank you for taking the time to teach me, to share with me, and to include me in your struggles. Your experiences have now been documented, and I thank you for having the strength to share such difficult times.

I thank Papa, Ngozi (and beautiful family), Felix, Congo, Uche, and Francis in Onipanu. Thank you for building the Prisoners Rehabilitation and Welfare Action (PRAWA) home and skills-sharing workshops with me, for sharing your stories, for remaining strong through all the hardships that have been thrown at you. In strength with you and all the Africans still imprisoned in European penal institutions on African soil, I will continue to fight for the abolition of all penal systems since they work to destroy all that makes us human.

I also extend a huge thankyou to all the academics and activists who contributed writings to this book. Without your research and your very important work, the experiences of prisoners in Nigeria could not have been contextualized and documented in such accurate and grounded accounts. Your academic and grassroots contributions to the everyday struggle for black liberation and racial emancipation are invaluable.

Adamoh, Nnenda, and Grace, my sisters. Without your friendship and support, I could not have lasted more than a day in Lagos. You always shared your honest thoughts and opinions, and your advice became my lifeline. We shared some really painful times, and we shared many beautiful moments. You are all incredible women, and every instant spent with you continues to be cherished in my thoughts.

Maggie, Afolabi, Michael, Malam, Kate, and Jonathon—all the time you took to teach me basic survival skills literally kept me alive. I thank you for all your help and for your patience with me as I transitioned from that spoiled, fragile woman who feared geckos and lizards into the flexible, durable, strong, and proud African woman who left Nigeria appreciating all living beings and accepting them as productive elements of the life cycle.

Saib, I thank you for your insights and your advice and for all those times you took to calm me down, to answer my questions, and to laugh with me when the insanity got to be too much.

Sunday, Prince, Voke, Julie, and Chuks—you all remained dedicated even when the world seemed to be in overwhelming opposition.

To all the PRAWA staff who participated, I will forever cherish the informal labour union we formed during the toughest months, and I will never forget the strike we were ready to embark on in order to survive very difficult and unstable working conditions. Our conversations of solidarity and our work toward maintaining each other's jobs formed the foundation of some of the most important life lessons I learned in Nigeria.

I extend a heartfelt thankyou to all the area boys in Onipanu and Palmgroove who kept me safe when there were conflicts, who gave me directions when I was lost amid the molwes, and who never took advantage of my lack of knowledge. You offered so much to me in terms of safety, and you never asked for anything in return. You proved to me that, even when the world looks down on you and ignorantly labels you, the human spirit can prevail through the stigma, and your sense of community trumped all the stereotypes people had imposed on our neighbourhood.

I would like to send out a huge thankyou to Annemieke, my friend in struggle and my spiritual sister. You pulled me through so many situations, and you reflected with me on oyeebo experiences. Thank you for sharing your wisdom, and for being such a strong and beautiful person.

Annick, Joline, and Tessa, I thank you for taking so many emotional and geographical journeys with me. We experienced parts of West Africa together that are so precious and untouched by Western imperialism; I could not have appreciated those places as much as I did had I not experienced them with you.

Nyi, my father through Voluntary Service Overseas (VSO), thank you for watching over me and for helping me when I needed help. Thank you for opening your home to me, and for struggling to keep VSO grounded in African traditions and values.

Renata, you made me a bridesmaid in the most beautiful wedding ceremony I attended in Nigeria. Thank you for accepting me as I am, and most of all thank you for proving to all those who work with you that African women are a force to be reckoned with. Your confidence in your people and your love for your culture inspired me, and made me want to push boundaries that should never have been established in the first place.

Martha, Nnenda, and Dick, thank you for opening your home, your family, and your lives to me. You provided sanctity and comfort when I was ill or homesick. You supported my work with prisoners when it seemed that the rest of the funding world did not care to provide non-colonized means of support. Patrick and Chike, you did the same, and for all that I thank you.

Benedict, in memory of your passionate and much too short life, I keep you in my heart and my thoughts. With Alan and the Jougla family I share the loss of a woman who was such a positive force in the lives of so many who knew her. The pain of her violent loss is immense, and I continue to be thankful for the privilege of having known and loved Benedict. Her passion for Nigeria was so genuine and heartfelt; if more Europeans opened their hearts and minds to Africa and Africans with the truth and love that she did, this world would be a much better place for us all.

To all my family and friends who supported me while I was in Nigeria, and who were there for me when I came back, thank you. Thankyou, Baba, for your understanding and support. All the incredible women in my family: Mama, precious Teta, Marianne, Sherine, Kayla, and Reham, you all bring immense meaning to my life. Thankyou to Leslie, Giselle, and Rebecca for timeless friendship and support. Thankyou, Ashanti, for inspiring me to bring Africa into North America in ways I never dreamed possible. Thankyou Veronica, Garlia, and Tiffanie, for supporting me through the writing of this book. To all my family and friends who were not with me during my Nigerian journey, please bear with me as I try to integrate my life and experiences there into a meaningful life here. It will not be easy, I know I have changed, but I also know that these changes were necessary.

FOREWORD

Julia Sudbury

In August 2002 prison activists and scholars from the United States, Canada, Australia, and across the African continent travelled to Lagos, Nigeria, for the Tenth International Conference on Penal Abolition (ICOPA X). Coordinated by Viviane Saleh-Hanna, then a staff member at Prisoners Rehabilitation and Welfare Action, the conference challenged those of us involved in prison activism and research to examine our unstated Western bias. Although often extremely knowledgeable about prison systems and anti-prison movements in the United States, Canada, and Europe, few of us knew anything about penal systems in West Africa. Indeed, we had most commonly defined the concerns, priorities, and goals of prison studies and anti-prison activism with no regard for the experiences of scholars and activists in the global South. Shortly before the conference the US government issued a warning suggesting that American visitors might not be safe in Nigeria, due to ethnic and religious conflict, and that Nigerian Airways was not up to international air safety standards, further discouraging travel. These warnings remind us that the lack of scholarly and activist engagements across the First World/Third World divide is a reflection of broader ideological and structural forces. Despite the shrinking of the globe and the emergence of a border-crossing cosmopolitan elite, significant barriers remain to meaningful and transformative transnational engagements in the field of prison studies and activism. Viviane Saleh-Hanna has therefore given us an important gift by gathering in these pages the experiences and analyses of African scholars, former prisoners, and human rights activists.

Colonial Systems of Control is a groundbreaking collection of essays. The book offers challenges for prison activists, and proposes new directions and methodological approaches for the field of prison studies. Viviane Saleh-Hanna brings together Western and African scholars, former prisoners, and human rights activists—a powerful approach that offers the reader a range of perspectives from which to approach the topic. The testimonies by former prisoners in particular provide a humanizing glimpse of the microlevel struggles for survival of criminalized African men and women, while the scholarly articles address the macrolevel social, political, and legal context. But the book is not just an analysis of what is wrong with the Nigerian penal system. Instead, the authors offer two possible alternatives to the status quo: a revitalization of traditional models of justice based on African cultural principles and penal abolitionism, and a model developed in Europe and North America but applied here uniquely to the African context.

Nigeria is home to immense wealth, enormous poverty, a decaying infrastructure, and blatant corruption. Lagos, a city of twelve million people, mostly Yorubas, Igbos, and Hausas, is a sprawling urban futurescape directly out of an Octavia Butler novel. Despite the billions of dollars each year generated by oil revenues, there is no reliable clean water, the roads are riddled with potholes deep enough to swallow a car, and, since garbage collection is infrequent, there are constant piles of smoking trash at the sides of the road. Thousands of cars burn leaded gas and churn out black fumes directly in the faces of the children selling every product imaginable to the drivers stuck in constant "go slows" (traffic jams). With the current government following the International Monetary Fund's (IMF) neoliberal agenda, and with widespread corruption of government officials, there is little hope of investment in roads, public transportation, water, or electricity any time soon. Victoria Island is a walled oasis within this urban mayhem. Reserved for "expats"—whites—and rich blacks working for multinationals such as Shell and Chevron, Victoria Island has modern restaurants, apartment blocks with their own generators and water supply, swimming pools, and expensive hotels.

Since the discovery of oil and the growth of incredible wealth inequalities, avoiding armed robbers has become an everyday part of life. It is not considered safe to drive outside town after dark, and Nigerians returning home from working abroad are frequently robbed. In desperation, communities have turned to vigilante gangs such as the Bakassi Boys, who carry out extralegal, on-the-spot executions of alleged culprits. In southeast Nigeria, where oil revenues and corruption make political positions goldmines, politicians are accused of having put the Bakassi Boys on the payroll. In the north, communities have turned to the harsh punishments given out under sharia law (traditional Muslim law), such as stoning and cutting off a hand. At first glance, we might be encouraged to believe that a study of prisons in a setting so different from the North American context would have little to teach a Western audience. It is critical, however, that we do not approach these essays as if they illuminate a fascinating yet distant experience, an exotic taste of otherness. Rather we can read these essays as a subaltern commentary on state violence, social control, inequality, and resistance. In this sense scholars and activists in North America and Europe have a great deal to learn from our Nigerian counterparts.

These essays make three critical interventions. First, they introduce the concept of "penal coloniality" and provide a detailed argument for understanding the emergence of prisons in Africa as an integral facet of colonialism. Essays by Ume and Saleh-Hanna and by Elechi demonstrate that precolonial systems of justice were based on concepts that are largely absent in Western models. These concepts included the belief that individuals who committed offences were harming the community or the spirit world rather than the state; that such offences could be made good through reparations to the affected family or community rather than through punishment; and that family and kin networks served as formal systems of social control, with banishment from the family and community to be used only as a last resort. The rise of the prison is then traced through the early and late colonial eras, as well as the postindependence eras of military and democratic rule. This genealogy demonstrates the shifting function of imprisonment and its close connection to relations of rule. By unpacking the history of the prison in this way, the authors encourage the reader to think critically about the role and function of prisons in contemporary societies. The Nigerian case study provides an opportunity to step back from the apparent inevitability and omnipresence of penal culture, and to study a society without prisons, a core concept developed in abstract terms by abolitionists in the West.

Second, these essays address the important issue of the relationship between the contemporary global political and economic order, the (neo)colonial state, and criminal punishment in the global South. There is a tendency in the scholarship on globalization to treat it as a new phenomenon arising entirely out of economic restructuring in the West, and the need for new markets and sources of labour. The authors gathered here bring an African lens to the social problems associated with globalization, and in so doing they establish the continuity of political, economic, and social dominance and exploitation from the beginnings of the trans-Atlantic slave trade through colonial rule, continental independence in the 1960s, and contemporary unequal global relations. The authors make a strong case that coloniality continues, transformed from direct rule by external colonial powers to oppression by an externally supported government structured by colonial principles of violence, militarization, and disregard for human rights. They argue against the conceptualization of the African continent as being in a state of postcoloniality and posit the colonial prison as evidence of its continuation.

The authors demonstrate that, at a local level, coloniality and globalization take the face of corrupt prison guards stealing rations meant for prisoners, police extorting bribes from terrified families of detainees, women incarcerated for mental illness, and soldiers imprisoned for complaining about poor conditions. They demonstrate that we cannot, as observers of the African continent often tend to, blame all the problems of poverty and human rights abuses on African governance. Equally, we cannot, as global justice activists tend to, ignore the abuses by African governments while pointing fingers at powerful Western nations, the IMF, and multinational corporations. Instead, this volume powerfully demonstrates the seamless interweaving of the local, national, and global, and finds the location of responsibility and accountability for the suffering of Nigerian prisoners at multiple levels.

Third, the essays gathered here address alternatives to criminal punishment in West Africa. Having demonstrated that prisons are a colonial invention that has little to do with African cultural traditions or principles of social organization, the authors come to the conclusion that alternatives must be found. However, rather than simply exhorting the reader to imagine a world without prisons, they provide concrete examples of alternatives and pathways to social change. One direction for change is to foster the development of indigenous justice models. Models such as "sentencing circles" in Aboriginal communities have been developed in Canada during the past decade, and there has been a plethora of research evaluating their effectiveness. However, there is little scholarship available outside the African continent on indigenous justice models in Africa. The authors make an invaluable contribution to scholarship on restorative and alternative non-punitive justice models. The chapter on ICOPA is particularly powerful because it documents the development of a transnational coalition of activists and scholars, including youth and former prisoners. This is the first detailed account I have read that documents the use of penal abolitionist discourse and praxis in an African context. These essays answer an important abolitionist question: if not prisons, then what?

In the United States the explosion in prison construction that occurred in the past three decades has sparked intense interest in whether prisons work, whose interests they serve, and what could be used in place of prisons. Increasingly there is an emerging consensus that US legislators have built themselves into a fiscal and social crisis by investing ever-larger sums of public money into incarceration and packing already overcrowded prisons with more and more non-violent offenders. In California, for example, the governor has recently declared a state of emergency in the state prison system and started shipping prisoners to other states, sparking a new round of debates about what can be done about the prison system. In Canada federal officials have tended to resist pressure to conform to US models of mass incarceration. However, expansion and privatization have occurred at the provincial level, and prison activists and the media have brought public attention to the Americanization of Canadian criminal justice, from the introduction of boot camps to the introduction of US private prison companies to run a jail in Ontario.

Prisons are rapidly becoming what Angela Y. Davis (1981) calls a panacea for all social ills, from mental illness and drug addiction to homelessness and poverty. This reliance on imprisonment touches not only the growing number of people who have a family member or friend in prison, on parole, or on probation, or who have experienced the criminal punishment system firsthand, but also those impacted by cuts in education, social services, and health care that occur as criminal justice budgets spiral upward. This reliance affects our everyday lives as we see formerly incarcerated youth and racialized minorities recycled through our inner cities, with no resources or support to establish a new life, gain employment, find housing, and secure treatment for addiction or mental illness. Despite the unsustainability of a social policy built on criminalization and punishment rather than on social investment and community infrastructure, politicians from both sides of the spectrum have been reluctant to envision real alternatives to mass incarceration. *Colonial Systems of Control* invites us to question the notion that caging people creates safety and to examine our assumptions about the efficacy of (state) violence in preventing (criminal) violence. It is a compelling and important book that will challenge the way you think about safety, crime, and punishment.

REFERENCE

Davis, Angela Y. (1981). *Women, Race, and Class*. New York: Random House.

CHAPTER 1

INTRODUCTION: COLONIAL SYSTEMS OF CONTROL

Viviane Saleh-Hanna

A long dirt road begins with the casual barrel of a gun, guarding a boundary, allowing selective access to outsiders and controlled exit to insiders. The few outsiders who are allowed to step past those guns and over the invisible, mysterious line in Kirikiri are faced with tall concrete walls inflicting visible boundaries and guns illustrating more clearly the visual and violent infliction of control. All visible boundaries within the Nigerian Prison 'Service' grounds are accentuated by the binding green gates built into the concrete walls, meant to function as points of transition between the two worlds: the world inside Nigerian prisons and the world outside them. The walls I see before me every time I enter a prison, anywhere in the world, are not just walls. They are symbols of degradation and violence; they are statements of disregard and dehumanization; they are perpetrators of myth and fear; and above all they are clear, concrete representations of the inhumanity capable of emerging in the name of euphemized humanities.

As I step beyond the gates and enter the world of prisons in Nigeria, I am faced with prison officials in green uniforms trying to maintain order among and control over convicted prisoners in blue uniforms. This is simply a world of green uniforms trying to keep blue uniforms behind the walls. Not as concrete but just as visible is the struggle to control all physical, mental, and spiritual undertakings. Colours mark power, not people: green uniforms taking shifts to monitor, control, and punish blue uniforms; blue uniforms fighting to exist as human beings inside a beast-like institution.

While I was in Nigeria, from October 2000 to November 2002, there were 142 prisons holding approximately 55,000 prisoners, sixty-two percent of whom were awaiting trial. While 20,000 prisoners (thirty-eight percent) had been convicted inside a courtroom, approximately 35,000 prisoners were imprisoned without legal representation or the chance to appear in court.[1] Those 35,000 people did not always have prison uniforms;[2] they wore the clothes they had been arrested in and, as the years went by, whatever clothes they had been able to get from those around them. I met prisoners who had served up to ten years awaiting trial and, if convicted, were not given "time served" recognition. An ex-prisoner I worked with at the PRAWA[3] office, a man I knew as Papa, often spoke about the ten years he had spent awaiting trial for a drug offence and the eight years he had been sentenced to serve. He had spent eighteen years in prison.

It is important to note the differences in conditions between awaiting-trial and convicted prisoners. It was clear that awaiting-trial prisoners are the most undernourished and maltreated people in most Nigerian prisons; in addition, the amount of time spent in lockdown is much higher compared with that for convicted prisoners. In the Kirikiri medium security prison in 2002, about 2,000 prisoners (seventy-four percent) were awaiting trial, while approximately 700 (twenty-six percent) were convicted. Warehousing approximately 2,700 prisoners, the Kirikiri medium security prison was originally built to imprison about 700 people. Many awaiting-trial prisoners in this prison told me they were given the chance to leave their overcrowded cell blocks (holding up to seventy-seven people in one room built to hold approximately twenty people) once a week for one hour. The amount of food awaiting-trial prisoners receive is much smaller compared with that for convicted prisoners, who already do not get sufficient servings. These conditions were confirmed by prison guards, who added that the lack of resources and staff to handle the thousands of prisoners necessitated such treatment.

In addition to the obvious injustice of loss of liberty suffered by all prisoners, awaiting-trial prisoners are imprisoned without the due process necessitated in a vengeful and violent *criminal* justice system. Representing one of the most vulnerable populations inside Nigerian prisons, awaiting-trial prisoners are subject to extremely harsh living conditions for many reasons. Primarily, and on the most concrete and logistical level, their maltreatment is often assumed to stem from their lack of representation in the Nigerian Prison Service budget: since they have not been convicted in court, they do not hold official prisoner status and are not represented in the budget.

Nigerian prison guards often claimed there was no option other than to warehouse awaiting-trial prisoners in inhumane conditions. Although this explanation (the lack of funds) may appear logical at first, it is not. The penal system is a violent system. How does putting more money into violence solve the problems that stem from the inhumane confinement of people inside cages? The United States has been throwing money at its penal system, but it has not humanized its prisons, it has only increased the number of people exposed to the inhumanity of the system. In 2006 the US Department of Justice had a monstrous budget of $20.3 billion.[4] More than a third of this money, approximately $7 billion, is spent on imprisoning people. In addition,

> the 2006 Budget includes $85 million to open three new prisons (one high-security, one medium-security, and one secure women's prison) and to expand two other facilities. When fully activated, these prisons will add a total of 3,164 beds.... $37 million is provided to pay for the added costs for food, security, medical care, and clothing of almost 4,300 inmates in existing BOP [Bureau of Prisons] facilities, and $20 million in initial funding is included for 1,600 new private contract beds. While additional prison space is being added, the Budget

continues a moratorium on additional new prison construction until the bureau completes an evaluation of its existing low- and minimum-security prison facilities for potential modification to house higher-security inmates.[5]

An increased budget for prisons in the United States has naturally and predictably resulted in the expansion of the prison system and imprisonment rates. The current result is a system that oppresses more people than any other penal system in contemporary and historical societies.

As of 2006 the worlds population had reached 6.6 billion,[6] meaning that the United States, with a population of almost 298 million,[7] has 4.5 percent of the world's population. Also in 2006 the world prison population reached 9.3 million, with the United States imprisoning 2,193,798 of those people. *This means that the United States houses 4.5 percent of the world's population and 23.9 percent of the world's prison population.* Nigeria had a reported population in 2006 of 131,859,731[8] and a prison population of approximately 55,000 people, meaning that *Nigeria is home to two percent of the world's population and under one percent of the world's prison population.* On comparing these statistics with the rest of the industrialized world, imprisonment rates continue to be disproportionately higher in the First World as compared with Nigeria. While Nigerians were imprisoned at a rate of 51 per 100,000 in 2002, that year the "incarceration rate in Canada was 116 per 100,000.... Canada's incarceration rate is higher than the rates in many Western European countries such as Germany (95), France (85), Finland (70), Switzerland (68), and Denmark (64) but lower than those in England/Wales (139) and the United States (702)."[9] *Agozino's (2003) suggestion that the West has much to learn from the so-called Third World when it comes to justice is well translated in these statistics.* For these reasons, this book presents the struggles and barriers of imprisonment in Nigeria while also presenting African justice models and alternatives that are not rooted in colonial responses to conflict.

Ironically, human rights violations that take place in Nigerian prisons are often presented as related to budgetary constraints.

Yet the increased funding for prisons in the United States has done little to humanize a fundamentally inhumane penal system. Evans (2005, 218) explains that money put into the prison system in the United States does not find its way into services for prisoners; rather, it is channelled into "guards' salaries and allocations for increased security measures." These conditions in the United States illustrate that putting more money into the penal system is not a solution. Nigeria does not need to "cage more people" as the United States does. The issues defined from within the confines of European penal rhetoric become questions of funding the efficient brutalization of people either through increased funding for imprisonment or through demonization of Nigeria's *inefficient* use of cruelty in Nigerian prisons. This line of questioning fails to address the fundamental brutality of penal justice. The answer to these ill-defined problems lies in fundamentally and collectively *rejecting* the notion that caging and dehumanizing people through penal, colonial institutions of control creates safer or more civilized societies.

From a perspective that questions these foundational issues of violence as *intrinsic* to the functions of the penal system, the struggles of Nigerian prisoners can be understood more accurately. In almost all Nigerian prisons death in custody is common. While there are no official statistics available, I witnessed many convicted prisoners assigned the harrowing task of carrying out for burial awaiting-trial prisoners' corpses (sometimes decayed) on rusted stretchers, wrapped in grey blankets. Many of these casualties were young men. *All* the casualties I witnessed had never been convicted. The issue again becomes a necessary and serious look into abolishing violent institutions that claim to provide justice as opposed to recoiling with shock and horror when the penal system's brutality is brought to the surface. Fundamentally, death in custody, although counterintuitive to our humanity, is not counterintuitive to the penal system's dehumanizing functions and foundational assumptions. Putting a person to death through formal due process in the United States or having a person die due to informal brutalities manifested through Nigerian prison conditions produces the same result:

the end of life as a result of state action. Whether this murder is sanctioned by a court or meted out in a prison yard is not focal; what is focal is the violent taking of life. The legal sanctioning of violence does not negate the seriousness of violence. And it certainly does not justify it. The legal sanctioning of violence through the penal system works only to subdue people into accepting that the state can and will use violence to implement power over those who are disempowered in society.

In European, North American, and South Pacific societies poverty determines imprisonment, but intersecting with classism are racism and sexism that embody criminal justice in industrialized nations. Penal systems are built on sexist, racist, classist, ageist, and heterosexist foundations: the institutionalization of these isms through penal justice results in the unequal distribution of violent penal justice. The United States represents the clearest case of institutionalized racisms and sexisms as integral to penal system functions: "If current trends continue, about one in three black males and one in six Hispanic [more respectfully known as Latino] males born today in the United States are expected to serve some time behind bars" (Gottschalk 2006, 19). This extremely high incarceration rate for men of colour in the United States exists in stark contrast to the imprisonment rates experienced by white men: "African Americans are imprisoned at more than ten times the rate of their compatriots of European origin" (Wacquant 2001, 83).[10] In addition, "nationally women are the fastest growing sector of the incarcerated population. The number of women in U.S. prisons has risen more than eight-fold since 1980.... The total number of women locked away in U.S. prisons and jails is now more than double the *entire* prison populations of France and Germany" (Gottschalk 2006, 19). The repercussions of mass incarceration in the United States have resulted in the daunting fact that "more than 1.5 million children in the United States have a parent in state or federal prison" (Gottschalk 2006, 19-20). These high levels of penal injustice have not been duplicated in Nigeria. Yet, despite mass inhumanity in the United States, Africans continue to be expected to turn to the United States and Europe for advice and guidance in the implementation of justice (Agozino 2003). This is a white supremacist expectation, implying that Europeans and their descendants in the United States, Canada, and Australia hold information and skills that are superior to those of people of colour when it comes to models of justice. In true white supremacist approaches, evidence of superiority is not proven but simply and unquestioningly assumed.

Intrinsic to white supremacist notions that criminal justice is a superior form of control is the assumption that, without reliance on European, centralized, and violent institutions of control, society would inevitably erupt into chaos and self-combustive violence. The same logic is present in the slave owner's psyche through the belief that enslaving African peoples helped to save their souls, and European war makers who colonized Africa assumed that their exploitation and military occupation of African lands could help to 'civilize' their peoples. Similarly, it is assumed today that the lack of European models of justice and control in Africa (or anywhere else in the world) would signify incivility and violence. Setting aside the faulty yet assumed superiority of white institutions, evidence has shown that European slavery, colonialism, and now the penal system are violent, vengeful, and exploitative institutions. Continuing to rely on the penal system for control is a perpetuation of penal coloniality, a concept further explored in Chapter 2. By implanting violence through *criminal justice*, the penal system overwhelms society with intense amounts of violence that obscure and bury actual violent issues between people amid the rubble of institutionalized structural and penal violence. The root of these issues is abstracted through faulty assumptions that the law is objective, and that European forms of violent penal justice are necessary and universal systems for equitable social control. If so-called civilized societies are serious about civilization, then white supremacy must be dismantled, and this requires the abolition of penal coloniality. To dismantle penal coloniality requires an analysis of who is most vulnerable to penal oppression: populations that have historically been colonized and enslaved by Europeans are the most vulnerable to penal colonialism.

While the average citizen is vulnerable to criminalization, a powerful minority of the world's population benefit from constructed immunities. In the same sense the majority of the world's population residing on continents colonized by Europe live in harsh conditions, while the minority in the industrialized world live in comfort. "The world's *500 richest people* have an income of more than $100 billion, not taking into account asset wealth. That exceeds the combined incomes of the *poorest 416 million*" people in the world (United Nations Human Development 2006, 269; emphases added). In addition, ninety percent of the people in the top twenty percent of global income distribution live in OECD countries,[11] while fifty percent of the poorest twenty percent of the global income live in sub-Saharan Africa (United Nations Human Development 2006, 269). The intersections of classism and racism that define power and wealth globally underpin the penal system's role in maintaining an enslaving and colonialist status quo.

To counter the constructed validity of this status quo, this book presents the lived realities of people inside European, colonial systems of control in Africa. In doing so this volume initiates a process of humanization. The reader is given the opportunity to open her or his eyes to the lived realities of the people in Nigerian prisons. Their struggles and their stories emphasize the contradictions of penal reform efforts in Nigeria. Central is the understanding that efforts for reform reinforce colonialism and need to be replaced with serious efforts to abolish penal forms of justice. Human rights efforts funded through colonizing nations' charitable funds will do little more than better equip the existing Nigerian penal system to hide and justify penal brutalities. *It is the structure that is inhumane,* and in Nigeria that inhumanity has nowhere to hide.

This book highlights the penal system as manifested in present-day Nigeria. In Chapter 3 Ume and I present a historical account of when and how the penal system became implanted in Nigerian societies. The roots of this system trace directly back to violent British invasions of West Africa. Chapter 4 by Agozino documents the role that militarized control has played in creating the current conditions suffered in Nigeria, importantly noting that the first centralized military power in Nigeria was a British one. Combined, the chapters in Section 1 provide an ideological, historical, and sociopolitical understanding of Europe's abusive and exploitative relationship with Nigeria. This backdrop is necessary in the presentation of penal coloniality in West Africa.

Section 2 (Chapters 5 through 12) presents the voices of Nigerian prisoners inside the Kirikiri maximum security prison in Lagos State. This section is the heart of the book. From these first published accounts of prisoners in West Africa we learn about the brutalities inflicted through the European penal system as it has come to function on West African soil. We are able to access the complex and intertwining consequences of racist colonial institutions and the corrupt African leaders who maintain them. These leaders and administrators are carrying on the legacies of colonialist exploitation through modernized, more contemporary penal coloniality in the region. These colonial oppressions can best be understood by those who are forced to live them. Through the struggles of Eribo, Akporherhe, Affor, Odibo, and Anagaba the reader can begin to conceptualize the violence involved in the construction and implementation of Europe's (and now North America's) primary model of *criminal justice*.

Section 3 delves further into the complex oppressions of penal coloniality, addressing the intersections of sexism, racism, classism, and the overpowering conditions that are produced. In Chapter 13 I provide details of the firsthand interactions I had with different branches of the penal system in Nigeria during the two years I spent there. Through these experiences I was able to better comprehend the intersections between poverty, youth, gender, and colonialism, and to expand my conceptions of oppression to include both formal and informal methods of unjust social control. In Chapter 14 Nagel provides a broader context of gender in Africa as it intersects with penal coloniality.

She provides examples of women in prison in Mali and Nigeria, and ties their oppressions into the larger context of contemporary globalization and human rights discourses. In this chapter, the interrelationships between microlevel struggles resulting from macrostructural oppressions are well illustrated. Agozino in Chapter 15 provides empirical facts that aid in an expansion of Nagel's analysis of multilevel struggles. He details the empirical realities of women in prison in Nigeria, and emphasizes the need to move toward a criminology that implicitly and consciously functions to counter colonialism. Wrapping up Section 3, Agomoh (Chapter 16) addresses the multiplicity of oppressions that are exploited through penal coloniality by providing details of the violence and inhumanity imposed on those who are mentally ill in prison.

The first three sections of this book provide details and contexts of the oppressions instituted through the power abuses and hierarchies of penal coloniality. Yet the book would not be complete without a section on how these brutalities and oppressions are defied, for Foucault (1972) emphasized that every site of power simultaneously produces sites of resistance. Section 4 therefore addresses resistance to penal coloniality as it has been implemented by women, musicians, students, and disempowered members of diverse Nigerian societies. Chapter 17 presents forms of resistance used by women in northern Nigeria who are oppressed through the Eurocentric and thus implicitly misogynistic laws that regulate their access to wealth and survival. Chapter 18 presents the life and struggles of musician and activist Fela Anikulapo Kuti, and illustrates how resistance through music can mobilize large masses against military dictatorships and their violent repressions.

Section 5 represents an extension of this discourse on resistance by providing more specific and concrete examples of African transformative justice models that have been used to compensate for the malfunctions and violence imposed through European penal systems in Africa. In Chapter 19 Ume provides examples of successfully implemented African justice models throughout Africa, and in Chapter 20 Elechi presents details of the Igbo democratic systems of justice and community-centred forms of social control. None of these models is presented as flawless, but they are in essence and in implementation community-centred and non-violent, and this is the starting point in the conceptualization of a world that can function without Europenal violence and coloniality.

The book concludes (Chapter 21) with a presentation of European academic theories on penal abolitionism and a summary of the tenth International Conference on Penal Abolition held in Lagos in August 2002 (Chapter 22). These last two chapters tie together the positive relationships that European scholarship and people in the West can build with Africans who continue to struggle with contemporary forms of colonial control. The concluding section emphasizes that European and Western industrialized societies have much to learn about the implementation of penal abolitionism by looking to Africa for practised and lived transformative justice.

In these concluding sections, we hope, the reader can conceptualize not only a world without prisons but also a world in which white and black nations (and the people within them) can come together to implement solutions and reparations that will initiate a healing process that effectively and necessarily addresses historical colonialisms, contemporary exploitations, and future potentials for humane and reciprocal coexistence.

These changes are necessary not only for those who suffer within or live at risk of penal coloniality in Africa but also for those who live in industrialized nations. The past few decades have marked an increased punitive approach to social problems, and this approach has resulted in a boom of prison construction in the United States and quickly increasing imprisonment rates throughout many industrialized Western nations. This trend has a disproportionately high impact on young people of colour living in societies structured on European and North American models of democracy: "Canada... seems to have followed a pattern of legislative change that appears similar to many other Western countries, including Britain, Australia, and the United States. In turn each of these jurisdictions have witnessed earlier child welfare models of juvenile justice wither away under the weight of punitive approaches to crime control that whet the public's appetite for a crack-down.... 'Getting tough' now underpins the administration of juvenile justice" (Hogeveen 2006, 51).

While in Nigeria, my understanding of the penal system as one of the major oppressive structures in contemporary societies was heavily reinforced. The stories and analyses presented in this book are meant to expose the depths of the brutalities that are the *foundations of the penal system.* The information shared in this book is meant to serve not as a critique of Nigeria but more broadly as a critique of the penal system. Nigeria happens to be the setting in which I saw the extremes and was faced with the violent capabilities of the penal system. Nigeria happened to be the geographical and political context within which I realized that any system capable of such brutality is in need not of reform but of demolition. While most of the authors in this book are African, they address European models of control. Their analysis, it is hoped, will heighten readers' awareness of the brutality encountered in Nigerian prisons, as a result of and in direct correlation to European colonialism and the European penal structures that have instituted *criminal* forms of justice all over the globe. Those on the receiving end of oppression can best explain the roots, experiences, and ramifications of oppression. Those in prison can best explain imprisonment, and those who have lived in colonized realities can best describe the connections between history and the present.

NOTES

1. Statistics gathered through PRAWA. Aside from these figures, I did not come across any official records on prison populations or imprisonment rates.
2. In all-male prisons I did not see any awaiting-trial uniforms; in the Kirikiri women's prison the awaiting-trial prisoners ironically

wore green (the Nigerian Prison Service uniform colour), while the convicted prisoners wore blue.
3 Prisoners Rehabilitation and Welfare Action is a Nigerian non-governmental organization dedicated to the struggle for human rights inside prisons throughout West Africa (including Nigeria, Ghana, and The Gambia).
4 See http://www.whitehouse.gov/omb/budget/fy2006/justice.html.
5 See ibid.
6 See http://www.census.gov/ipc/www/worldpop.html.
7 See https://www.cia.gov/cia/publications/factbook/print/us.html.
8 See https://www.cia.gov/cia/publications/factbook/geos/ni.html.
9 See http://www.csc-scc.gc.ca/text/pblct/basicfacts/BasicFacts_e.shtml#Context2. Figures for the United States are for incarcerated adults only.
10 White men, though, are imprisoned at higher rates in the United States than in any other democratic or industrialized nation.
11 The Organization for Economic Cooperation and Development, predominantly controlled by Europeans and their descendants, is a governing body with thirty member countries. The OECD functions to produce "internationally agreed instruments, decisions and recommendations to promote the rules of the game in areas where multilateral agreement is necessary for individual countries to make progress in a globalized economy." See http://www.oecd.org/home/0,2605,en_2649_201185_1_1_1_1_1,00.html.

REFERENCES

Agozino, Biko. (2003). *Counter-Colonial Criminology: A Critique of Imperialist Reason.* London: Pluto Press.

Evans, Linda. (2005). "Playing Global Cop: U.S. Militarism and the Prison Industrial Complex." In *Global Lockdown: Race, Gender, and the Prison-Industrial Complex,* ed. Julia Sudbury. New York: Routledge, 215–230.

Foucault, Michel. (1972). *Power/Knowledge.* New York: Pantheon Books.

Gottschalk, Marie. (2006). *Prison and the Gallows: The Politics of Mass Incarceration in America.* Cambridge, UK: Cambridge University Press.

Hogeveen, Bryan. (2006). "Unsettling Youth Justice and Cultural Norms: The Youth Restorative Action Project." *Journal of Youth Studies, 9:1,* 47-66.

United Nations. (2006). *Human Development Report 2006: The State of Human Development.* New York: United Nations.

Wacquant, Loïc. (2001). "Deadly Symbiosis: When Ghetto and Prison Meet and Mesh." In *Mass Imprisonment: Social Causes and Consequences,* ed. David Garland. London: Sage Publications, 82–120.

SECTION I

CONTEXTUALIZING NIGERIA

To discuss penal coloniality in Nigeria, it is first necessary to present the context in which Nigeria exists today. Colonialism and the slave trade are major tenants in the recent history of the country. The past is not the past as privileged people choose to believe. The past is the foundation upon which contemporary conditions of privilege or underprivilege are built. A complex past has left Nigeria with complex contemporary demographics. Structural oppression and economic exploitation functioned officially in colonialism and slave trading through European laws, but they also functioned unofficially through racial demonizations and abstract academic cultural degradations. As a result the official facts about Nigeria do not represent a complete picture of the Nigeria I came to know and experience.

This Nigeria was both complex and honest. That honesty resounded in the openness through which society functioned: problems are not obscure, corruption is not shielded, struggles are not hidden, and above all criminal justice is exactly that: a *criminal* way to conduct justice. The *criminal* justice system addressed in this book is a system of injustice, and it is wholeheartedly an invention of European and North American governments and their agents. Western institutions in Nigeria are naked. They are unable to hide behind Western propaganda and illusions of justice. I travelled across the Atlantic Ocean, and I lived in Africa, and there I found the truth that is *criminal* justice.

CHAPTER 2
PENAL COLONIALITY

Viviane Saleh-Hanna

Because colonialism is such a highly complex and intrusive process, defining it and articulating the depths of its brutality have been a struggle as difficult as the sociopolitical fight for liberation from it. The definitions of colonialism presented in the 1950s continue to be highly relevant and accurate in capturing what Africans experience today. Furnivall stated in 1956 that "colonization originally implied settlement, but the tropics have been colonized with capital rather than men, and most tropical countries under foreign rule are dependencies rather than colonies, though in practice both terms are used indifferently" (1). This understanding that imposed dependencies are forms of colonialism seems to have disappeared in a world that continually mistakes charity (by formerly colonizing entities) for justice (for formerly colonized people). Also lacking is the general understanding that physical withdrawal of Europeans from African governance did not minimize but instead expanded European and North American control over Africa.

In contemporary Africa and the diaspora there is an understanding that colonialism has transformed into neocolonialism. Nkrumah (1975, 199) explained that neocolonialism is "imperialism in its final and perhaps its most dangerous form." He added that the fundamental nature of neocolonialism is "that the State which is subject to it is, in theory, independent and has all the outward trappings of international sovereignty.

In reality its economic system and thus its political policy [are] directed from outside" (199). This definition of neocolonialism has much in common with the dependencies described in 1956 by Furnivall. In that sense I question how the prefix *neo* can be added to the word *colonialism*. *Neo* is a Greek word meaning "new," and in defining neocolonialism Nkrumah defined new transitions that further implanted European economies and laws in the domination of West Africa. Inaccurate in this analysis is not the definition he provided but the prefix he used—*neo* assumes "newness." Conversely, colonialist strategies have illustrated many policies and experiments in exploitation since inception. What Nkrumah calls "neocolonialism" is in fact the European decision to transition traditionally recognized forms of colonialism into more sustainable, abstracted colonialisms based on already practiced models that exhibited successes and profits in non-settler colonies historically referred to as dependencies.

This expansion into more sustainable European colonialism is evident in contemporary Africa. All over the continent European colonial uniforms remain, once worn by white bodies from Europe but now worn by black bodies in Africa. White people still live in plush condos in Ikoye and Victoria Island in Lagos, and their high socioeconomic status continues to be reliant on the oppression of Africans and the exploitation of African resources. Colonial institutions and white supremacist attitudes remain. They are engrained in the functions of everyday life and are legitimate in the eyes of the Nigerian government. Colonial institutions continue to colonize and oppress Nigerian people. Only within the realm of white supremacy can such exploitation and abuse continue for 500 years. And only within the context of white privilege can these exploitations change immensely in language and so little in structure.

In Ngũgĩ's (1982, 13-14) acclaimed novel *Devil on the Cross*, European colonialism in contemporary Africa is accurately presented through a recurring nightmare suffered by a central character:

And now Warĩĩnga was revisited by a nightmare that she used to have.... She saw first the darkness, carved open at one side to reveal a Cross, which hung in the air. Then she saw a crowd of people dressed in rags walking in the light, propelling the Devil towards the Cross. The Devil was clad in a silk suit, and he carried a walking stick shaped like a folded umbrella. On his head there were seven horns, seven trumpets for sounding infernal hymns of praise and glory. The Devil had two mouths, one on his forehead and the other on the back of his head. His belly sagged, as if it were about to give birth to all the evils of the world. His skin was red, like that of a pig. Near the Cross he began to tremble and turned his eyes towards the darkness, as if his eyes were being seared by the light. He moaned, beseeching the people not to crucify him, swearing that he and all his followers would never again build Hell for the people on Earth.

But the people cried in unison: "Now we know the secrets of all the robes that disguise your cunning. You commit murder, then you don your robes of pity and you go to wipe the tears from the faces of orphans and widows. You steal food from the people's stores at midnight, then at dawn you visit the victims wearing your robes of charity and you offer them a calabash filled with the grain that you have stolen. You encourage lavishness solely to gratify your own appetites, then you put on robes of righteousness and urge men to repent, to follow you so that you may show them paths of purity. You seize men's wealth, then you dress in robes of friendship and instruct them to join in the pursuit of the villain who has robbed them."

And there and then the people crucified the Devil on the Cross, and they went away singing songs of victory. After three days, there came others dressed in suits and ties, who, keeping close to the wall of darkness, lifted the Devil down from the Cross. And they knelt before him, and they prayed to him in loud voices, beseeching him to give them a portion of his robes of cunning. And their bellies began to swell, and they stood up, and they walked towards Warĩĩnga, laughing at her, stroking their large bellies, which had now inherited all the evils of the world.

Ngũgĩ wrote this book while imprisoned in Kenya. He was in prison for using his literary genius to critique African governance and the continuity of European corporate control of African resources. While reflecting on colonialist control, Ngũgĩ lays out a nightmare describing the superficial transitions that have taken place in Africa. He is defining not a *neo*colonialism but a euphemized colonialism that is abstracted on superficial levels and thus further engrained on more concrete levels. At the root of this nightmare is the fact that African independence from European colonialism has never been achieved. While societies have changed due to European and Euro-American globalization, these changes have not been, according to the Eurocentric evolutionary framework, for the better. Since so many of these changes have not been tied to black liberation, the transition from colonialism into *neo*colonialism signifies European transitions, not African ones. In addition, the implication of *newness* may apply to details of life (e.g., communication technology, the growth of Eurocapitalism through globalization, etc.), but it should never be mistaken for newness in structure. The 500-year-old nightmare continues in Africa. Due to the euphemized nature of contemporary colonialism, the struggle includes bringing this nightmare into waking consciousness.

Articulating limitations imposed through *neo*colonialist and *post*colonialist discourse, Farred (2001) presents an anti-postcolonialist discourse with a "primary ideological loyalty" that incorporates and renovates "the program of genuine social transformation that undergirded the anticolonial struggle, even as it attempts to make history under very different conditions" (245). In anti-postcolonialist discourse, Farred critiques the pitfalls of neo- and postcolonialist discourse while emphasizing the need to identify the "new class of 'enemies'" (245). What has changed, according to this discourse are "the terms of the struggle"; as a result "anti-/postcolonialism has to address itself to that. It is a mode of struggle that has to explain its genesis, be self-reflexive, 'permanently' vigilant about the project it is (de/)constructing, and explicate how it came to constitute itself as not only an oppositional mode of politics but a different political formation. Most important, anti-/postcolonialism—as a history, a series of practices, and a theory of resistance—has to become its *own* political modality and discourse. It has to produce itself... as a new form of politicized knowledge" (245).

In contributing to the anticolonialist struggle, I suggest that a starting point be a more concise multidimensional articulation of struggles against contemporary colonialisms. *Post*colonialism implies that colonialism existed in the past. *Neo*colonialism is broad, it is abstract, and it implies newness. I did not witness historical colonialism or new colonialism in Nigeria. I witnessed expansion and abstraction in who maintains the colonial status quo. I saw the black businessmen in Ngũgĩ's novel. They came dressed in human rights caps looking to reform and strengthen European criminal justice in Africa through foreign aid. They came dressed in police uniforms reinforcing a status quo that keeps poor people in prison. They came dressed in expensive Nigerian clothes speaking of big changes but only exploiting those who do not have power to self-determination. I came across these forms of colonialism because I worked predominantly in the area of criminal justice. Had I worked in a bank, or a corporate setting, I am sure they would have come dressed in business suits, as described by Ngũgĩ.

For these reasons I use the term "penal colonialism" in reference to contemporary conditions when discussing criminal justice in Nigeria. In addition, I prefer to rely on terms such as "economic colonialism," "political colonialism," "educational colonialism," "cultural colonialism," "geographical colonialism," "spiritual colonialism," and "psychological colonialism" when discussing other areas of colonial oppression. The violent reality is that colonialism has infiltrated and dominated entire social structures in Africa. In dealing with this violence we must first articulate it in its entirety. To do so we must stop relying on unidimensional languages.

In the realm of penal coloniality, I start by stating the obvious: colonialism was legalized by the same criminal system that legalized slavery. So-called *neo*colonialism was legislated through the same laws that legalized economic exploitation of Africa. Contemporary criminal justice systems (in Nigeria and the world over) were born out of a system that legalized slavery and colonialism. Not being conscious of the racist and violent foundations of the penal system restricts comprehension of violence in Nigerian prisons and prisons everywhere else. This lack of consciousness allows many to demonize Nigeria (representing blackness) for its struggles, while ignoring Europe's (representing whiteness) implicit role in this violence.

GEOGRAPHICAL COLONIALISM: CARVING UP AFRICA FOR A EUROPEAN THANKSGIVING

Nigeria as a nation-state exists only because Europeans held a conference in 1884–1885. The Berlin conference to divide Africa was meant to minimize European bloodshed in competition over African resources—it was a preventative strategy meant to avoid World War I as the British Empire and the Prussian (German) Empire (attempting to consolidate) competed for world domination. In attempting to minimize European bloodshed in this violent competition, Europeans sat down in Berlin and savagely carved up Africa, allocating to each other different pieces. This was done regardless of already existing social structures, political economies, and ethnic societies.

As I travelled throughout West Africa, it became apparent that current national boundaries were designed, not according to ethnicity or already existing African nations (or empires, as oral tradition records), but according to colonial interests and access to shores for trading and commerce purposes. Starting in Nigeria and moving west into the former French colony of Benin, I found that the Yoruba nation extended beyond the boundaries of Nigeria, along the southern coast, and that the Hausa nation extended beyond Nigerian national boundaries and spanned the northern regions of neighbouring countries. The official lines had been drawn vertically by colonialists, allowing access to the coast for trading purposes, but the unofficial nations still exist through language and practised traditions of people who live horizontally across several colonially defined nation-state boundaries.

In 1572 Abraham Ortelius, one of the most famous European cartographers and the producer of the first modern European atlas, printed a map of Africa[1] (outlined on the left below). A similar map was published in 1707,[2] illustrating that ethnic and sociopolitical organization in Africa relied on horizontal designs primarily defined by environmental conditions (coastal, Saharan, tropical, and so on). While each major section had a multitude of ethnicities within it, they were tied together in lifestyles and social organizations that relied on environmental necessities. After the imperialist Berlin conference in 1884–1885, Africa was carved up vertically and excessively to allow Europeans access to costal regions (outlined on the right below).

Each section of the map on the right was taken by a European nation. As a result, already existing social structures and economies were destroyed. Intense military and imperialist domination

Map 2.1
Africa in the Sixteenth Century

Map 2.2
Africa in the Nineteenth Century

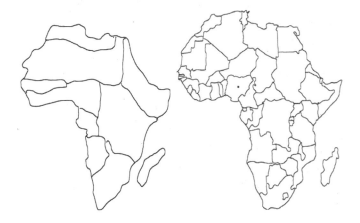

ensued through a colonialism reliant on the fragmentation of Africa. The racist and capitalist actions of Europeans over 100 years ago continue to define and impact Africa today. The map on the right continues to be the *post*colonial or the *neo*colonial continent. For this reason Nigeria (marked on the map on the right with ▪) literally exists within European boundaries and colonialist strategies. Living through those definitions for two years reinforced to me that the past is *never* just the past.

NIGERIAN DEMOGRAPHICS: OFFICIAL AND UNOFFICIAL FACTS

Here I present the resulting demographic composition of Nigeria. The country was taken over by the British. It is important to note first that Nigeria lies on a land mass of 924,000 square kilometres,[3] making it more than three times the size of the United Kingdom, with its land mass of 241,590 square kilometres.[4] The countries neighbouring Nigeria to the east (Cameroon) and the west (Benin) were "taken" by the French, resulting in the division of ethnic groups otherwise connected by language, tradition, history, culture, and social organization. Replacing these similarities and historically aligned societies, Nigeria now exists in a state of disparity, working to represent and unify hundreds of ethnic groups, all of which continue to be forced to surrender economic and sociopolitical control to European and North American banks, corporations, and foreign policies.

For these historical, geographical, and economic reasons, Nigerian demographics are highly political and complex. The numbers of people and the percentages of people that populate the ethnic groups comprise a political hotspot since power (in an assumed democracy) should be distributed according to majority representation. As a result, depending on the source, numbers change. The nation's population in western documents is officially (and by "officially" I am referring to the CIA *World Fact Book* but not deferring to its accuracy) reported at 133,881,703.[5]

While living in Nigeria, I heard unanimous reports estimating the population to be closer to and most likely exceeding 200 million. The Federal Republic of Nigeria reports a population approaching 140 million.[6] Western reports do state accurately that Nigeria is "Africa's most populous country" but inaccurately that it is composed of approximately "250 ethnic groups."[7] Oral history and information passed on to me while I was living in Nigeria documented that more than 515 ethnic groups live in Nigeria. The Nigerian Embassy reports at least 374 ethnic groups living in the country.[8]

According to Western records and international politics, "the following are the most populous and politically influential [ethnic groups]: Hausa and Fulani (29%), Yoruba (21%), Igbo (18%), Ijaw (10%), Kanuri (4%), Ibibio (3.5%), Tiv (2.5%)."[9] I do not take these numbers too seriously since I am fully aware of the political implications of these distributions. The fact is that the number of people belonging to each ethnic group is not well recorded. It is a highly controversial issue—so controversial that in 2006, when the Nigerian government tried to conduct a census, violence broke out, and many people refused to participate in it.[10] On one level, people do not trust governments, and thus refused to submit information on ethnic affiliation and location. This reluctance may be because the first so-called *democratically* elected president of Nigeria to take office, Olusegun Obasanjo, was a former military dictator (February 14, 1976, to October 1, 1979). He very reluctantly stepped down in the summer of 2007 after eight years in office. He was replaced by Umaru Yar'Adua, General Shehu Musa Yar'Adua's younger brother. General Shehu Yar'Adua was Obasanjo's deputy during his military regime in the 1970s. On another level, the political ramifications (especially in relation to the oil regions) would be massive if documented ethnic groups (largely underrepresented in the revenues gained from oil exports) in that region tried to claim their share of profits. The only unanimously agreed-on statistic in both Western and Nigerian records is that one out of every five Africans is Nigerian,[11] making Nigeria the most populated country in Africa.

According to mainstream politics in Nigeria, and according to numerous discussions I had with Nigerians (from various segments of governmental and non-governmental communities), the three most influential and recognized ethnic groups are the Yoruba, the Igbo, and the Hausa. This information is accurately reflected in official Nigerian statistics as presented by the Nigerian Embassy.[12] This demographic is best understood within the geographical divisions in the country relying implicitly on the original organization of Africa, pre-carving by Europeans. The vast majority of Nigerians (*all* whom I came in contact with during my two years in the country) recognize that the north is Hausaland, that the west is Yorubaland, and that the east is Igboland. The oil region is referred to unofficially as "south-south" and officially as the Niger delta. It is known to belong to several influential ethnic groups, the most influential, according to the people I spoke to, being the Ogoni and Ijaw peoples, although these reports of majority population came to me from members of those groups. Also worth noting is what was unofficially referred to as the "middle belt," an area between Igboland and Hausaland that was recognized as home to many minority ethnic groups, the Tiv and the Fulani claiming the majority of that minority. It becomes clear, as I attempt to present the basic demographics of Nigeria, that it is a complex region with many official uncertainties, and unofficial and very rich traditions. There is unanimous recognition of the fact that Nigeria is one of Africa's richest nations due mainly to high-quality oil in the Niger delta, and to its size and population, dwarfing surrounding West African nations. In stating that Nigeria is a rich nation, I am not stating that these riches are reflected in the lives of Nigerians. A monopoly of wealth, enforced through economic colonialism, continues to exist, with the majority of Nigerian wealth sustaining economies abroad.

SPIRITUAL COLONIALISM

When presenting the religious demographics of the Nigerian population, Western records state that Muslims make up fifty percent of the population, that Christians make up forty percent, and that ten percent of the population officially practise indigenous beliefs.[13] Many Christians in the country would dispute these numbers, claiming that it is a fifty-fifty split. Many Muslims have told me they comprise more than fifty percent of the population, and, in reference to the ten percent who practise traditional African religions, it became clear to me that the taboo attached to African spirituality has forced many into secrecy. Such taboos are direct remnants of colonialism and missionary impositions on the region, and represent one of the many dimensions of spiritual colonialism. In trying to understand the religious dynamics in Nigeria, I found myself researching the official statistics but listening closely to the records passed on orally. Politically and socially, I found that ethnic affiliations and loyalties transcended religious ones, especially within the context of violent confrontations. These political and ethnic conflicts were often referred to in Western mainstream media as religious clashes. The ethnic and political contexts that overshadowed almost all clashes, and transcended religious divisions, felt like a nationally understood phenomenon but an internationally kept secret.

LEGAL, POLITICAL, AND ECONOMIC COLONIALISM

Historically, the Portuguese were the first to arrive in Nigeria. By 1486 they had established major trading in ivory, gold, and enslaved people. "After 1650, the Dutch, French and British trade competition undermined the Portuguese" (Loew 1996, 812). This competition intensified as Europeans travelled farther inland. In 1830, as Loew notes, the British Lander brothers "reached the Niger River delta from the interior. By the mid-1800s [the Berlin conference came later], this penetration had led to major trade links between north and south along the Niger and Benue rivers" (812). After the conference in Berlin the British established a monopoly in Nigeria. By 1879, Sir George Goldie had established the National African Company, and in 1886

> Goldie's group established a wide governmental and commercial authority along the coast. Great Britain also established the Oil Rivers Protectorate in 1885.... It was renamed the Niger Coast Protectorate in 1893. *At the same time, the threat of German and French expansion from the north forced the consolidation of British inland territories.* In 1900 the British government withdrew the Royal Niger Company's charter of 1886 and established the Protectorate of Northern Nigeria. Frederick D. Lugard was appointed high commissioner and assumed full responsibility for Northern Nigeria. At the time, Northern Nigeria was a vast territory with limited resources. Forced to rule the country through the agency of its African leaders, Lugard's policies gave rise to the method of "indirect rule" which became the model for British colonial administration elsewhere in Africa.... In 1906, the British government established the Colony and Protectorate of Southern Nigeria, including Lagos Colony, and [the] Protectorate of Southern Nigeria existed separately from 1906 to 1914, though both were administered as a single unit. In 1914, the two regions were unified into the Colony and Protectorate of Nigeria with Lugard as governor general.
>
> Between World War I and World War II, *regional animosities emerged* between the north and the south and between the southwest and [the] southeast. *Conflicting economic interests and religious differences contributed to these animosities, though most of the hostilities between the Yoruba, Ibo and Hausa were based on ethnicity.* Increasing pressures for self-government resulted in a series of constitutions between 1946 and October 1960. The constitution of 1954 firmly established the federal principle and substantially reduced the powers of the governor.... Constitutional conferences in London in 1957 and 1958

prepared the final steps and set the final dates for the change from colonial self-governance to independence.... On October 1, 1960 Nigeria became the sixteenth African state to achieve independence. (812-813; emphasis added)

As shown in the emphasized text of this Western version of history in Nigeria, "the threat of German and French expansion from the north forced the consolidation of British inland territories" and drove many of the policies associated with the extraction of African resources for European gain. Lacking in this version of history (and in many Western accounts of African history) is the Berlin conference of 1885-1886. Also lacking is a connection between European invasion and the redrawing of boundaries in the conflicts that emerged between World War I and World War II. Instead, Western history attributes these conflicts to "religious and ethnic conflicts," void of European interventions and economic monopolies. These attributions continue to dominate conversations about conflicts in Nigeria. This is one example of the continuity of colonial logic in the construction of Nigeria through a Western lens. Since Euro-defined independence of Nigeria in 1960, the country has had twelve military and a few civilian)dictators. Olusegun Obasanjo is the current (and officially first but unofficially second) democratically elected president, as of May 29, 1999. He is Yoruba, and his vice president, Atiku Abubakar, is Hausa. Over the years, much like politics in the United States, Canada, and Europe, ethnic representation in governance has not included oppressed populations. In this sense, European colonialism has succeeded in reproducing Westernized democracy in Nigeria.

Since each ethnic group in Nigeria has its own language, culture, and traditions, the people of this former British colony communicate with each other in English, emerging in various forms throughout the country. Nigerian forms of English are known as pidgin or broken English. The officially recognized languages in Nigeria are English, Hausa, Yoruba, Igbo, and Fulani. The unofficially recognized languages are British English for the privileged and broken or pidgin English for the masses, with Lagos having a specific dialect of pidgin English encompassing many Yoruba words and expressions. Hausa is predominant in the north, Yoruba in the west (mainly southwest), and Igbo in the east (mainly mideast). The number of languages aside from these recognized languages is massive, with estimates ranging from 200 to more than 500.

PENAL COLONIALITY IN NIGERIA: OPPRESSING THE POOR AND MAINTAINING THE COLONIAL STATUS QUO

As illustrated above, the social structures of Nigeria were defined by European laws meant to exploit Africans. As a result the official legal system in Nigeria is based on "English common law, Islamic Shariah law (only in some northern states), and traditional law."[14] My work and experiences in West Africa brought me into contact with all three segments of the legal system, and gave me the opportunity to witness the mobilization of many community forms of justice (some violent, most reconciliatory) to address conflicts in ways that superseded the criminal justice system. For good reason, the criminal justice system, with its roots heavily embedded in European exploitation, is ideologically mistrusted. Administratively, the *criminal* justice situation in Nigeria is best described as inhumane, highlighted by the visible injustices occurring through official and unofficial (yet highly visible) criminal justice procedures.

Chomsky (1995) provides a Third World model through which non-Western nations become structured after historical colonialism has been implanted. He explains that this model incorporates contemporary "sectors of great privilege [with] growing numbers of people sinking into poverty or real misery, and a superfluous population confined in slums or expelled to the rapidly expanding prison system." In Nigeria the penal system's prison and police branches enforce a rapid criminalization of poverty, while social conditions, historical contexts, and contemporary politics promote violence among ethnic groups: if the people are fighting each other on a continuous basis, then the government and the small wealthy class can continue to exploit the country's massive resources with little opposition.

This is the role of penal justice in Nigeria: penal coloniality promotes divisions and stigmas that keep poor populations in fear of each other, thus unable to form a solidarity that can effectively challenge oppressive conditions. These functions of the Nigerian penal system[15] are similar to the functions and roles of the criminal justice system in the West; in Nigeria, these functions felt and appeared more obvious. It seems like a straightforward correlation found in a universal status quo: "the rich get richer and the poor get prison" (Reiman 1990). In Nigeria this status quo has foundations in generations of oppression and millions of dollars spent on illegal land occupation, degradation, and control. What appears to be a simple relationship is a complicated and highly politicized structure that is not ambiguous in mission.

The reasons for brutalities and human rights violations were clear to me in Nigeria's society of visible extremes. Nigeria was transparent—the direct benefits of corruption and oppressions were obvious, openly discussed, and understood by the average person. While I was there, Nigeria was not a place of comfort and superficial senses of security. It was a place where the rich, the poor, those in prison, those not in prison, the employed, the unemployed, the homeless, the landlords, the students, the teachers, the cab drivers, the bank tellers, the market women, the lawyers, the prison guards, the police officers, area boys (homeless youths living near bus stops in each neighborhood), the human rights activists, the government officials, and the journalists all seemed to understand that *government does not represent the people, that the penal system does not exist to serve and protect the people, and that the criminalization of the poor is a reality that is not debatable.* Yet, in facing all these indisputable realities, the people continue to fight each other through ethnic conflicts and continue to scapegoat street crime as the largest threat they face. Although most of the people seemed to be aware of the corruption and oppression inflicted on them as a direct result of the Nigerian government and the international corporations and nation states it works with to exploit Nigeria's resources, it seemed that few had the resources to fight back. I found myself coming face to face with oppression, witnessing its intricate functions and its truly disempowering demeanours. When day-to-day survival is a struggle, and when history is so merciless, organized efforts of resistance, although more vital than ever, become more difficult and for many seemed to border on the impossible. These feelings of hopelessness were often combatted in the lived resistance I saw on a microlevel by prisoners who formed communities to help each other in prison. Market women organized to resist police brutality in the workplace. Bus drivers went on strike to protest police extortion of bribes at each bus stop. On an individual and at times communal level, I found hope. On a macrostructural level, and on an international level, I am overwhelmed with the immensity of exploitation. To deal with this I work diligently to understand colonial domination.

WHAT IS COLONIALISM?

In attempting to study, or formulate an understanding of, colonialism, I find myself asking questions and facing conceptual barriers that are vague, difficult, and invisible, yet strong and real. In a quest to understand the absence of self-determination in Africa, I find it necessary to focus on the colonial justice system there since it presents some of the most visible remnants of colonial institutions. In searching for an accurate picture of what colonialism is, I found Fanon's (1964, 81) assessment of Algeria and the revolution against the French colonial government illustrative: "Colonialism is not a type of individual relations but the conquest of a national territory and the oppression of a people: that is all. It is not a certain type of human behavior or a pattern of relations between individuals. Every Frenchman in Algeria is at the present an enemy soldier. So long as Algeria is not independent, this logical consequence must be accepted." Within the context of occupied territory, colonialism comes forth as a dichotomizing force, enforcing oppressor and oppressed roles and, in revolution, forming enemy and ally status. Within this realm, I have come to see colonialism as the formal implementation of war, international wars disguised as civil conflicts, occurring within specified and foreignly defined national boundaries. An extension of these dichotomies exists today, as Hecht and Simone (1994, 18) describe the current geographical boundaries as central to an understanding of colonialism.

Considering that it was the European colonial governments that defined these boundaries, the official languages[16] of each nation-state, and their existing political and social structures,[17] it is important to place contemporary African nation-states within this context. While physical occupation of the land has legally ceased to exist, the co-optation of African social structures continues to occur, not only institutionalizing oppression within communities but also exploiting international relations while destabilizing continental associations. Merry's (1991, 890) assessment of colonialism presents an accurate summary of such intricacies: "Colonialism is an instance of a more general phenomenon of domination. Events that happened in the past, such as those in the period of colonial conquest and control, can provide insights into processes of domination and resistance in the present." Furthermore, Merry explains that an understanding of colonialism allows for an assessment of "domination at the periphery of the world system."

Merry (1991) and Tamanaha (2001) present two definitions of colonialism: one general and one narrow. Tamanaha's (2001) general definition, which I find to be accurate, relates to an assessment of the unequal distribution of power that occurs when one group endeavours to impose its command on a group it has defined as inferior. Merry's (1991, 895) narrow definition, which encompasses a more traditional view of colonialism, asserts that "the term refers to the European political, economic, and cultural expansion into Latin America, Africa, Asia, and the Pacific during the last four hundred years. Although similar processes have been going on for thousands of years, it is the recent European expansion, intimately connected with the spread of capitalism and the search for land, labor and markets, which has shaped the contemporary world". Tamanaha's definition of colonialism is the most relevant to the contemporary era because it is not specific to geographical land occupations and is based within a context of global power relations. It incorporates a definition that allows for an assessment of the continued existence of colonial institutions as a form of continued colonialism in Africa.

Césaire (1972, 13) presents an assessment of colonialism that is painful, more heartfelt, and, in my opinion, more functional in defining what the study of colonialism can achieve. He states that the study of colonialism allows society to "*decivilize* the colonizer, to *brutalize* him in the true sense of the word, to degrade him, to awaken him to buried instincts, to covetousness, violence, race hatred, and moral relativism." In conjunction with Césaire's switch of attention from colonized to colonizer, Hecht and Simone (1994, 18) assert that colonialism was as much about disordering Africa as it was about ordering and stabilizing the West, claiming that the consequences of colonialism must be studied both in the destruction of African sociopolitical systems and in the settling of the West more comfortably into itself today.

WHO ARE THE COLONIZERS?

Western European nations quickly come to mind when colonialism is brought up: the British Empire in particular, with some awareness of the colonial exploits of France, Spain, and Portugal. In a more current context, the Americanization of the Middle East, the wars in Palestine, Afghanistan, Lebanon and Iraq, the overthrow of governments, and the implementation of new democratic (i.e., US-compatible) structures in occupied territories are forms of colonization but are seldom discussed in mass media as such. The relationships between history and the present do not often enter the conscious political and cultural conversation. This is because colonialism has inappropriately been relegated to historical categories.

Although colonialism has been relegated to a historical timeframe, like a mistake from the past, assumed to have ended when the British Empire became less powerful in relation to the American Empire, Césaire explains otherwise: "I make no secret of my opinion that at the present time the barbarism of Western Europe has reached an incredibly high level, being only surpassed, it is true, by the barbarism of the United States.... And I am not talking about Hitler, or the prison guard, or the adventurer, but about the 'decent fellow' across the way [believing that society has progressed and civilized itself], a sign that cruelty, mendacity, baseness, and corruption have sunk deep into the soul of the European bourgeoisie" (1972, 26). It is not only the extreme regimes of the past that imposed brutality and oppression. Hindsight is important in noting such extremities. But a true understanding of history and the cycles of mass violence the West is participating in with Africa illustrate that present conditions and wars are also brutal, violent, racist, exploitative, and *colonial*.

The imposed historical connotations of colonialism have several implications. First, they place colonialism in a safe space, allowing colonial tenets and practices to continue — but outside the reach of contemporary criticism. Historical connotations function to disallow the colonized territories to point mainstream fingers at history, bringing to light the true cycle of power, and the continued degradation and exploitation of colonial practices. Second, they place contemporary colonizers in a more righteous position of power, making their actions void of historical context and thus more difficult to assess according to learned lessons, thus perpetuating and enforcing global cycles of violence. In reflecting on these cycles, Bourdieu's (1991, 163-164) assessment of symbolic power is applicable: "Without turning power into a 'circle whose centre is everywhere and nowhere,' which could be to dissolve it in yet another way, we have to be able to discover it in places where it is least visible, where it is most completely misrecognized — and thus, in fact, recognized. For symbolic power is that invisible power which can be exercised only with the complicity of those who do not want to know that they are subject to it or even that they themselves exercise it." The symbolic power of colonialism today lies in discourses of *post-* or *neo*colonialism. This is a language that implies change and thus assumes progress. This is a function of the evolutionary element most scholars apply to their understanding of history, assuming that a progression in time can be equated to a progression in conditions. It is always easier to assume that contemporary times are much more civilized than the barbaric past. While this assumption may aid the creation of positive identities for privileged groups, I do not find that it aids in the accurate representation of contemporary global conditions. These global conditions have left the colonizer sorry, but richer and stronger, and the colonized broken and poorer. I question the accuracy of this broken image, and the impact of the victim label on colonized nations, since much of victimization (in the Western context) seems to be associated with helplessness, backwardness, blame, inefficiency, and lack of dependability, carrying with it an infantilizing connotation that keeps the aggressor in control.

WHO ARE THE COLONIZED?

Writing during the era identified as colonialist, Memmi (1965, 91) claimed that mythology and dehumanization of colonized populations played a functional role of control, and he explained that "the myth is furthermore supported by a very solid organization; a government and a judicial system fed and renewed by the colonizer's historic, economic and cultural needs." Thus, even if colonized peoples maintained an African identity and resisted elements of degradation, "how could the colonized escape the low wages, the agony of his culture, the law which rules him from birth until death?" This question brings forth an assessment of resistance, but within the grander scheme of colonialism, what role does resistance play, and how successful has the colonized world been in maintaining and regulating its role in global politics? In a very warped world survival and success include submission to European and North American structures that historically and today are racist and violent. Struggles become defined through these domineering structures. In this sense those who are colonized are forced to submit to their domination in order to reach for an unattainable dream of success, or they are forced to reject that system of minority control, and become relegated to the outskirts of an already struggling economy and infrastructure. The colonial experience predicates racist exploitation. If you are a person in Africa, that exploitation maintains a heavy international inequality. If you are Black in America the same struggle exists, but instead of the international maintenance of injustice you are subject to internal colonization that presents a larger dream of success but provides no sustainable access to it. Who are the colonized? They are the people all over the world who are forced to live in poverty so that very few Europeans and their descendants can maintain power and wealth.

IMAGERY ASSOCIATED WITH COLONIALISM

Memmi (1965, 79) explains that, "just as the bourgeoisie proposes an image of the proletariat, the existence of the colonizer requires that an image of the colonized be suggested." It is within these images, largely supported by and promoted through Western versions of science,[18] that excuses and justifications for brutality emerge; void of this imagery, "the conduct of a colonizer, and that of a bourgeoisie, would seem shocking." It is the same imagery that I find consistent from the official cross-Atlantic slave-trading era, through colonial times of occupation (during which Africa was relegated to occupied territorial status), to the so-called era of African independence. The continued implementation of such imagery keeps the North/West deluded with self-identities of civility and development. In this process the negative imagery of the South/East must be enforced to maintain such delusions, for without beliefs in the inferiority of Africans the superiority of Europe and North America cannot construct itself. The imagery of colonialism is white supremacist. It is a normalized imagery that transcends derogatory white supremacist languages and lives through contemporary white supremacist institutions, policies, and economies that function in normalized and privileged cultures reproduced through Hollywood and constructions of the American Dream. It is a white dream, and its existence relies on the nightmare described by Ngũgĩ.

Gilroy (2000, 56) presents an assessment of colonialism within the context of racism that emphasizes this connection between the African nightmare and the American Dream. He explains that colonialism implemented an ideology that consigned Africans to prehistoric and prepolitical status. He asks, "in what sense does modernity belong to a closed entity, a 'geo-body' named Europe? What forms of conscious solidarity, and located subjectivity, does it solicit or produce?" In addressing such identities, he concludes that the process of colonialism provided an avenue through which "racially differentiated groups no longer shared the same present. The dominant groups could enlist their irresistible momentum of history on their side and treat the apparently anachronistic subordinates as if they belonged to the past and had no future" (56-57). Today the overwhelming majority in the West subjects Africa to a primitive image, one that encompasses pictures of a used-up victim of circumstance, too broken to participate in a future that was taken away through colonialism and slavery. Through these Eurocentric attitudes and institutionalizations of knowledge, the racist imagery that Gilroy addresses transcends oceans and enters the consciousness of mainstream citizens in Western societies.

Upon my return to North America from West Africa, discussions with friends, family members, acquaintances, colleagues, university students, and professors brought forth, with few exceptions, an overwhelmingly consensual response: Africa *is* perceived as a wounded continent occupied by broken people. This imagery contradicts my experiences in West Africa. I left Nigeria with a sense of empowerment, understanding that the West Africa that I experienced is a surviving realm, which, despite immense exploitation and imposed brutalities, stands tall, not broken, but scarred. In facing the contradictions between the negative consensus in the West and my empowering experiences in Nigeria, Benin, Togo, Ghana, and The Gambia, I found myself thinking back to the tribal marks on a Yoruba friend's face. The scars were deep and numerous, and I remember first reacting to them with surprise—scars are not often displayed in the plastic world on this side of the ocean. As I got to know him and saw more tribal marks on people's faces, I came to appreciate the beauty they accentuated in the physical features of a person's face, and I came to understand that scars (much like wrinkles), while seen as unsightly in the West, are signs of survival, healing, and wisdom in Africa. So when I say Africa is a scarred continent, I am placing that comment within an understanding that scars are signs of healing and that unhealed wounds beside them are connected to past injustices: the social, economic, and communal wounds that I did see and experience are not beyond the realm of control; they, like old wounds, would one day become attractive scars.

LINGUISTIC COLONIALISM

The negative Eurocentric imagery associated with Africa as discussed above is ingrained and most prevalent in the type of language used when discussing Africa academically, politically, economically, and (though less in these politically correct times) culturally. Through my discussions with people in the academic and human rights contexts, I found myself compiling a list of the double standards that are implemented and illustrated in the type of language utilized and normalized when referring to Africa and other continents that have mass colonial histories. The list is an ongoing venture and is nowhere near comprehensive, but it is representative of the discussions in which I have engaged. It starts with an international focus and ventures into an African national and criminal justice/law context.

Table 2.1

THE SOUTH and EAST	THE NORTH and WEST
1. *Under*develop*ed* or Develop*ing* Third World Nations	1. Developed, Industrialized, *First* world Nations
2. Tribal and Religious *Clashes and Riots*	2. War
3. Tribes	3. Ethnic groups and diversity
4. Brutality in Justice: Human Rights *Violations* – the problem is in how people treat each other	4. Brutality in Justice: *Shortcomings* in the penal system – the people do not hurt each other, its just that the system cannot be perfect
5. *Traditional* Justice Systems	5. *The* Criminal Justice System
6. Community Justice (informal/Localized)	6. *Common* and Civil Law (common, natural, universal)
7. Aid and Education *Campaigns*	7. Civil *Rights*
8. *Corrupt* Leaders	8. Leaders who make *mistakes*, are *misunderstood* or *misinformed*
9. International Corporate *Initiatives* and *opportunities*	9. International Trade *Agreements*, *Free* Trade and Capitalism

These differences in wording illustrate a double standard both in the definition of issues and in the implementation of solutions to these issues. In the hierarchical sphere of power, Africa continues to come in last (third place); in the economic realm Africa continues to represent a pot of gold that should be grateful for the exploitation of its resources; and in the human realm violence on African soil is associated with communal clashes, while violence on Western soil is serious enough to warrant international wars and global attention.

It has become clear to me that the value of life in this global order is related to power, and that privileged citizens of a powerful nation are entitled to anger and revenge when the lives of their loved ones are taken, while citizens of the Third World caste are not. Their anger is relegated to tribal clashing,[19] while the anger of powerful governments is used to justify illegal wars and expanding colonial conquests. The double standards are so engrained that they are present in the 'politically correct' language of this era. While it is no longer okay to call Africans primitive (in most contexts), it is now okay to refer to them as underdeveloped. I do not see a difference between the two terms. I do see a continued colonial mentality that justifies contemporary colonialism.

On another level, the informal approach to African issues, as illustrated in the language used, can be associated with resistance to assimilation, illustrating a flexibility of African societies that is complex in comparison to the simple rigidity of Western standards. When those rigid standards are not met, an informal relegation is accorded, and, while this informality appears degrading in the industrialized and corporate context, within a different context the inability to formally define structures in Africa can be seen as an African triumph. According to Chabal and Daloz (1999, 4),

> it is a consequence of the fundamentally instrumental concept of power which marks out what we call the informalization of politics on the [African] continent. There are, in consequence, good grounds for thinking that the weak character of the state in Africa may be more perennial than has hitherto been envisaged. It may well be... that the state in contemporary Africa will durably fail to conform to our own Western notions of political modernity.

While this lack of conformity can be viewed as a failure in the West, it came to represent empowerment and survival during my experiences in West Africa. It also came to illustrate that, when the West cannot understand or control something, dehumanization and degradation are tools it uses to regain control; while First World governments and institutions continue to use such tools to control their own citizens and to justify their own brutalities in relations with Africa, they cannot help but relegate themselves and their people to a dehumanized status. As justifications arise, brutalities expand, and, as brutalities expand, the First World becomes comfortable economically and politically, but socially perpetuates cultures of greed and deluded supremacies.

WHAT IS LEGAL PLURALISM IN RELATION TO COLONIALISM?

Legal pluralism is the academic field of study that formally recognizes that different types of legal systems can and do function in one society at the same time. This field of study arose within academic institutions during recognized colonial times when European governments invaded Africa and began to work to realize and attempt to categorize what traditional practices they could define as law. Different forms of legal pluralism have been defined and utilized over time. Classical legal pluralists, working during early colonial times, were largely a group of legal scholars and anthropologists schooled in the Eurocentric mindset that Western scholars had the academic tools through which African societies could be studied and understood. Their successors formed the new legal pluralist school of thought that worked to address such Eurocentric notions, but in doing so they did not address racism in academia but instead worked to address shortcomings in previous works. Legal pluralism, as a field of study, has spent much time observing, defining, and categorizing African societies. It emerged as a study of law within the classical legal pluralist framework and evolved into a study of culture in the new legal pluralist framework. The following is a presentation of how contemporary scholars discuss, define, and conceptualize legal pluralism.

According to Tamanaha (2001, 115), legal pluralism as an ideology was initially formulated by legal anthropologists who were researching law and society in the wake of colonialism. Their work brought forth what can be referred to as classical legal pluralism. This form of legal pluralism encompasses a general understanding that defines specific situations (e.g., colonialism) in which "two or more legal systems coexist in the same social field" (Merry 1988, 870). Hountondji (1983) assessed the emergence of pluralism in Africa within the cultural realm, asserting that cultural pluralism existed in Africa before colonial governments institutionalized themselves. He contended that pluralism as a scholarly notion emerged as a dichotomizing and simplifying force, artificially reducing pluralism to a confrontation between two extremities.

The new legal pluralism as defined by Merry represents Hountondji's pluralism. It represents an ideological shift that assumes that "plural normative orders are found in virtually all societies" (Merry 1988, 873). Within this understanding state law itself is recognized as plural in nature (890), thus allowing for the unequal distribution of harsh consequences; in addition, an understanding of power is implemented in this ideology, thus allowing for an assessment of the "penetration and dominance of state law and its subversion at the margins" (886).

New legal pluralism implements a developmental approach to understanding knowledge, reassessing research that emerged during the recognized colonial period, within the context of the political era. The study of African law vis-à-vis Western law continues to be central in this field. In these comparisons/ contrasts several new legal pluralist scholars have reached the conclusion that African "'customary law' itself was a product of the colonial period, shaped by efforts of 'native' modernizing elites to create law attuned to the new market economy and the efforts of European officials to preserve traditional culture and the power of tribal political leaders" in works to maintain control of occupied territories (Merry 1991, 893). In assessing anthropological literature and contemporary scholarly research, Merry concludes that native courts are not a function of precolonial law but a historical construct emerging during the colonial period to address issues of powerlessness among colonized populations and struggles between the colonized and their colonizers for land and resources: "The nature of law changed as it was reshaped from a subtle and adaptable system, often unwritten, to one of fixed, formal and written rules enforced by native courts" (897).

In these assessments Western scholars are able to recognize that colonial governments imposed their own definitions of law on colonized societies. What Western scholars are unable to recognize is that they continue to compare and contrast in a hierarchical manner, relegating what they do not understand to an informal status that implies lack of organization and structure. Assessing changes implemented by traditional modes of social control through the colonial process must be accompanied by a contextualization of contemporary social structures of control in Africa. Gilroy (2000, 41) stresses the need to recognize that *colonialism was a military enterprise* and thus implanted militarizing foundations for control. Abashi (1998) traces this militarization as an implementation of British colonial rule and assesses the constitutional building of a judiciary that has the discretion not only to access traditional laws when necessary but also to refer to martial law when needed. He illustrates the contemporary implementation of such constitutional regulations by bringing forth the kangaroo trial on November 10, 1995, in which Ken Saro-Wiwa and eight Ogoni activists were hanged on murder charges that did not allow for appeal after conviction.

These works illustrate the contemporary relationship between civil society and colonial legal institutions in Africa. It becomes clear that colonial and criminal justice models in African society are central in the processes that maintain oppressive conditions in Africa. The impositions of colonialism are brutal not only due to the racist attitudes to which they gave birth; they are brutal not only due to the uneven distribution of resources and wealth they reared; they are brutal also because of their militarization and criminalization of a continent that continues to struggle to deal with such histories and continues to struggle to purge itself of such abusive experiences.

WHAT WAS THE ROLE OF LAW IN THE COLONIZATION OF SUB-SAHARAN AFRICA?

The role of law within the colonial process encompassed mass justifications of racism and the legalization of exploitation. The same laws that legalized slavery and colonialism have been used to legalize globalization and criminalize resistance. Tamanaha (2001, 112) explains that the law implanted by colonizers was largely encompassed by regulations for economic enterprise. He also outlines the transition that occurred from laws initially meant to govern the colonizers (and to keep them accountable to their European governments) to laws transplanted to facilitate the exploitation of colonized people's resources.

Merry points out that "European law was central to the colonizing process but in a curiously ambiguous way. It served to extract land from precolonial users and to create a wage labor force out of peasant and subsistence producers. Yet at the same time, it provided a way for these groups to mobilize the ideology of colonizers to protect lands and to resist some of the excessive demands of the settlers for land and labor" (1991, 891). *The law used to oppress was also presented as the only legal means through which rights could be obtained.* In this ambiguity the law becomes both oppressor and liberator, thus placing within its realm the power to define liberty, take liberty, and shape liberty. In the colonial setting this power extends beyond liberty, and has come to encompass economic, political, cultural, and social consequences that not only enforce colonialism today, but also continue to keep the wounds from historical repression wide open. In the continued implementation of law as defined by colonial Europe, African societies continue to struggle to achieve freedom and autonomy, as defined by such laws.

In an assessment of the literature on law and society in the colonial context Merry concludes that "these works show how law served the 'civilizing mission' of colonialism—transforming the societies of the Third World into the form of the West" (1991, 894). In studying these missions scholars have focused on the points of intersection between traditional systems of conflict resolution and colonial legal systems, the new forms of law that emerged as a result of this interaction, and the points of resistance to co-optation that took form through traditional means of implementing legal and social control during colonial periods: "Colonial officials saw the decline in traditional authority as a threat to the stability of the colonial regime" (Merry 1991, 898). Law in this assessment becomes a reinforcement of colonialism. It institutionalizes cultural, economic, social, and political degradation. The continued implantation of such laws and criminal justice institutions on African soil will only aid in the continuation of a colonialism that may not physically or legally exist in Africa but structurally and institutionally thrives to impose a status quo that keeps colonial governments in first place and African societies in third place.

Merry also stated that "colonialism typically involved the large-scale transfer of laws and legal institutions from one society to another, each of which had its own distinct [precolonial] sociocultural organization and legal culture" (1991, 890). These transfers led to the implementation of what legal pluralists like to refer to as dual legal[20] systems and the emergence of an ideology that accepts their coexistence. What Merry and other Western legal scholars fail to recognize is that this coexistence is not the result of a mutual agreement, or a mutually reciprocal arrangement, but the result of a military enterprise that dominated one group through the occupation of homeland territories. Merry asserts that the implementation of dual systems (one for colonizers and another for colonized) has resulted in the emergence of a conflict in postcolonial societies, one that is centred on the struggle to "fashion a unified legal system out of this duality" while reviving and implementing precolonial traditions and laws (1991, 890).

My time in West Africa illustrated to me the simplicity and inaccuracy of such assessments. The duality of legal systems is not the centre of the conflicts that have arisen—the existence of colonial legality is the centre. While African civil societies continue to be exposed to colonial social structures and colonial criminal justice institutions, and the colonial corporate exploitation of their resources, African government officials are able to employ capitalist endeavours, making a significantly small portion of the population richer while driving the majority into poverty. This form of wealth distribution mirrors that which exists in the civilized Western worlds, and, while it manifests itself in more extreme forms in Africa, these extremities are not the main problem: the main problem is the very existence of a Eurocapitalist structure that nationally keeps the majority of

Africans poor and globally keeps former colonialists and their colonizing descendents rich.

HAS COLONIALISM BEEN ABOLISHED IN SUB-SAHARAN AFRICA?

Tamanaha (2001, 115) assessed the role of law in the contemporary context and found that, while the revival of traditional law was "one of the leading slogans of the worldwide decolonization movement of the 1950s and 1960s," the decolonization process kept much of the legal regimes "virtually intact through 'transnational' clauses that continued existing colonial law until repealed," and such repeals, if they were pursued, involved a lengthy bureaucratic process outlined in colonial languages and falling in line with colonial goals. Tamanaha also placed the role of Western law in decolonized settings within the context of international politics. He found that, "under the prompting and influence of international aid agencies, of transnational banks and other corporations that required familiar legal regimes as conditions of investment," and in the best interests of capitalism as "partially inspired by Weber's argument that formally rational law best suits the needs of capitalism," Western legal systems continued to implement control not only over the previously colonized peoples but primarily over their national resources (2001, 115). Africa as a continent is rich in resources but poor in wealth. Europe and North America, while not so bountiful in resources, continue to maintain control over global wealth. This legal construction of wealth through the capitalist structuralization of global politics is key in maintaining a colonial and exploitative status quo.

Through these assessments current global order is understood as built upon European colonialism. An understanding of contemporary situations void of the context of colonialism would thus constitute an incomplete and inaccurate representation. Hecht and Simone (1994, 17) explain that "colonialism was meant for the West to redefine itself in relationship to the world. And the work for which African bodies were captured during slavery has much to do with the West's efforts to change itself, to construct new kinds of economics and identities," forging a journey through which the West erodes opportunities for oppositional competition in the contemporary capitalist world order. In addition to these assertions Hecht and Simone outline the manner in which the African continent, in its "underdeveloped" nature, represents the potential, "not only to survive, but [also to] restructure and reinvent itself within a context of global realities" (15). Within this framework the dichotomization of the problems in Africa becomes difficult.

Resistance becomes a necessary function of oppression, and simultaneously oppression grows to become a tool through which resistance can manifest itself. Despite the Eurocapitalist and thus colonialist structures that maintain an uneven distribution of wealth, and despite the inhumane behaviour of Western 'civilized' states, resistance is not impossible, and oppression is not insurmountable. A starting point for resistance lies in the dismantling of the illusions that the West has constructed in its conceptions of Africa. The strength of such illusions lies greatly in the dichotomization of issues. In fragmenting and ignoring the interrelationships that tie historical and contemporary issues together, the imposition of dehumanized and inferior images of Africa can continue to be manifested.

An example of these fragmentations is the debate on the problems associated with capitalism. Chabal and Daloz (1999) outline the more traditionally dichotomized debate among scholars and politicians who discuss colonialism. This debate tries to decide how to address the assumed problematic nature of African political institutions. On the one side, some argue that political institutions have precolonial roots in the continent and thus are destined to fail; on the other side, others argue that political institutions in Africa are in the process of development, and naturally should face problems and downfalls. Hecht and Simone (1994, 31) bring this debate together, stating that "the power of African colonialism[21] was not so much to disrupt the internal dynamics of household, kinship, and social life but to disrupt the wide-ranging interconnections that existed among communities and people across often vast distances," adding that colonialism relegated the continent to an inflexible condition, devastating but not eliminating its political structures and internal economic cohesions.

Central to these analyses are not the functional or dysfunctional political institutions that exist in Africa but more the context within which Africa now exists. The reasons for the existence of problematic institutions in Africa are not simply a tenet and natural extension of historical oppression, nor are they due to the struggle to rebuild from the destructions imposed by an oppressive history. The problems are shaped (problematically for the West) by the attempted destruction of an entire continent's social, political, and economic structures. This attempted destruction is perpetuated through a debate assuming that destruction was successful and continues in discussion about why such destruction was successful, and what can be done about it. In resisting such unproductive and elitist debates, one can begin to restructure the conversation. What did Europeans achieve in their colonial brutalization of Africa (thus shifting the focus from what Africa is suffering to what the West is gaining)? How can Africans survive such brutality (thus focusing on the struggle as something that must be overcome)? What are Africans facing today in relation to the continued brutalities and exploitations of the former colonizing governments and corporations? How can Africans continue to survive (thus emphasizing that Africans are not victims but survivors)?

Instead of focusing on whether or not the rebuilding of Africa should mirror precolonial social structures, scholars may want to begin addressing contemporary Africa, and its interrelationship to history, culture, tradition, and strength. The proposed rebuilding process is problematic because it keeps Africa within a development framework assuming that destructions of African structures were successful. This is also problematic because people who engage in these debates continue to assess Africa through a Western lens: "Many discourses on Africa lament that the continent has lost its 'traditions' and become a dumping ground for the world's social and cultural waste. But in practice, Africans don't so much defend their traditions as allow tradition to take its own course, into terrain that is often neither recognizable nor acceptable" to the Western world (Hecht and Simone 1994, 23). In accepting their Eurocentric inability to conceptualize the survival and strength that Africa has displayed in resistance to colonial and slave-trading brutalities, Western scholars can begin to learn from not trying to describe African politics and social structures. The learning process may begin through an in-depth assessment of current domineering nation-states and their reliance on colonial racisms.

These colonizing nation-states have been unable to maintain their boundaries and national identities in West Africa in ways they were able to achieve in Europe and North America. The dilution of statehood in Africa is visible at the national borders that separate African nations but fail to separate African ethnic affiliations.[22] Between Nigeria and Benin, although laws exist to regulate trade between the two nations, "the border is the site of rampant smuggling, where unregistered markets provide a livelihood for many.... The illicit exchange is crucial to the economies of both countries. Officials are forced to turn a blind eye or risk further undermining the regions' precarious infrastructures" (Hecht and Simone 1994, 21). The rigid borders defined by colonial governments continue to be ignored by African peoples. The unacceptability of African social structures in Eurocentric eyes places Africans in a position of advantage. Because unacceptability is dealt with through a lack of understanding in the West, Africans can continue to be unacceptable in Western attitudes and non-conformist in practice. All of these factors prepare Africans for a globalization that appears to be dissolving notions of statehood, and transitioning nationhood to corporate and economic control.

While the imposition of colonial borders on African nations is formal and legal, these borders are meaningless in the face of fluid African structures able to adapt to rigid and centralized impositions. The non-elastic colonial national borders snap when confronted with the elasticity of African organizations and social structures. Although the laws that regulate trade between nations are being compromised, Hecht and Simone (1994, 19) explain that, while African societies have become "underdeveloped in the web of advanced capitalism," what they have essentially accomplished in this underdevelopment is the ability to slip "further out of either comprehension or control. Post-colonial regimes from Khartoum to Lagos have no idea how many people live in their metropolis, let alone how, with little or no employment or services, millions somehow survive." And it is in that survival that invisible governance emerges, confusing, sometimes frustrating, but in general destabilizing Western analysis of social structures, while empowering Africans enough to endure and transcend the hardships associated with displacement, oppression, and colonialism.

CONCLUDING COLONIALISM

Has colonialism ended in Africa? Has it transitioned? I have demonstrated that it has not ended and has not transitioned enough to warrant the use of new terms to describe current conditions. I suggest that, on an international and continental level, it thrives, that on a national level it is well defined in the structures erected to regulate Nigerian society, but that on an individual level I saw that people continue to resist colonialism and continue to exist. So legally, yes, the same system that legalized colonialism has now outlawed it, implementing legal independence for African governance. But what is legal is clearly not representative of what is applied. Economically, socially, and politically, colonialism still has a strong hold on the continent. And on the level of micropolitics, resistance continues: the oppressive living conditions of civil society continue to carry an emblem of survival against all odds. It is within this context that Nigerian prisoners live, and it is within these historical and contemporary conditions that their experiences can be appropriately and accurately understood. Outside this contexts, the colonial demonizing and projecting of political and social ills can continue. From within a contextualized understanding of oppressed and imprisoned populations, their struggles function as tools for understanding oppression as well as opportunities to gain wisdom on resistance to a dominant penal coloniality in these times of mass incarceration, private prisons, awaiting-trial prisoners, and abuses of political prisoners in military prisons all over the globe.

NOTES

1   See http://alabamamaps.ua.edu/historicalmaps/africa/index.html (W.S. Hoole Special Collections Library).
2   See http://bell.lib.umn.edu/historical/Hafrica.html (James Ford Bell Library, University of Minnesota).
3   See https://www.cia.gov/cia/publications/factbook/geos/bn.html.
4   See ibid.
5   See http://www.cia.gov/cia/publications/factbook/.
6   See http://www.nigeria.gov.ng/Welcome.aspx.
7   See http://www.cia.gov/cia/publications/factbook/.
8   See http://www.nigeriaembassyusa.org/thisisnigeria.shtml.
9   See http://www.cia.gov/cia/publications/factbook/.
10 See http://www.npr.org/templates/story/story.php?storyId=530 1389.
11 See ibid.
12 See http://www.nigeriaembassyusa.org/thisisnigeria.shtml.
13 See http://www.cia.gov/cia/publications/factbook/.
14 See ibid.
15 A system that functions primarily to keep a minority of the population wealthy and thus powerful at the expense of the majority, who are rendered poor, not powerful, and thus vulnerable to the processes of criminalization.
16 These languages continue to be used, facilitating territorial determinism of contemporary economic relations in Nigeria to England and the United States in general, in Cameroon to France, and in Angola to Spain and Portugal; in addition, "past" colonial Western nations tended to have the largest embassies in the African countries they previously "inhabited."

17 These structures are highly visible in the types of criminal justice systems currently institutionalizing each African "nation."
18 The Western fields of science provided Western "knowledge," which defined Africans as "inferior" biologically and culturally during times when Europe needed to justify its oppressive colonial regimes in Africa. The descendants of such scientists, now identifying themselves as (Western) "positivists," continue to do so in "research" that racially profiles African Americans as "criminal" and African societies as "developing."
19 The term "tribe" carries with it Eurocentric connotations of primitive cultures, while the term "ethnic groups" carries with it connotations of diversity in contemporary, civilized societies.
20 Legality is a Western phenomenon used in conflict resolution, becoming imposed upon traditional precolonial modes of conflict resolution. The transition from conflict resolution to "legality" often gets taken for granted, thus ignoring the structurally and ideologically imposed co-optations that took place.
21 This would more accurately be referred to as European colonialism, since it was the Europeans who colonized.
22 The Yoruba are present in southwestern Nigeria and neighbouring West African nations, while the Hausa people in northern Nigeria span northward into Niger and westward into Benin, Togo, and Ghana.

REFERENCES

Abashi, C. (1998). "The Military and the Administration of Justice in Nigeria." In *Special Military Tribunals and the Administration of Justice in Nigeria,* ed. F. Okoye. Kaduna, Nigeria: Human Rights Monitor.

Bourdieu, Pierre. (1991). *Language and Symbolic Power.* Cambridge, MA: Harvard University Press.

Césaire, Aimé. (1972). *Discourse on Colonialism.* Trans. John Pinkham. New York: Monthly Review Press.

Chabal, Patrick, and Jean-Pascal Daloz. (1999). *Africa Works: Disorder as Political Instrument.* Bloomington: Indiana University Press.

Chomsky, Noam. (1995). "Letter from Noam Chomsky." *Covert Action Quarterly,* 54. http://caq.com/CAQ54chmky.html.

Fanon, Frantz. (1967). *Toward the African Revolution.* Trans. Haakon Chevalier. New York: Monthly Review Press.

Farred, Grant. (2001). "A Thriving Postcolonialism: Toward an Anti-Postcolonial Discourse." *Nepantla: Views from South,* 2:2, 229–247.

Furnivall, J. S. (1956). *Colonial Policy and Practice: A Comparative Study of Burma and Netherlands India.* New York: New York University Press.

Gilroy, Paul. (2000). *Against Race: Imagining Political Culture beyond the Color Line.* Cambridge, MA: Harvard University Press.

Hecht, David, and Maliqalim Simone. (1994). *Invisible Governance: The Art of African Micropolitics.* New York: Autonomedia.

Hountondji, Paulin. (1983). *African Philosophy: Myth and Reality.* London: Huchinson.

Loew, Eric E. (1996). "Nigeria." In *Historical Dictionary of the British Empire K-Z*, ed. James S. Olson and Robert Shadle. Westport, CT: Greenwood Press, 812.

Memmi, Albert. (1965). *The Colonizer and the Colonized.* Boston: Beacon Press.

Merry, Sally Engle. (1988). "Legal Pluralism." *Law and Society Review*, 22:5, 869–896.

---. (1991). "Law and Colonialism." *Law and Society Review*, 25:4, 889–922.

Ngũgĩ, Thiong'o Wa. (1982). *Devil on the Cross.* Oxford: Heinemann Educational Publishers.

Nkrumah, K. (1975). "Neo-Colonialism: The Last Stage of Imperialism." In *The End of the European Empire: Decolonization after World War II*, ed. T. Smith. Lexington, MA: D.C. Heath, 199–208.

Reiman, Jeffery. (1990). *The Rich Get Richer and the Poor Get Prison.* 3rd ed. New York: Macmillan.

Tamanaha, Brian Z. (2001). *A General Jurisprudence of Law and Society.* New York: Oxford University Press.

CHAPTER 3

AN EVOLUTION OF THE PENAL SYSTEM: *CRIMINAL JUSTICE IN NIGERIA*

Viviane Saleh-Hanna and Chukwuma Ume

This chapter looks at the historical circumstances that came together to implement the Nigerian Prison Service and how they have affected its performance. What challenges has the institution been confronted with? The chapter also attempts to offer scenarios for the future. The first section looks at the justice system that existed before the advent of colonialism, the second section compares colonial penal systems and postcolonial penal systems, while the third section examines present penal systems and indicates options for responses. In laying out this history, we refer to geographical locations in Nigeria, and the following map will serve as a guide to these references.

TRADITIONAL MODELS OF NIGERIAN JUSTICE

Generally, crime in precolonial Nigerian societies was limited to serious violations of standard behaviours, customs, and traditions of the various communal groups. What was traditionally considered a crime or offence included behaviours generally regarded as abominations: murder, theft, adultery, rape, incest, and suicide. The definition of abominations was diverse according to the different cultures that exist in Nigeria. Offenders in these categories of crime were held responsible according to community sanctions. These sanctions were sometimes extended to their families and close relatives. Individualism was not, and

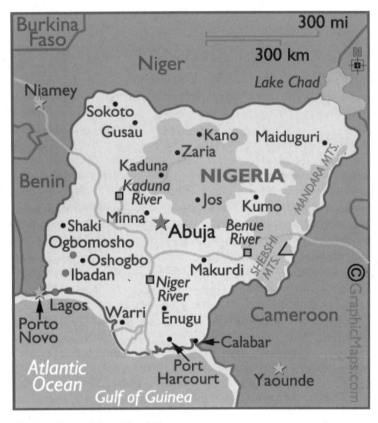

Map 3.1: Federal Republic of Nigeria

still is not, a central tenet of Nigerian society. For example, those who committed suicide were punished through the denial of decent burials (Igbo 1999). Any family member who violated such injunctions was in danger of being ostracized by the community until reparations and prescribed rituals of purification were undertaken by the family. In this way the extended family kept a close watch over the activities of its members to ensure good behaviour and compliance with societal norms, so as not to drag the name of the family into the mud for selfish or other personal reasons. However, for a recalcitrant or uncontrollable member of the family the last resort was to disown him or her, thus exonerating the family from any charges of complicity or cover-up. As one looks at the history of our culture, one learns that social control in most traditional Nigerian societies and customs was exercised by the community and the family, not by the state.

Banishment or execution of offenders by the community (today what we use prisons to accomplish) *was always a last option*. It was saved particularly for repeat offenders who participated in violent behaviours. In general, there were three broad classifications of offences: those against individuals, those against the community, and those against the gods or spirit world. Each classification has its own set of punishments. But what remains significant is that, apart from the extreme punishment of banishment or execution, there was no consideration of incarceration, particularly in southeastern Nigeria.

THE PENAL SYSTEM IN NIGERIA: COLONIAL AND POSTCOLONIAL ERAS

Imprisonment as a form of punishing offenders is alien to Africa's core values in the administration of justice. For the vast majority of cultures in Nigeria, imprisonment was not considered a valid form of dealing with conflict. To a small number of communities in Nigeria before the colonial era, separation of the offender from the community was employed. For instance, different communities in the western and northern parts of Nigeria did use various forms of imprisonment: the Ogboni House among the Yorubas in the west, the Ewedos among the Edos of Benis in the northeast, the Fulanis in the north, and the Tivs in the middle belt. In addition, the *Lagos Blue Book* indicates the existence of a place of confinement at Faji where offenders were imprisoned and employed mainly in street cleaning (Jarma 1998). These places of confinement functioned on small scales and were used to handle issues of banishment from the community. Stigma and demonization of prisoners were not a function of these houses. Total separation through high-security cultures was not central. The purpose of these forms of confinement was to secure community safety, and there was never a total separation of offenders from the community for extended periods.

It was only during the formal annexation and subsequent colonization of Nigeria by the British that penal institutions were manned by trained and commissioned officers[2] in 1861 (Elias 1964). By 1872 the first formal prison was built by the British colonial government to hold 300 prisoners. It was known as Her Majesty's Prison and was built in what is currently known as Broad Street in Lagos State. As the colonial invaders extended their frontiers, the number of prisons increased in areas where the British sphere of influence could be felt. Some of the prisons built around that period include Ewedo prison, originally built by a traditional ruler[3] (Elias 1964), rebuilt and expanded by the British in 1910, and then moved to Oko village to assume greater responsibilities and capacities. In 1900 Sapele prison was built under the Oil Rivers protectorate before amalgamation with the Lagos colony in 1906. In 1890, Calabar prison was built to detain convicts from the Calabar Rice Scheme. It was destroyed, however, during the civil war in Nigeria and thereafter rebuilt by the British.

The notions of "convict" and "criminal" were imposed by the British as they implemented their criminal codes. Prior to this time offenders were people who offended. As the British colonial government extended its power over the Nigerian region, it also extended the imposition of its criminal justice institutions and its demonization of our offenders, who now came to be defined as criminals. The separation of an offender from the community took on a new aspect as that person became a criminal through British law. In addition, the number of acts that could be defined as offensive to a community grew as the British implemented their colonial laws.

For traditional forms of justice to be recognized by colonial governments, they had to become institutionalized. With the establishment of what the British came to call "native courts," an expansion of prison building was undertaken. Abeokuta prison was institutionalized in 1900, while Owo prison was established in 1911 at Ifon and transferred to Owo in 1925. Ijebu-Ode came into existence in 1895; Agodi was established in the same year under the Prison Ordinance of 1884, with only two cells, to accommodate only a few male prisoners. Similarly, Kano central prison was set up in 1903 and was later moved to its present site in 1910, while Kazaure was established in 1908 to accommodate fifty prisoners. Like the prison built by an *oba* (king) in Bini Kingdom, Zaria and Kafanchan prisons were initially accommodated in the *emirs'* ("princes'") palaces.

The vast majority of the current prisons in Nigeria were built in the first two decades of colonial rule. Abinsi (now Makurdi) prison was built in 1918, Gboko prison built as a Native Authority prison in 1932, and Oturkpo prison institutionalized in 1924 and briefly administered from Enugu before the creation of a divisional headquarters. Others include Gwoza in 1920 and Biu in 1910 (moved to its present site in 1923). Nguru was built in 1928, while Maidugiri was first built in 1920 and rebuilt in 1954.

With amalgamation of the northern and southern protectorates by Lord Lugard in 1914, the Prison Ordinance of 1916 and the Prison Regulations of 1917 were promulgated. The ordinance gave extensive powers to the governor to establish and regulate prison administration throughout Nigeria. It also gave powers to the governor to appoint directors and other officers to manage prisons,[4] while the native authorities were operating at the local level and under the local district officers. Consequently, there was no uniformity in prison administration because of the difference in the mode of governance in northern and southern Nigeria. For instance, while prisons in the north were managed by *yaris* ("chief warders"[5]), in the south there were three categories of prisons: the provincial prison, the divisional prison, and the convict prison for those serving sentences above two years. The total institutionalization of a criminal justice administration had not yet occurred.

It is imperative to note that, although there were many ordinances and orders made by the colonial government to regulate prison administration between 1920 and 1960, it was not until 1966 (six years after independence) that the Nigerian federal government made concerted efforts toward the unification of prison administrations throughout the federation. These reforms worked to mirror what the British had institutionalized in Europe. With implementation of their institutions during colonialism, it was said that the best way to "work with what they had left behind" was to better institutionalize their laws. These transitions into a federally regulated prison service were encouraged, guided, and funded by Western (mainly European) governments. Thus, what we have today as the Nigerian Prison Service functioning under a centralized administration was established on April 1, 1968, following the Gobir Report (Jarma 1998) on unification of the existing central and native prison administrations. *The unification of administration, among other implications, signalled the beginning of the gradual withdrawal of British officers who hitherto had manned prisons in Nigeria.* As colonial institutions looked more like their own, they felt more comfortable in their withdrawals. Subsequent reorganizations in the prison service led to the promulgation of Prison Decree No. 9 of 1972. The decree chiefly placed the British prison system in the hands of Nigerians.

It is important to point out that the circumstances surrounding the period under review were also affected by sociocultural and economic changes. Crime rates had risen. Ugly incidents attended urbanization, and the creation of a British nation-state named Nigeria in West Africa had dire consequences. The exploitation of our economic fortunes and resources entered trade agreements with the industrialized world. Poverty was on the rise; so was crime. It was after the British pulled out of Nigeria that the economic situation here began to dwindle; as they deoccupied our government positions, they continued to occupy economic agreements and relied heavily on the institutions they had put in place during colonialism to maintain a European status quo. Consequently, during colonialism there was no recurring record of prison overcrowding, with its attendant consequences. Tools and facilities (particularly at designated vocational skills acquisition centres within the prison) were enough to carry out sentence planning of prisoners. In the *post*colonial era, when the British no longer occupy Nigeria, our resources extend further into the European economy, leaving Nigeria and Nigerians in greater distress. As the British left Nigeria, they took with them control over our livelihood. They expanded access to our oil reserves and in so doing destroyed our agricultural lands. They imposed a capitalist economy that keeps many poor and a few rich. And they left behind their *criminal* justice institutions, which could take care of those who did not fit well into the British capitalist economy.

THE NIGERIAN PRISON SERVICE TODAY

Against the backdrop of a series of efforts aimed at restructuring and positioning the prison service in Nigeria to meet up with its ever-increasing demands, particularly enacting Prison Decree No. 9 of 1972, another major shift took place in 1992. The Nigerian Prison Service became recognized as an important and strategic security agency. It was consequently removed from the civil service structure and made to incline more toward a paramilitary service.[6] The prison service became retained under the Ministry of Internal Affairs under the aegis of the Custom, Immigration, and Prison Services Board.[7] The board was mandated to manage and formulate general policy for the three paramilitary services, appoint and discipline all categories of staff for each service, and make regulations and standing orders for paramilitary services. The institutionalization of imprisonment through the centralization of criminal justice in Nigeria aided in a shift from safety of the community in precolonial Nigeria to security for the state in contemporary times.

Administrative Structure of the Nigerian Prison Service

Currently the Nigerian Prison Service has six directorates created to ensure and enhance specialization and institutionalization of the *criminal* justice bureaucracy in Nigeria. The directorates comprise:

- operations;
- administration, personnel management, and training;
- finance and supplies;
- inmate training and productivity;
- medical and welfare services; and
- works and logistics.

Each directorate is headed by a deputy controller general. At the apex of the structure is the controller general of prison,[8] the chief executive of the service, responsible for the formulation and implementation of penal policies. He is answerable to the president of the Federal Republic of Nigeria through the minister of internal affairs.

There are eight administrative zonal commands into which prisons in the thirty-six states, plus the Federal Capital Territory of Abuja, are clustered for proper coordination and supervision. Each zone is headed by an assistant controller general of prisons, a rank next to that of deputy controller general of prison, who heads the directorates at the headquarter office. Following the assistant controllers general, each state command is headed by a controller of prisons, who supervises the activities of the various prison formations at the state level.

Functions of the Nigerian Prison Service

According to the Federal Ministry of Internal Affairs annual report for 1997, the main functions of the Nigerian Prison Service are:

(1) to keep safe custody of people who are legally interned;
(2) to identify the causes of their antisocial behaviour, and to treat and reform them to become law-abiding citizens of a free society;
(3) to train them toward their rehabilitation on discharge; and
(4) to generate revenue for the government through prison farms and industries.

To implement any or all of these functions, the penal system is currently endowed with 148 prisons, 83 satellite or lock-up prisons, 10 prison farms, and 9 cottage industries for inmates' vocational training (Agomoh et al. 2001). However, the achievement of these tasks by the prison service today has not been easy, especially when viewed from its background and other historical antecedents, vis-à-vis the present scope and operations throughout the federation, coupled with the ever-dwindling fortune of the nation's economy.

The rate of recidivism, and the rate of deaths (or permanent disabilities) occasioned by malnutrition, long incarceration in the "single" or overcrowded cells, contagious diseases, and the generally poor welfare in most of the prisons in Nigeria today, indicate that prisoners are living in dangerous environments and, when they need it, are not receiving treatment or rehabilitation. In fact, the problems militating against the effective realization of these functions in the prison service today are many. Admittedly, most of these problems—overcrowding/congestion, high remand population, poor and dehumanizing ways of treating prisoners (health and welfare), poor planning and logistics—were ostensibly not in existence during and shortly after the recognized colonial period, for reasons initially outlined.

With the benefit of hindsight, it is obvious that there was no consideration or contingent plan for any or many of the problems affecting the prison system today. The concern then was primarily to contain a few dissident voices against colonial rule or the pocket sizes of Nigerians in the employ of the British institutionalized commercial and capitalist interests. Nevertheless, some of these problems could and should have been handled by the various successive Nigerian administrations, while others are linked to other agencies of the government. Unfortunately our options in Nigeria included ostracization from the international community through rejection of Western institutions and economic structures, or ostracization of our people through the continued implementation of European economic and social control structures and institutions. Like the leaders of many nations in this position, our leaders have chosen the latter, either out of fear of the wrath of Western military aggressions,[9] or out of greed for Western capitalist and imperialist wealth, or a combination of both greed and fear.

OUR TOMORROW: EMERGING ISSUES AND SUGGESTIONS

Despite all these problems, hope has always been kept alive. Over time there have been a series of interrelated efforts aimed at correcting some of these identified anomalies. We identify areas considered key for any meaningful reorientation and refocusing of the Nigerian Prison Service.

- In 1998 the federal government's Taskforce/Committee on Prison Decongestion and Reforms adopted a sector-wide approach and determined criteria for the *release of prisoners*, and by the end of the exercise some 8,000 prisoners were released nationwide. Regrettably, though, this exercise has not been sustained, only ad hoc. Those 8,000 prisoners were quickly replaced, and other prisoners have yet to be immediately released at such necessarily high rates.
- We believe that, rather than this approach, a more insightful method of prison decongestion such as alternatives to imprisonment or non-custodial

approaches should be embraced. Again, there should be a review of some of the obnoxious laws that enable law enforcement officers to arrest and detain suspects without having a reasonable conclusion of investigation by the police. There should also be some functional mechanism that allows our African values to re-enter justice through encouraged contact between prisoners and the community.

- As a starting step, we hope to implement a legitimate external non-governmental monitoring mechanism for the Nigerian Prison Service, conducted by independent observers who have the power to criticize and address brutality in prisons. Without external observation the prison system will be allowed to continue in its brutality toward and demonization of prisoners. External observation will allow us to concretely define brutality while abstractly allowing for questioning of the philosophies of imprisonment and its relevance to Nigeria. These approaches will put in place more sustainable solutions to the congestion of prisons in Nigeria because they will allow for identification of excessive use of power in imprisonment.

- Similarly, while we make the call for decongestion of the prison population, there is also every need for the prison system in Nigeria to consider urgent steps toward structural rehabilitation and provision of other related facilities. While we still have prisons in Nigeria, we need to address the immediate needs of the people inside them. Structural rehabilitation would include renovation of cells to allow for more healthy spaces (i.e. air ventalization) to combat disease and may include the reconstruction of wells to provide clean drinking water for prisoners.

- Also, in view of the dwindling economic fortunes of the country, coupled with the fact that we never have relied and likely never should rely on the state to fix our problems, it remains imperative that members of the community should quickly come to the aid of prisoners and become more involved in the issues relating to prison management. It is time to shift back to community safety and away from state security as central to justice in Nigeria. If the "decay" in justice continues unarrested, other social structures will continue to be affected to the extent that no meaningful life will be allowed to take place. The interconnectivity of our social structures is recognized and accepted by Nigerians. If we begin to address the problem of imprisonment, we can start the journey toward healing the rest of this colonized, lived existence.

CONCLUSION

The Nigerian Prison Service occupies a primary place in the colonial *criminal* justice system. The problems associated with the ineffective operations of the service have been enumerated here and elsewhere (Agomoh 1996; Odinkalu and Ehonwal 1991; PRAWA 1998). Some of the options for intervention highlighted in this chapter would enhance empowerment of Nigerian communities and hopefully lead to prison decongestion (and eventually penal abolition) as a first step toward addressing penal coloniality in Nigeria. On a more specific and immediate level, we need to work to ensure an improved welfare system for prisoners. We need to work back toward employing a system that addresses conflict and harm in a manner that centralizes integration of all peoples into our communities.

The structural decay that the criminal justice system has imposed on our African societies must be arrested. It is our hope that a turnaround can be achieved within a reasonable period of time as we make further journeys into the new millennium. Nigeria has endured slavery, Nigeria has endured colonialism, and Nigeria continues to endure penal colonialism in all its forms. We are concerned not only about *prisoners'* rights but also about a society that respects *human* dignity and inclusion; as long as we have prisoners, we are not free; as long as we have prisons, we are not postcolonial.

NOTES

1. See http://worldatlas.com/webimage/countrys/africa/bwmaps/ngbw.htm.
2. The officers were commissioned by Governor H. S. Freeman.
3. Oba Ewedo was the fourth *oba* who ruled the Bini Kingdom from 1255 to 1280. The prison named after him was rebuilt and made a maximum-security prison to accommodate 608 beds.
4. For more details on the ordinance, see Order 60 of 1922. It is also important to note that the first director of prison appointed after the amalgamation was B. Dolan, who inclined toward the reformation and rehabilitation of prisoners. Much credit was also given to him for his efforts in initiating the classification of prisoners in Nigeria.
5. Here we see the mixing of a traditional African term (chief) with an early colonial term (warder). The term "warder" rather than "warden" is still used in Nigeria, reflecting the early British colonial influence.
6. See Federal Government Circular B.63755/11/8311 of July 10, 1993, and compare Regulations 5 and 6 of the Draft Prison Regulations.
7. See Prison Decree No. 14 of 1986.
8. The controller general of prisons used to be the director of prison as initiated by the colonial administration. This became unfashionable in line with some of the restructuring that took place in the prison service.
9. History and contemporary events show that those nations that do not "coincide" with the demands of the West become demonized and attacked. If our political, economic, and cultural structures do not match those of the West, either we become "uncivilized" and in need of "liberation," or we become "dangerous" and in need of "attack."

REFERENCES

Agomoh, Uju. (1996). "Decongestion of the Nigerian Prisons: Practical Strategies for the Remand Population." Lagos: PRAWA.

Agomoh, Uju, A. Adeyemi, and V. Ogbebor. (2001). "The Prison Service and Penal Reform in Nigeria: A Synthesis Study." Lagos: PRAWA.

Elias, Oluwale Taslim. (1964). *The Prison System in Nigeria*. Lagos: University of Lagos Press.

Federal Ministry of Internal Affairs. (1997). *Annual Report*. Abuja: Federal Ministry of Internal Affairs.

Igbo, E. U. M. (1999). *Introduction to Criminology*. Nsukka: Afro-Orbis Publishing Company.

Jarma, I. M. (1998). "The Evolution, Management, and Development of the Nigerian Prison Service in the Colonial and Post Independent Era." Paper presented at the workshop on Nigeria Prison System: Issues and Ideas for Reform, Abuja, November 10–12.

Odinkalu, A. C., and L. Ehonwal. (1991). "Behind the Walls." Lagos: Civil Liberties Organization.

PRAWA. (1998). "Agenda for Penal Reform in Nigeria." Lagos: Prawa.

CHAPTER 4

THE MILITARIZATION OF NIGERIAN SOCIETY

Biko Agozino and Unyierie Idem

INTRODUCTION BY DR. KAYODE FAYEMI

The dominant wisdom, a year and a half after Olusegun Obasanjo assumed office as Nigeria's president in May 1999, is that the country is now a democracy. It is true, of course, that elections were held and that candidates vied for various positions on the platforms of political parties, as a consequence of which a democratically elected government, along with a National Assembly and its counterparts in the states, are now in power. As I have argued elsewhere, however, polling booths and voters are not all that make a democracy. Indeed, democracy, at its core, is a state of mind, a set of attitudinal dispositions woven into the fabric of a society, the concrete expression of which are its social institutions. Undemocratic social institutions cannot, therefore, sire or sustain democratic governments, no matter how often the ballot box ritual is enacted.

This is the kernel of the argument advanced by Biko Agozino and Unyierie Idem in this important chapter, which takes a hard look at the country's social fabric: the institution of the family, the educational system, the economy, the military, the judiciary, and traditional communities.[1] It concludes that the more than thirty years of rapacious military dictatorship, which the Nigerian people have been forced to go through, have left an indelible mark on the collective psyche. This psyche has been so militarized that it now embraces force and routine violence, and instinctively shies away from debate and dialogue, the two all-important props without which a truly democratic edifice cannot stand.

Employing the refreshing method of participant observation, and using the descriptive tools of anecdote, personal narrative, and eyewitness account, the authors offer us a graphic and troubling picture of a country at war with itself, where children are brutalized by parents, students are terrorized by teachers and government officials alike, and traders and other economic actors are engaged in a vicious war of cat and mouse with rivals, armed robbers, and security agents on the make. In churches and mosques the talk is of spiritual warfare and *jihad,* cudgels, bows and arrows rather than the tools of persuasion and conversion. Military decrees have banished judges and the rule of law to the margins of social life, and guns have usurped legal tomes as the final authority.

It is an unflattering portrait of a society in a state of anomie, a society where, to quote the Nigerian scholar Attahiru Jega (1997), whose work is cited in this paper, the "prolonged nature of military rule has constricted democratic space, entrenched authoritarianism, and nurtured nihilism."

Is it possible, then, for democratic politics and the institutions that sustain it to take firm root and blossom in this harsh landscape? This is the burden of this chapter. Agozino and Idem's contention is that Nigerians need to undergo a process of "demilitarization" akin to a detoxification exercise that will make them unlearn and discard the military ethos they have unwittingly acquired over the years since 1966, before the journey toward a truly democratic country can properly begin. The main strength of this chapter is how the authors take great pains to succinctly demonstrate how Nigerian society became infected with the "military" virus. They implicitly argue that what is learned can be unlearned, that society is not atavistically bound to violence, and that, given the right mix of programmes and policies, what is damaged can be made whole again.

And therein lies the importance of this chapter. It refuses to take the country's new democratic dispensation for granted, preferring to see it as a tender sapling that requires plenty of water and sunshine to take root and flower. And this water and sunshine are the country's social institutions that, as the authors make clear, are so battered and bruised that they are more likely to smother the sapling of democracy than nurture it if they are not reformed within the appropriate policy framework. Agozino and Idem have outlined the steps that, if taken conscientiously, not only will safeguard Nigeria's nascent democracy but also may be exported to neighbouring West African countries still grappling with dictatorship and militarization of the communal psyche.

This chapter makes a demand not only on Nigeria's political and civil society leaders but also on the international community, particularly policy-makers in Europe and the United States currently involved in the important work of rolling back military dictatorship, civil war, and poverty in Africa. If there is one thing that this chapter makes clear, it is that bad economics breeds poverty, and mass poverty in turn invites military dictatorship. Dictatorship, as Africa's recent history has abundantly demonstrated, is a key cause of civil war. And where there is war, democratic politics flies out the window.

The battle to shore up democracy on the continent must therefore adopt a holistic strategy, integrating the economic, social, and of course political in a marathon designed to firm up the institutional structures that ultimately must support democratic governance if it is to have any chance of surviving beyond the ballot box ceremonial.

CONTEXT AND METHODOLOGY

Between December 1998 and January 1999 we conducted an ethnographic study in six states in Nigeria on behalf of the Centre for Democracy and Development. While campaign groups in the country at the time directed their attention to the return of the military to the barracks, we focused on militarization as a process that goes beyond the military, permeating the whole of civil society. And while donor agencies encourage a definition of civil society that refers specifically to non-governmental organizations (NGOs), we adopted a sociological definition that embraces the institutions of the family, education, religion, economy, community relations, and justice. Finally, while many commentators assume that Nigeria is unique, we assume that Nigerians have a lot to learn from and to teach their immediate neighbours in West Africa about the means of democratizing a militarized civil society.

This project aims to highlight the obstacles to democratization due to the institutionalization of a militaristic ethos in Nigerian culture and society. The project attempts to identify ways and means of strengthening civil society through a structured process of democratizing Nigerian culture and politics.

The project focused preliminarily on six states in the country: Enugu State in the east, Cross River State in the southeast, Lagos State in the west, Plateau State in the middle belt, and Kaduna and Kano States in the north. Approximately one and a half weeks of archival research, observations, and interviews were conducted in each of the six states. The fieldworkers also established contact with experienced researchers in these states who wanted to collaborate on the more definitive project.

While most campaign and research organizations in the country concentrated on the military handover to a civilian administration, we observed the militarization of family and kinship relations, with men assuming a militaristic attitude toward women and children, resulting in widespread domestic violence, abuse, and anti-democratic tendencies in civil society. Children were beaten all the time by adults, men beat women, some women were killed or maimed, while the culprits were accountable to no one.

Yet the institution of the family remains one of the strongest supporters of the struggle for democracy in the country. At a time when it was easy for political activists to be betrayed, family members stood by their own in most cases. Also, in spite of the authoritarianism within the institution of the family, it remains one of the most open democratic spaces where genuine criticism is expected and given without fear of censure. We would like to extend this observation to the rest of West Africa to see if the countries that are less militarized are also less authoritarian in gender and kinship relations compared to the more militarized ones.

The educational system in Nigeria reinforces the authoritarianism of the family not only by widespread use of security officials to run institutions of higher learning but also because of the authoritarian orientation of the civilian educational administrators and government officials, who ban legitimate staff and student unions. In the reigning atmosphere of insecurity, intimidation, and frustration, some students and lecturers join or form secret cults through which they vent their pent-up feelings by murdering, raping, maiming, and terrorizing fellow students and sometimes staff.

Paradoxically, as in the case of the family, the educational institutions remain one of the gateways to democracy in the country, given their capacity to serve as places of open criticism and debate in spite of attempts to muzzle critical scholarship. This is evident in the fact that Nigerian students, lecturers, and many university administrators remain in the vanguard of the struggle for democracy even when a majority of their colleagues remain silent supporters of the repressive system.

The religious institution is also militarized. Members of religious organizations whom we interviewed emphasized that they were engaged in spiritual warfare, and this is not always too far behind actual wars against rival religious organizations. This strong militaristic ideology inherent in all organized religions needs to be studied in greater detail with a view to increasing the democratization of religious practices and beliefs. After all, underlying every religious faith in the country is the assumption that people should love one another, indicating that this divisive institution could yet be made to deepen democratic beliefs, more so as key members of the priesthood and some clerics have been advocating the advantages of democracy in the country.

The legal institution in Nigeria is militarized through the role of special military tribunals in the trials of civilians; the widespread use of armed soldiers and police officers to shoot suspected criminals on sight, resulting in the killing of innocent people; the appalling conditions in overcrowded jails, where detainees are held without charge; the use of capital punishment; and the lack of democratic accountability by security agents. These issues will be explored further to find ways of demilitarizing Nigerian law and enhancing its democratization because the law remains one of the chief instruments of challenging authoritarianism in the country, albeit in a limited fashion.

The economy is one of the most militarized of Nigerian institutions. Traders speak of the practice of using army officers to collect debts or settle scores, the use of hired killers to murder rivals, and the use of religious rituals and sorcery in the spiritual warfare that is thought by some to accompany trade. Nigerian workers receive brutal treatment at the hands of employers and the government. Then there is interference with trade union activities resulting in seizure of the unions and their administration by government-appointed sole administrators, the sponsorship of rival unions often armed and used to attack genuine representatives of workers, the horse-whipping of striking workers and their summary dismissal, and the deprivation of the communities around industrial locations and the use of "carrots" to divide such communities, resulting in internecine conflict.

These conflicts sometimes spill over and affect industrial installations, thus giving security agents the excuse to use live ammunition against unarmed demonstrators. Are the economies of the rest of the Economic Community of West African States any less militarized than the Nigerian example?

Transportation companies routinely hire armed escorts to protect the passengers from robbers, but the armed men that the passengers usually encounter are at the countless military and police roadblocks, brazenly extracting illegal tolls from every passing driver, thereby inflating transportation fares. While some traders kill innocent people for "money medicine," others take the law into their own hands and execute suspected criminals, referred to by Aba traders in the eastern part of the country as "mice."

These issues require a closer look to find alternative consensual ways of running the economy rather than perpetuate the militarization of this vital institution of Nigerian civil society. As in the case of the other institutions mentioned above, the militarization of the economy sits side by side with free-market beliefs and the deep-rooted democratic practice of haggling in which the buyer is encouraged not to be intimidated by the dictatorship of the trader but to make an offer based on a sense of fairness and decency, unlike supermarkets in the West, where the prices of items are not open to bargaining.

Some communities have adopted the barracks mentality of "might is right," especially in the contest for elective political office characterized by thuggery and violence. Some traditional rulers run secret cults with which they intimidate people in rural areas and extort money from them as fines without due process. Young people who are thought to be delinquent are rounded up, blindfolded, and tortured with threats that they could be executed. At night armed vigilante groups patrol the streets with what one informant called "enough guns to wage a war." Even in the cities the streets are barricaded, and armed watchmen take over at night. Indeed, people live in a state of war. Rather than resigning ourselves to this state of affairs, it is wise to search for alternative ways of policing the community that would be more democratic and less militaristic, given that many Nigerian communities have age-old traditions of democratic republicanism in the true sense of that phrase.

We propose that the questions raised about lessons from other parts of West Africa be pursued by extending the ethnographic research to the rest of the region. We also recommend that a group of three researchers/activists be set up in each of the six

Nigerian states visited and funded for three years to continue the process of observation and analysis, and to coordinate the implementation of the practical implications of the project in their areas. They would employ two full-time research and education officers (twelve altogether) from the fund. These hires will ensure that the paradoxical observations highlighted by the preliminary trip will be investigated more closely and documented in greater detail for the purpose of developing an educational programme that could help to disseminate the findings of the research and thereby help to end the militaristic ideology in civil society.

The education programme would be implemented through a series of radio programmes that would broadcast, in pidgin English and Nigerian languages, issues of democracy and "literacy." A monthly journal could be funded for all the groups to contribute articles to and for discussions of the curricula of the weekly grassroots democracy literacy classes. An annual democracy literacy conference should also be funded for all the groups and the foreign-based partners to review progress and plans.

UNDERSTANDING MILITARIZED CIVIL SOCIETY: ANALYTICAL FRAMEWORK

Military rule in Nigeria seems to be the norm rather than the exception. The military has ruled the country for more than thirty years in its forty years of independence. According to Attahiru M. Jega (1997), "this prolonged nature of military rule has constricted democratic space, entrenched authoritarianism, and nurtured nihilism, while economic crisis and structural adjustment have battered Nigerians, and has indeed led to the increasing questioning, if not challenging, of the legitimacy of the State." Such a crisis of democracy is compounded when the government becomes even more militaristic and authoritarian in an attempt to silence dissent.

This project focuses on the administration of justice, the conduct of trade and industry, the conduct of private life, the practice of religion, organized political activity, and the politics of traditional forms of authority. This empirical focus was complemented by interviews with individuals and archival research to determine to what extent the military style of exercising power has permeated civil society in the country. We interviewed experts and members of the elite, but went beyond their opinions to interview ordinary urban and rural dwellers to highlight the lessons that Nigerians need to learn about how to deepen the democratization of civic life.

The ongoing communal conflicts in Nigeria that threaten the process of transition to civil rule in the country make such a project urgent to ensure that the military is kept out of Nigerian politics. Previously, discussions focused only on the military in politics (Bell 1968), but by focusing on militarization as an issue that goes beyond the military the project stands a chance of making an innovative contribution to the search for solutions to the democratic crisis in the country. Ways of achieving such a goal were explored through interviews with ordinary Nigerians and experts alike, direct observation, and archival research. The implications of the findings for West Africa and the rest of the continent are highlighted in this chapter, and hopefully will be followed up in further research.

In the course of the research for this chapter we sought answers to questions of how to democratize a militarized civil society from diverse sections of Nigerian society, with a focus on how much civil society has been militarized. Answers to such questions were previously sought in the way to limit military involvement in politics or how to seek accommodation of the military in politics.

No matter which society we care to examine, the assumption that militarization is an essential aspect of social life goes largely unexamined. The few who have examined this link have restricted themselves to an examination of the role of the military in politics. Some argue that the military as an institution is needed for the defence of the territory of the state. Others point out that the interests of the state are often interpreted from the point of view of the interests of the ruling classes. Some have argued that, when their nation is at war, they are duty-bound to support their country and fight in defence of the fatherland or motherland. Others point out that the defence of the homeland has been used as a slogan even when the competing interests of the ruling groups, especially in commercial activities, lead to war in which ordinary people are expected to back their country. Still others add that, even in aggressive wars or defensive ones, it is always the poor who are forced to fight one another in the interests of the ruling classes.

Consequently, some call for all the poor people of every country to refuse to fight one another just because they happen to live within different borders. They call for the poor to boycott all wars and mutiny once the ruling classes declare war on the working people of a different country. They also call on workers who are not in the army to support the soldiers by going on strike in order to force the belligerent ruling classes to settle their disputes democratically.

This approach has been dismissed as "heroic folly." It is all very well, it has been pointed out, for soldiers to desert as soon as war is declared. It is also heroic to call for workers to go on a general strike in opposition to imperialist war. However, this idea is sheer folly because it plays into the hands of the ruling classes, which could use martial law to suppress the working people. It is also folly to wait until war has been declared before opposing it.

This heroic folly has been contrasted with "opportunistic cowardice" among those who call for unqualified patriotism in defence of the homeland. Accordingly, those who adhere to this form of social chauvinism are accused of forgetting that the days of progressive national wars have been replaced by imperialist wars and that the working people should always try to turn these imperialist adventures into civil wars in their individual countries (Lenin 1974).

So even those who oppose militarism have focused on the army and on warfare. The present project aims to analyze the extent to which militarism has gone beyond the army and warfare to penetrate and militarize civil society. We focus on different social institutions in turn to see how democratic they are and, if militarized, how to go about demilitarizing and democratizing them. At the risk of oversimplification, militarism is defined here as *the use of force to settle any disagreement or to enforce order instead of relying on intellectual and moral leadership to command respect or obedience.*

Eminent sociologist Stuart Hall (1996), in a paper originally presented to a colloquium on Theoretical Perspectives in the Analysis of Racism and Ethnicity, organized in 1985 by the Division of Human Rights and Peace, UNESCO, Paris, follows Italian intellectual and politician Antonio Gramsci in offering a clear view of a militarized civil society that is similar to the one adopted in this project. Gramsci (1971) argued that the intellectual or moral leadership of a class, or what Lenin called working-class hegemony, over other classes is exercised not only by the working class, who need to win the support of the peasantry and other exploited classes (by moral and intellectual leadership rather than by force) in their struggle against the exploiters (especially in underdeveloped economies such as that of Nigeria, where the industrial and office workers are numerically weak), but also by the ruling class, who are too few to rule by force alone and are thereby forced to lead as well, though not entirely without force.

Furthermore, according to Hall (1996, 426), such moral and intellectual leadership differs from pure domination, coercion, and economic-corporate monopoly over the legitimate forceful means, not because they are completely absent in a hegemonic situation but because "hegemony is not exercised in the economic and administrative fields alone, but encompasses the critical domains of cultural, moral, ethical and intellectual leadership." Hall goes on to add that "it is only under those conditions that some long-term historic 'project'—for example, to modernize society, to raise the whole level of performance of society or transform the basis of national politics—can be effectively put on the historical agenda."

According to Hall, this clarification by Gramsci of the nature of hegemony is based on an important distinction Gramsci made in the *Prison Notebooks* (1971), the book he wrote when the fascist dictatorship of Mussolini clamped him into jail for his working-class politics. In the essay "State and Civil Society" Gramsci argues that, contrary to the assumption of liberal social contract theorists such as Thomas Hobbes and John Locke that civil society is a state governed by rational civic law as opposed to anarchic natural law in the state of nature, there are two types of civil society in capitalist society, and both of them are extremely militarized. The first type is characterized by modes of struggle that Gramsci called the "war of manoeuvre," in which the struggle between classes is concentrated in one decisive battle where strategic victory is won "in a flash" by breaching the defences of the opposing class. The second type of militarized civil society is characterized by modes of struggle that take the form of a "war of position." This type of struggle is more protracted, taking place on many different battle fronts, so it is impossible to win the struggle through any single breach without taking into account the whole structure of society. These complex positionalities suggest that the struggle to democratize Nigerian civil society, for example, must abandon the antiquated tactic of the war of the trenches or the war of manoeuvre because these "wars" have a tendency to centralize and focus on a single issue: soldiers, regionalism, classes, or corruption. The war of position demands a careful look at the militarization of "the voluntary associations, relations and institutions of civil society—schooling, the family, churches and religious life, cultural organizations, so-called private relations, gender, sexual and ethnic identities, etc.—[which] become, in effect, 'for the art of politics... the "trenches" and the permanent fortifications of the front in the war of position: they render merely "partial" the element of movement which before used to be "the whole" of war'" (Hall 1996, 428, expanding and quoting Gramsci 1971, 243).

Our approach extends the limited perspective of Gramsci by including the judiciary, one of the more coercive arms of the state, in the conception of civil society. We do so deliberately to emphasize that juridification always goes beyond the law courts and that, even with specific reference to the courts, it is necessary to emphasize that civil society does not begin where the state ends but actually remains a part of the state, where leadership is or should be based more on consent (but never without force at all) than on force (with or without consent). By adopting the definition of a militarized civil society advanced by Gramsci and extended by Hall, we warn that Nigeria is not the only country with a militarized civil society. The problem of militarization is global, and differs from country to country and from time to time. Thus, our study of Nigeria offers important lessons on how to democratize militarized civil societies throughout the world.

We apply this broad conception of civil society in our project. A similar approach was adopted by Momoh (1998) in a paper presented at the Workshop on Comparing Experiences of Democratization in Nigeria and South Africa in Cape Town. He is critical of those influenced by "ahistorical and Eurocentric ideology" who deny the existence of civil society in Nigeria and of those who claim that civil society emerged in Europe before the state. To him, civil society has always been an arena of different forms of struggle—social, cultural, economic, and political. Mamdani (1995) also reviewed the misleading dichotomization of state and civil society in Africanist studies, and concluded that African problems should not be seen simply as evidence of primordial influences. Our focus on militarization illustrates that this is a global problem with African dimensions.

PRELIMINARY NOTES FROM THE FIELD

Before travelling to Nigeria at the end of November 1998 for the field trip, we needed to go to the Nigerian High Commission to renew one of our passports. There were only seven of us at the High Commission by 9:30 that morning. As soon as the receptionist signalled that it was time for us to queue, a fight broke out between a man and a woman over who should be the first to be attended to. She slapped him, and he struck her in return. The woman began to cry: "You call yourself a man, and you are fighting a woman!" She struck out at him again and again, with her handbag, with her palm. He tried to strike back, and another man pushed him aside. They squared off and started a boxing match.

Tempers calmed down after a while, and the man apologized to the embassy staff. We suggested that he apologize to the woman as well. He did so, but the woman said that an apology was not enough. The receptionist said that it was too late in any case because he had called the police. The police came and took statements. It was not until one o'clock in the afternoon that the man returned to join a much longer queue, but the woman was nowhere to be found. Perhaps she had immigration problems and she was detained for further questioning by the police. At about three o'clock we saw the woman outside the High Commission gesticulating and talking animatedly with another man.

The lesson is that, even with only seven Nigerians queuing up to go into an office, there will be a rush to see who will be the first. It would have cost the man and the woman less time to allow the other to be attended to first. Much later, in a different context, the Nigerians waiting all day for their applications to be processed started offering explanations about why they were frustrated. Some said the reason is that Nigerians do not love one another. They said that, when you go to the embassies of people who love their country, you are not made to wait all day. They also said that, when foreigners come to the High Commission, they are treated better than Nigerians themselves.

How true is this idea that we do not love ourselves? Is it connected to the fact that we have been brought up under undemocratic regimes where people got nothing unless they were willing to fight for it? How do we encourage Nigerians to avoid *gra-gra* ("machismo") and settle their disagreements democratically when national problems are being settled dictatorially?

SIX MILITARIZED INSTITUTIONS

The Family

The family is the most ancient and most civil of civil society institutions, but ironically it is the most militarized in Nigeria. During the pilot study for this project we visited and observed a young Nigerian family with four lovely children, the eldest of whom was not yet five. We were surprised to find that canes were kept in the house for the punishment of the children. One was reserved for the father's special use. The mother regularly threatened to use the cane. The maid used it freely, and the three aunts caned the children too. Two visiting uncles used the canes freely, and even family friends were allowed to use the cane whenever they thought fit. We raised this issue with the family, and they said that the children "do not hear" (are disobedient) until they have been beaten.

The logic is that if they (the children) are not disciplined corporally they will turn out to be delinquents. The father gave the example of a neighbour who returned from England with his family. According to him, the parents were so permissive that their children had no manners at all. The son of that family never carried out any chores until his father started "dealing" with him the "Nigerian" way by beating the devil out of him. The climax came when the teenage son shot his sister twice with their father's shotgun and nearly paralyzed the girl. His father beat him nearly to death, with the result that the boy learned his lesson. Now he is of exemplary character.

One of us argued that treating children violently at home is partly why they themselves become violent. We suggested that the family should try to listen to the children more and talk to them gently rather than threatening them with force. The family agreed with our suggestion that many cases of corporal punishment of children are unnecessary, and that beating children makes them cry more than usual, thereby making the parents restless. As a result, the children were no longer beaten while we were there. However, the threat of "I go beat you o!" (I am going to beat you) was still liberally used.

We also suggested that the parents try telling their children they loved them (something we never heard), because there was no doubt they loved the children, instead of telling them all the time they would be beaten. At one point we were being recruited into the disciplinary regime by the parents, who threatened the children that if they did not behave uncle or aunt would beat them. To this we usually retorted that we would not beat them because they were really lovely children, and this was true.

This issue was observed even among human rights campaigners who were worried about the inhumane treatment of prisoners in Nigeria yet were ready to forcefully discipline their toddlers for throwing tantrums in public. We came to the defence of a toddler by saying that she was simply being assertive, that adults threw worse tantrums without being beaten in public, and that even the law, with all its insensitivity, would not think of "punishing" a child who had no sense of right and wrong.

Greater manifestations of this use of force or militarism within the family came in the form of news reports that husbands had gone beyond what one newspaper called the "traditional right" of disciplining their wives through beating to the savage practice of disfiguring them with acid. Some of the women were attacked in this way simply because they were good breadwinners when their husbands lost their own jobs. The jealous men figured that their wives must have been seeing other men; otherwise, how were they able to sustain the family?

We saw campaign posters around the country (issued by the Legal Research and Resource Development Centre [LRRDC]) proclaiming, "YOUR WIFE IS NOT A PUNCH BAG. STOP WIFE BEATING TODAY!" The poster depicts a bare-chested man whose right hand has struck a woman with fright in her eyes and plasters on her face, while the children look on sadly in the background. The suggestion here is that wife-beating is a hobby enjoyed by some sadists rather than a premeditated strategy of command and control in the patriarchal family. The punching-bag metaphor oversimplifies the problem of militarized gender relations within the family. However, the LRRDC is likely using the metaphor mainly as a reference to an object to be dominated and beaten without any fear of retaliation or challenge. Even if some sadists see wife-beating as a hobby, it is because it is, first and foremost, a means of controlling the woman, or so they think.

A more direct manifestation of militarism in the family is the intimidation of family members by agents of the state when one member of the family (usually the man) is suspected of having done something disapproved of by the state. Indirect pressure can be applied by influential in-laws who might informally warn their son-in-law to stop confronting the authorities. Also, the wife can be arrested and detained until the husband gives himself up for arrest.

The militarization of the family is most clearly represented by the ceremony in military weddings during which a sword is offered to the groom by his colleagues in the regiment. At one such wedding that we attended the explanation given was that, although the sword is an agent of destruction, the groom should use it to protect his family. Similar symbolism (though not identical) is found in some traditional marriage ceremonies in which cannons are fired to celebrate the marriage of a daughter. In one that we witnessed the groom's party was escorted by a uniformed soldier to get past the numerous road blocks routinely mounted by security officials to extort money from drivers.

Concerns with the family as a militarized institution of civil society are summarized in a comic-strip poster produced by the Women, Law, and Development Centre, Lagos. The comic strip is captioned "VIOLENCE AGAINST WOMEN: SAY NO TO..: childhood marriage, wife beating [though the picture is that of a fight in which the woman is clutching the man's crotch in apparent self-defence], sexual harassment, female child labor, rape, female circumcision, and negative cultural attitude" (illustrated with a woman carrying a baby on her back and an overloaded basket on her head while a man carries only a hoe and a gun). This poster is a clear illustration of how militarized family relations easily spill out into the wider society. However, the poster focuses on women as a unidimensional group, listing a wide range of struggles and violent experiences under one category. While this focus draws attention to women's struggles, the framework cannot take into account the diversity of struggles that women in diverse positionalities (e.g., age groups, socioeconomic classes, marital statuses, etc.) experience. Their struggles and violent experiences cannot be properly defined or addressed through the unidimensional, fragmented nature of this framework.

The poster highlights various campaigns that were going on in Nigeria, such as the Gender Specific Litigations and Protection Strategies Workshop organized by the Gender Action Project of the Shelter Rights Initiative (June 1998); the publication of *Beasts of Burden* in April 1998 by the Women's Rights Project of the Civil Liberties Organization; the *Status of Women in Nigerian Police*, a special issue of *Law Enforcement Review,* April-June 1998, a quarterly magazine of the Centre for Law Enforcement; and the Democratic Alternatives Workshop on Women's Participation in Politics, November 21, 1998, to mention but a few.

The militarization of family gender relations is summed up by Namiji in her article "Harmful Traditional Practices Affecting the Health of Women from Childhood." In answer to the question "who is a man?" Namiji (1998) writes that "he is the boss of the woman... He is the commander-in-chief of the family and rules and regulations are established and maintained by him as a woman has no say in running the affairs of the house." These issues were prominent in interviews with activists and researchers, and they will be taken up in greater detail to promote the democratization of family and gender relations.

The Educational System

We were still in high school when the distinguished historian Professor Ade Ajayi was dismissed from his post as vice chancellor of the University of Lagos, Nigeria, in 1978. That was also when Dr. Edwin Madunagu was dismissed from his post as a mathematics lecturer at the University of Calabar and the late Dr. Ola Oni, an economist, from the University of Ibadan. They and others were removed because they expressed sympathy for students who were protesting against the killing of their colleagues by soldiers during the demonstrations against the commercialization of education that year. The students were demanding a candle-lit procession to bury their murdered comrades, but General Olusegun Obasanjo's administration saw this as evidence of insurrection because the students also called for the resignation of the education minister, an army colonel. Army officers with horse whips were sent to all the high schools in the country to act as disciplinary officers, and they ended up acting as gate men who arrested students for coming late to school and punished them corporally. Some students resisted this military discipline by deliberately sneaking out of the boarding houses at night to attend parties in nearby villages, just to prove that even army sergeants could not restrict their freedom of movement.

All the campaign groups, activists, and researchers whom we encountered during the field trip expressed profound faith in the ability of education to serve as the principal tool for the democratization of a militarized civil society. To provoke a critical evaluation of this faith, we pointed out that the militarists are often very educated individuals and that the educational institutions are militarized. We were told in response that a democratic educational programme has to be a special programme, but all agreed that educational institutions in Nigeria are in dire need of democratization and demilitarization. As Toyo (1998) put it,

> only the ideological education, organization and political action of the masses can get the country near democracy. Only the self-governance of the toiling people and their self-education through this can make democracy evolve. The foolish notion that democracy can result from someone's magic wand, wizardry or manipulation must be cast into the rubbish heap. The current antithesis is between military rule and responsible

and truly national civilian rule, not between military rule and democracy. With all the goodwill in the world, it is a gross error—to say the least—for military officers to stay long in office and excuse their doing so by the chimers that this will ensure a "transition to democracy."

The militarization of education takes two principal forms: (1) a lack of accountability and an authoritarian attitude among administrators who issue orders with "immediate effect," undermine student and staff unionism, and seem to be scared of dialogue, and (2) the widespread use of secret cults to intimidate and attack activists on campuses, kill or maim rivals, rape female students, and intimidate staff.

During our fieldwork Professor Eskor Toyo told us that people mistakenly talk about the collapse of the educational system. According to him, the system has not just collapsed; it is dead, and academics were busy writing its obituary. A detailed analysis of Professor Toyo's thesis is provided by Professor Idowu Awopetu (1998) in "The State and Democratisation of Education: Obstacles and Prospects of Independent Student Unionism under Military Dictatorship." Awopetu argues that education is a human right and not a privilege. He outlines the historical struggles of Nigerian workers to expand educational opportunities as part of the struggle for political independence. These efforts resulted in a huge expansion of education, but when the military took power it began to commercialize education in the country.

This process came to a head in 1978 when the government of General Olusegun Obasanjo announced a threefold increase in the cost of feeding and housing students, resulting in the "Ali Must Go" protest (named after the military minister of education at the time) in Nigerian universities. The government responded with force, resulting in the killing of some students and the closure of the universities. The tribunal of enquiry set up by the government recommended sacking many renowned academics for expressing sympathy for the students. Government-employed journalists were also sacked, and many students were expelled. From this time onward the military saw student unionism as a threat and routinely banned the National Union of Nigerian Students and the Academic Staff Union of Universities. Given the overall atmosphere of intimidation and authoritarianism, according to Awopetu, it was not surprising that secret cults had mushroomed in the universities and were fast spreading into the secondary schools.

The *Sunday Tribune* (Nigeria) of August 16, 1998, ran a story on the "rising menace of campus secret cults." The paper reported that some of these cults in Nigeria's tertiary institutions were "Pyrate Confraternity, Buccanneers, Maplates, Blood Suckers, Black Cat, Eye Confraternity, Vikings Fraternity, Mafia, Red Devils, Black Beret, Green Beret, Trojan Horse, Neo-Black Movement, Musketeers, Black Axe, Temple of Eden Fraternity, Mafiosi, Osiri, Burkina Fasso, Revolution, Mgbamagbu Brothers, Scorpion, Dragon, Panama Pyrate Confraternity, Airwords, Ku Klux Klan (KKK), Amazons, Barracudes, Wairus, Black Heart, Maphites, Mgbamgba, Ozo, the Pink Ladies, Frigates, Himalayes, Canary, Marpiates, Pirate, the Blood Spot, Ibaka, Ostrich, the Eagle, the Flamingo, the Woodpecker, even the Dove and the Seadogs!" According to the newspaper, "there have been frequent clashes between members of these cults and violent fights over matters as trivial as space for holding nocturnal meetings or rallies. Daggers have been drawn over such mundane issues as 'ownership of girls.' Moreover, they employ the auspices of their clubs to settle private scores with non-members by subjecting them to acts of terrorism, intimidation and brigandage. Besides, self destruction results from violent inter-personal clashes resulting in their own deaths and those of innocent persons."

According to Professor Muyiwa Awe (the *Post Express*, March 30, 1998), when he and Professor Wole Soyinka formed the first secret cult in 1953 as students of University College, Ibadan, they had no sinister motive. All they wanted was a covert way to oppose the colonial administrators of the university on policies that went against the interests of student welfare.

Their cult, Pyrates Confraternity, remained the only one active in the universities until 1968, when the rival Eye Confraternity emerged with the aim of resisting oppressive government policies countrywide. Professor Awe blamed the militarization of campus cults on political violence and thuggery that led to the bloody coup of 1966, the pogrom against easterners in the north and west of the country, and then the civil war that nearly dismembered the country.

The violent clashes between these cults in the institutions of higher learning result in increased militarization of the campuses. Armed police officers are dispatched to the campuses to maintain order, and some people call for the setting up of special military tribunals to try cultists. Daily newspaper headlines tell the story graphically: "Nsukka Varsity Shut over Cult Crisis" (the *Guardian,* May 11, 1998), "Cults: Police Boss Accuses EDSU Administrator [a military-style sole administrator appointed by the Abacha dictatorship as an alternative to a vice chancellor) of Complicity" (the *Guardian,* May 29, 1998), "Police Return to LASU, UI as Cultists Clash" (the *Guardian,* August 27, 1998), "Oyo, Ogun Expel 256 Students over Cultism" (*Vanguard,* February 18, 1998). The above stories are only a sample from a big file on secret cults in the library of one of the daily newspapers.

In a contribution to a Committee for the Defence of Human Rights publication *Nigerian Students and the Challenge of Leadership,* Dr. Kola Babarinde (1998) argues that, although secret cults are found in different Nigerian traditional societies, student cults can be explained thus:

1. Students' mass protest is a worldwide phenomenon that differs from secret cults.
2. Government interference with students' activism through repression of organized student bodies has encouraged inexperienced and ill-disciplined students who were frustrated or ambitious to join underground movements.

3. There is a link between the militarization of the society and an upsurge in cult activities on campuses.
4. The history of cultism and underground movements is linked with periods of political repression.
5. A lasting solution can only come through the democratization of the entire society.
6. Nigerian youths have a role to play in the democratization process.

During the African Studies Association meeting in Philadelphia, where this section of our chapter was presented as part of a panel honouring Nigerian history professor Ade Ajayi, he commented briefly on the details of events that took place at the 1998 convocation ceremony at the University of Ibadan, where he was then a research professor emeritus. According to Professor Ajayi, one of the staunch supporters of the Sani Abacha dictatorship in Ibadan attended the convocation ceremony with a motorcade of three bullet-proof limousines. The students allegedly got suspicious and decided to search the limousines to see why anyone would be visiting a university in bullet-proof vehicles. It turned out that the local politician had a cache of weapons. Outraged, the students burned all three cars. Later the then head of state, General Abdulsalami Abubakar, sent word to find out if it was safe for him to visit the university for the occasion, and the students sent word back to say that it was safe since they had destroyed the weapons brought onto campus by a corrupt politician. It was shortly after this incident that some alleged cult members killed a number of students at the university, raising suspicions that the killing had been sponsored by external forces in retaliation against the students for "disgracing" local politicians.

The repression in Nigerian universities attracted the attention of activist musicians such as Fela Anikulapo Kuti. This was also the case with the late Jamaican singer Peter Tosh, who reasoned that, if education was for domestication rather than liberation, one should not blame youths for acting like gangsters. According to Iyorchi Ayu[2] (1986), the conditions under which Tosh was teaching were similar to those of Kuti in Nigeria. He analyzed the aesthetic and the political in Kuti's musical education of the people, and concluded that it remains a powerful instrument for advancing the resistance of Nigerians against neocolonial fascism. Kuti was repeatedly brutalized, like many ordinary Nigerians, but he maintained his reputation as a social critic and popular educator until his death in 1997.

Community Relations

Interviews with scholars, journalists, and individuals in addition to archival research revealed the widespread use of force and violence to settle communal disputes in various parts of Nigeria. Members of the ruling class fall back on their respective ethnic groups to mobilize support. Even when they come from the same ethnic group, they still manage to manipulate different gangs of mainly unemployed youths into harassing and fighting one another. At other times false propaganda peddled by competing groups of rulers incites people into spontaneous violence against their fellow oppressed.

This was the case when British officials blamed severe economic hardship following the Second World War on the uncompromising attitude of the nationalists. Since the radical labour movement led by Michael Imoudu was openly aligned with the National Council of Nigeria and the Cameroons (NCNC), the leading nationalist movement, the British accused Nnamdi Azikiwe, the party leader, of inciting workers to embark on the 1945 general strike during which Imoudu was jailed without trial. The Hausa community in Jos came to believe that Igbo traders, against whom they competed for trade, were responsible for the shortages and high costs of commodities. In December 1945 ethnic rioting broke out in the Jos market between Hausa and Igbo traders.

This scene was repeated after Anthony Enahoro moved the historic motion for independence in 1956. Alhaji Ahmadu Bello, leader of the Northern Peoples Congress and the Sarduana of Sokoto, countered with a motion for independence "as soon as practicable." The northerners were called unprintable names, and their leaders adopted an eight-point programme of "northernization" that sounded like secession. Southern leaders concluded that their northern counterparts were imperialist stooges who did not represent the views of ordinary northerners. Thus, the Action Group sent a team led by S. L. Akintola to campaign openly in the north for independence in 1956. However, when rioting broke out at a Kano rally, the Hausa attacked mainly Igbo supporters of NCNC, perhaps because they were the more numerous and more conspicuous southerners in the north.

The Tiv had also rioted in 1947 against the imposition of a Yoruba as the chief of Makurdi. However, the major crisis in the middle belt was that of 1959 following the federal elections. In alliance with the Action Group, Joseph Tarka's United Middle Belt Congress (UMBC) appealed to the Tiv to leave the Hausa–Fulani-dominated Northern Peoples Congress (NPC). The UMBC won by a landslide, and the NPC resorted to scapegoating. UMBC supporters were sacked from their jobs en masse, and they embarked on civil disobedience. They refused to pay taxes and started attacking Native Authority policemen who were used to intimidate them. The situation became worse between August and November 1960 when 30,000 houses of NPC supporters were burned, 20 arsonists were killed by landlords and the police, and 5,000 "Tarka"-chanting Tivs were arrested.

History repeated itself in the western region following the elections of 1964. The NPC government had frustrated the efforts of United Progressive Grand Alliance (UPGA) candidates to file their nominations in the north, paving the way for sixty-seven Nigerian National Alliance (NNA) candidates to be returned unopposed. This tactic forced Dr. Michael Okpara, leader of the UPGA, to call for a total boycott of the elections. The boycott was total in the east but partial in the west, north, midwest, and Lagos. In spite of the boycott, victory for the NNA was announced, but the UPGA refused to accept the results. Dr. Nnamdi Azikiwe could have used his powers as president to appoint a caretaker administration until a fresh election was held, but he struck a compromise instead and got the NNA to concede some appointments to UPGA politicians.

The federal elections were followed by the October 1965 regional elections. The western region rejected Akintola and his unpopular Nigerian National Democratic Party at the polls, but Akintola went behind the scene to announce, over the government-controlled mass media, that he had won and that the winners had lost. The west went wild. Operation "Wetie" (or soak him with petrol and set him ablaze) became a rallying call. That was when the federal prime minister, Alhaji Abubakar Tafawa Balewa, chose to declare a state of emergency, but not before wondering aloud why people were saying that there was trouble in the west when Lagos, a part of the west, was calm (Nnoli 1978).

This was the last straw that brought five patriotic majors to attempt to shoot some "democratic" sense into the body politic (Ademoyega 1981). However, either by design or by error, their victims fell into an ethnic pattern, and the Hausa-Fulani were once again incited against the Igbo. This anger resulted in a countercoup and one of the bloodiest pogroms in human history. The civil war that followed this unscrupulous power struggle by the ruling class is now history, yet no lesson was learned by the politicians of the second republic, who tempted the military back into power (Falola and Ihonvbere 1985). However, even under the military, several parts of the country were convulsed in intercommunal conflict.

In Osun State in the west, during the preliminary fieldwork at the end of 1998, the people of Ife were fighting their Modakeke neighbours over the siting of a new local government headquarters. In Delta State in the south the Ijaw were fighting their Itsekiri neighbours for a similar reason, and in Ondo State in the west the Ijaws were fighting their Ilaje neighbours. In Taraba State in the northeast the Kuteb were fighting the Jukun and Chamba.

Toward the end of 1999 members of the Oodua People's Congress were fighting northerners and Ijaw youths in Lagos.

Yoruba people in the north and the south were being attacked in retaliation. In Lagos factions of the same organization fought one another and engaged the police in armed confrontations, to the extent that the state governor was waylaid and nearly killed, and the Nigerian president, Olusegun Obasanjo, threatened to impose emergency rule. In Odi, Bayelsa State, some police officers were kidnapped and killed, and the military descended on the town, raping, looting, and killing the people, and eventually flattening the town.

According to a human rights lawyer interviewed in Kaduna, these ethnic conflicts reflect undemocratic conditions that do not allow for the peaceful resolution of disputes. The *Human Rights Situation Report* for July-October 1998, published by the Human Rights Monitor, stated that, although some of these conflicts revive ancient animosities between the warring ethnic groups, we must not forget that those communities were living peacefully, by and large, until the current crisis of democracy led to mass frustration and a loss of faith in legal institutions. These conflicts are worsened by discriminatory government allocation of facilities. Even after setting up public commissions to advise on the locations of those facilities, the government ignored the advice and submissions received, and went ahead to balkanize the communities in the name of local government creation.

The above observations are supported by activist and social theorist Dr. Edwin Madunagu (1998), who states that

> Nigeria is a country of hungry, desperate, betrayed and cynical people. It is a country where public authority is completely alienated from the people, where there is no iota of faith between the governed and those that govern them. It is a capitalist country but one with an extremely corrupt, bankrupt and philistinic ruling class and which combines all known maladies, inequalities, insensitivities and irrationalities of capitalism namely, oppression, poverty, disease, exploitation, ethnic domination and arrogance, religious manipulation, unemployment, armed robbery, drug trafficking, social anomie

and moral despair. It is a country of dialectical extremes: extreme of poverty and extreme of wealth; a country where some individuals are stingingly rich, but the society as a whole is very poor; where there are mansions, but no roads to get to them; where water is as scarce as petrol.

The Ogoni struggle and the Ijaw youth protests differ from the many ethnic wars slightly because, when they were not fighting their neighbours over ownership of oil-rich land, they were marching against the international oil companies and the military government that preside over the exploitation of natural resources from a land that they consider their own, without any compensation or reward for the people whose sources of livelihood have been damaged by oil spillage and pollution. Interviews with journalists who visited the Ijaw area indicate the bravery of the young people but also the devastating military repression that the government unleashed on them. Yet all are agreed that democratization would be a major step in settling the conflict.

Religion

The right to freedom of thought, conscience, and religion is enshrined in the Nigerian Constitution. Section 35 of the 1979 Constitution, section 38 of the 1999 Constitution, and Article 8 of the African Charter on Human and Peoples' Rights (Ratification and Enforcement)[3] all contain elaborate provisions for the freedom of religion. Section 35(1) of the 1979 Constitution states that "every person shall be entitled to freedom of thought, conscience and religion, including freedom to change his religion or belief and freedom (either alone or in community with others, and in public or private) to manifest and propagate his religion or belief in worship, teaching, practice and observance."

This provision was copied uncritically by the 1999 Constitution, but there are problems even with this basic provision. Freedom of religion seems to be narrowly defined as the freedom to choose a religion. Implicitly, the freedom to choose not to have any religion does not seem to be protected by the Constitution. The greater problem is with young people under the age of eighteen whose freedom of religion is to be exercised on their behalf by parents, who must choose the religion that they should be taught at school. Their choices ignore the militarized nature of family relations that could manifest here in the form of torture, physical and mental, of those children who do not share their parents' religious beliefs. Once again the family and the educational institutions are being used to regulate the freedom of religion without examining the anti-democratic character of these institutions.

Although Nigeria is a secular state, there have been efforts to identify the country as a religious state, but these efforts have been successfully resisted to some extent. Biko Agozino and others conducted research for Mass Mobilization for Social and Economic Recovery (MAMSER), a government agency, on the politicization of religion and its consequences in countries such as India, Pakistan, Spain, Ireland, Sudan, and Lebanon as a warning to those who were bent on politicizing religion in the country (Toyo 1989). The continuing politicization of religion in the country has resulted in many "religious clashes," such as the "Maitatsaine riots, the Zangon Kataf, Kafanchan and Tafawa Balewa riots" in northern Nigeria (Sako and Plang 1997).

Contributors to *Ethnic and Religious Rights in Nigeria,* edited by Festus Okoye and published in Kaduna by the Human Rights Monitor (1998), contend that the increasing incidents of religious conflict in the country are linked to manipulation of religion by colonial officials followed by politicization of the volatile issue by neocolonial elites. In the first chapter of the book Sam Egwu argues that religious identity should be recognized as a problem instead of being seen simply as a taken-for-granted fundamental human right. Another contributor, Y. Z. Yau, analyzes the parties involved in most religious conflicts: the state and polarized religious groups. Yau argues that, far from being neutral, the state should be seen as a partisan actor in these conflicts. He warns that the state should not treat migrant beggars (Almajerai) who flock to religious zealots for alms as repressively as it treats religious militants.

Most of these religious conflicts take place in the north, but the phenomenon of secret cults that are no less religious in character takes place mostly in southern universities. Also, in the north and the south, superstitious beliefs in spiritual warfare abound. People decorate their houses with charms or blood-stained paintings of Jesus Christ to ward off evil spirits. Books that teach people how to fight and win spiritual "battles" sell very well. The consequence is not only lack of trust in other people but also loss of faith in the ability of Nigerians to solve their own problems. Families are torn apart by accusations and counteraccusations of sorcery and witchcraft or demonology, resulting in high rates of mental illness and even murder.

Also in the south, some traditional rulers use secret cults to intimidate citizens in their localities and extract fines from them for offences such as playing music all night long or harvesting new yams from their own farms before the ruler ordains that the harvest is ready. Some of these cases end up in court, with the citizens claiming that they no longer indulge in nature worship and that the traditional ruler was abusing their human rights by forcing them to abide by such rituals. In many such cases the churches provide lawyers for the defence of their members in court.

It is for such reasons that the Political Bureau set up by General Ibrahim Babangida to moderate the national debate on the political future of Nigeria reported that most Nigerians rejected notions of diarchy (civilian-military joint rule) as well as triarchy (civilian-military-traditional rule). According to the report of the Political Bureau, "as regards traditional rulers, we cannot see in which way their inclusion can provide a unifying force... They compete against the nation for allegiance, represent a force against the principle of popular democracy and are dysfunctional reminders of national differences" (1987, 78-79).

Just like the educational institution, the religious institution helps to sustain the militarization of the family by preaching doctrines that recognize the man as the undisputed head of every household. The duty of the woman is always that of obeying and serving the commander-in-chief of the house, and his only responsibility is to love and care for her.

The dangers of militarizing religion in the country were highlighted by the ongoing adoption of sharia as the dominant law in many of the northern states of Nigeria. Christians all over the country and pro-democracy activists have been calling for a halt to the adoption of what they regard as Islamic fundamentalism in parts of the country. Muslim politicians who are making a case for sharia have tried to reassure them that it would be applied only to Muslims. Agozino and Anyanike (1999) have contributed to the debate by arguing that it is wrong for some of the governors to declare that their states have become Islamic states, since Nigeria is governed by a secular Constitution that is supreme. Although sharia has always been allowed to operate as a customary law, it was restricted to civil matters, while the Nigerian penal code was applied in cases of criminal offences.

The declaration of sharia by some states in the country has been followed by vigilante groups who try to enforce strict adherence to segregation of men and women in public, even though such segregation was required only in the homes of Muslims in the past. It is feared that the vigilantes might begin to demand the segregation of public transport according to gender, to the disadvantage of women, who would have their freedom of movement curtailed. Moreover, a strict enforcement of the dress code might lead to the sexual harassment of women, Muslim and non-Muslim alike, who prefer not to wear the veil. Already one of the local governments in a state that adopted sharia has ordered unmarried women and widows to get married as proof that they are not prostitutes or face ejection from the local government area. The sharia issue is part of the overwhelming militarization of civil society in Nigeria.

Kayode Fayemi, in a paper presented to the DFID West Africa Governance Team in April 2000, has explored this sharia controversy from a more holistic perspective that encompasses all of the social, economic, and political underpinnings of the phenomenon. For him the sharia debate has to be located first within the problematic identity politics prevalent in the country. In this regard the central question has revolved around the nature of the Nigerian state and the definition of citizenship. These fundamental issues, debate on which has hitherto been suppressed or scuttled by successive military administrations, are now openly expressed by the newly found democratic freedom in the country. Fayemi goes further to conceive of the sharia phenomenon in terms of the power struggle that has engulfed the country since the return to democratic rule. This power struggle has pitched the "political north," which dominated national politics for much of the postindependence period, against the rest of the country. "Disappointed" northern elements that were the forces behind the presidency of Obasanjo now use sharia as a weapon to deal with him.

Yet another explanation for the sudden rise of the issue has been linked to the perceived leadership vacuum in the north and the possibility that the propagators of sharia are using it to fill this void. One of Fayemi's (2000) many explanations that corroborated our own position on this issue is that sharia represents "a response of Islamic fundamentalism to a growing Christian fundamentalism under a 'born-again' Christian President." A disturbing thing about this Christian fundamentalism, from the standpoint of Muslims, is its fundamental opposition to Islam, unlike the stance of established denominations such as the Catholic, Anglican, and some Pentecostal churches, which have been more accommodating in this regard. That these Christian fundamentalists have dubbed the present government as God's government—in clear violation of constitutional provisions designating Nigeria as a secular state—does not help matters in any meaningful and peaceful way.

Finally, the sharia question, according to Fayemi, must be understood in socioeconomic terms as a demonstration of the lack of faith in the "democracy dividend" by those involved in the sharia carnage, most of whom have been the greatest victims of the political and economic mismanagement of the country. All of these explanations are credible and carry enormous weight. Our contention, however, is that the militarization of the "national psyche," again to borrow from Fayemi (2000), makes it impossible for Nigerians to initiate democratic processes to address and resolve these fundamental issues.

The Judiciary

Ideally, the judiciary is one of the bastions against arbitrary power. In Nigeria, however, the institution has become completely militarized. Apart from the usual doubts about the independence of the judiciary, especially under a military regime in which the executive and the legislative arms of government are one and the same, successive military regimes in the country have tried to colonize this vital organ as well by using special military tribunals to try cases that would ordinarily be handled by normal courts. This issue was addressed by lawyers and activists in a book published by the Kaduna-based NGO Human Rights Monitor (Okoye 1997).

In the first chapter, "The Military and the Administration of Justice in Nigeria," Chris Abashi (1997) traced the history of the search for justice in Nigeria from colonial days to the present. He noted how the administration of justice became increasingly militarized under British rule with the introduction of both armed force and militarized law enforcement agents, in contrast to precolonial societies. He analyzed section 6 of the 1979 Constitution, which vested the judicial powers of the federation in the courts: the Supreme Court of Nigeria, the Court of Appeal, the federal High Court, the High Court of the states, the High Court of the federal capital territory, a Sharia Court of Appeal of a state, and a Customary Court of Appeal of a state.

The Constitution did not mention magistrates, customary and sharia courts, or special military tribunals specifically, but subsections VIII–IX cover "such other courts as may be authorized by law to exercise jurisdiction on matters with which the National Assembly may make laws" and "such other courts as may be authorized by law to exercise jurisdiction at first instance with respect to which a House of Assembly may make laws." These were the subsections abused by successive military regimes by authorizing the trials of civilians in military tribunals. The most notable instance was the kangaroo trial of Ken Saro-Wiwa and eight other Ogoni activists who were hanged for murder following a conviction that did not allow any appeal.

Abashi (1997) also reviewed the Bill of Rights provisions in the Constitution designed to safeguard due process in the judiciary. Nigerian military regimes, he discovered, flouted every one of these provisions, including the simplest one, that cases should be heard in public. According to Abashi, judges now decide cases in their chambers without regard to due process. A panel headed by a justice emeritus of the Supreme Court, Kayode Esho, produced a report in 1997 detailing numerous problems ranging from corruption to excessive militarization of the judiciary. Up to the time of writing this chapter, the civilian government had not released an official report of the panel.

The trend was set by the Constitution (Suspension and Modification) Decree, 1966, which stated that

> any decision, whether made before or after the commencement of this decree, by any court of law in the exercise or purported exercise of any powers under the constitution or any enactment or law of the Federation or any state which has purported to declare or shall hereafter purport to declare the invalidity of any Decree or of any Edict (in so far as the provisions of the Edict are not inconsistent with the provision of a Decree) or the incompetence of any of the government in the Federation to make same is or shall be null and void and of no effect whatsoever as from the date of the making thereof.

It is noticeable here that "Decree" and "Edict" are capitalized, while "court of law" is not.

Abashi (1997) noted the irony that, in spite of their authoritarianism, the standardization of the courts in Nigeria was accomplished by military regimes. Moreover, the excesses of the military are quite understandable, given that soldiers are trained to use force to resolve matters speedily and efficiently. This sounds like the ideal bureaucracy of Max Weber, but, as his critics have shown with the example of the Nazi Holocaust, an institution or process that is fast and efficient does not necessarily guarantee justice. The sad situation in Nigeria is that even the police are authorized to shoot suspected criminals on sight. Also, due to speedy arrests without sufficient evidence, the prisons are overcrowded, with the majority of inmates awaiting trials for years on end.

Arguing that more democratization is the only guarantee for the rule of law, Abashi (1997) quoted the late dictator General Sani Abacha to emphasize the decay in the Nigerian judiciary. According to Abacha,

> a just and fair society must enjoy a trusted judiciary. A judiciary that is not insulated from political control or financial pressures is soon weakened and put in disarray. Under such conditions brigandage replaces societal orderliness and the right to life and property. The judiciary is a vital custodian of our individual liberties. While no constitutional system or the instruments that govern it can be perfect or made watertight against human abuse, we demand that our judges be courageous, impartial and honest. In recent times our judiciary has been especially subjected to the strains and pressures arising from ethnic, political and social considerations. The events immediately preceding the annulled presidential election illustrate the aberration, which ha[s] intruded into our judicial process. We had the puzzling and unpleasant experience of our High Courts delivering contradictory judgments on the same issue within the same period, depending on where the litigation was instituted and by whom. (Abashi 1997, 24)

A careful reading of Abacha's speech reveals an attitude of loathing toward the judiciary. Nigerian soldiers refer to civilians as "bloody civilians," meaning that they are not disciplined and thus not efficient. It is part of the military's self-appointed task in politics to discipline Nigerians, including judges, to make sure that they deliver judgments with immediate effects as in wartime. Abacha was surprised that the courts gave contradictory verdicts, but that is part of the democratic process that the courts must uphold. That is why there are appeal courts and the supreme court, but dictators will not trust independent-minded judges, which is why they make decrees ruling out the possibility that any court will challenge them even on the ground of incompetence. Yet the problem is not caused only by the military. Corrupt judges and lawyers, after all, draft the draconian decrees that help to militarize the Nigerian judiciary.

Just as Nigeria inherited its legal rules from imperialist Britain, so too the law courts in neocolonial Nigeria continue the colonial policy of administering repression and maintaining inequality by force. This oppressive legal practice was opposed by Nigerians right from colonial days by refusing to go to court and preferring to settle disputes in traditional settings or by venting their anger on the infrastructure of the courts. This was the case when Aba market women burned down Native Authority courts in 1929. The defiance of Nigerians later manifested itself in the refusal of the Zikists, a group of fiery young nationalists, to plead before a colonial judge. They were convinced that the colonial court had no jurisdiction to try the case because the matter was between Britain and Nigeria. More recently, Ken Saro-Wiwa advanced a similar argument when he was tried by what he called a kangaroo court.

As the United Nations Fact-Finding Mission to Nigeria stated in 1996, the Civil Disturbances [special tribunal] Act of 1987, under which the Ogoni nine were judicially murdered, was not valid because it violated the right to a fair trial. Although the Nigerian Constitution had a provision for such a tribunal to be set up, it required a commission of enquiry that was never set up in their case. The defendants faced enormous prejudice, given the fact that they were tried in two separate groups for the same charge. The request by the defence to play a tape in which the military governor of Rivers State pronounced the men guilty even before commencement of the trial was refused by the tribunal, showing how biased it was. Similarly, the tribunal refused the introduction of contradictory video evidence given by a prosecution witness. That the defendants were denied the right of appeal made the trial deficient in the dispensation of justice.

The haste with which the Provisional Ruling Council (PRC) confirmed the death sentences indicated that the outcome was determined in advance. Moreover, the PRC confirmed the sentences even without receiving the transcripts of the trial. The failure of the tribunal-appointed lawyers to present a case for the defendants before the PRC (after their own chosen lawyers had withdrawn due to military interference) indicated that the appointed lawyers were not representing the interests of the defendants. The fact that a military officer was a member of the tribunal meant that its independence was compromised. Even when the defendants instituted a suit in the High Court asking for a suspension of the tribunal, the tribunal ignored it and continued (Campaign for Democracy 1998).

It is not surprising that the Nigerian military prefers a repressive role for law. This, however, is not an exclusively military practice, given that the colonial and neocolonial civilian administrations share this preference. One of the first things that the Tafawa Balewa government did in office was pass the Banking Act of March 1961, aimed at liquidating the National Bank of Nigeria, on which the opposition government depended to finance its activities. Fortunately for the opposition, Justice Daddy Onyeama was bold enough to rule that the law was null and void. But that marked the end of judicial independence in the country.

The judicial crisis deepened when Samuel Ladoke Akintola was constitutionally removed from office as premier of the western region, following a petition by the majority of the members of the Western House of Assembly to the governor, Oba Adesoji Aderemi. Rather than respect the Constitution, Akintola sat tight and announced that he had unilaterally removed the governor. The newly appointed premier, Chief Adegbenro, then took the case to the House of Assembly, seeking a vote of confidence in himself. Before any vote could be taken, the supporters of Akintola started a fight that ended in the breaking of the mace. Prime Minister Tafawa Balewa promptly ordered the police to disperse the members with tear gas. He went on to summon parliament, which declared a state of emergency in the western region, with Sir Moses Majekodunmi, a federal minister, as the administrator.

With the help of the NPC-NCNC alliance, Akintola was reinstated as premier, while the regional NCNC leader, Chief Fadahunsi, became the new governor. The federal government did so even though the matter was still *sub judice.* Akintola had gone to court, during the emergency, to challenge his removal. As expected, the federal courts nullified his removal, but the case went to the Privy Council in London, which ruled that the removal was constitutional and that Chief Adegbenro was the legitimate premier of Western Nigeria (Agozino 1989).

The ruling of the Privy Council was ignored by Balewa and Akintola, and instead the plan to annihilate the opposition was rigorously pursued. Thus, in September 1963, Justice Sowemimo told the nation that his hands were tied and that he had no choice but to convict Chief Awolowo and his co-leaders of the opposition to long terms of imprisonment for alleged treason. If the strong and mighty could be bruised in the internal struggles of the ruling class, then one can only imagine the fate of the powerless masses. An example is the case of Tiamiyu Banjoko, who was arrested on suspicion of breaking a windowpane. He was still awaiting trial for the seventh year when the chief judge of the former western region released him (*This Week,* March 28, 1988).

The courts seem to understand their role as that of maintaining order by keeping the people in check without worrying much about the actions of the rulers and their agents. This is especially the case under military regimes when all manners of unchallengeable decrees are heaped on the people. The only serious effort to control elite crimes came with General Murtala Muhammad's Corrupt Practices Decree of 1975, which created the Corrupt Practices Investigation Bureau and special tribunals to try those suspected of corrupt practices.

However, before the tribunals were established, the 1979 Constitution replaced the decree with the toothless Code of Conduct Bureau and Code of Conduct Tribunal. The same military government that was hesitant to prosecute millionaire thieves did not waste time in storming the popular musician Fela Anikulapo-Kuti's home with soldiers, who caused the death of his mother, a foremost leader of Nigeria's struggle for independence (Martins 1998). The same repressive measures awaited students who protested that the government of General Obasanjo was trying to commercialize education.

The second republic inherited and maintained this tradition of judicial repression. With the excuse of looking for the gunmen who had snatched some money from a multinational company in Apapa, the police gathered sixty-eight innocent poor people, detained them overnight, and then squeezed them into a security vehicle meant for a maximum of twenty-eight. They were driven to court and left in the scorching sun all day, and fifty of them suffocated to death. This was on March 3, 1980. Public outcry forced the government to bring the police officers to trial, but, as expected, none of them was convicted of any wrongdoing. Six weeks later, on April 26, more than 120 peasants were murdered in Bakolori. Their crime was that they had dared to ask for adequate compensation before multinational companies could take over their farmlands. Not even one police officer was brought to trial for this crime, even though the president of the country came from the same state as the farmers. The same police force was to stand watch while what one of the officers described as a "cooperative mob" burned Bala Mohammed, special political adviser to the governor of Kano State, to death on July 10, 1981 (Usman 1982).

These are mere snapshots from the judicial records of the second republic, a regime that was inaugurated by judicial fraud. To settle the quarrel among the leading bourgeois contenders for power, the Supreme Court "discovered" a new mathematical law claiming that two-thirds of nineteen states equal twelve. This method of winning elections became fully developed during the 1983 elections, when some petitions alleging fraud were dismissed on the technical ground that they were not properly filed, while other petitions with similar technical defects were allowed. The same internal struggle among the elites was the reason Jim Nwobodo used the colonial law of sedition—the crime of the Zikists—to jail Arthur Nwankwo, the author, who was lucky to be freed by the federal High Court on the ground that the law on sedition was contrary to the freedom of expression guaranteed in the Constitution.

Generals Muhammadu Buhari and Tunde Idiagbon overthrew the second republic, and then got tough with millionaire thieves and innocent people alike. They launched the War against Indiscipline (WAI) on the assumption that ordinary Nigerians lacked discipline, and that they needed to be regimented and taught basic sanitary practice by force. The two dictators sacked many judges, allegedly on health grounds. Chief Justice Sowemimo confessed to *This Week* of March 28, 1988, that the judiciary was "sick" and that what the government was doing was "an exercise to rekindle the credibility of the judiciary."

The regime made drug-trafficking a capital offence and immediately executed three young Nigerians as a deterrent. The militaristic tribunal that tried them did not allow any appeal. Under the two dictators a judge went to the hospital bed of Fela Kuti to beg forgiveness for sentencing him to prison on the orders of the military when there was no evidence against him. In almost all the states of the federation today there are armed patrols of soldiers and police officers authorized to shoot to kill on sight all those suspected of criminal behaviour.

Soldiers and officers still go on rampages against the civilian population, justifying this abominable behaviour with the excuse that they were trained to be "mad dogs." Idiagbon and Buhari had jailed many second republic politicians for corrupt enrichment, until General Ibrahim Babangida overthrew them in August 1985 and gradually released all the politicians, before locking up journalists and executing those whom military tribunals found guilty of trying to overthrow his government. General Abacha drove this militarization of the judiciary to the extreme extent of using tribunals to settle old scores and eliminate rivals in his bid to succeed in office.

The Economy

The militarization of the Nigerian economy dates back to the scramble for territories by European multinational companies. The Royal Niger Company was the first colonial power that owned the country, ran its own army and police, and fought to repress resistance to the penetration of the interior by British traders at the end of the slave trade. When the British colonial administration took over the coercive role from the company to help maximize its profits and competitiveness against other European rivals, the colonial police and colonial army became the instruments for the repressive economic exploitation of Nigerians.

Evidence comes from the Women's War against Colonialism in Eastern Nigeria in 1929. The women were not simply protesting against attempts to tax them without democratic representation, but also directly attacking the properties of the multinational companies in the region, destroying local authority courts, and attacking the stooges of colonialism otherwise known as warrant chiefs. The women were massacred by the colonial police because they dared to challenge the double squeeze of Nigerians by the colonial economy, which guaranteed steady increases in the prices of manufactured goods and steady decreases for raw materials such as palm oil, from which the women earned the bulk of their incomes. A similar fate awaited the coal miners at Iva Valley in Enugu, who were mowed down for daring to demand a fair wage in support of the struggle for independence from Britain.

The Campaign for Democracy (1998) concluded its *A Special Report on Nigeria* by stating that "the state of the economy profoundly veers off the path of sanity. Like a rogue economy it is like a bandit state where consumption overlaps production, reward is to the indolent, order is macabre and reproduction is only of looting of future credit." In fairness, observers will say that this is a most unmilitary state of affairs, given that the military is usually associated with discipline, order, and efficiency. Sadly, when an economy is run like a battlefield, the result is that there will be widespread demolition of basic infrastructure, general disregard for the rules, an atmosphere conducive to looting and pillaging, and an attitude of winner takes all.

The above view was strongly demonstrated in a paper presented at the International Conference on New Directions in Federalism in Abuja, Nigeria, March 15-18, 1999, by J. Kayode Fayemi of the Centre for Democracy and Development (CDD). In his paper, "Entrenched Military Interests and the Future of Democracy in Nigeria," Fayemi argued that, contrary to the received wisdom that Nigeria was democratizing irreversibly, there were indications that military officers were scrambling over booty and that the influence of militarism in Nigerian politics went beyond the handing over of power to a retired army general whose party won the presidential election of February 1999. Given the overwhelming role of the military in the transition process, Fayemi pointed out that there was a need to go beyond the simplistic debate over whether the military is the armed wing of the oligarchy or the oligarchy itself. Instead, the military "mindset" itself should be explored to see how militarism has become hegemonic in spite of the individual intentions of specific military officers. Fayemi suggested that the emergence of the "bureaucratic-economic militariat" could be traced back to the discovery of crude oil in the country, and the way in which the military tightly controlled the oil industry for the purpose of political patronage and primitive accumulation of capital, sanctioned by decrees that claimed to be making the economy more nationalistic at the same time that it was increasingly being cornered by the military top brass and their cronies.

In fairness, some will argue that senior military officers and leading politicians all over the world are always targeted for recruitment by big companies, precisely because they can use their strategic skills and government contacts to help such companies become more competitive. The difference in the case of Nigeria is that one retired army officer is able to own and control a conglomerate of thirty-five companies with interests in banking, shipping, textiles, and, of course, oil.

Further evidence of the militarization of the economy comes from the London-based newsletter *Africa Confidential* in its edition of April 2, 1999, which reported that, prior to their retirement, Nigerian army officers used their dictatorial powers to line their pockets and those of their families and friends. The report indicates that the president elect at the time, General Olusegun Obasanjo, was not happy because General Abudulsalami Abubakar awarded eleven oil exploration blocks and eight oil-lifting contracts soon after the presidential election. Out of the eleven exploration blocks only one went to an indigenous company with a track record in the industry, Amni International, whose chairman, Sani Bello, is the father-in-law of General Abubakar's eldest daughter. Emmanuel Edozien, the economic adviser to General Obasanjo's winning party, is a director of the company.

Other companies were awarded similar licences due to their military connections, including Anchorage Petroleum (Chief of Defence Staff Air Marshal Al-Amin Daggash), Dajo Oil (Chief of Army Staff General Ishaya Bamaiyi and leading oil trader Mike Adenuga), Ozeko Energy Resources (Chief of General Staff Vice Admiral Mike Akhigbe), Totex Oil (Brigadier Anthony Ukpo and Texaco), Malabo Oil (former Minister of Oil Dan Etete, who uses his Ghanaian pseudonym, Kweku Amafegha, and senior diplomat Alhaji Aminu). Many of these companies lack expertise in oil exploration. However, according to the *Guardian* of May 11, 1999, the Nigerian military dissociated Al-Amin Daggash and Ishaya Bamaiyi from the controversial awards.

No matter how brazen the primitive accumulation of capital by military officers appears in Nigeria, we must not forget that the problem goes far beyond the military as such to include militarization of the wider civil society, even when military officers are not directly involved. There are widespread reports that the multinational oil companies have their own armed security guards, and that they import weapons for the police and the army to use in intimidating the people in their areas who are demanding compensation for the degradation of the environment. This is in addition to the lopsided spending on "security" in the national budget, as Table 4.1 shows.

Discussions with traders in Nigeria during our fieldwork revealed a militarized mindset that threatens the democratic tradition of haggling in the open market. According to the traders, police officers routinely arrest them and threaten to shoot them unless they part with their goods or money. Those who resist are intimidated by tales of people whom the police have shot and later claimed to have been armed robbers. Young traders often succumb to this intimidation and lose their money or goods. The traders themselves imbibe the ideology of force by arming their own vigilantes to keep watch over their shops at night and execute as "mice" those who trespass with the intent to steal.

On a different level, organized labour is subjected to dictatorial regulation even when it is simply challenging corruption that is killing the economy. This was the case during our fieldwork when it was reported that workers at the Enugu State-owned *Daily Star* had gone on strike to demand more financial accountability from the army-appointed director of the company. The managing director reacted by sacking the striking workers, including senior journalists on the editorial board. The workers rightly pointed out that only the board of directors had the power to hire or fire them. The managing director reported the incident to the military administrator of Enugu State, and he drove to the scene "with immediate effect." On seeing him the workers naively started cheering, thinking that he had come to support their call for accountability at the newspaper, which had been reduced to

Table 4.1: Federal Recurrent Budget in Million Naira

	1997	1998
Total budget	102,637.7	116,542.9
Presidency		
Chief of general staff	292.9	337.3
National security adviser	35.2	35.2
Police affairs	120.9	155.3
Other security		
Defence	12,974.7	15,134.8
Police formations	9,744.4	11,734.4
Internal affairs	4,316.9	5,281.1
Total	27,455.0	32,677.8
As % of total	**26.75**	28.04
Social services		
Women's affairs	136.4	231.8
Water and rural development	350.3	407.5
Education	12,632.2	13,928.3
Health	4,720.4	4,860.5
Youth and sports	2,011.0	3,187.2
Total	19,850.3	22,615.3
As % of total	19.34	19.41

Source: Federal Republic of Nigeria, Budget of Transition Press Briefing (cited in Ibeanu 1998).

an occasional weekly due to financial mismanagement. To their surprise, the administrator asked the workers to step to his right if they wished to go back to work or to remain on his left if they did not wish to return to work. Of course, everyone wanted to return to work, but the military administrator was not satisfied. He asked for a list of the ringleaders of the strike and called out their names one after the other. The strike leaders were publicly humiliated and horsewhipped before being told that they had been fired. The workers went to the state High Court, and it ruled that their sacking was null and void and of no effect. The military government refused to accept defeat and went on to appeal the ruling, until a visit by judges of the Court of Appeal to the state house managed to convince the administrator to withdraw the case and reinstate the workers with compensation.

This form of repression becomes more severe when workers become vocal about the need to democratize the whole society instead of concentrating on the usual demands for fairer wages. This was the case when the National Union of Gas and Petroleum Employees went on strike along with the National Union of Bank Workers in protest against the undemocratic annulment of the June 12th presidential election that Chief Moshood Abiola had won. The union leaders were clamped into jail without trial for more than five years, and because the Nigerian Labour Congress, the umbrella workers' organization, supported the pro-democracy strikes the military government sacked the executive of the congress and appointed a sole administrator to run it for five years, 1994-1998. Unfortunately, as always, some trade unionists collaborated with the military by supporting decrees that disqualified experienced professional trade unionists from standing in union elections. Such anti-democratic unionists have also been reported to use intimidation and outright violence to silence their opponents in the unions, while others even try to bribe union members with food and other gifts for votes.

CONCLUSION

Follow-up of this information could be conducted in the form of further research combined with democracy literacy classes, national seminars on the democratization of everyday life, and an international conference on the relationships between militarization and civil society.

Seen as a whole, the project is a democracy audit of the country, starting with pilot fieldwork and a report highlighting issues to be included in the curriculum for a series of democracy literacy classes in selected locations. Proceedings of the national workshop and the international conference, along with the original report of the fieldwork, will be published as a guide to groups and individuals who may wish to build on the findings by carrying out similar audits of democratic processes in an educational framework broadly defined.

We recommend that a group of three researchers/activists be set up in each of the six states visited and funded for three years to coordinate the project in their areas. They would employ two full-time research and education officers (twelve in all) from the fund. This would ensure that the paradoxical observations highlighted by the preliminary research will be investigated more closely and documented in greater detail for the purpose of developing an educational programme. The proposed programme could help to disseminate the findings of the research and thereby help to stem the spread of militaristic ideology in civil society.

As stated above, the education programme could be implemented through a series of radio programmes that addresses the public issues of democracy. This could be accomplished through the implementation of thirteen episodes of thirty minutes each on Radio Nigeria Kaduna because of its wide reach, with possible syndication by other radio stations in the country. This should be expanded at some point to include television programming to reach wider audiences. A monthly literacy journal could be created to allow all the groups to contribute articles addressing the curricula of grassroots democracy literacy classes. This would also include monthly enlightenment lectures through which face-to-face discussions could occur.

An annual democracy literacy conference should also be funded for all the groups and the foreign-based partners to review progress. The preliminary researchers should be retained to serve as consultants on the project, and to act as the foreign-based partners of local researchers and educationists.

This project and related activities will, we hope, bridge the gaps between academic and organic intellectuals in the local communities in the way that Walter Rodney (1969) suggested, by holding "family discussions" in the universities and schools, over the radio and television, on the pages of newspapers, but also on street corners, in back alleys, in places of work, and in market squares.

NOTES

1. The critique of gender politics within the Black Panther Party by Michelle Wallace, author of *The Black Macho*, informed our decision to share this project equally, even though it was originally contracted to one of us. We thank the Centre for Democracy and Development for funding this project at short notice. Thanks also to the Criminal Justice Group in Liverpool, John Moores University, for providing one of us with replacement teaching during a sabbatical, affording ample time not only to finish editorial work on a book on migration patterns but also to travel to gather material for this chapter. We also thank colleagues, family members, and friends whose generous support and assistance supplemented our limited resources during the field trip.
2. The fact that Ayu later went on to serve a military regime as the education minister who challenged the University Staff Union was not lost on us.
3. Act Cap 10 Laws of the Federation 1990.

REFERENCES

Abashi, C. (1998). "The Military and the Administration of Justice in Nigeria." In *Special Military Tribunals and the Administration of Justice in Nigeria*, ed. F. Okoye. Kaduna: Human Rights Monitor.

Ademoyega, A. (1981). *Why We Struck*. Ibadan: Evans Publishers.

Agozino, B. (1989). "Political Modalities in Successive Regimes." In *Political Practice in Nigeria*, ed. Eskor Toyo. Calabar: Community Development Partners.

Agozino, B., and I. Anyanike. (1999, November 28). "Sharia and the Nigerian Constitution." *Guardian*. (Also published in *Black World Today*, February 1999.)

Awopetu, I. (1998). "The State and Democratisation of Education: Obstacles and Prospects of Independent Student Unionism under Military Dictatorship." In *Nigerian Students and the Challenge of Leadership,* ed. J. Ogunye, S. Jegede, and B. Olasupo. Lagos: Committee for the Defence of Human Rights.

Ayu, I. D. (1986). *Essays in Popular Struggles.* Oguta: Zim Pan-African Press.

Babarinde, K. (1998). "Cultism, Campus Violence, and Students' Developmental Process in Nigeria." In *Nigerian Students and the Challenge of Leadership,* ed. J. Ogunye, S. Jegede, and B. Olasupo. Lagos: Committee for the Defence of Human Rights.

Bell, M. J. V. (1968). "The Military in New States of Africa." In *Armed Forces and Society,* ed. J. van Dooren. The Hague: Mouton.

Campaign for Democracy. (1998). *A Special Report on Nigeria.* Lagos: Campaign for Democracy.

Egwu, S. (1998). "The Political Economy of Ethnic and Religious Conflicts in Nigeria." In *Ethnic and Religious Politics in Nigeria,* ed. F. Okoye. Kaduna: Human Rights Monitor.

Falola, T., and J. Ihonvbere. (1985). *The Rise and Fall of Nigeria's Second Republic.* London: Zed Press.

Fayemi, J. K. (2000). "Entrenched Military Interests and the Future of Democracy in Nigeria." Paper presented at the International Conference on New Directions in Federalism, Abuja, Nigeria, March 15–18.

Gramsci, A. (1971). *Selections from the Prison Notebook.* London: Lawrence and Wishart.

Hall, S. (1996). *Critical Dialogues in Cultural Studies.* London: Routledge.

Ibeanu, O. (1998). "The Nigerian State and the Politics of Democratisation." Paper presented at the Workshop on Comparing Experiences of Democratisation in Nigeria and South Africa, Cape Town, May.

Jega, A. M. (1997). "Organizing for Popular Democratic Change in Nigeria: Options and Strategies for Consideration." In *Strategic Planning Workshops on Democratic Development in Nigeria: Report of Proceedings.* London: Centre for Democracy and Development.

Lenin, V. I. (1974). *Against Imperialist War.* Moscow: Progress Publishers.

Madunagu, E. (1998). "The National Question, the Power-Blocs, and Popular-Democratic Transformation of Nigeria." In *In Defense of History: A Journal of the Centre for Research, Information, and Documentation.*

Mamdani, M. (1995). "A Critique of the State and Civil Society Paradigm in Africanist Studies." In *African Studies in Social Movements,* ed. M. Mamdani and E. Wamba-dia-Wamba. Dakar: Council for the Development of Social Science Research in Africa.

Martins, B. (1998). *World Press Tribute: Fela Anikulapo-Kuti Eda 1938–1997.* Lagos: Music Foundation of Nigeria.

Momoh, A. (1998). "Civil Society in Nigeria: Towards a Reconceptualization, Reinterpretation, and Substantive Discourse." Paper presented at the Workshop on Comparing Experiences of Democratisation in Nigeria and South Africa, Cape Town, May.

Namiji, A. (1998). "Harmful Traditional Practices Affecting the Health of Women from Childhood." *Women's Advocate, 3.*

Nnoli, O. (1978). *Ethnic Politics in Nigeria.* Enugu: Fourth Dimension.

Okoye, F., ed. *Ethnic and Religious Politics in Nigeria.* Kaduna: Human Rights Monitor.

Political Bureau. (1987). *Report of the Political Bureau.* Abuja: Mass Mobilization for Social and Economic Recovery; Federal Government of Nigeria.

Rodney, W. (1969). *The Groundings with My Brothers.* London: Bogle-L'Ouverture.

Sako, R., and D. Plang. (1997). *A Basic Guide to Fundamental Rights for Nigeria.* Kaduna: Human Rights Monitor.

Toyo, E., ed. (1989). *Political Manipulation of Religion: Case Studies.* Calabar: Community Development Partners.

---. (1998). "On Democracy and Human Rights." In *In Defense of History: A Journal of the Centre for Research, Information, and Documentation, 1.*

Usman, Y. B. (1982). *Political Repression in Nigeria.* Zaria: Gaskiya.

Yau, Y. Z. (1998). "The Participation of Shiites and Almajirai in Religious Conflicts in Northern Nigeria." In *Ethnic and Religious Politics in Nigeria,* ed. F. Okoye. Kaduna: Human Rights Monitor.

SECTION II

NIGERIAN PRISONERS: VOICES FROM INSIDE

The following chapters were written by men forcibly confined in Kirikiri medium and maximum security prison in Lagos. All the authors were given the option to use pseudonyms or their real names in this book. They all chose to publish under the names given to them by their families. Many thought that their stories and their names needed to be heard. Through this book their lives are no longer anonymous numbers trapped inside prison yards. These chapters (with the exception of "Patriotism: Illusion or Reality?" by Osadolor Eribo) were handwritten in Kirikiri in 2003. I transcribed them and then translated them from Nigerian pidgin English. The chapter by Clever Akporherhe was verbally stated in the PRAWA office (upon his release) while I transcribed it, verbatim on his behalf. Major efforts were made to maintain the original messages and aesthetics of these writings. These are men who exhibited immense amounts of courage and integrity while I worked with them in Kirikiri. Despite the hardships they face each day, they continue to work toward educating those who are not in prison about the inhumane realities of their lives.

CHAPTER 5
ANOTHER FACE OF SLAVERY

Osadolor Eribo

After the abolition of slavery and the slave trade towards the end of the eighteenth century, people around the world, particularly the black race, were gladdened in body and in mind because it marked the beginning of the end of a savage and barbaric era. But little did the people of Africa and Nigeria in particular know that in less than a century would come a period of decadence, a society that is reminiscent of the era of slavery. The "elites" in Nigerian society returned to the continent and came to see themselves as our messiahs, sent here to guide and take us safely to the promised land—an epic of civilization; instead, they led the larger society astray with their selfish and uncompromising attitudes. The attitudes of the political bigots in this country have created a riotous environment, an unparalleled state of insecurity. There are fewer moral values now than ever before. Nigerians now see vices as virtues. We live in a society that has legalized tribalism[1] by calling it "the quota system." We live in a society that sees "crimes" only as actions committed by armed robbers, while actions committed by bureaucrats and the powerful people in this society—such as forgery, 419 (fraud), looting of the government's treasury and land resources, misappropriation of funds, and dissemination of false information to the general public—are not regarded as crimes.

This is a society that openly and readily denies its citizens "justice." There is always one sort of governmental interference or the other in the court of law, which is supposed to symbolize truth but is now a vehicle of violence. Nigerian society is openly ruled by a particular class of people, and it has been that way since the beginning of the postcolonial era, the so-called era of African independence. Nigeria has become a nation that refuses to give youths a chance. It has become a society with leaders who are over seventy years of age, who were once military dictators but now are "democratically" elected "presidents" wearing the best fabrics, showing off the newest designs, owning and flaunting brand-new Rolex watches, estates, and fleets of cars both in Nigeria and abroad. These are men who live gluttonous lives in fabulous houses. They have become models of fashion and design, often appearing on the front pages of this country's national newspapers and magazines. All this they have achieved with taxpayers' money and with this country's rich resources. Strangely enough, they do not seem to make the link between their lifestyles and poverty in Nigeria. They do not make it their responsibility to alleviate the suffering of the masses, most of whom live in abject poverty. The attitude of "monkey dey work; baboon dey chop" is rampant.[2] Sociopolitical and economic insecurity, social injustice, unprecedented rates of violent crime, and mass human rights violations are another epoch of slavery in this African society.

The rulers of our present society have been able to achieve such a remarkable feat in their pursuance of oppression by capitalizing on the weakness of the people. Poverty and illiteracy are the tools they use to keep the masses oppressed and their own bellies full. The Nigerian Prison Service's role in this oppression is instrumental. A Nigerian prison yard is where I am currently held captive. Ninety-five percent of the prisoners who are currently behind bars are from poor homes and are illiterate. They are people who have been pushed to the edge of a cliff by life's frustrating factors created by the elites of this nation. Most of the victims of this society got involved in crime as a result of their frustrations and the lack of opportunities to survive through "legitimate" means. Many felt dejected and hopeless without shelter and food, pushing them into the "other side of life" and engulfing them in it: the side of life people call "criminal." Worse still, upon arrival in prison these people are shown cruelty, depravity, inequality, and sheer wickedness. All basic rights are denied: food, clean drinking water, and medical attention come to mind immediately. Food that the government sets aside for prisoners is almost always "diverted elsewhere." Prisoners here are being subjected to physical and mental torture, which starts in the police stations and continues inside the prisons. Some prisoners arrive here half-crippled from the torture they endured inside police stations or as a result of a hard life on the streets, the unavailability of affordable polio vaccinations, the lack of nutrition, or "accidents" along the way. On being brought to prison they are subjected to psychological torture as a result of their disability.

One question I keep pondering over is this: are these people the most dangerous offenders in our society? If they are not, why are they treated in this inhumane manner? Every time I ponder over these questions, I find myself reaching the same conclusion: they treat us like this because they can, because we are among the poorest, most uneducated, and underprivileged people in Nigeria. My pondering also helps me to reach a second conclusion: the prison in the Nigerian context is not an instrument of reformation but an instrument of perpetual slavery and persecution employed by the privileged against the underprivileged. It is a dumping ground for police "suspects," it is a place to keep those people whom society has rendered worthless, and it is a place to incapacitate the poorest masses. This incapacitation is achieved not only through imprisonment but also through gunshots and chains under the pretense of interrogation: too many prisoners have been physically crippled through such brutalities.

Nigerian prisons are also an instrument for silencing patriots who refuse to compromise themselves for the social ills in this society. It is a place where innocent citizens are held captive to cover up the misdeeds of the government. It is no surprise to most people in this country that their "government" and police "force" have not been able to crack down on any assassination cases here. So many protesters have been assassinated, and not one case has been brought to justice. The murder of Dele Giwa, editor of *News Watch* magazine; the assassination of the defunct National Democratic Coalition (NADECO) chairman Pa Alfred Rewane; the recent killing of Minister of Justice Chief Bola Ige; these are but a few of the cases.

The Nigerian prison is like an ugly monster created by those in powerful positions to destabilize (physically and mentally) the youth and underprivileged of this nation. The penal system's work is ensuring that this nation is left with a future too similar to its violent past. The Nigerian prison is a mirror of Nigerian society, where cruelty, depravity, hunger, inequality, social injustice, and basic wickedness are the order of the day. I have seen no clearer picture of mass inhumanity than that of the Nigerian prison environment, and I have been a soldier at war in several nations in my life.

Prisoners given sentences ranging from ten years to life in prison for Indian hemp (marijuana)–related cases are still languishing behind bars, even though the laws that put them behind bars have been amended by the Nigerian "democratic" government as one of the implemented changes from military to civilian rule. Are such sentences not at variance with our present Constitution and law? Why are these people still in prison? It is a shame that innocent men charged with the murder of Pa Alfred Rewane are in jail even after countless revelations and confessional statements by government agents confirm that the government itself is responsible for his death.

It is even more disheartening to know that veteran soldiers, who served as Nigerian contingents under the ECOWAS[3] monitoring group ECOMOG,[4] with various physical disabilities as a result of gunshot and bomb blast wounds sustained while on peacekeeping missions in Liberia and Sierra Leone, are still languishing in jail simply because they spoke out against the poor medical care they received and the non-payment of their *estacode* ("allowances"). Some are still waiting for medical treatment and are in need of surgery, which they will likely never receive.

The cases I list here are but a few among so many appalling ones I come across every day inside this prison. The typical Nigerian prison is a place where mortal beings are metamorphosed into lesser beings. Prisoners are stripped of the natural power of choice endowed upon humanity; they are shown hatred and violence. They are haunted by stigmatization both within and outside the prison. They begin to feel dejected and hopeless. After spending most of the productive years of one's life in prison, one is sent back into society without any incentive or hope for the future, and many have been maimed from torture. When they leave prison they become "savagely wicked and cruel" in the eyes of Nigerian society. It is shocking that so many people know of the inhumanities and the cruelties that take place here, yet are puzzled at the inability of ex-prisoners to become "better citizens" of this corrupt and lethal society.

In light of all this, I find it necessary to reinforce this capability: irrespective of the traumatic experiences both inside this Nigerian prison and outside within the harsh Nigerian society, there are those of us who continue to take back the power of choice. We choose to resist corruption and oppression; surprisingly and unrepentantly, we choose to remain patriotic to the nation that has robbed us of our lives. There are some of us who still look forward to the day when positive changes will occur within *our* society.

"And the moon's fine to look at when the sun isn't there." So says the tale of Shakespeare "Treason". At this crucial point in time, I wish to commend the efforts of the humanitarian-minded people and the various human rights organizations nationwide, the non-governmental organizations, the religious bodies, and of course the international communities for their awareness programmes and immense contributions, morally and financially, toward the attainment of a just society and, more so, for the level of love you have been able to give to those who feel dejected inside these prisons. Your networks have been our only source of love, hope, inspiration, and "moon" to look at when the sun is conspicuously absent.

When I look at the good and wonderful handiwork of nature around me, the ever-green landscape of our geographical setting, the fertile soil, and the brilliant men and women who live in this African nation, alongside the corrupt and selfish ones, I tend to have a vision of truth: one where inequality and perversion of truth will be replaced by equal rights and true justice; where the looting of Nigerian resources and government treasuries will be replaced by pride and nation-building; where old and egocentric political bigots will be replaced by young, dynamic, and invigorating leaders; where economic depression will be replaced by industrial revolution; and, above all, where hatred and political violence will be replaced by peace, serenity, and equal rights. The key to achieving these dreams lies in revolutionizing the entire social structure, in refocusing on education, in reorienting this nation's people through the use of intelligible and relevant African methods with a logic that can penetrate deeply into the fabric of Nigerians and break the shackles of this continued colonial slavery.

NOTES

1. Tribalism is discrimination according to tribal ethnicity.
2. "Monkey dey work; baboon dey chop": That is, one person works, while another eats the fruits of that labour.
3. The Economic Community of West African States (ECOWAS) was formed in 1975 by several West African nations to strengthen the West African region's economic structures.
4. ECOMOG (Economic Community of West African States Monitoring Group) or ECOWAS Monitoring Group (ECOMOG) is an armed monitoring unit set up by ECOWAS (Economic Community of West African States) in 1990 to implement peacekeeping missions in West African countries experiencing civil wars and other violent internal conflicts.

CHAPTER 6

MY NIGERIAN PRISON EXPERIENCE

Clever Akporherhe

I, Clever Akporherhe, stayed in Kirikin medium security prison for a period of one year and six months. On the day of my admission I became seriously sick. I complained to the officer or warden, but I was told that I would be taken to the clinic on Monday. I arrived on Friday. In reality I was never taken to the clinic.

On arrival I was taken to the "welcome cell" meant for new inmates. There the prison "INTERPOL" tortured us with whips and asked us to bend our heads while sitting on the floor. We were about 250 men, all new prisoners courtesy of "Operation Fire for Fire" [a police squad working the streets of Lagos]. We were locked up in a cell meant for twenty-six people. We sat like that for most of the day. At about 9 p.m. the general of the prison, with headphones and a walkie-talkie, spoke to us and issued a warning that those of us with hidden money, whether in our anuses, pockets, or anywhere else, should hand the money over to them immediately. Fear gripped me for the first time, and I quickly dropped my N2,100 (equivalent to Canadian$ 21), along with my Rapido wristwatch worth N2,500 (equivalent to CA$ 25). Upon release they gave me N300 (equivalent to Canadian$ 3), and I never saw the watch again. At the time several other persons dropped various sums of money. Later we were all searched again and asked to excrete — to "make sure" that no one was hiding money inside his anus.

The sleeping arrangements were terrible, as we were lined up like sardines on the ground. We did not receive any food that day; they said that, since we were *alejos* ("newcomers" to prison), we were not entitled to eat yet. Inside the welcome cell there was one big bucket of water for the 250 prisoners, who were squatting like sardines. They were calling us up two at a time and giving us one cup of water each, which we had to drink immediately and then return to our spots. If you asked for a second cup of water, they gave you a whip instead. We were not allowed to go near the bucket of water or even ease ourselves at the lavatory. Inside the cell, if one of us needed to use the toilet, a big plate was given to him to piss in before the convicted prisoners who are made to supervise the welcome cell poured it into the sink. This, they said, was meant to avoid making the sink smell bad, but in reality it was meant to dehumanize their "new" prisoners.

We were woken up very early the next day, around 5 a.m., and asked to pray. Before the end of prayer the "morning baked beans," as they call them, were brought to us, not more than twenty beans with dry *garri* (a staple carbohydrate in the Nigerian diet) scattered on top. We were not allowed to wash our hands before and after eating; no utensils were provided. Two hours later we were brought out and given cutlasses (machetes) to clear the area where a lot of human waste was buried and grass had overgrown. After the morning's backbreaking labour we were taken back to the welcome cell without bathing.

The warders and officials are not very friendly unless they think they can get something from you. They are usually friendly if they know that "your people" (family or friends) will be coming to visit you—they hope to get a piece of whatever your people bring for you.

There was a time while I was in prison that all the mango and fruit trees in the yard got chopped down due to the unavailability of firewood for cooking. The contractor supplying the wood had brought nothing. So used tires and fresh wood were used to cook, and it took a long time to prepare the food for the 2,400 prisoners in Kirikiri medium security prison at the time. This is a prison built to accommodate 788 people. While the shortage of firewood was going on in the prison, they served dry *garri* twice a day—once in the afternoon and once in the evening—for about three months; our food supply was getting smaller and smaller because they did not have a means of cooking for us. Even before this situation, a lot of the prisoners, especially the ATMs (awaiting-trial males), were underfed and looked very undernourished.

Before the shortage of firewood, the main food was dry *garri* soaked in water from wells contaminated with larvae: worms and insects can clearly be seen with the naked eye in the water. As for the health clinic, there is nothing to write home about. It's a mere dispensary unit: no doctors examine prisoners, and all complaints are met with tablets when they are available—this for prisoners who are fortunate enough to visit the clinic. Any prisoner who wants to go to the clinic must make it to prayers on time; any latecomers are denied medical help. Those prisoners who are fortunate enough to have visits from their families or friends and are fortunate enough to get medicine from them have it seized by the prison officers at the gate. They confiscate it, stating that the doctor did not prescribe it in the hospital, even though doctors rarely examine prisoners in the clinic. After confiscating the drugs they never help you to go to the clinic for medical assistance. Only one person is taken from each cell for treatment each day; it does not matter how many people in that cell need medical attention.

Daily reports of death from various cells frightened me, and one day I complained to the authorities about our living conditions. I was immediately taken to the solitary cells called *angola*. These are cells where prisoners are punished for one offence or the other. The cells are built for one person, but they cram about six or seven people in. My survival was due to the Christian churches that came for fellowship and brought in food.

Most of the food meant for prisoners was carted away by the officers. Aside from that, the same warders who are supposed to "correct" us supplied bunches of Indian hemp for prisoners who in turn sold the drugs to other prisoners on a retail basis. After being divided into "pinches," as they called it, a wrap of Indian hemp worth N10 (10 Canadian cents) in the free world could be sold for N60 (60 Canadian cents) inside.

Current conditions do not provide clean drinking water, a good toilet system, or proper medical aid, and there is overcrowding and too much torture of prisoners by warders. Even on Sundays prisoners are asked to manually clear grass for labour. The conditions are dehumanizing and fatal. In view of the above facts, I appeal to the general public and to this audience to do something for those imprisoned in Nigeria.

CHAPTER 7

MY STORY

Chris Affor

On April 24, 1994, I heard a knock on my office door. Before I could even say "come in," two men entered. One of them was my boss; I tried to read the expression on his face, but it was blank, and I knew right away that I did not like the air around either his looks or the looks of the man standing next to him. That man was following closely behind my boss, not allowing any distance. Initially that did not have any meaning to me. My boss's voice echoed, "Mr. Chris, I don't know what it's all about. I just can't understand the message. This is a police officer, and he would like to see you at the station. You better go with him for a better explanation. I don't get mixed up with such stuff, don't expect me around." Then he continued, "Constable, this is Mr. Chris; he stands a better chance of giving whatever explanation you need." With two strides he was out of the office.

The constable said politely, "Sir, your attention is needed at the station for a little briefing on a certain matter that requires your attention. You only need to come with your car, just to make things easier for the both of us. I promise to give you a helping hand where necessary. I am waiting."

I had no prior experience with police stations. Neither could I remember or think of anything in my life that would give them reason to want or need to speak with me. I raised my head to speak to the constable, but no words emerged. Like most people in Nigeria, I was terrified of the police. That fear is especially escalated among those who do not have massive life savings. I allowed the policeman to drive my car in order to regain my composure. He parked the car in a parking lot I had never seen before. I looked at the inscription on the wall of the building; it was bold enough to convince a fool: Barbeach Police Station. The words I had wanted to say were no longer available or necessary. I had entered their turf. I swallowed my words and without even a gesture followed him inside.

Four men were called out from the police cell. We were arranged in a single row before the station officer. I recognized one of the men as the man who had sold me my car, Segim Oladokim. He was my neighbour about two years ago. I lived in a building that had four flats [apartments]. The man who sold me the car occupied the two flats upstairs, while the two flats downstairs were occupied by my work colleague Ademola, Mr. Williams, and me. Oladokim had five cars in our parking lot, among which he placed one for sale. We agreed on the price, and documents were handed over to me after settlement. Two days later Oladokim himself brought certified papers on "change of ownership" and handed them to me. All the while I had nothing on my mind, no doubts about the legitimacy of this sale—it did not occur to me to raise any suspicion. He was a good man, managing a big business, but at the time I didn't know his secret.

It dawned on me as these men confessed that the car that Oladokim had sold to me was not only stolen but also sold to me under the pretense of doctored documents. The car was connected to a criminal case investigation in Alagbon, Lagos State, of robbery and murder. After being tortured for some time, the men had confessed to this robbery.

I spent two weeks in the police cell, unaware that these were days of grace given to me to find whatever [monetary] "settlement" I could for a job well done by the police. It was unfortunate, but I didn't understand the smallest signals and secrets of this procedure and the affairs in which I found myself. My level of understanding at the time had no reference to how the criminal justice system is run in this country. I got to know about it at court, through a tip offered to me by one of the police officers (that, if I had found "settlement" for the police officers, I would not be on my way to jail), but at that point it was too late. Naively, I expected to be released, believing that my role in their murder and robbery case had been cleared before the police through the "confessions" made by the robbers, leaving me with little or no statement to make: their "confessions" had, as far as I knew, answered all their questions. If wishes were horses, I would have collected an "award" for innocence. I never knew then that my journey was just about to begin.

On May 8, 1994, I was taken to court. That morning the police officer in charge of my case called on me and said, "My hands are tied, the case is the sensitive type.[1] I have to charge and take you to court to defend your case. You better make necessary preparations for your bail. We shall be at the court in the shortest time." I brightened, believing the case was over. I was ready to "pay" the police constable some money to show my appreciation; he had refused to accept any money from my wife. I did not know then that the offer made by my wife was too small and that he considered it an insult; thus, he had already decided to "deal with me." He never knew I was poor. He had concluded from the size of my office and from his personal scale of assessments given my appearance that I was not. How I wish I was as big as that empty office and as powerful as the misconceptions that led to my misfortune.

The story changed in court. I heard the judge say "that you, Mr. Chris Affor, on the 17th of May, 'robbed' one Mr. Anerson Ebere of Mob Odade Street, Agege Lagos, a 505 Peugeot Saloon car valued at 'N500,000.' You are hereby to be remanded at Kirikiri medium prison without bail under section... of the Constitution of the Federal Republic of Nigeria awaiting DPP [Directorate of Public Prosecution] advice." This essentially meant that I would be sent to prison on a "holding charge" to await trial, and that I would wait until the DPP brought me to court for trial. I turned to look for the policeman who once promised to give me a helping hand if necessary. He was nowhere to be found. I have no words to describe the type of rings [shackles] they hooked upon my hands and legs. The weight alone is enough to frustrate a beast.

In my head I could not understand what was going on. What shall I say to my people? Will they hear that their son is now a robber? The stigma associated with that in Nigeria is too much to carry. Whom shall I call for explanations? Who will listen to my voice? Is it possible to believe me instead of the police and the judge? Who is the liar—the police, or the judge, or the man found with the stolen car? Possibly, they will know the truth later. Who will convince them? The police? Who will solicit on my behalf? Will they believe him? I must be a dreamer if I believe I can easily be vindicated. The evidence appears so obvious in this court of law, but no one is ready to decode the real facts. How I wish the ground could have opened and swallowed me up just to satisfy the intensity of my desire for a hiding place; even the world is too small to contain me. I was absolutely devastated. My job? My wife and kids? All gone? Is there a God in heaven? Why should he fail to intervene in this case? Possibly he is not aware. But he knows all things. Why must my case escape his eyes? Possibly it is my fault. But what is the fault? Too many questions—and not a single answer.

From that moment on, nothing else seems to have stayed in my memory for long. I noticed it was drizzling outside; after that my memory is absolutely blank. The only thing I can recollect was when I was guided by two strong hands through a mighty gate made with some rugged type of iron, part of which was used to construct the railway. I heard myself answering certain questions absentmindedly, and I later found out they were the correct answers. The police here seem to have forgotten how to smile, staring as if they have nowhere to go, and they also seem to have forgotten what it means to be decent in appearance. The world immediately began to feel very different, a place where too many things occur that are absolutely unnecessary.

My wife immediately arranged for a lawyer. She received assistance from the policeman in charge of my case, the same man who had arrested me and promised to help me, also the same man who had promised to release me from prison within a month. According to that police officer and the lawyer he had helped us to find, my robbery charge was pending, and a "holding conviction" by the judge made it possible for them to keep me in prison as long as need be. That "conviction," I am told, was later determined unconstitutional by the Court of Appeal. The lawyer was paid, and hopes for release were high. To cut a very long story short, we found out that the lawyer was a duper, conspiring with the police to extract money from people in prison, abandoning cases early, and claiming he had been "trying his best," eventually forcing people either to pay him more money or to begin looking for another lawyer out of frustration. He abandoned my case after it went through the Court of Appeal, so my release proceedings were left without representation. I ran out of money, so my only option was to begin looking for another lawyer after my wife gathered up more funds.

The second lawyer we hired could not produce results because he did not possess a passing idea on the series of protocols and procedures made in a holding charge by the Nigerian judiciary, despite the fact that it had been deemed unconstitutional by the Court of Appeal. He was what we call "a baby lawyer": we knew him to be a lawyer, but quickly learned that lawyers have credentials regarding the type of cases they can handle. He was not a criminal lawyer and did not disclose this information at the time of consultation. I know now that he is a divorce lawyer and never knew how to produce results in criminal justice proceedings. At this point I had spent three years in prison, still believing stories from lawyers, and their words of assurance and reassurance, all to no avail. I eventually understood that I needed to find a different path.

My wife and I decided to consult a Nigerian human rights activist as a result of our lack of funds. His response to our lack of money was "Goodbye." To cut that long story short as well, the DPP had not "looked" at my case for eight years. The judge refused to make any efforts in my case, claiming that it was illegal for him to interfere with the activities of the DPP even though it had failed to perform its "duty" for eight years. It is illegal to interfere in the activities of the DPP, even as a judge, after eight years as a matter of protocol? But the same protocol failed to recognize as illegal my detention without trial. Who is to blame, the man in detention or the chains of judicial impropriety? Who is to bear the brunt of this inactivity that receives the blessings of government protocol?

A detailed look into the actions of the Nigerian criminal justice system brings to light incredibly ironic occurrences. Right now I have been in prison for ten years without trial. "Visiting judges" come into the prison to listen to the complaints of prisoners, especially those awaiting trial for ten years or more. This exercise is performed four times a year and includes official visits by chief judges for the state. They come into the prison, promise to look into the "affairs of the awaiting-trial inmates," once in a while they release a few people, and then they leave. Too many of us have been awaiting trial for more than ten years; too many of us continue to wait for a trial or for a judge to have mercy during a visit and let us go.

We have come to learn that the presence of these judges is only one among a series of government protocols. It has nothing to do with release. Can you imagine judges inside these prison yards, parading themselves around in the presence of absolute injustice? And not seeing the irony of their actions because they are so wrapped up in the name of government protocol? They claim to "sympathize" with prisoners weeping for want of justice and suffering from illegal detentions signed by *those same judges.* How can they reconcile my situation and sympathize with me when my detention warrant has been declared unconstitutional? Is the judiciary divided? Do they not communicate with each other? Where is the supremacy of the Court of Appeal over lower courts? Why does the penal hierarchy enforce only itself inside the prison while failing to keep its police officers from brutal behaviours and its courts from imposing unjust sanctions?

I believe that the lower courts, the high courts, the Court of Appeal, and the Supreme Court are all under the same judiciary. What brought about the differences in their applications of the law? If judges are helpless in the presence of absolute injustice, then what chance do I, a prisoner, have of ever getting out of this prison?

I strongly believe that, if judges wanted to access authority to redeem the filthy judicial situation and its misuse of the prison system, they would know precisely how to obtain such power. They say that their hands are tied, and they say that in the presence of prisoners awaiting trial? Whose hands are tied? Besides, if the hands of judges are tied, judges who are still sitting in the seats of judgment, who are still being endowed with the power to interpret and apply the law, then is the law itself tied? Who shall restore justice?

It is important that the actions of these judicial powers be brought to light before one can determine measures to restore authority and reinstate absolute independence worthy of a constituted judiciary of a nation. And this "investigation" needs to occur before international penal reformers come here to "help" us build a more efficient system of justice. Does a more efficient system give judges more power? How can we trust them, in light of how they have misused their power already, not to implement a more brutal system? It is irrelevant to talk about the existing incremental impropriety, because when things have fallen apart this badly the centre can do nothing to hold things together. Little wonders come forth when one sees the Court of Appeal declaring certain rules unconstitutional while the higher court and the lower court, the police, and the prisons continue to implement a holding charge. My "learned friends," where is your knowledge?

I do not know when I have ever been as extensively discouraged or depressed as I have been with my experiences of the failure of justice in this country. It is frustrating to meet up with the predator's objective and the perpetrator's mandate. Prison has no particular agenda for implementing anything good. It is meant for dumping and wasting natural potentials and human resources, purposefully built to deprive the poor of the right of real success and in fear of possible future rivals for power in society. Prison retains that social mantle of authority and kingship that allows for a very limited and predetermined number of heads to wear the crown.

This system does not have an agenda for reformation or rehabilitation. It is a system of practical exploitation and subjugation through constant pressure. The threat under law has a hidden purpose, and that is to subdue the poor by reducing them to a state of irresponsibility and slavery. As prisoners fight for their rights and their needs, those who wear the crown continue to ignore us.

The public has become too willing to accept as true anything the people in authority claim to be true. What they do not know in detail is that prison life is dreadful and would frighten a lion. Nothing is normal here. Nothing makes sense here. What a confused world. The meals are tasteless. The food is constantly undercooked and permanently cold, and portions seem to have a way of reducing themselves constantly. We don't eat food, we swallow food like pills with our eyes closed. We have no choice; it is our only source of survival. We eat what we hate and enjoy what we dislike, all in the name of survival. If I were a criminal, all this might be a reminder of the magnitude of my actions. My situation, along with those of thousands of awaiting-trial prisoners, is unique. We have come to see how this system is deliberately cruel and openly oppressive. How can I live without past reflection? How can I not think that this raw distribution of injustice can be deadly if the raw desire for vengeance is not properly checked? How can I, or anyone for that matter, begin to look for rehabilitation within the realm of a revenge-based system?

Criminal justice in Nigeria is not concerned with guilt or innocence. In this system the police are experts at "getting confessions" out of individuals and continue to do so to improve their own careers as efficient officers. Receiving injustice from the seat of justice, from discredited social and justice systems, is not only corrupt but has also left too many citizens in this African motherland in colonial prisons. We are here through the measures of the Constitution that is meant to protect us. It is the same Constitution that legalized colonization and the slave trade. How does a constitution-based system relate to Africa? It never has had, and most likely never will have, our best interests in mind.

I long to see the day when the law shall avenge the poor and bring justice upon the ruling class, which for too long has subdued and subjugated the less privileged to a state of social, economic, and psychological breakdown. Their political ambitions are not rivalled by those of the lower class, and never will be as long as they continue throwing us into prison with the help of *their* laws and *their* institutions of "justice."

If you go around the prison, a little personal survey will tell you that the man you see is either a poor man or the son of a poor man. The wealthy are not here. All the so-called accused rich people we see in the media who have been arrested for fraud and brutality have rarely been seen inside Nigeria's prisons. The law has a way out for them. It is a selective distribution of justice, always in favour of certain classes of people: "corporate criminals" with "corporate immunity" by "corporate law" for the "corporate class."

An illustration of what I am trying to express about Nigeria today is found in the Kirikiri maximum security prison in Lagos State, the number one prison in Nigeria, they say. As of today, despite a series of celebrated criminal cases in the media, and despite the newspaper headlines reporting fraud, duping, drug-dealing, and political and economic corruption, this prison holds six "political" detainees from the Abacha [military dictator] era for human rights violations. Where are the others? They say that in theory "nobody is above the law." They also say that there is "equality before the law." But *practical justice* continues to exonerate the rich. And if the lower courts fail to keep the rich out of prison, the higher courts can exert their power and release them. If the higher courts delay a rich man's freedom, then the Court of Appeal will restore that freedom almost immediately, without preambles or delays. Before you can finish saying "Where is the man?" he will be back in his luxurious family home feasting on fresh fish pepper soup. Their cases are often discharged and they are acquitted for "want of substantial evidence" and "lack of proof." Justice in this country is for "just us" — just the poor in prison and never the rich accessing the power of higher courts. This system values money over human life and dignity, exonerating corporate criminals and condemning powerless individuals to years of jail time.

The solution to this problem of discredited justice is still far from being defined. Do we now sit back and rely on the corporate and politically powerful class to reform their own system? They know that the imbalance of power is exploitative. The privileged person who is not vulnerable to justice might think that prisons give the government power to curtail crime and make their society safer. I agree: it makes *their* society safer by safeguarding a small rich population, keeping just that population less vulnerable to competition for power. To remain safe, they must continue to subjugate the poor in a perpetual state of slavery.

The irony for me is that all these conditions come with "civilization." The same system that was brought to us by "civilized" British colonialists represents one of the more brutal aspects of life in Nigeria. I still wonder how long I will be held behind these walls. I still wonder about my future. I wonder what this system is really doing and where it is all going. And sometimes I find myself wondering what this system is maintaining and why.

NOTES

1   "Sensitive" in Nigeria because armed robbery is the worst crime a person can commit or be accused of committing. Armed robbers are viewed as one of the most immediate and lethal problems in the country.

CHAPTER 8
A TRIBUTE TO SOLIDARITY: MY OASIS

Chris Affor

I regret that I don't have the words to express the depth of my gratitude; I would have started to write a heart-felt appreciation long overdue that put "golden tears" on my face even at a dreadful point of emotional and psychological breakdown, when I was eaten up by pessimism and despair, attracting insanity and suicide. There came a turning point, the PRAWA Circle,[1] which introduced prisoners to calculated, sifted, and refined reconciliation, social reformative measures aimed at diluting tension, anger, depression, and raw desire for vengeance. We prisoners together have learned to survive as one. Words do not come close to describing how happy I, as well as many others, feel, and we recognize and respect the presence of solidarity, as if it was divinely destined to comfort dejected souls like cold water on a thirsty tongue and like good news about home from a distant land.

Prisoners are rejected people, abandoned by society and ignored by the world as a whole. Social discomfort with the unknown leaves those "tagged" as prisoners to become the representation of deadly character descriptions, meant for beasts. As a prisoner in Nigeria I feel enslaved by events and life circumstances so unfavourable that humiliation and dejection are evident enough to form sweat on squeezed faces like those of the Caihdihh Ancestral Shrines.

It is not possible to interpret this experience through words or facts, for when one is not free true expression of the self and of experiences is tantamount to crossing an ocean in your own room. Those who have travelled along this particular road can better tell the story, for my life has left a mark on my palm, a constant reminder of the bitter past of cultural imbalance, yet I still maintain hopes for days of plenty. I must not fail to confess that solidarity here has altered my life for the better, giving me a restoration of identity, dignity, and self-esteem. But I have been emotionally, physically, and psychologically discredited by the judiciary, and my imprisonment has been the result of judicial impropriety through selective distribution[2] under the rich colours of the law.

In light of oppression, solidarity among prisoners and those from the outside world who work with us gives us the strength to deal with the negative public sentiment in regard to prisoners. I continue to believe that something good can come out of all this. The sad reality is that in here there is an overabundance of fertile minds, of vision-oriented and talented people, hidden behind bars. We are unduly isolated because of "unknowns," with derogatory and even deadly security measures meant to put our credibility as human beings in question.

Whom can you believe? The convicted and disreputable fellow with more than substantial evidence to attract a position behind bars, or a respected public servant with a standing reputation in the court of law? It is not simple. We refuse to let you believe that it is simple. This is a puzzle that requires considerable scrutiny to solve. There is one standing assurance: our longevity must speak for our survival in moments of severe deprivation and degradation. It is incredible that solidarity can accomplish something real inside the walls, bringing support to prisoners to survive psychologically, physically, socially, and emotionally, constantly giving prisoners new energy to keep fighting back in the war for power and control. In recognizing our present state as pawns in the hands of our criminal justice predators, we gain power. Always less than satisfied with the "barter criminal justice system" (the perpetrators' choice), we remain aware.

True solidarity inside prison includes sustained efforts to put out the contemporary penal inferno, which serves the ruling class, the political predators, those few individuals who have privatized the seat of power, representing their interests while misrepresenting the poor and the decency of all people regardless of social position.

In the end heartfelt smiles from prisoners inside these dungeons go a long way toward repairing deadly emotional and psychological damage inflicted by punitive people and their systems. In here, lingering at the corner of life's destitution, living at the heart of life's wilderness, we are dedicated to putting smiles and optimistic looks on the faces of the poor and helpless victims of this unjust system.

Sincere solidarity among prisoners makes me feel like a human being in the midst of my life's wilderness. Solidarity among prisoners and members of our human rights community is proof that walls cannot distance us from society for long, and every time community members sit with us, every time they do not distance themselves from us, every time they fail to show signs of distaste or disgust in our presence, every time they are comfortable in our company, so lively that they seem to have forgotten we are prisoners, we are reminded that we continue to be human beings.

Solidarity does not allow us to feel like lesser people. In a prison yard, inside the grasp of the law, meant to humiliate the less privileged, we look upon solidarity with community activists as the closest thing we have to brothers and sisters. Solidarity gives us a certain degree of confirmation, reminders of our humanity, touching our spirits. It is special and now deeply engrained in my heart.

My oasis comes through my recognition of the humanity around me. No matter how hard the prison works to dehumanize us, when I look at the *people* in prison with me I experience humanity. As we sit inside this prison yard, hungry but in discussion with each other and sharing knowledge, we find ourselves instilling a great and versatile presence of mind, defining success, and getting a sense of accomplishment by helping each other. Presenting each other with the fact that knowledge is power, and realizing that power cannot be circumvented by circumstantial disasters and tribulations, we learn that the light of knowledge knows no failure. Life is a stormy career from creation until death, but the gift of unconditional planting is the mother of unconditional harvest. Solidarity inside this prison is the unconditional planting of life.

Whatever we have done as people becomes our identities and is instituted as a perpetual reference for recognition—positively or negatively. It is human to respect people from whom we can gain something positive. The giver in us is to be honoured for the wonderful aspect of giving. Recognition of this giver brings a happiness that cannot be wholly reciprocated at the other end of the spectrum.

How I wish I was gifted with better language to decode and express my experiences, and the power I have seen in solidarity. For now, I continue to refuse to be broken emotionally and psychologically. I am covered by this oasis and have found immunity.

The authorities have tried to subdue the poor in this country to a breaking point where there will be no future available to us. They are wasting the natural resources of my nation, and I along with the others who are less privileged cannot see the light in our lives beneath the walls of this unjust criminal justice system. It does not have a legal agenda; its practical purpose is exploitation and subjugation through constant pressure and threat under the colour of *their* laws. With this agenda against the poor, the criminal justice system is purposefully aimed at reducing people to a confused social, emotional, and psychological state.

The law that is supposed to uphold, maximize, and update the interpretation of justice does not cast a light that shines on the poor in this nation; the law is an instrument of deliberate injustice and practical corruption. The judge's gavel has been sold for a cut of the "national cake." The truth is now for sale, with a price tag that only the wealthy can afford. You need to be a millionaire to contend for your rights in a country where no one cares. The "fundamental human rights" of people who do not have money have been buried and forgotten. We see rules and regulations and constitutional rights on posters displayed on walls in police stations, prisons, and government houses, and on streetlight poles, paid for by foreign funders in another "awareness-raising" campaign. Some of these fundamental human rights are pasted on the walls in several police stations I sat in. Those posters say that bail is free, that you should not give or collect bribes, and that the police are your friends. All that took place in those police stations underneath such signs contradicted these messages.

It is painful that, despite all these posters and campaigns, the Nigerian police, judiciary, and prison system can keep a suspect in prison for ten years without trial and no means of earning bail. In the name of a "holding charge," even after the Court of Appeal has declared such a charge and subsequent detention unconstitutional, we continue to sit behind prison walls.

If some of us succeed in raising our heads above these waters of injustice, and find a way to leave this prison yard, after all the years our families and friends (those of us who have them) spent raising fortunes to get us out, there is no compensation for wrongful imprisonment, for years lost in prison without trial. In the hands of police, lawyers, and judges lie our uncertain fortunes.

I take some satisfaction from knowing that my truth has been told. My power lies in speaking out: while the constitutional justice system is credited permanently to the rich in our society, the poor remain voiceless because they have "nothing to offer." I know I have something to offer. My experiences speak volumes about the nature of the law and how it functions to oppress the underprivileged.

I am a Nigerian, but at times I find myself daydreaming about reasons to doubt my citizenship. If I am a Nigerian, or a citizen of any nation, then where is my access to fundamental human rights as accorded to me through my citizenship? I feel as if I belong to no country in particular. I think that prisoners all over the world must feel like this. If we do belong to a nation, then we should have access to an embassy for help, a source outside the system that could properly represent *our* best interests. If I were a true citizen of this nation, then I wouldn't have been "used" to implement colonial injustice. My citizenship has nothing to offer me. I have been used in this "African" experiment with "constitutional and colonial justice," subjected to rules that have been abused by a series of "according to taste" constitutions, meant to subjugate the poor while fulfilling some kind of established "unconditional pledge for national loyalty."

NOTES

1   The PRAWA Circle is a programme that Viviane Saleh-Hanna implemented in several Nigerian prisons to enhance solidarity among prisoners and aid in building survival tactics for those serving time in Nigeria. In addition to community-building, the programme allowed prisoners to identify their own needs and to work toward helping each other meet them. In Kirikiri medium security prison prisoners suggested the implementation of a literacy component to the programme; as a result prisoners who had literary skills began to teach others who did not. In the maximum security prison literacy was not a concern; community-building was considered to be the main priority; thus, its circle programme consisted of discussions and debriefing sessions.
2   The distribution of "justice" targets the poor and allows the rich to prosper.

CHAPTER 9
JUNE 14, 2003

Igho Odibo

Greetings,

I am Mr. Igho Odibo, forty-two years of age, and am currently held in Kirikiri maximum security prison in Lagos, Nigeria. I was a student in Germany, studying computer assembly, before I contracted HIV/AIDS and was deported back to Nigeria in 1998. I was handed over to the Nigerian federal government for medical treatment, but they did not provide any. I have started to battle with the federal government along with battling my illness. I am currently in prison, where there is no medical treatment available to me at all. It's only some non-governmental organizations and human rights agencies that once in a while give me assistance and care for me. I have become a Christian in prison and have handed all hope over to Christ. I am currently in prison for an alleged robbery offence but have yet to face trial. In Nigeria, if you don't have money, you cannot come out of prison, sometimes for life. I have nobody coming to see me and nobody to take care of me, it's only Christ Jesus.

Mr. Igho Odibo
Kirikiri Maximum Security Prison
Lagos State, Nigeria

CHAPTER 10

THE SYSTEM I HAVE COME TO KNOW

Sylvester Monday Anagaba

June 18, 2003

I was arrested on April 17, 1992. I was taken to the Lagos State Police Command in Ikeja, where I was hung like a monkey from the ceiling, with my hands holding up the rest of my body. This was done to me twice for long periods of time in one night, all in the name of "investigation." The second time they strung me up to the ceiling I passed out, only to wake up the next morning with my hands and legs paralyzed from the hanging, and my whole body covered with bruises and blood. I was ordered at gun point to sign a statement. I do not know who wrote it or what it entailed. I refused but was hit with a police baton. My IPO [investigating police officer], Sergeant Otein, was the man beating me; he even threatened to kill me if I refused to sign the statement. I did sign it later. That same day the leader of the team of men [police] handling my case came into our cell (there were many of us in one cell that night). They chose thirty people and sent them out to be killed by the OCSARS [officer in charge of special anti-robbery squad] in the Lagos State Police Branch. Since they believed I was innocent, they told me that they did not want to kill me but at the same time could not release me "free of charge," as bail is not free in *their* police station. They asked me to contact my family and to ask them to bring N40,000 [approximately CA$ 400] for bail. I did contact my family, and they did manage to collect the money, and my family did pay the "king" of the other policemen in that station.

On April 21, 1994, very early in the morning, I was taken to court by my IPO, Sergeant Otein. When I tried to enquire why I was not being released, he told me that I had given the money to his superior. I should have given him the money, because his boss had eaten the lion's share of that money; for that reason I will suffer more than Job [the biblical figure]. At court they charged me with stealing a necklace from a woman. I have been remanded, by the magistrate, to Kirikiri maximum security prison on a "holding charge."

I was taken to Area F Police Station at Ikeja on court order because I raised up my hand at the court to demand my adjournment. At Area F Police Station I was put inside cells with hardened armed robbers. It was like hell, because I have never in my life had cause to be behind a police counter. I was pushed into a cell that afternoon. The police had informed the suspects inside that cell that I had refused to give them money. I was mocked by the other prisoners and told what the future had in store for me. I was eventually able to make an impression upon the hearts of that hungry mob, and we had a conversation. They had been deprived of their freedom, most for years ranging from one year to four years. They had been in police custody, warehoused inside police cells the whole time. I spent five months and two weeks in that police cell. I paid N10,000 to be taken to court on September 20, 1994. That was my ticket out of the police cell and into the maximum security prison in Kirikiri. I have been here on a "holding charge" awaiting trial ever since.

At the "reception" of this penal institution, which the guards on duty call "country no vex" (i.e., "Welcome to the country where you cannot get angry"), everybody registered under his family name. After the exercise of recording our identities was complete we were taken to the "solitary blocks." We were put into cells, eight of us in an eight-by-ten-foot cell. It stunk like hell; the odour was so overwhelming that five of us vomited immediately upon entering it. It was like entering a hole that was a natural extension of hell. In the cell there were no mattresses, there was no toilet and no means of getting water, the floors were littered with cigarette butts, ash, and spider webs covered with dust and sweat from the prisoners who had used the cell before we arrived. The place was hot; there was no ventilation except the door with crossed iron bars. Worst of all, there was no light, and we had no food. The guard claimed that our number was not included in the rations for that day. They took all the money any of us had and made it clear to us that ownership of money is not allowed in prison.

The next day we were put in blocks [small halls filled with people]. The sight of my roommates was sickening. I remember one man in particular who was not dead but decaying. Scabs covered many people, from head to toe, and some even had scabs on their palms. My block was another eight-by-ten-foot cell, but this time we were fifteen in number. Now I knew why the first cell was called the "solitary cell."

That night my journey of exile in this country began. I couldn't sleep, as we were packed in like sardines. At one point we were told that we would be taking turns sleeping, since there wasn't enough room for us all to lie down on the floor. When five people were asleep five would mount sentry, while the remaining five would sit down. At about two in the morning I was still standing when one of my new friends, Felix Okoedion, fell over. All efforts to revive him were fruitless. We shouted for the guards to come, and they asked us to "handle the situation" until daybreak. Felix finally gave up at 3 a.m. We rang the iron door with our feeding pans but to no avail. The next morning we were beaten with batons, gang-chained with shackles, and taken to solitary confinement, where we spent three months without questions or medical care, and we were given half of the measly rations of the miserable food they give to the rest of the prisoners. These are just some of the experiences I have had with the penal system in Nigeria; they are the ones that come to mind when I reflect upon my time here. It has been difficult.

CHAPTER 11

MAN'S INHUMANITY TO MAN

Sylvester Monday Anagaba

Game hunting is a jungle sport, but in this inside world known as maximum security prison men are still being hunted like game. It is a cruel, dehumanizing mechanism they call rehabilitation; it is a system that is nothing more than a refined method of slavery — all the ethics of enslavement are very much alive, mostly in the blood of the colonial slave drivers known as wardens or prison guards.

I have been in this prison for nine years now, but something that I cannot forget until they put me inside a grave took place on May 20, 1995. On that fateful day there was a slaughter like I have never experienced before or read about. Forty-three men were murdered: that is, they were executed while on death row, and their executions were meant to appease the then military governor of Lagos State, Colonel Oyinlola. He ordered the killing of men who, by legal rights, still had their appeals or the rest of their trials to go through. They were killed in cold blood by the blood-thirsty men who rule the affairs or dictate the events inside this prison and the society in which this prison functions.

On that day the yard was peculiarly cool and deserted. Even the officer in charge of morning feeding and the checker who confirmed prisoner numbers each day never performed their routine activities. It was not a usual morning. At about 9 a.m. there were sounds of chains, as if a gang of slaves were being led from one section of the yard to the other to be taken out for execution.[1] They started firing at 10 a.m., but by 1 p.m. there was a break, as a quarrel had erupted between the state governor and some radical lawyers who were protesting the deaths of their clients, people whose cases were pending in the Court of Appeal. Surprisingly, at 1:30 they continued their slaughter, and by 4 p.m. they had killed forty-three men. The prison yard became a mortuary that day, and it was an experience I can never forget. The next day we saw thick blood on clothes and watched human meat being chopped [cleaned] off the bullets that had just executed many men.

Years later, on May 5, 2003, my lawyer filed a suit at the Federal High Court on fundamental human rights challenges, asking the court if they intended for me to perpetually remain in prison. All efforts to secure freedom had been thwarted by that court for so many years. In most cases the Nigerian court uses long adjournments and bureaucratic jargon to frustrate lawyers who actually try to help prisoners.

But I must keep persevering, I cannot languish in this place. Lately, I once again filed a third motion at the Ikeja High Court, asking for information on the standing status of my case, only to learn once again that the Directorate of Public Prosecution (DPP), the police, and the court have yet to locate a case file for me. They do not even have a charge sheet, and, worst of all, my name did not appear in the computer in the Ministry of Justice. The judge ruled that, since she does not know what they are charging me with, she cannot give me bail. When I read that judgment I became physically ill.

The warders [prison guards] here don't want us to leave. It is clear in their actions and their attitudes. They cannot help us, and when we try to help ourselves they try their best to frustrate us. There are minimal prisoner welfare facilities. Most help comes from Nigerian non-governmental human rights organizations. Some provide us with written materials, but few provide medical care, which is most needed since so many prisoners are sick, and the few who manage to go to the prison hospital seldom get checkups and too often are told that there is no medication available. If medication is available, they ask us to buy it from them. Those who cannot afford it die. The federal government does supply some medication for prisoners, but too often prison guards take it home for personal use or for resale—it's their "Christmas bonus." This year (2002) so far, eight people have died in the prison hospital due to the unavailability of drugs or neglect by the nurses, who come to "work" to sell clothes, shoes, and wristwatches to prisoners and staff, not to take care of sick prisoners.

In a phrase, in here it is about survival of the fittest, and the fittest are defined through monetary wealth. The richest of the poor people in prison are the ones who have a chance. If you do not have money, you cannot survive, as the food in here is minimal and horrible. The government does supply prison staff with some soap, mattresses, slippers, insecticides, and so on for the maintenance of prisoners, but all these things seem to belong to the prison guards. They continually tell prisoners to just use what we have and to buy what we need or want. Extortion is a way of life here. Prison guards tell us that the government has not paid them salaries for months, and, if we the prisoners have some money somewhere in our possession, they will find it. When they don't get paid we get searched, and family members get harassed for money if they come to visit. In order to see us they always have to pay the guards for access anyway. This is one of the reasons there was a riot on April 13, 2003, at Kirikiri medium security prison. Prisoners are sick and tired of such harassments. The situation is tough for us, and what keeps some of us alive is the hope that it will end some day: one way or the other, it will have to end some day.

Sadly, Motivating Monday, as the prisoners and community organizers and activists used to call him, passed away in 2004 inside the maximum security prison hospital. Prisoners have confirmed that he was told before he died that he had earlier been diagnosed with AIDS. Prison officials failed to inform him of that diagnosis until shortly before his death. They did not provide him with any medication; in fact, medication made available to prisoners has been consistently sold by the prison guards who work in the Kirikiri maximum security prison hospital. May Motivating Monday's soul rest in peace. His smiles will always be remembered. His positive attitude, despite all the hardship, oppression, and injustice, prevails in the minds of those of us who met him, got to know him, and were inspired by his strength.

NOTES

1 Outside the walls of Kirikiri maximum security prison there is a wall of metal barrels between the wall and a long line of poles that have been dug into the ground. This is the shooting range set aside for executions. While the barrels prevent most of the bullets from hitting the prison wall, the sounds of death echo throughout the prison yard while the executions are taking place.

CHAPTER 12

PATRIOTISM: ILLUSION OR REALITY?

Osadolor Eribo

> Under a government that imprisons any man unjustly, the true place for a just man is also a prison.
> —Henry David Thoreau

The epoch of political instability, chaos, ethnic rivalry, and the continued existence of colonial boundaries defining nations in West Africa gave birth to a period of armed insurgence and war in the West African countries of Liberia and Sierra Leone. This unrest culminated in military peacekeeping operations by many West African countries, and these efforts were spearheaded by Nigeria.

As a patriotic person with the burning desire to ensure that the world can provide dignified life for all, irrespective of class or nationality, I saw it as an honour when I was short-listed by my country's army for military peacekeeping operations in the war-ravaged countries of Liberia and Sierra Leone. These peacekeeping operations can best be described as *peace enforcement* operations, which proved to be worse and more complex than any outright war. During the process of peacekeeping/enforcement, on behalf of defenceless citizens, we were met with stiff resistance from full-fledged combat engagements. As soldiers we saw it as a point of duty to defend innocent and defenceless citizens and their properties. In short, these countries were under severe rebellious torrents.

The atrocities and crimes against humanity that we witnessed were appalling. We saw the burning of people's homes, the looting of properties, the raping of women, child soldiering, and the maiming and cutting off of hands and limbs of defenceless citizens. These actions were perpetrated by the various rebellious factions, who met outright condemnation by the international community and the United Nations. Hence, the ECOMOG Operation, to act as a counter against all odds, worked to restore normalcy, peace, and stability, and to create room for democratic governance as sanctioned by the international community. But little did we, the peacekeeping soldiers, know that we were acting on our own, and at our own risk, not on behalf of the Nigerian government. Time and the events that transpired eventually proved this to us.

We encountered stiff resistance from rebellious factions carrying the same deadly weapons that we carried. The result was massive death tolls and injuries incurred by both parties. I happened to fall into the category of "wounded in action," with a comminuted fracture of the right femur. I still don't know how I managed to be among those who remained alive; I limped away with much pain and grief as a result of this world's apathy toward human life.

Those of us who were injured were taken to Cairo, where the Nigerian army refused, first, to pay us medical severance and, second, to provide us with sufficient medical treatment. On our return to Nigeria, rather than addressing the plight of the wounded ECOMOG soldiers, the state and the army began discrediting our complaints, stating that the soldiers had not channelled their complaints through the army properly. How could we have channelled our complaints through the same institution about which we were complaining? Consequently the soldiers were charged with mutiny, conduct contrary to good order and service, lack of discipline, and disobedience to particular orders. We were found guilty as charged, illustrating the state's and the army's total disregard for fundamental human rights.

The wounded soldiers who were patients at the military hospital, Yaba-Lagos, were all forcefully ejected to face court martials even though they were all in very bad physical states: shattered bones with physical disabilities, nervous breakdowns, battered souls with feelings of having been betrayed by the army. On the day of judgment of the court martial a letter was passed on to the president of the General Court Martial (GCM), who insisted on having copies made available to the other army generals presiding with him. I think the letter itself was the judgment of the case, and only God knows where it originated from—perhaps it came from a very high authority, higher than that of the army. When the president of the GCM was passing his oral judgment on the case he said, "the way and manner I find you guilty is nothing I can explain." And with that, all twenty-three wounded ECOMOG soldiers were sentenced to life imprisonment by a "kangaroo court."

Paradoxically, I, a patriotic citizen of his country, a disciplined soldier who has had no reason to be tried by the military for any act of indiscipline or insubordination, automatically found myself in the "inside world," the lowest ebb of life where mortals are reduced to nothing: the prison. Reasons for my imprisonment: simply for complaining to the appropriate quarters of the state about fraud I encountered in army practices and medical negligence, a complaint that both the state and the army authorities validated.

This was daylight robbery of justice by the state and the army. It was sheer wickedness and barbarism! Soldiers who had paid their dues and served humanity to the best of their abilities, to bring about peace and political stability in neighbouring West African states, were being treated as infidels and worthless beings. Rather than giving God the glory for sparing the lives of the soldiers from the torrents of bullets and shells, they chose to dishonour, chastise, and persecute them, and even try to kill them psychologically by incarcerating them incommunicado. I believe these proceedings were manipulations by the state to cover up the corruption of some influential and powerful people;

hence, the wounded ECOMOG soldiers were used as scapegoats. If not for their injuries as a result of service in Liberia and Sierra Leone, these soldiers would not be where they are today.

Despite the high level of moral decadence that seems to have consumed the world today, it gladdens my heart to know that there are still traces of truth. The inhuman treatment and persecution meted out to the wounded ECOMOG soldiers met stiff opposition from a few notable individuals and human rights activists, who saw the entire process as not just an act of injustice but also a slap on the face of humanity, scuttling the democracy we have all been working so tirelessly for. Notably, Chief Gani Fawehinmi, a human rights activist, challenged the verdict of the GCM in the Court of Appeal in Lagos. With Fawhemi pressing for litigation in the Court of Appeal, and because of pressures and criticisms from human rights organizations, the army and the state had to commute the life imprisonment sentences imposed on the soldiers. This took place in the seventh month after the original verdict was passed. These were the new sentences: fifteen of the soldiers were "awarded" one year in prison, five others were "awarded" three years in prison, and three others were "awarded" five years in prison. These revisions of the original sentences caused the army to relocate the soldiers from the military police cells at Arakan barracks (where they had been held hostage for seven months incommunicado) to the Kirikiri maximum security prison.

As one who had been convicted by the state and sent to prison, supposedly a correctional facility where citizens are to be remoulded into better citizens, I found out, to my greatest surprise, that the prison has failed totally to serve as an instrument of rehabilitation/reformation. I went on a fact-finding mission; it began to dawn on me that I had been kept alive by divine providence just to witness this social blight that is called prison. Contrary to my patriotic beliefs before incarceration, I discovered that the state needs more help than does the average prisoner. The state that created the prison institution has got to be, for lack of better words, absolutely sick in the mind. Prison is vindictive and violent, an institution that seeks vengeance and punishment. The colonial government that "invented" it and brought it to African soil surely was anything but "civilized."

Everything about prison is counterproductive and a million steps backward from this present age of *Homo sapiens*. The state claims that my ways are not good enough, that my behaviour is antisocial, so it threw me into prison to be reformed and shown better ways to live my life? At first I decided to be receptive to the good things the state had to offer me. But little did I know that I was at the threshold of doom and death. All that the state/prison system has to offer its prisoners is marijuana, trickery, treachery, deceit, bribery, and corruption, along with a host of other social vices. In seeing this I realized that the state in conjunction with the prison authorities works to massacre the spiritual and psychological makeup of the masses. The plan of the prison system is simple: lock up the prisoners, throw away the keys, allow them to smoke their heads off (but make sure to catch them once in a while to punish and torture them), and render them demented and dispirited without any sense of belonging. The system also renders prisoners docile for the remaining parts of their lives.

My experience as a prisoner was like that of a slave, and it was insulting to my human existence. Rather than being receptive to their "rehabilitation," I decided to shut the doors of my mind against the invading toxins of the state/prison system. I had to be on guard and put all my survival instincts to use to stay afloat, much like I had to do when I was at war. The vile strategies adopted by the state/prison system in the breakdown of the average prisoner served as a challenge to me to value the life I had prior to incarceration, and I dredged up every ounce of strength I had within me to stay alive.

I speak of the prison system based on the Nigerian context in which I am living. I have not been a witness to the prison systems around the world, but I know that prison is prison no matter how you paint the picture. In the Nigerian context, sixty percent of the prison population are Awaiting Trial Inmates (ATMs), while the

Convicted Inmates (CMs) constitute a fraction of this population. It was revealing for me to learn that the prison system targets the helpless, the hopeless, and the underprivileged in society. Children, particularly boys in this country, are vulnerable to this penal attack. Those whose parents cannot afford to shelter them are being raided in the streets by the police and thrown into prison on trumped-up charges of armed robbery. There is another category of prisoners that I have come to know as ATM lifers, those who have been held hostage awaiting trial for as long as ten to fifteen years.

Prisoners have been stripped of all rights to livelihood, including the right to eat. Food is being siphoned and taken home by members of the prison staff, and at the end of the day prisoners are left with very little to eat. When they go to the hospital to report sickness they are told that there is no medicine available, yet the prison authorities sell medicine to those prisoners who can pay for it. Basically, prisoners exist because of visitors who bring food, medicine, clothing, toiletries, and so on. Meanwhile, prison guards constantly extort money from visitors, and they do so as they stand under the sign at the entrance gate that in boldprint states that "all prison visits are free." Prisoners "pay" to survive inside Nigeria's prisons, and they don't just pay in the loss of their freedom or in the unconstitutional denial of court appearances; they literally pay money to stay alive.

Another disgusting thing about the prison system that struck me is the differential treatment imposed according to class, how the rich and the poor within the confines of the same prison walls live such different lives. Class segregation is the order of the day: the rich flout prison rules and get away with it freely, while the poor are severely dealt with. The rich are entitled to numerous privileges, ranging from self-feeding (getting food from the outside) to having sex with their female visitors in the administrative building. In a nutshell, the rich control not only society but also prison.

Religion also plays a role in how the prison is run. It seems that religion is the only means of rehabilitation and reform available to prisoners; more so, it is the only option left for prisoners to get themselves busy, and, most importantly, to get relief through the religious visitors and the supplies they provide: All other rehabilitation "programmes" in prison, such as workshops or trade learning centres, are either grounded or ill-equipped. In such conditions prisoners go to church or to mosque from dawn till dusk. The doctrines presented there do not have meaningful effects for a large number of prisoners; they simply go to pass the time and to get access to resources.

My vision for rehabilitation efforts for the average prisoner goes beyond mere teachings of religious doctrines — it is all about giving people an alternative roadmap for life. The key lies in empowerment, not in religious rituals. Rather than implementing workshops and programmes, thereby creating avenues for the acquisition of vocational skills as a way of empowering prisoners, the state is busy building churches and mosques in prison yards. Hence, many prisoners today nurse the ambition of becoming pastors after imprisonment, and I believe that is due to their lack of access to other vocations. When religion becomes the only avenue for livelihood the level of tyranny becomes more problematic. They have hijacked our freedom, and now they have co-opted our spirituality. Of course, I cannot say there is too much "wrong" with society having a lot of clergy, but the unfortunate thing within the context of religion inside Nigerian prisons is that, by the time prisoners are released (if at all), and find their way to those churches that came to see them and provide assistance in prison, they are often treated with a cold shoulder. With nowhere else to go, and having left prison with nothing but faith, prisoners end up feeling disappointed when the church does not provide support in the community. So many have lost hope on so many levels, and so many, feeling dejected and duped, fall back into crime. While in prison they were not empowered; they were "spiritualized." It is one thing to quote Bible passages to someone asking him or her to refrain from crime; it is another thing for the person to fully believe and accept the passages as solutions to life's problems.

Ironically, even when some of us are busy trying to find better solutions to this social menace of crime and punishment, the criminal justice system is simply not doing likewise. It is busy frustrating the thinkers and the serious-minded prisoners with a show of full-blown apathy. Its administrators think that they already have the answer. They think that, because they have an institution, the problems are being addressed. I must commend the non-governmental organizations working on prisoners' rights, particularly Prisoners Rehabilitation and Welfare Action (PRAWA), for their attempts to train prison officers about rehabilitation and prisoner empowerment. These efforts have actually gone a long way toward sanitizing the prison environment in terms of physical abuse of prisoners by prison staff—although they had started flogging prisoners again just before I left in 2003.

Much is still expected of the human rights groups, especially prison-focused NGOs such as PRAWA, in terms of sanitization and education of the average prisoner in the Nigerian prison system. While I was in prison my heart bled every time I walked by posters designed by PRAWA for prisoners with messages such as "if your rights have been abused, please report or write to so and so office"; eighty percent of the prisoners around me could not read that message, let alone write to report abuse. The posters are not conspicuously placed, and they are of no importance because the average prisoner has yet to be educated about his rights. So even if his rights are being violated on a daily basis, he may not know it. Worse still, the prison system has socialized its prisoners into believing that writing letters voicing complaint or seeking redress is a crime; in fact, it is the gravest sin a prisoner can commit, so much so that when caught fellow prisoners are ready to lynch the culprit. As a result, while the posters are a great gesture, and while the concept of prison officers behaving humanely while working in an inhumane system is well-intentioned, prisoners either don't know how or don't want to be involved in grievance procedures.

I can still recall an incident that transpired in 2002 when a team of Amnesty International (AI) employees visited Kirikiri maximum security prison for a fact-finding mission. Normally, when visitors of such calibre visit the prison the authorities, because they have so much to hide, ensure that all prisoners are in lock-up, except for those few inmates working directly with the system. In this instance, while the AI team was walking with the prison warden I saw one of the AI employees having a chat with one of the privileged prisoners who was not in lock-up that day. After the visit I walked up to the prisoner (a lifer) to inquire about the nature of his discussion with the white man. He said, "Oh, he was just trying to know from me about the general condition of the place and whether or not our feeding is good enough." I quickly asked, "And what did you tell him?" He smiled broadly, his eyes filled with light, and he answered, "Oh, of course I told him the food is good, and everything is OK." I was silent for a moment and could not utter a word; I almost choked, for then I knew that his broad smile was that of betrayal, and I too forced a smile and said, "Oh! It's OK. You're right." I had no option but to play it cool with him, for if I had opposed him he would have made the matter known to the prison authorities, and I need not divulge what that could have entailed for me.

The prison system is so complex that, for the masses to devise a catalyst with which to break it down, all hands must be on deck. There needs to be a concerted effort among prisoners, ex-prisoners, and civil society in bringing about an alternative to the present criminal justice system. Unfortunately there tends to be a wide margin between the people concerned. One reason the Nigerian prison system is waxing stronger and stronger as an oppressive mechanism is simply that there are no prisoners' rights groups or programmes in prison. There also tends to be a wide gap between ex-prisoners and current prisoners.

While I was busy resisting my period of penal colonization with non-confrontational and non-violent means, litigation was going on in the Court of Appeal on behalf of the twenty-three wounded and convicted ECOMOG soldiers. On March 18, 2003, the grounds for appeal paid off, as the soldiers were discharged and acquitted of all the charges against them by the GCM. The decision of the Court of Appeal was unanimous, yet it took eleven days for the prison to enforce the decision of the Court of Appeal by releasing I and two others whose sentences were commuted from life imprisonment to five years imprisonment. Whereas, those (20 others) whose sentences were commuted to one year and five years respectively had already served their terms.

Currently I and my military colleagues remain in a state of distress since nothing seems to be in the works, either by the state or by the army, in terms of our progress. Particularly, our medical predicament is huge, since some of us still need medical attention for injuries sustained during peacekeeping operations. The stigmatization and intimidation we are now faced with, both within and outside the military environment, are massive. Our freedom and our lives are perpetually threatened.

Consequently I now have a contrary view of warfare: no matter how refined the rules may appear, it is an archaic and uncivilized philosophy. I have come to understand that not all ancient philosophies are outdated and that not all modern philosophies are civilized. In these "modern" times we use guns to repel fighting and a repressive penal system to repel crime. It is an act of sheer folly to use violence to repel violence, for violence is violence irrespective of how it is painted, so no person or group of persons, even if they are members of a state, is eligible to be the custodian of violence.

Although the ECOMOG peacekeeping operations incorporated elements of mediation and dialogue, in a bid to reconcile the various warring factions and to bring about normalcy, these efforts were not fully appreciated or sufficiently used. Maximum use of these alternatives to violence would have averted the humanitarian catastrophes that ensued, resulting in too many dead bodies and the irreparable effects of war on those who survive it. "Modern" society is still very capable of conducting witch hunts and evil rituals. The same phenomenon is illustrated in other wars fought in other parts of the world. It is not an element "special" to Africa.

When one makes a critical appraisal of war and the penal system one sees how interwoven they are in terms of the violent solutions they offer to their respective "dilemmas," and the devastating effects they have on all whom they touch. Hence, both problems may need to rely on similar solutions if true change is to occur. Such solutions need to be non-violent in both nature and structure.

While I was an inmate at Kirikiri maximum security prison I got to work with Viviane Saleh-Hanna, working under the aegis of Voluntary Service Overseas and placed for two years in West Africa with Prisoners Rehabilitation and Welfare Action (PRAWA). Through her I got to know about transformative justice and penal abolition. Her work in the prison during her time with us in Nigeria was most beneficial through the programmes she initiated in the maximum and medium security prisons. Her dedication and service to humanity have greatly affected my life and inspired me to believe more in myself, a feeling that is shared by so many members of the programmes she brought in through PRAWA. We all love you and miss you greatly! And we hope that more people will become involved with prison work and the penal abolition movement. It has empowered many of us to think for ourselves and to revolutionize our minds, and it has shown us that there are segments of the global population who are working to truly change oppressive mandates.

Given the circumstances that surrounded my incarceration and the experiences I had while imprisoned, I now understand the urgency in opposing this present form of criminal "justice." The state seeks vengeance on and punishment of the poor, the illiterate, and the underprivileged—people whom the state has failed by subjecting them to these conditions in the first place. Unfortunately the larger society fails to appreciate the fact that many prisoners behind bars are social rebels, people who fight against the oppressive system that does not want to see them exist. Since the Nigerian government and the United Nations can negotiate with rebellious militias, why can't they extend this practice to the average criminals and offenders in the street? Must these rebels against poverty become rebels who challenge the political power structures, not just the economic ones, before they are asked relevant questions and spoken to like real human beings? Or is their discerned poverty an excuse to render them helpless and unsophisticated—and thus not worth the effort?

More functional and healthy modes of justice are not about creating an escape route for criminals or about fostering an opportunity for the government to compromise with evil; rather, the concepts of transformative justice and penal abolition provide an avenue through which everybody in society gains equal access to opportunities and rights. I do not believe that hundreds of years ago West Africans had a worse method of solving conflicts in society; frankly, I believe that the methods of conflict resolution of precolonial Africa were far better than the "modern" penal system, and this is why I also believe that ancient philosophies are not less civilized or wrong in our era. It is true that stagnation is the greatest enemy of nature, but for humanity to take a step further and assume the status of Civilization we must put under appraisal the past and the present. We need a change away from the present penal system.

Today's society seems ever so keen to make the Western penal system the only permanent form of justice. This system is so big and so powerful, so controlling, that for any major changes to come about we must all work together in unison, like one family with diverse members who have different strengths to offer. We must be very careful of the kind of change we wish for and how we go about achieving it, lest we become like the overzealous politician or revolutionary who wants change at all cost, either by rigging the ballot or pointing the gun. The present penal system, compared with traditional African modes of justice, rather than taking humanity a step forward, has proven to be a step backward and a betrayal of civilization. Therefore, whatever the alternative to the penal system may be, it must be devised in line with various traditional sociocultural settings of peoples of the world.

Whether or not we have been abused by war or the present penal system, or overall by government policies, we must not be indifferent to issues affecting humanity in general. Change needs to occur now for the benefit of future generations. Let us replace indifference with concern and apathy with empathy, so that we can leave behind an inspired legacy for generations to come.

I strongly believe that care, love, empathy, and morality are all encompassed in the phenomenon of patriotism, and that it cannot stand silent in a state where irregularities have gained wide acceptance as a normal way of life. As true Nigerian patriots we cannot fold our hands and stand akimbo to watch while the rich and self-centred people of the world deprive us of our power, and violate our rights to choice and survival. As a virtuous and patriotic citizen of the world, I believe that true patriotism should be viewed, not only as a duty we owe to the countries we are citizens of, but also as a duty we owe to ourselves and to generations of unborn people, and the global village into which we are developing.

SECTION III

COLONIAL SYSTEMS OF IMPRISONMENT: GENDER, POVERTY AND MENTAL HEALTH IN PRISON

Penal colonialism is a concept that brings forth the perpetuation of colonialism in "former" European colonies through the contemporary existence and use of colonial legal and penal institutions. Colonialism implemented a form of social control that divided, dehumanized, degraded, and conquered those people whom colonialists aimed to exploit; it is important to recognize that colonialists not only degraded and brutalized those populations targeted for colonialism, but also, in that process, created the *illusion* of superiority and *civilization* for their people and their people's creations. Among those creations was the penal system.

It is not surprising that nations responsible for the atrocities that occur(ed) during colonialism are also responsible for the creation, implementation, and widespread use of the penal system. It is a system that relies on the degradation and dehumanization of those whom it targets, and by their very nature the penal system's institutions and codes target those populations that are most vulnerable in society. Aside from the overrepresentation of poor people and people of colour in *all* penal institutions, those people who are most vulnerable among vulnerable populations struggle and are prone to suffer grave consequences. This section presents the experiences of those who live in poverty, those who are developmentally challenged, and women within the penal system. Penal colonialism, while atrocious and harmful to African societies on many levels, imposes a high degree of oppression upon those who are least able to defend themselves.

CHAPTER 13

NIGERIAN PENAL INTERACTIONS

Viviane Saleh-Hanna

INTRODUCTION

The reflections presented in this chapter emerge from a daily journal I kept during my time as a community organizer and activist inside Nigerian prisons. The experiences I had were inundated with visual brutality, mental stimulation, and political conversation. In attempting to keep myself grounded, and in trying to grasp the larger picture, I found myself creating mental snapshots of the details that eventually combined to form a mosaic that made sense to me, according to the things I saw, heard, and thought while I sat inside prison yards and conversed with Nigerian prisoners. These words are an attempt to present that mosaic.

From October 2000 to November 2002 I lived in Onipanu, Lagos, Nigeria, and worked as a community organizer and activist with Prisoners Rehabilitation and Welfare Action (PRAWA) through Voluntary Service Overseas (VSO).[1] Leaving Nigeria was one of the most difficult things I have had to do. My culture shock was greater upon returning to the West than it was upon arriving in Nigeria. For two years I lived and worked in a country that was extreme at all levels; it was an incredible learning experience, a discovery mission that changed my life. I discovered more about my own and other people's boundaries than anything else. When a person who has grown up in the privileged world of the West lives in Nigeria, where people are suffering and struggling to get the most basic things in life, one cannot help but learn from that struggle.

I saw people struggle to get nutritious food and clean drinking water. I saw people go to work every day on roads full of potholes and on buses packed with people. I saw people work in offices and banks without access to telephones, other communication equipment, or constant electricity. I saw people of all ages struggle all day in the scorching sun to sell what they could so they could take food home to their families. I saw elderly people get killed crossing the expressway because there are no crosswalks. I saw children gathered around a single kerosene lantern at night because there was no other light to do homework by, and I saw too many children who did no homework because their parents could not afford to send them to school. I saw the same children on the streets working day and night to sell what they could so their families could survive. I saw babies die of malaria because their parents could not afford inexpensive medication. I saw young people who were physically disabled because they did not receive polio vaccinations. They were living on the streets, and they were using handmade skateboards to mobilize themselves just enough to beg for money. I saw people persevere and struggle just to get by. Yet I saw a lot of smiles and joy throughout that process of survival, along with the frustrations and the despair. I saw the basic human soul make the best of unnecessarily harsh living conditions in one of the most fertile, oil producing nations on the African continent. In Lagos, my home for two years, the basic infrastructure is simply not functioning—and it is home to more than fifteen million people.

The things that people did to help me, the tolerance levels I saw them exhibit for each other's struggles and for my struggles, were massive. The identification of struggle as a collective phenomenon was immense. There were times when people piled in on each other's laps on buses because there was a fuel shortage in Lagos, the most populated state in an oil-producing nation. During these fuel shortages the number of buses on the road for public transportation was never enough to accommodate the number of people needing to get to work or go home or just go, so people piled in on top of each other. I remember my first few months in Nigeria when I watched in awe and kept a silent but defensive air on the bus: "Try and get on my lap, and I will 'deal with you-o'"! But as the months went by and I understood more about the struggle to get by and the need for collective efforts in accessing basic resources, I saw myself changing. That change became conscious when a woman I sat beside on the bus one day explained to me how selfish I was for putting my comfort level above the need for someone's mother, father, son, or daughter to get home before dark. I quickly realized that the Western outlook on life is self-centred and self-prioritized. I realized that not allowing a complete stranger to sit on my lap on the bus meant that one less person made it home before the Lagos streets became dangerous at night,[2] and I quickly learned that this little inconvenience for me was nothing in comparison to that of the person who got stranded on the street. The journey of learning had begun.

The little things that I saw changing in my thought patterns grew beyond everyday life and brought me into a whole new mindset. That mindset looked at the larger political scheme and opened my eyes to the self-interests and self-promotion of Euro-supremacist systems of governance and resource control in relations with the global South. It got to a point where I was dreading a return to a world that is so sufficient and so convenient and so gluttonous with the consumption of *everything* that on the surface it is able to revolve around a delusional, extremely introspective, individualistic mentality. And I got to a point where I became very conscious of the imperialist *fact* that those comforts for the minority in the world are built on the backs and discomforts of the millions who comprise the majority. I came to realize and experience the fact that most of the people on this planet live in violent poverty *so that* the minority can (not should) live in excess.

My work inside the prisons enabled me to meet people who have been "rejected and neglected," as prisoners used to tell me, and I came to see on a new level that the ideals and ways of the West are now ingrained in the control institutions and economic structures in Africa. The *criminal* justice system that functions in the self-promoting West is the same system that is being forced upon black people in Africa. It is foreign, and it is dehumanizing, and it is malfunctioning: people wait in prison for years before they go to court, medical care is almost non-existent, malnutrition and disease are killing people every day. The Western world, the same world that colonized Africa and other continents, is putting money into penal, social, and political reforms, and into what is called *human rights* work: these reforms maintain colonial systems on African soil, and the work of human rights as implemented through European and American governments and corporations ensures that the West remains well within its comfortable role of the patriarch in Africa. I came to the harsh realization that colonization still exists within the strong structures of global economic control and resource exploitation. Slavery continues in the degradation of African cultures, in the exploitation of African resources, and inside the cells of European prisons in Africa. Meanwhile, genocide among ethnic groups is being promoted by the national boundaries and the capitalist global economies that the Western world has implemented.

Living and working in Nigeria, and coming to these realizations, forced me to admit that the so-called civilized segments of the world of today are more dangerous in their illusions of political correctness and assumed universal moral schemes than the uncivilized, slave-producing, colonial world of not so many years ago. If *this* is civilization, I continue to fail to see civility. If *this* is justice, I continue to see the criminality of justice in *criminal* justice institutions. The state we are in now, as a global community, is oppressed and broken, much like the state that our global society was in hundreds of years ago, but at least in the past people knew what they were up against, people knew what and whom to fight against: they were the colonial governments and their arrogant white employees, they were the slave catchers and the slave traders, they were the white men who researched Africa and named it primitive, tribal, underdeveloped, and barbaric, and they were the white-robed missionaries who demonized African spirituality. In today's world the oppressors are your friends and allies: Western *funding* agencies, international diplomatic *allies,* European *colleagues* who control organizational agendas, and *fellow* human rights activists who work to reinforce European economic and political structures and institutions. In the meantime, as this beast they call civilization works to abstract oppression and blur the boundaries of freedom, the majority of people in Africa (and on all continents recovering from European occupation through colonialism) continue to struggle; unfortunately, most can no longer see on a concrete level what exactly it is they are struggling against. The white-robed missionaries now have black skin underneath those white robes. The government that maintains the European exploitation of Africa now gives public speeches wearing expensive *agbada* and *asoke* (African clothes), carrying African last names. Gone are the European top hats and straight trousers, but not gone are the European systems of control that continue to allow the West to rob Africa blind.

Financial and political corruption is rampant in the non-governmental, non-profit, human rights world. I came to learn that this corruption is intimately linked with the continued imposition of Western structures, institutions, attitudes, and financial regulations upon Nigeria. The quest for human rights in Nigeria is still defined and controlled by Western governments and European institutions and structures *at the root* of the upheavals that Africa continues to face. Also at the root of this human rights discourse and work is the assumption that Africans can get life and dignity from Europeans—a fallacy that has strong foundations in savage European slavery and colonialism. The commodification of all that is human is exemplified in this human rights discourse, which assumes that humanity can be "given" and "taken."

While the West continues to flourish and grow, Africa continues to struggle, and leaving Nigeria knowing that was difficult. I felt torn between worlds. I knew I was coming back to a capitalist, corporate, imperialist North American reality, and I knew that this reality is built on the backs of entire nations and millions of people of colour. I did not know if I could handle coming back to the West, but I also knew that in Nigeria I was *oyeebo, baturia,* and *enyatcha* ("a foreigner"). In North America, as an immigrant, I often feel like a stranger. People may not call me "foreigner" to my face, but there are many ways for them to reinforce my separate category as a woman of colour. I belong to a large generation of people who have been displaced from the South and placed in the West — involuntarily forced to live in the belly of the beast, no longer belonging in Africa (because my family was forced out), yet never being "included" in the West.

So what is home for me, and what is home for most people in this miserable, corporate, forced migration existence? I found myself questioning many things that people in positions of white privilege, economic superiority, and Western citizenship often take for granted. Am I pretending to come back home? How do I walk away from the people I have struggled beside for two years? In the grander scheme of oppression, how does one not just survive but also fight back and maintain self-dignity through that fight? How can people of privilege come to understand the implications of their privilege for the underprivileged? And as I got ready to leave Nigeria, I could not reconcile myself with the fact that, despite the struggles and the hardships, Nigeria had become home to me, more so than any Western society in which I had lived. The same people who called me *oyeebo* in Nigeria embraced me as one of their own. Being different in Nigeria is not degrading, as being different in the West is. I had never felt more at home than I did in Lagos. Why was I leaving? Did I join the Nigerian world temporarily so I could test myself, all the while knowing deep inside that this immediate struggle would not be a permanent reality for me? And what is more important, the physical comforts of the West or the emotional comforts of inclusion that I experienced for the first time in Africa? Why is it that in this fragmented and broken world so many of us are forced to have one or the other? Why are so many black people living such broken and incomplete lives?

In the West people have the option to ignore the harsh realities of oppression. In Nigeria I did not meet a single Nigerian[3] who had that privilege. Even if someone lived in a privileged compound with generators to supply electricity during NEPA[4] outages, and even if someone had an air-conditioned car with a driver, and even if someone maintained a high income, that person still had to confront the realities of those who did not have any of those things. Nigerian society has not yet developed the ability to hide its problems and to completely segregate those who have from those who have not.

As I witnessed and experienced these social realities, questions continued to engulf my thoughts. Why is the distribution of resources, opportunities, and comforts so unbalanced? Is this form of capitalist imperialism going to go on for much longer? Forget about whether it is "fair" — is it sustainable for so few to have so much while so many have so little? Can the minority who own so much sustain that wealth? And at what cost will they fight to maintain the global monopoly of resources? I know it cannot last forever, and I know this only because change is the only constant element of this global existence. I found comfort in that understanding, but I also felt anxiety: will change bring about equality and freedom, or will it continue to promote and abstract and reinforce the same inequalities? What has my being in Nigeria really done in the grander scheme of the world and oppression? I know it has done more for me as a human being than anyone else. I have learned so much, and I console myself with this thought: now I know more, and, yes, this knowledge is violent and painful, but I still prefer to know rather than never to have had the opportunity to learn.

Here I present some of the experiences I had while in Nigeria. These experiences shaped my understanding of the world, and for the first time I began to feel as if I had access to something real. It was not sugar-coated. It was not commercial. It was not an adventure that could be commodified. It was real life for millions and billions of people. And I am grateful to have accessed it, even if for just a moment. And I am responsible for spreading it as far and as wide as I can: I leave Nigeria with a readiness to share this knowledge with whoever is willing to learn it.

Nigeria has shown me that life is about survival. For some it is physical survival; for others it is emotional, cultural, and spiritual survival. For me it became a combination of all those things. There were times when I feared for my physical safety, but those times were few and insignificant. The most significant experiences for me were the times when my belief systems and perceptions of life were put in question, when my thoughts no longer made sense, when my priorities were drastically challenged and renumbered. Nigeria was a place of growth and truth for me, and that has been survival. In that survival I found moments of freedom. In a place where the leaders are lying and the average person is dying, I had to search for truth and ways to keep growing, and I learned that, even in the midst of upheaval and struggle, the human spirit prevails. I left Nigeria with a sense of hopelessness for the world as we know it, but with a renewed sense of hope in the human capacity to collectively resist and survive through community.

PENAL INTERACTIONS WITH THE COMMUNITY

A criminal justice system that was not made by or for West African societies continues to be imposed upon Nigeria—its inefficiency reflects the inefficiency that rules the country's general state. This state reflects the injustice that Western social structures impose upon all societies "structured" by them. The end result? People get caught in a grinding machine that destroys all that it touches. I have come to see the penal system as a tool by which colonial structures are implemented among those whom the national and international corporations cannot "employ." The more time

I spent working with Nigerian prisoners, and the more I was confronted with open police brutality on the streets of Lagos, the more convinced I became that the penal system in Nigeria is the most visible symbol of the continued colonial presence in the Nigerian mental state and the Nigerian governmental structure.

My Nigerian journey became a time when I had to ask a lot of questions and engage in a lot of discussions to make sense of my surroundings, and, at times, to survive in those surroundings. Those questions, discussions, witnessed events, and experienced moments were pivotal in creating an awareness that continues to challenge how I perceive the penal system and society in general. In Nigeria I did not learn just about Nigeria, I learned about the foundations of all *criminal* justice institutions, and I learned about the functions and behaviours of all *criminal* justice agents.

GOVERNMENT CORRUPTION: THE ISSUE OF PAYING SALARIES

It would be unfair to present my interactions with the Nigerian penal system without presenting the situations with which Nigerian governmental agents are faced. When discussing corruption and brutality with prisoners, prison guards, police officers, and community members, many in Nigeria understand that the government does not pay its employees salaries for many months at a time. It is believed that the money is kept to accumulate interest in private bank accounts. Many claim that this lack of constant and reliable income is the main cause of theft and corruption among prison guards and police officers in Nigeria. Corruption extends beyond the penal system, and affects schoolteachers, local government staff, court-appointed magistrates, doctors, nurses, and so on. Demanding bribes for services becomes the main method of earning money for many government employees. In Nigeria the infectious nature of state brutality is visible and constantly observed. I preferred this openness to the delusional propaganda that promotes state institutions as existing to "serve and protect" the people.

The political, economic, and penal structures in Nigeria have turned many groups in society against each other,[5] and thus play a large role in the functions of social control: confusion and animosity are powerful modes of divide-and-conquer frameworks. Benefits for the state are both financial and political. While money is accumulating in private bank accounts, the people struggle against each other to survive; the community breaks down; unity and solidarity are weakened; and organized resistance to the situation becomes more and more difficult. While salaries are used as a method of social control in Nigeria, and while the lack of consistent salaries seems to result in increased corruption, the lesson I learned was that this specific situation in Nigeria only illustrates the modes through which the state divides, oppresses, and conquers.

Police brutality and prison guard sadism occur in *all* criminal justice institutions, and they are not a function of a few bad seeds. Such violence is a function of the criminal forms of justice that penal structures impose. This violence is not limited to Nigeria. It just happens that in Nigeria the dysfunctioning of bureaucracy disqualifies justifications for criminal justice, making the problematic and violent nature of criminal justice more visible.

THE MEDIA

In Nigeria the national newspapers often gave accounts of police brutality and government corruption. The prisons, being less visible, did not make the headlines as often, although when they did the accounts were critical and exposed the brutality that takes place. My experiences with the media in Nigeria came primarily through reading newspapers, several television interviews I participated in, and interactions with newspaper journalists. Every morning I read the national newspapers, and every morning I had the same reaction: too many rich people buy up too many pages to advertise their birthdays, anniversaries, retirements, graduations, or promotions. The space left for news was generally critical of the government, and critical of the economic situation in Nigeria, but rarely looked to the international forces that support, encourage, and benefit from Nigerian corruption.

The portrayal of people engaged in street crime demonized and vilified them. The escalation of "jungle justice" (violent means employed by community members to kill people caught stealing) was rarely portrayed in a critical manner. It was often accepted as a necessary means of protecting one's community. On a more political level, articles that supported and glorified high-level politicians were read with a grain of salt.

My discussions with many Nigerians illustrated such attitudes. In a society where corruption is openly practised people were free to assume that bribes and gifts inspired such articles. This level of transparency in relation to corruption in Nigeria allowed the masses to function in a more critical and socially aware mindset. At the same time, journalists whom I met were, like most of the people, struggling to survive. They wrote about such struggles, and when they got incentives (i.e., bribes) for writing otherwise the public understood why. In relation to the penal structure the media in Nigeria presented a skeptical and weary picture. It is my opinion that such portrayals were made possible through the above-mentioned inability of the criminal justice system in Nigeria to mask its oppressive realities and functions.

GENERAL ATTITUDES TO CRIME IN NIGERIA

In Nigeria the worst crime a person can commit is armed robbery. If a person is identified and labelled as an armed robber, the chances that he or she will survive street justice, police raids, or prison time are slim. Those who do survive are rarely given a chance to re-enter society. My discussions with many Nigerians (including taxi drivers, university professors, market women, youth on the streets, people sitting next to me on the bus, neighbours, doormen, heads of human rights organizations, students, and others) on their views of the penal system, and specifically the institution of imprisonment, showed me that on the surface they support it, but any discussions beyond superficial slogans revealed an understanding that incorporated the economic context. Some of the facts shared as common knowledge among the public included the following. Armed robbers generally rent guns from the police force and use them to rob the community. The average person in prison for armed robbery is violent because he or she was pushed to rob to survive. The minority who are given the opportunity to attend and graduate from university will most likely have a very hard time finding a job, let alone one that will pay enough to sustain them or their families. That is why some of the armed robbers in Lagos are university students trying to pay school fees or university graduates who are unable to find work.

The myth behind justice through a criminal justice system has been largely revealed in Nigeria, but too many are too busy trying to survive to work against it. While demonization of armed robbers, and open verbal and physical attacks on them, were common, I did not meet a single person who discussed such attitudes without placing them within the proper social and political context of Nigeria at the end of that discussion. It was those discussions that formed my views and understandings of crime in Nigeria. Many whom I spoke to understood this: if they are robbed, there is a chance they won't eat that month. They cannot trust the police to protect them, and therefore they turn to vigilante justice for protection; if they do not adequately address the possibility of an armed robbery, or deal with the experience of being robbed, they can end up in severe financial trouble, along with the families they have to support and the neighbours who also got robbed. Because armed robbers generally worked through neighbourhoods in Lagos, when one home suffered it usually suffered with the homes around it. It was understandable why armed robbers were so feared and so hated: they represented the most visible and most immediate threat of the short-term loss of money or life. They were less predictable than the government, which has established a traditional method of extorting money from the country. The lack of stability in Nigerian socioeconomic structures does not present people with many options for safety. These circumstances, in my opinion, naturally lead to an extremely angry outlook toward armed robbers.

This hatred, and the increasingly violent reactions from community members and vigilante groups toward armed robbers, have led to an increasingly violent method of robbing. Awaiting-trial and convicted armed robbers whom I spoke to in Kirikiri medium and maximum security prisons explained that, to ensure survival of street justice (what is often called jungle justice), which ultimately leads to a horrific death by burning, armed robbers began adopting a more violent approach to robbing. While the initial purpose was to steal money, more and more armed robberies now end in violence. The armed robbery suspects and convicts I discussed this with explained that leaving survivors who may recognize them only increased their risk of getting caught and likely killed. This cycle of violence is vicious and one of the many contributing factors in a reported increase in the number of deaths related to street crime in Lagos State (among other states).

When the people have little or no faith in the police or the government they work for, violence often becomes a reaction that appears to be necessary for survival, not because there are no peaceful means of resolving these conflicts, but because Nigerians continue to live within the penal and corrupt structures that colonialism imposed. When penal structures reinforce state behaviours that encourage revenge as a mode of addressing conflict, such structures also encourage revenge as an acceptable method through which those people whom the state has failed should address conflict. In Westernized nations the state has been able to monopolize the right to avenge, punish, and brutalize. In Nigeria the state's inability to do so has aided in exposing the consequences that criminal justice and imperialist economic practices bring to a society. While citizens of Westernized nations continue to blame each other for social problems, Nigerians appeared to be more aware of the larger issues and were more able to identify the roots of their problems as residing in state (in)actions.

RELIGION AND COLONIAL CONTROLS

The vast majority of Nigerians identify themselves with either the Christian or the Muslim religion. I came to understand that a large number of Nigerians still have ties to the traditional religions of their ancestors, but such ties are shunned and viewed as demonic. It was ironic to note that so many religious people relied on colonial religions as protection against black magic, also referred to as *juju*. The irony lies in the contemporary colonial mindset, which seems to have a strong spiritual hold on the country. Colonial religions continue to be perceived as pure, while West African spirituality is viewed as black and evil. Aside from reinforcing missionary and colonial degradation of African spirituality, the institution of religion also plays a key role in distorting the international understanding of Nigerian society.

Conflicts in Nigeria are often presented in the international media in a highly simplified form: they are often referred to as religious conflicts or clashes. The historical and political contexts of conflict are rarely illustrated. I came to learn that religious conflicts are primarily conflicts between ethnic groups and are almost always linked to a political or economic cause. In addition to the simplification of historical and contemporary ethnic relations, the international media have little understanding of the upheavals that European colonial boundaries impose upon African nations: the lines drawn by colonialists now define African nation-states, not according to precolonial African kingdoms and empires, and not according to ethnic affiliations to specific land spaces, but according to coastal land spaces, primarily created for European trading purposes. "The Berlin Conference [1884] was Africa's undoing in more ways than one. The colonial powers superimposed their domains on the African continent. By the time independence returned to Africa in 1950, the realm had acquired a legacy of political fragmentation that could neither be eliminated nor made to operate satisfactorily" (Rosenberg 2004). In colonizing Africa, European nation-states created African nation-states according to European agreements that allowed European access initially to trading ports along the coast and eventually to interior land spaces on the continent: "What ultimately resulted was a hodgepodge of geometric boundaries that divided Africa into fifty irregular countries. This new map of the continent was superimposed over the one thousand indigenous cultures and regions of Africa. The new countries lacked rhyme or reason and divided coherent groups of people and merged together disparate groups who really did not get along" (Rosenberg 2004). Many of the religious conflicts occurring in Nigeria today are intimately linked with these colonial measures of exploitation. Conveniently, such recent acts of oppression are not publicized in the international media. All the global community learns about are the religious clashes that take place.

The only religious element of such clashes is associated with the imposition of missionary inquisitions on the continent. In addition, the highly publicized religious conflicts are often used to divert attention away from the roots of these problems, not only by diverting attention away from the war crimes that Europeans participated in during colonialism, but also by directing attention toward these colonially introduced religions and the tensions that arise as a result of their divisions. In the end the Western corporate exploitation of African resources is not in the limelight, and neither are the criminal actions of European nation-states. The focal point, conveniently for the West, becomes the actions of people in Nigeria who continue to struggle with the consequences of colonialism, missionary impositions, and globalization.

The use of religion inside prison played a key role in social control. The prison, a colonial institution, imposed mandatory identification with colonial versions of religion. Several ex-prisoners informed me of the signing-in process that required them to check off on their entry form their association with either Christianity or Islam. Those who did not officially associate themselves with either religion were assigned one; those who did not participate in religious ceremonies prescribed by the prison did not gain access to the donations of food and medicine provided through churches and mosques.

Two ex-prisoners whom I worked with as colleagues in the PRAWA office spoke to me in detail about their experiences with religion inside Nigerian prisons. Both had dreadlocks upon entry, and both practised traditional religions. Once imprisoned, they were forcibly shaved bald and made to choose from one of the two available religions: Christianity or Islam. Upon choosing Christianity, they were identified as Christians in prison records and for the remainder of their imprisonment attended church services and listened to sermons. They celebrated Christian holidays and special occasions, and occasionally received food or medicine through church donations. Both returned to practising their traditional religions upon release. In a few instances, ex-prisoners who established strong religious affiliations (both Christian and Muslim) while in prison received community support from churches or mosques upon release. These conditions and circumstances, often reinforced through colonial penal structures, highlight the intrinsic need to associate with colonial religions in order to survive.

Inside Kirikiri medium security prison, the first prison in which I implemented the Prisoners Support Circle Programme, I was told by both prisoners and guards that it was the first programme that did not have religious and/or legal connotations. It was the only programme that did not start and end in prayer, and it was the first programme that did not require religious affiliation for participants. Many prison guards and staff in Nigeria emphasized religion as an essential part of the rehabilitative procedure. There were many prisoners who benefited spiritually from these religious programmes and were happy to participate in them, but there were many prisoners who felt coerced and exploited.

The prevalent attitude of prison guards and prisoners' rights activists toward prisoners who practise any form of traditional Nigerian spirituality is compliant with the missionary attitude that colonizing nations exported to Africa: these prisoners are demonized and ostracized. These attitudes also mirror the outspoken opinion of the general public as I came to hear it. Often, when conversing with prison guards and church organizations inside prisons, I was told that "souls need to be saved," and I often found myself silently and sarcastically thinking "and what better place to do such saving than in a colonial prison institution where people have few options or choices and where they are struggling to survive?" I still have images of hundreds of malnourished awaiting-trial prisoners crouched in tight neat rows on the dirt of the prison yard, chanting and praying as missionaries in white robes led them in song, standing over them, clapping and preaching in English, often in a loud manner that consisted of shouting religious "truths." Sitting beside the missionaries on the floor were large bags of rice and *garri*.

I still have memories of some circle programmes I ran that were disrupted by loud missionary and other church group preachers, and louder songs in reply by hungry prisoners. Sitting in a colonial prison yard, built to maintain a colonial *criminal* justice system, listening to colonial religious chants, while black men and women in colonial prison uniforms guarded over all proceedings, and witnessing Africans maintain all these colonial structures felt tragic, to say the least.

INSTITUTIONALIZED POVERTY

Criminalization of the poor is not a secret or disputed topic of debate in Nigeria. It is an accepted fact. Within the Nigerian prison and police cells one rarely found people whose families had money. Those who had money were efficiently bailed out; those who did not remained inside. In the streets of Lagos poverty and homelessness were rampant. Unlike in North America and most Western nations, where the poor are segregated within certain neighbourhoods, and generally kept out of view of the middle and upper classes, in Nigeria one found poverty everywhere one looked. The state in which I witnessed the most extreme levels of poverty was, ironically enough, Bayelsa. This state, in the southeastern region of Nigeria, is one of the richest states in terms of resources. When one defines wealth through natural resources, Bayelsa State is crucial in the provision and production of oil. I visited a remote village called Eniwari. It was located far into the Delta River region and could only be accessed by boat. To the governor of the state it was made accessible by helicopter. To the people it was made accessible through different types of boats—smaller ones with engines for those who could afford them and larger, much slower, boats for those who had very little money.

Along the river, on the way to Eniwari, I was struck by the level of poverty in the villages. I was further struck by the unavailability of fuel for boats. I was angered by the natural gas flares of the oil refineries that burned twenty-four hours a day, seven days a week, depriving the surrounding villages of clean air to breath, clean water in the Delta River (the only access to water in the region), and the comforts of a dark nightfall. Frustrating was the fact that the majority of these villages had no electricity or access to phone lines. I began to wonder why the natural gas flares were not being transformed into a source of power for these villages and quickly came to this conclusion: hook-up costs for electrical connections cannot be that high, but the human potential to organize can be. If people are left to struggle to find food and clean drinking water in the oil-polluted fields and rivers, they will have less energy to organize and struggle against oppressive economic and international corporate oil structures.

Despite such obstacles, there is a strong movement developing in the area among the people in protest of their living conditions. Oil pipes are visible everywhere. These pipes have been built through villages, homes, schools, whatever is in their way: oil pipes are built over the ground for economic reasons, as opposed to underground for safety purposes, and instead of diverting their course any building or vegetation on the closest and most convenient path is destroyed. These visible oil pipes are often vandalized, and international oil company workers face kidnappings for the purpose of ransom collection. It has become so common that major oil companies, such as Shell, Chevron, and Mobil, have set aside specific amounts of money to deal with ransom demands. It has been found that paying ransoms is cheaper than following safety regulations in extracting oil. Unfortunately for the people, the amount of money set aside by these companies is far less than the amount of money they stand to lose if organized resistance attacked and shut down the oil-producing process in Nigeria. Their attempts, while inconveniencing these corporations, do not threaten corporate existence or divert corporate actions away from the destructive consequences faced by the people who have lived in that region for generations.

A stronger, more visible police and military presence exists in this area of Nigeria, more than I found in other states. This was yet another clear connection between the suffering of the people and the use of the penal structure's personnel to protect and maintain colonial structures that benefit from a status quo that sustains Western corporations and their monopoly over African resources. Under such conditions one cannot help but see the immense economic gains that the powerful minority accumulate on the backs of the vast powerless majority. One also cannot help but see the clear role that the penal system's mechanisms play in assisting the powerful by oppressing the powerless within the context of economy, finances, and armed control.

THE POLICE

My knowledge about the Nigerian police force comes mainly through direct contact with the police through my work with (ex-) prisoners, through my contact with the police while commuting around Lagos, or through stories prisoners and ex-prisoners told me about their experiences with the police. This section outlines some of my direct interactions, the stories passed on to me, and some of my thoughts and conclusions about what I witnessed, heard, and experienced.

My Experiences with the Ajegunle Police

To present the situation with the police in Nigeria and their interactions with the average (and poor) Nigerian, I will share an experience I had, starting on July 19, 2001. An ex-prisoner, Florence, whom I had been working with since my arrival in 2000, was living in the poorest neighbourhood in Lagos. It is called Ajegunle and is referred to by Lagosians as "jungle city." It is an overcrowded, concrete, urban jungle with very few running water facilities, very sparse electricity, and dilapidated buildings as homes. Florence worked hard to find rent money, and this neighbourhood was the only one she could afford to live in. One night she got into an argument with her neighbour and was making a lot of noise. Another neighbour got involved, and in his attempts to reduce the noise level he beat her severely. That night (July 18, 2001) she was taken to the police station and put in a police cell for the night.

The next morning Florence's husband asked for my assistance in bailing her out. In Nigeria bail is not legally supposed to include the transfer of money. All police stations have posted notices stating that bail is free. Bail is granted when a responsible person signs on behalf of the person being held. When that person signs bail forms he or she is admitting responsibility for the released prisoner. Should that person not appear in court at the appointed time, the police have the right to arrest and imprison the person who signed the bail forms.

Upon arrival at the police station in Ajegunle I was met with screams and shouts from inside the interrogation room. There was only one room, and that was where I was taken to meet with the investigating officer for Florence's case. Upon entering the room I found a young teenager topless and handcuffed on the floor, being beaten with wooden rods by a policeman. The policeman was hovering over the trembling teenager screaming, "Are you ready to speak yet?" As we walked in, the policeman motioned for his suspect to take a seat on the bench beside me. He was facing his investigating police officer, and I was facing Florence's. I could feel his shoulders trembling beside me. As they discussed his case, Florence was brought into the room. There was an open wound on her head, and blood was dripping down her face. This, she explained to me, was from the beating her neighbour had given her the night before.

As she sat down beside me, the teenager's family entered the room and began discussing his case with the police officer. Ironically, that officer was sitting directly beneath the "BAIL IS FREE" sign. He had an open copy of the Nigerian Criminal Code in front of him, and was eating *moimoi*[6] and porridge for lunch as they discussed details of the case. The police officer claimed that he had arrested the teenager for the theft of a fridge from under a bridge in Lagos. The teenager insisted that the policeman had picked him up off the street randomly. The policeman ignored him, and continued explaining to the teenager's family that he had arrested "this boy" and was charging him with theft of the fridge. This crime carried a sentence of up to seven years, he stated, but he added that he believed the boy had stolen the fridge at night, which could lead to a life sentence. I do not know if this is the case in Nigerian law, but the policeman seemed to be confident that it was. He proceeded to tell the teenager's family that, if they had N5,000 (approximately CA$ 50), he was willing to forget the entire matter. The family discussed the situation among themselves and concluded that they had no means of gathering such a large sum of money. They had no choice but to leave. The teenager sitting beside me broke down crying, and the policeman continued to eat his lunch.

As all this was happening, I was trying to convince the investigating policeman for Florence's case that he should release her from custody because he did not have a charge against her.

His responses to my questions and comments were not related to the case at all: he wanted to know if I was married and what I was doing in Nigeria. To my surprise the policeman who had been dealing with the teenager and his family in such a brutal and corrupt manner stood up in my defence, and asked his colleague to be reasonable and to show me some respect. It was concluded that, if a resolution could be reached among the neighbours, the police would let Florence go. The neighbours all gathered, and we reached a resolution, but the police refused to sign any papers or release anybody until I left the station.

They delayed the procedure for days, and after I had travelled out of Lagos for (ironically) an Access to Justice workshop in the middle belt region of Nigeria, they released Florence. A few steps out of the police station two women screaming "Thief!" grabbed Florence. The police arrested her again, and put her in a cell with the property she had allegedly stolen (clothes) and the tools she had allegedly used to break into the home of the supposed victims. They took her picture with the evidence and told her she was going to pay for bringing a foreigner into the police station to help her out. "Are you trying to get us stripped of our badges?" they asked her.

Upon my return to Lagos I was informed that Florence had been taken to Kirikiri prison for women to serve time as an awaiting-trial prisoner on theft charges. After hiring a lawyer, and bribing several officials and officers, she was released on July 27, 2001, before a holding charge could be imposed upon her. This was the only time during my stay in Nigeria that I succumbed to the pressure to bribe somebody, and I did it because I felt personally responsible for her false imprisonment. The experience showed me how quickly and efficiently imprisonment can be used and reversed in Nigeria. As for the teenager they were torturing when I arrived at the police station, I never found out what happened to him. Like so many others, he was likely either shot by the police or imprisoned indefinitely as an awaiting-trial prisoner.

Illegal Raids

An ex-prisoner named Uche, whom I was working with at the PRAWA office (he is a sculptor and artist, and trained ex-prisoners and youth at risk through our trades and skills work programme), disappeared for a week. No one knew where he was, and, knowing the situation with the police and illegal raids in Lagos, I was worried. He eventually showed up on March 2, 2001, and told me what had happened.

He was in the market the prior week and was picked up by the police. He did not have enough money to give them, so they arrested him. They threw him into the back of a van, and one of the policemen took his trousers. He was left exposed from the waist down in the van. Another policeman commented on how savage he was, walking the streets naked, and would not accept any explanation about the missing pants, even though his colleague was standing beside him holding them. Uche and about fifty others were taken to a local police cell, where they stayed for a few days. They were not given any food and had to beg for water, which they were given sparingly. One of the other detainees managed to get the message out to his family that he was in that particular police cell—he had convinced the police officers that if his family found him they would be able to pay for his release. When the family arrived Uche was able to convince them to help him too. They helped as many as they could and took messages out to the families of the rest of the people being held there. Those whose families were contacted and had the money to pay for release were taken home; the rest were taken to prison on awaiting-trial charges.

In the two years I spent in Nigeria there were three separate incidents of jaywalking that resulted in the imprisonment of people I knew either through work or through my community. I went to the local government's holding cells in Onipanu, a place where all jaywalkers were kept until they paid their fine of N500 (CA$ 5). At N500 a head, these government workers were making quite a bit of money; they told me they picked up hundreds of people a day. I managed to talk to the local government staff who had arrested these people, and because I was a foreigner they humoured me and released them without taking money from me.

I took my time with the discussions and learned that the people I was talking to were not police officers. They were local government staff who used this as a means of making money to subsidize themselves while they were waiting for their salaries to be paid. They had built cells in their offices (complete with bars). They were in charge of the main highway (Ikorodu road) near my home and office. Ikorodu road has overhead foot bridges that can be used for crossing the road, but they are few and far between. It was a long walk to the overhead bridges, and most people just crossed the main road by running to avoid the fast-moving vehicles. A problem with using the foot bridges was that they were not well maintained and thus not safe; they were made of thin metal and often had large holes (sometimes covered with large rocks to help people avoid stepping into them) that one had to walk around to avoid tripping. Thousands of people used them to cross the main road every day.

While I was living in Onipanu, one of the overhead bridges broke and sent many people to their deaths, either from the impact of the fall or from the traffic below. The number of people who died was never officially reported. I remember discussing this incident with the local government staff who were arresting people who did not use the bridges, and the response I got was simple: it is our job to make the main road safer, and we must arrest people who insist on running across the road instead of using the overhead bridges. The dangers that the poorly maintained overhead bridges posed were not their concern—that was another government department's responsibility.[7]

To provide some perspective on the safety of these foot bridges, I present an experience I had using one to cross the Ikorodu road one afternoon in the middle of August 2001. The foot bridge nearest to my home was beside a gas station. While I was crossing the bridge, the police had come to use the gas station to fill up their vehicles. They were transporting money (which included special armoured cars and many armed escorts), and to scare away any potential armed robbers they started to fire (while in the gas station) rounds of ammunition into the air. All of us on the bridge had to run for safety. I remember the people around me, the racing cars below me, the sound of gunshots, and the sight of smoke. It was surreal to me but so normal and expected to those around me. It is what the police do, and all those who get in their way must learn to move fast or suffer.

Bribes: Happy Weekend!

Often in Lagos, and many other parts of Nigeria, the police set up traffic check points where they flag cars down and "check to see if all is well." What generally happens is that they ask for money, take what they can get, and move on to the next car. On the weekends this request is verbalized through a widely known and understood phrase: leaning into each car's window, holding his gun, the police officer, with a smile, exclaims "Happy weekend!" I came to understand this as meaning "Make it a good weekend for me by giving me money." These police check points, set up both on the weekends and during the week, usually led to many traffic jams and sometimes ended in violent confrontations.

Aside from police check points on the road, the police also take over almost all major bus stops in Lagos and request bribes from all taxis, buses, or *okadas* (motorbikes used for public transportation) passing through. There were many violent incidents in Lagos related to this police presence at public bus stops and motor parks. There were countless accounts of public transportation bus drivers or *okada* drivers being shot and killed by the police for failing to give them bribes at the bus stations. There were several times when all public transportation workers went on strike to protest the police bribes they had to pay at each bus stop. These strikes have not succeeded in stopping the police from vilently robbing bus drivers in Lagos.

From a Military State to a Police State: A Cab Driver's Incident

My experiences with the police check points involved a lot of discussion and many questions. Generally, when they found that I did not respond with money quickly enough they asked me to move on. I always felt that my foreign status kept me safe from violent confrontations. Contemporary global power dynamics put people with European or North American identifications in positions of privilege, and in Nigeria I came to experience such privilege. While in the West, as a person of colour, I am constantly struggling to achieve recognition, respect, and benefit of the doubt, in Nigeria the global elements of oppression played out in my favour.

On the night of March 22, 2002, I did experience one incident that was not so peaceful. I was alone in a taxi around 9 p.m. after a concert in Ikeja, on the Lagos mainland. My taxi driver had tried to avoid a police check point (to avoid giving them money) by doing a U-turn, but was spotted by the police. Four of them surrounded the car, and one started to whip the taxi driver's hands on the steering wheel. These actions succeeded in immobilizing the car. Policemen with batons, whips, and guns[8] surrounded the car. While one policeman was whipping the taxi driver's hands (resulting in cuts and open wounds), another stuck the barrel of his gun inside the car against the driver's head. The policeman was shouting angrily, threatening to kill the taxi driver. We immediately pulled over to the side of the road, and the taxi driver was taken to the side and surrounded by several policemen.

I stepped out of the car and initiated a discussion with the police officers standing nearby. I wanted to talk about what had just happened and what we were going to do to resolve it. I tried to convince them to let us go. My argument was that it was late and that the streets were getting more dangerous, as armed robbers may be nearby (in my silent opinion, the streets were getting more dangerous because of the heavily armed and volatile policemen). During our discussion one policeman turned to me and said, "This is not a democratic state, the military regime is gone: the police are now in charge. If you want democracy, go back to your country, let us deal with this man." I was constantly aware that Nigeria had been transformed into a police state after the military regimes were removed. I was surprised to hear this thought verbalized by a policeman in uniform. Besides, he reminded me, everyone in Nigeria still remembers Olusegun Obasanjo (the current democratic president) when he ran the country as a military tyrant. It became clear to me that a change in appearance (i.e., uniform) rarely means a change in structure. The president of Nigeria now wears plain clothes instead of a military uniform; the streets are now terrorized by armed men in black police uniforms instead of armed men in green military ones.

In North America the masses tend to believe otherwise. In North America people put a lot of faith in appearance and political correctness. Presidents and leaders of nation-states may have corporate backgrounds, but they are not viewed as businessmen, since they make decisions on behalf of the state. In Nigeria the situation does not allow any segment of the population to live in such superficial comforts. In Nigeria, I discovered, the vast majority of the people do not live within an illusion of democracy and rights. It is understood that the state functions to control its citizens, to subdue them so that the rich can get richer, while the poor continue to struggle. A policeman, armed and dressed in uniform, explained these things to me. Despite my anger at the situation, and my fear for the taxi driver, I respected his honesty, and was struck by his political awareness and understanding of society. He did not need a university degree to understand issues of power and institutional affiliation to historical oppression.

That night I had several short political discussions with police officers who were not directly involved in the argument with the taxi driver. This kept me occupied until the taxi driver was able to give the rest of the policemen enough money to let us go. In the car the taxi driver thanked me for staying with him — had I left and taken another taxi, he did not know what would have happened to him or if he would still be alive. It is a sad and scary state of affairs — the police control the streets with guns and intimidation. Aside from the threat of death or grievous bodily injury, there is always the threat of prison and awaiting-trial prisoner status.

Torture: Stories from a Nigerian Prison Yard

A lot of my knowledge of police brutality in Nigeria came through experiences I heard from prisoners who were tortured in police cells prior to being taken to prison. I met prisoners who had both arms broken as a result of being hung by their arms from the ceiling for weeks. The pressure from their bodies resulted in bone fractures in their arms. Once taken to prison, these prisoners rarely received medical attention; all the prisoners I met in this condition were awaiting-trial prisoners. Most of them had been held in the notorious SAS (special armed robbery squad) detention centre, known to be one of the most brutal and violent detention centres in the country. I met many prisoners who had been shot and tortured by the police prior to being taken to prison. My work with those who had experienced police brutality before being imprisoned helped me to understand how health is managed in prison, while raising my awareness in relation to police brutality. The two issues are intertwined: police brutality usually results in injuries for which the prisons, after receiving prisoners from police cells, do not provide medical attention.

One awaiting-trial prisoner named Enmeka was nineteen years old when I met him inside Kirikiri medium security prison. He had been arrested early in December 2000 (at age eighteen), and shot in the back of the leg while being made to lie down on the floor in a police cell beside seven others who had been arrested with him. The police had shot four of them; two had died instantly. Enmeka had received no medical attention for his wounds; occasionally he was given painkillers. I met him on September 5, 2001, eight months after he had been shot. The bullet had hit the bone in his upper thigh, causing it to splinter; he had been in prison the entire time, and the bone fragments in his right thigh were causing an infection and resulting in immense amounts of pain. When I met him he was lying on the dirt in the prison yard verbally wishing death upon himself. After talking to him I tried to bring in doctors to see him and to buy antibiotics for his infection. I quickly learned that the prison medical staff was unwilling to help him because he was suspected of being an armed robber and thus considered unworthy of their limited resources. He was in Kirikiri medium security prison located on the same grounds as Kirikiri maximum security prison in Lagos. The maximum security prison had a hospital, while the medium security prison had painkillers donated by a church.

The medical staffs of the two prisons refused to cooperate with each other. The maximum security prison staff refused to take Enmeka into their cleaner hospital without access to painkillers (which they did not have), and the medium security prison staff, who did not have access to the cleaner environment of a prison hospital (they had only a small clinic), did have access to painkillers, but were not willing to give any to the maximum security prison hospital. They were low on supplies already. As a result Enmeka was held in solitary confinement in the medium security prison, occasionally receiving painkillers when his complaints of pain got too vocal. He was in solitary confinement not for humane but for practical reasons. Putting him in the overcongested awaiting-trial cells was impossible because he was unable to squat or stand for long periods of time due to his injuries. He was sharing a cell built for two with five other prisoners, and in his opinion this was a luxury; at least he was not in a cell built for twenty with seventy-six other prisoners.

On September 7, 2001, I spent the entire day discussing and negotiating Enmeka's situation with both the medium and the maximum security prison guards. We finally reached a compromise: the medium security prison guards agreed to give

Enmeka painkiller pills (not injections) to take with him, and the maximum security guards agreed to admit him to their hospital. This compromise was reached after the wardens of each prison persuaded their staffs to comply. When it came time to transport Enmeka from the medium security prison to the maximum security prison I was informed that there were no vehicles available. I was told that "There are rotting corpses in the prison vehicle, which we have not taken to the mortuary yet, and so he will have to wait until tomorrow to be transferred." Not wanting to risk a change in anyone's mind, I suggested we move him in the PRAWA office vehicle. The prison guards were disgusted, and told me that he had scabies and would most likely infect the car. I asked for blankets to place on the seat for him, and they informed me that all blankets available for prisoners' use were infected with scabies as well. I decided to continue with the transfer nonetheless. Two convicted prisoners were assigned the task of carrying him to the car (which we drove into the prison yard), since he was unable to walk and the guards did not want direct contact with him. An armed prison guard accompanied us in the car, and we drove down the street on the prison grounds to the maximum security prison, where convicted prisoners carried him into the hospital.

When we arrived at the clinic they did not have a bed ready for him, and Enmeka was dumped onto the concrete floor while they prepared one. Over the next few months I worked hard to raise money for him to buy medication and antibiotics for the infection, but his injury was not in my expected and planned budget. After raising money and finding authentic medication[9] I took it in to Enmeka.

On November 14, 2001, I learned that half of the medication had been confiscated by the prison medical staff (who are all uniformed and thus prison medical guards), and sold for their own profit. Since Enmeka received only half of the medication he needed, his infection took much longer to heal. Eventually I was able to raise enough money to subsidize an x-ray for him and learned then that the bullet was not in his leg (it had gone right through), that the bone fragments were the cause of his infection, and that the antibiotics were helping his body to expel them one by one: they were being released in the pus that was forming around his wounds. Enmeka would gather the bone fragments and save them in a tissue each day. He kept count of how many pieces were exiting his wound each day, and would show them to me and share with excitement the proof of not only his injury (prison staff had often told him that there were no bone fragments in his leg) but also healing. He stayed in the maximum security hospital for many months, and before his wounds completely healed he was sent back to the medium security prison, much to my protest: his wounds had not healed properly and in the medium security prison environment would only become infected again. My protests were futile.

By the time I left Nigeria Enmeka was able to walk while applying partial pressure on his leg. He was still wearing bandages and hoping that he could keep the wound clean outside the hospital setting. I was able to get a lawyer to take on his case (since he had no legal representation when I met him, like so many awaiting-trial prisoners). I hope that one day he can at least be taken to court and, if not released, then sentenced so that he has a definite number of years to serve and thus a chance of being released from prison one day. However, as far as I know, and from what people released from Kirikiri maximum and medium security prisons have told me, the lawyer whom I knew and had worked with in PRAWA did very little for Enmeka after I left the country.

Recently I was informed by some prisoners who managed to be released from Kirikiri maximum security prison that Enmeka was transferred back to the maximum security prison because he had been involved in riots protesting living conditions in the medium security prison. His leg has completely healed, and he is happy to have resisted the amputation that the hospital staff had constantly threatened him with during his first year in prison. As for his case, he continues to await trial.

THE COURTS

The court system in Nigeria is backlogged and inefficient. It remains foreign to most of the people in the country. The logic of English common law has failed to implant itself upon the consciousness of this African nation. While I view that failure as a triumph against colonialism, I also saw the impact that such disconnection between the people and the social structures they are forced to live within can have. It is an oppressive reality that not only enforces dysfunction but also works to degrade a population already alienated through poverty.

Language

On June 27, 2002, during an Alternatives to Violence Programme (AVP) training workshop in Lagos, I met a court magistrate who was a participant in the workshop with me. We struck up a conversation about the cultural dynamics of the Nigerian criminal justice system. She told me about the tensions that lead to violence in Nigeria and the language barriers that exist between ethnic groups. She explained that often, in her Lagos-mainland-based courtroom, defendants do not speak formal English, and generally do not understand the basic tenets of European legal codes and procedures.

She mentioned a specific case that she had encountered. The man (defendant) standing before her spoke very little English and had no understanding of how the court or the criminal justice system works. He had spent years in prison awaiting trial. On his court date his family managed to get enough money together to get him a lawyer. He was acquitted of all charges. When the magistrate made her decision and announced it in court the defendant standing before her did not understand. She had to translate the court's legal jargon (acquittal) into pidgin English, commonly used in Lagos ("You are free, make you dey go"), so that he knew it was time for him to leave the courtroom. At first this story surprised me. In the west, we are bombarded with criminal justice knowledge in the media. As I spent more time in Nigeria I realized that the irrelevance and inefficiency of the court system in Nigeria were topics of discussion mainly among lawyers and judges. While inaccessibility to language is a visible disconnection between people and the criminal justice system, it is symbolic of a much larger disconnection: the logic of criminalization, community separation, and stigma is incongruent with most cultures in Nigeria. Conflict is not commonly dealt with through such degrading and barbaric rituals. Conflict is generally addressed through communication, representation, and solutions/problem-solving models.

Inefficiency: Technology, Funding, and a Backlogged Bureaucracy

All records in the Nigerian penal system, at all levels, are kept manually. Computers and recording devices are inaccessible, not only due to expense but also due to the lack of constant electricity. All records are handwritten and filed. If an awaiting-trial prisoner's file goes missing, the chances that prisoner has of ever going to court or leaving prison are almost non-existent. I met many prisoners and ex-prisoners whose life circumstances have been greatly affected by such inefficiencies. I came to see that, while the Western industrialized world has been able to adjust its penal bureaucracies to a level that gives an air of functionality, in Nigeria that functionality is constantly challenged, and in that challenge lies the true dysfunctions of the penal system. I often wonder what it is about the penal system that keeps it so strong. I find that a lot of the bureaucratic jargon flogged at us in the West allows the institutionalization of brutality to hide behind segments of processes and procedures.

In Nigeria these processes and procedures in no way justify criminal justice; instead, their inefficiency exposes the weakness of penality as social control. So where does the justification for the penal system come within the West African context? I came to understand that the West continues to flog cultural supremacy and assume criminal justice civility that suggests superiority in its dysfunctional bureaucratic systems of control. It is in the expectation that a more efficient system may implement more justice that Africa maintains penal systems irrelevant to its societies. Colonial powers continue to exert control over the continent through assumed superiority in implanting systems of social and crime control. The penal system in Western societies assumes a monopoly in conflict resolution and harm-defining roles. In Africa, colonialism brought in such monopolies, and imposed its penal institutions and mindsets upon nation-states and citizens. Despite the failure of penal systems to produce safety and crime reduction in Western societies, the colonial mindset of superiority continues to justify attempts to make the penal system work in Africa. As justifications fail, and as the penal system continues to implement a criminal form of justice the average African continues to bear the brunt of such practices.

A Man Shares His Story: Prison and Court Brutalities

On April 30, 2001, late in the afternoon, an elderly man named Felix who had been released from Kirikiri maximum security prison that morning came to the PRAWA office. He told me that he had just come from the courthouse, where he had been informed, after nine years of awaiting trial in prison, that his case had been thrown out of court three years ago. "No one told you?" the judge had asked him. He had been free to go for three years, but no one had noticed or told him. Upon hearing what he called the bittersweet truth, he had been released. The prisons and the courts had not given him enough money to pay for transportation off the prison grounds. He had walked all day and eventually found his way to the PRAWA office. He was seeking assistance. Felix explained that too many people released from prison after many years behind bars are not given any money for transportation home, and often have to steal to get themselves home to their families or friends.

The majority of ex-prisoners often have no home to go to: the stigma attached to imprisonment is so strong that it does not differentiate between awaiting-trial and convicted prisoners. Nigerians are aware of the problems that push people to break the law or expose people to police brutality and wrongful imprisonment, but at the same time they see prison as a mysterious and scary place, so, despite the reasons that led a person there, upon release that person also becomes mysterious and scary. Many ex-prisoners end up living on the streets and eventually go back to prison. Felix had lost all contact with his family and had nowhere to go. My office did have a home for ex-prisoners to use as a transition point after prison, but the rooms were never enough for the number of people who needed them. We did have a room for him at the time, and he stayed there for the entire time I was in Nigeria. I am not sure what will happen to him if that home can no longer be sustained by PRAWA.[10] Felix's experiences and the time we spent discussing them during my stay in Nigeria illustrated firsthand how imprisonment breaks up a community, not only stigmatizing prisoners but also separating them from families and friends for extended periods of time. This process weakens community strength and reinforces a divide-and-conquer mechanism of social control. Now when I read or speak about security and criminal justice, I put them within that context. The state secures its status quo and strengthens itself at the expense of the community, which becomes fragmented and weakened.

THE PENAL SYSTEM QUESTIONS AND EXPOSES ITSELF

The penal conditions presented, while brutal for those who suffer from them, illustrate that the penal system does not just make mistakes occasionally but is built on a foundation that is vengeful and dangerous. While the human casualties in Nigeria continue to mount, I found that these problems prompted discussions that allowed Nigerians working in criminal justice to question this system and its relevance to their society.

Awaiting-Trial Prisoners: Bureaucratic Finger-Pointing

As stated above, most prisoners in Nigeria are awaiting trial. I had the opportunity to discuss this specific issue during several DFID-funded[11] Access to Justice workshops held in July 2001 in Makurdi, Benue State. These workshops were attended by the police force, the prison service, the Nigerian Bar Association, judges, magistrates, and community members. Upon attempting to find the root cause of the disproportionately high prisoner population that had not been taken to court for years, it became clear that a criminal justice system with a weak infrastructure does not provide shelter from the bureaucratic administrative legitimizations of inhumanity that take place in Western-based criminal justice institutions functioning within more rigid and defined infrastructures. Blame for the large awaiting-trial prisoner population in Nigeria was passed from one sector to the next. The bureaucratic reality set in as it became clear that the root cause of this problem is not linked to a specific segment of the criminal justice system in Nigeria, but results from the collective efforts of all branches involved. Unfortunately, within the context of bureaucracy, responsibility for shortcomings gets distributed into an ambiguous, insoluble, unfortunate situation.

The magistrates and lawyers who work in the courts openly blamed the police for arresting too many people indiscriminately and unjustly, while at the same time pointing fingers at the government's refusal to provide them with proper resources (technological recording devices, non-payment of salaries, and so on) to deal with such high numbers. The prison guards also blamed the police for such misconduct, while pointing fingers at the courts for their inability to speed up the entire process. The police pointed fingers at the lawyers and the court officials, who, they claimed, are not working efficiently enough and thus causing a backlog in the penal structure, which results in a large awaiting-trial prisoner population. A large number of the prison staff who participated in these Access to Justice workshops openly stated that they believed the prisons are dumping grounds for the penal system's inefficiency and injustice. The police force claimed that society has become so violent that they have no choice but to arrest as many people as they do. The prison guards, lawyers, and magistrates disagreed with them. The magistrates and lawyers stated that they are the scapegoats for inefficient structures and inappropriate police actions. The community continues to suffer at great expense, and the penal structure continues to expose itself through the constant failures and degradations it imposes upon all those whose lives it touches. Community leaders who participated in these workshops pointed fingers at all branches of the inefficient and criminal justice system.

"Jungle Justice": A Violent Solution within a Violent State of Penality

One disturbing and rigorous reaction to such tensions and failures in the criminal justice system has caused many to turn away from the penal structure. These issues were also discussed in the Makurdi workshops in July 2001. Unfortunately the justice most visibly utilized throughout the country maintains the penal structure's violent and revenge-oriented mentality. This is what many Nigerians have come to refer to as" jungle justice." The mistrust that so many feel toward the penal system's official structures has caused people to turn to pockets of organized political groups who serve as neighbourhood watchers.

These groups have resorted to violent means of dealing with armed robbers in certain neighbourhoods. Because most Nigerians do not have access to guns, the concept of necklacing has been introduced. When an (alleged) armed robber is caught, a tire is thrown around his or her neck and brought down to his or her arms. The vigilante group proceeds to douse the person with kerosene and set the person on fire. The bodies are usually left on the streets as warnings to others that they have entered a community that does not tolerate armed robbers. It was unanimously stated by community participants in the Access to Justice workshops that this has been the only way communities can protect themselves. If they choose to take the people they caught robbing them to the police, they fear that the police will be bribed, and the released armed robber will come back to find them and most likely kill them. On the other hand, those charged with and convicted of armed robbery in prison have stated to me that this jungle justice has resulted in their need to use more violence while robbing. They fear that leaving people alive can result in their getting caught and their inevitable necklacing. The cycle of violence grows larger and more dangerous under these conditions. In addition to such factors, the politics involved with these organized neighbourhood watchmen are violent. Many are organized based on ethnic groups and various political party affiliations.

As discussions progressed in these workshops in Makurdi, I learned that both the community members present and the police agreed that jungle justice is necessary and just. Discussions went as far as to suggest that the police should seek the assistance of such groups in dealing with the violent situations now overwhelming the nation. In responding to this violence, the police officers present at the workshop pointed fingers at the government for its refusal to provide them with proper resources to do their job, stating that an alliance with such political and violent groups may be their only chance to deal with the violence they face every day. They complained that they lacked access to functioning guns, proper vehicles, and working telephone and communication services. Even uniforms have to be bought by police officers who want to wear them while on duty. As these discussions progressed between different agents of criminal justice, the use of violence to address problems was natural and expected, not because the people who work for the system are violent but because violence to address conflicts has been normalized in Nigeria through the implementation of criminal justice. The culture of criminal justice and the institutionalization of penalty have resulted in a reliance on violence and dehumanization to address conflicts and social ills.

THE PRISONS

My most direct contact with criminal justice while in Nigeria was with the prison system. Prison guards were more accessible to me, and were less confrontational and violent than the police I confronted on the streets. In conferences and workshops the Nigerian Prison Service representatives were the most progressive in their attitudes toward prisoners, possibly due to increased contact with prisoners over longer periods of time. While I found that prison guards who hold high positions in the Nigerian Prison Service were progressive in their politics, I also found that those prison guards who worked directly with prisoners often mistreated and brutalized them.

Health in Prison: A Religious Experience

Inside Kirikiri medium security prison the convicted prisoners' cell blocks hold up to twenty prisoners, while the awaiting-trial prisoners' cell blocks (they are approximately the same size) hold seventy-seven. These blocks consist of one cement room with small windows on either side of the walls. In other parts of Nigeria such windows do not exist, and ventilation is much worse than it is in the dilapidated conditions in Kirikiri medium security prison. The awaiting-trial prisoners do not have beds or mats to sleep on, and the conditions are so congested that they must take turns sleeping on the floor. On all occasions I had to visit the health clinic in Kirikiri medium security prison I saw an overwhelming majority of the awaiting-trial prisoners seeking medical attention. I was told by an awaiting-trial prisoner that each day only one prisoner per cell block is allowed to seek medical attention. Prisoners allow whomever they think is in the most need to emerge for help. Those who make it to the clinic are made to sit on the ground outside the clinic as they wait for access to health care. Those prisoners who do not come in time for prayers are not allowed to visit the clinic that day.

On several occasions I witnessed prison officers herding a group of ill prisoners with sticks and beating those who did not move fast enough, and most of the time I saw them beating prisoners on the head. I heard those prisoners seeking medical attention being made to shout and scream their amens and hallelujahs prior to seeing the nurses. It is those prisoners who look like walking skeletons, half-naked and sitting on the ground, who are made to sing, clap, and chant as they wait to be seen by the nurse.

Inside the clinic, where I spent an entire day (September 7, 2001), I noticed that the medical staff do very little assessment of sick prisoners. Several convicted prisoners (serving as medical assistants) were made to check if the ailments existed (if there were complaints of visible illness), and one medical staff nurse, upon the order from the matron (head nurse), gave a shot of painkillers to a prisoner, who was made to drop his pants in front of everybody. Any prisoner who showed any fear of the needle or hesitated in dropping his pants was ridiculed and threatened by the prison's medical guards.

Food and Water in Prison

Because an official budget does not exist for awaiting-trial prisoners, there are no budgetary provisions for their imprisonment. Convicted prisoners wear blue uniforms, while awaiting-trial prisoners are made to wear the clothes in which they were arrested. Most of them no longer fit those clothes due to the overwhelming weight loss and malnutrition they suffer during their imprisonment. Upon discussing the issue of food with some of the convicted prisoners, they explained to me in a letter how the system works. They explained that the Nigerian Prison Service hires a contractor who supplies the food to the prison. Before supplying the food the contractor takes his or her cut and then passes the food on to prison headquarters in Abuja, the federal capital. In Abuja prison officials take their cut and then pass the food down to each of the state controllers of prison, who in turn take their cut and then pass the food down to the controllers of each prison, who of course take their cut and then pass the food down to the yard, where the chief of the yard takes his cut and then passes the food down to the kitchen, where the guards in charge there help themselves to their cut and then pass the food down to the convicted prisoners who cook it, and who admitted to serving themselves and their friends bigger portions. What is left of the food then gets distributed to the rest of the prisoners in the yard, first to the convicted and then to the awaiting-trial prisoners. Some prisoners also explained in a letter that, during a prison visit by Obasanjo's[12] special assistant on prisons to assess living conditions in Nigeria's prisons, prison officers brought in twelve extra bags of *garri* for him to see as available food for prisoners, and after he left they took back thirteen bags.

These accounts and stories helped me to better understand how prisoners in Nigeria have come to experience such malnourishment. On an ironic note, prisoners have pointed out that the car used to move dead bodies[13] from the prison yard to the mortuary is the same car that prison officers use to move the food from the prison yard to their homes.

In addition to malnutrition, other factors contribute to the poor health of prisoners. In the majority of the prisons there is no access to clean water to drink: wells are dug into the ground and are not properly maintained. Upon looking inside the wells, one can often see the insects and the worms that live inside and around them. In the overwhelming majority of the prisons those wells are the only source of water for drinking and for bathing. They are also a breeding ground for mosquitoes, among other insects, and this has created an increase in the number of prisoners who suffer from malaria. While diagnosis and treatment of malaria are cheap and readily available in Nigeria, it has been stated that untreated malaria is one of the main causes of death in the country. In prison testing and medication for malaria are not readily available, and, since there are very few official records outlining cause of death for the many who die inside prison, the number of people affected is not available.

Tuberculosis in Prison

Another problem prisoners face is the lack of medicine for diseases such as tuberculosis (TB). In Kirikiri medium security prison in 2002 there were eighty-three prisoners suffering from

TB. These prisoners were segregated into the TB cell because it is a contagious and lethal disease. They were given medicine when it was available (mainly through donations from churches or other charitable organizations), and when they ran out of medicine the treatments stopped until the next batch of medicine was bought or donated. This inconsistent treatment has created a group of prisoners who have developed a form of TB that is immune to medication. If released alive from prison, they will spread this form of TB among the community. Considering that TB is a highly contagious disease spread by sharing the same air space, the possibilities for disaster are massive.

The ironic detail here is that in Lagos State, where Kirikiri medium security prison is located, TB medication is free. This was one of the promises that Governor Tinubu made to the people when he was elected in 1998. The problem in receiving the medication is that proof has to be given that the patient is suffering from TB, and the tests are very expensive. The high cost of these tests (along with the minimal prison health care budget) results in prisoners being moved to the TB cell without proper testing and diagnosis. Any loud coughing may result in transfer to the TB cell. After entering this cell most prisoners are never released back into the general population because (1) they almost never get the full dose of treatment and thus rarely recover to full health and because (2) the few who do get the full dose, through friends or family members who provide the medication, cannot be sent back to the general cells, since other prisoners fear contracting TB and do not trust the authorities to have treated infected prisoners properly. Prisoners who enter the TB cells rarely leave them alive; those who are discharged during their confinement in TB cells leave the prison very sick and rarely survive, due to lack of money or the immunity they have built up to TB medication while in prison.

Beatings in Prison

While most of my knowledge of torture came from the stories I heard from prisoners, and from their visible scars, there were several occasions when I witnessed beatings of prisoners by prison guards. Beatings often took place in front of the chief officer's office in the prison yard, where all prisoners could see and hear exactly what was happening. Discussions with and questions to the prison guards about these beatings led me to learn that they were over infractions of prison rules, and were almost always linked to drug-trafficking in prison. One of the most horrific beatings I saw a prisoner get was given by the chief guard in charge of the yard himself. He was teaching his officers how to beat a prisoner properly.

On a hot Wednesday afternoon, May 16, 2001, I witnessed a highly disturbing and degrading moment. It happened during a programme I ran beneath a tree in the yard with convicted prisoners. Two awaiting-trial prisoners were allegedly caught dealing drugs inside the prison, and the guards felt they had to make examples of them. Within sight of the majority of prisoners in the yard, they were made to kneel handcuffed, shackled, and topless in the burning sun for hours. They were stripped down to their underwear. The kneeling was followed by brutal beatings with wooden sticks and whipping with leather whips. The handcuffed and shackled men were then forced to stand up and hop from the guard's office to the white-painted doorway leading to solitary confinement, a section in the yard that prisoners refer to as Angola. As the prisoners were made to hop to Angola, guards were mimicking them, hovering around them, imitating their actions and their postures, walking as they were walking with the shackles and hopping around behind them as they hopped their way to solitary confinement. The scene was degrading, horrific, and violent on physical, mental, and emotional levels. This was one of several times I witnessed prisoners being beaten by guards in Kirikiri medium security prison.

I did not witness a lot of violence between prisoners. The only incident of violence among prisoners that I did see occurred on September 10, 2001. The chief of the yard called me into his office to show me what two mentally challenged prisoners had done to each other. One had given the other an open head wound; the wounded one was shackled, and the assailant looked very confused. The chief was leading them with a stick to the clinic. He explained to me that they had six mentally ill prisoners and that he was seeking funds to have them transferred to the Yaba psychiatric hospital. Despite the beatings I saw him inflict upon prisoners, I also witnessed him providing his own home for ex-prisoners who did not have a home upon release, and I witnessed several occasions when he personally bought clothes for those who did not have sufficient clothing upon release. The contradictions in the prison system in Nigeria once again illustrated that, despite the brutal structures of this violent system, there were a few times when humanity and a sense of African community managed to prevail.

The beatings that I witnessed inside prison generally occurred while I was running the Prisoners Support Circle Programme in the prison yard, and I often discussed with the prisoners who witnessed the beatings with me what could be done in that situation. I was told that going to the guards and interrupting them would result in harsher beatings for the prisoner after I left. I had to resort to talking to the prison guards about it after they finished, when I was on my way out of the prison. Discussion had to be carefully worded. I did not want to put the prisoners at risk of further torture and punishment. The overwhelming response from the prison guards who did engage me in discussion fell back on the penal system's crime and punishment rhetoric. Once again the Nigerian penal system succeeded in illustrating the violent and degrading potentials that the people who work within it can reach, while emphasizing the justifications that allow and encourage the institution of violence.

Overcrowding: Baroness Helena Kennedy's Visit to Kirikiri

On April 26, 2001, Baroness Helena Kennedy was in Nigeria for a visit organized by the British Council. During this visit she spent some time in the Kirikiri prisons in Lagos. Inside the medium security prison we walked through the convicted and awaiting-trial sections of the yard. The awaiting-trial section had been cleaned up for her visit, yet what we saw was horrific. Inside each cell block holding over seventy prisoners each were half-naked, skeleton-like men staring at us through the bars. Some tried to get her attention, pleading for help. The entire scene made me angry, both at the inhumanity of the conditions and at the power differentials exhibited. Most prisoners in this section of the yard rarely see people from the outside, and thus any chance to be seen or heard represents the chance to briefly exist. In addition, many prisoners thought that, if white people saw what was happening to them in this white institution, brutality would cease.

The smell in this section of the yard was overwhelming. Unclean water holes were left exposed, and people had been locked up for days, maybe weeks. There are no words I can find to describe the sensation. The baroness and the British Council's executive director for West Africa (at the time) were mortified by their prison visit. Upon returning home, I was informed by my Nigerian colleagues, the foreign visitors were physically ill and vomited after seeing the prisons that day — and they saw the prison yard in its best, cleaned-up condition. I wondered that night if the foreigners who entered Nigeria's prisons thought about colonialism and why such institutions exist in Africa as they sat back in their comfortable first-class seats back to Britain.

Women and Children in Prison

There is only one prison in Nigeria that exclusively imprisons women. It is located on the Kirikiri prison grounds between the medium and maximum security prisons. The Kirikiri female prison incarcerates on average 150 to 200 females. I met some prisoners who were fifteen years old and others who looked even younger. On average there were between eleven and fifteen convicted women, while the rest were awaiting trial. The Kirikiri female prison has only female guards working in it, and it is not as overcrowded as the neighbouring male prisons. It is also the prison that I had the hardest time gaining access to, and the prison where I saw some of the most brutal forms of punishment being imposed.

Maintaining the stereotypes of how women are expected to behave, most of the punishments and oppressive tactics involved emotional manipulation and degradation, while physical torture was kept to a minimum. I witnessed women being made to kneel on the ground in the scorching sun for hours in the prison yard. They were being punished for being involved romantically with each other. I met women who were in prison with their babies — they were either pregnant upon arrest or had their children with them at the time of arrest and did not have anywhere to leave them before the police took them to prison. Some of the babies I met in this prison had never seen a man. The women told me about an Amnesty International visit that included several male visitors. One of the toddlers was so confused and scared by the sight of a man that she cried for hours.

The female prison was the only prison in Nigeria that did not allow me to donate food directly to prisoners; I had to leave all donations with the prison guards, which they distributed after I left; prisoners reported not receiving full portions of what was left for them. The level of disrespect and resistance I received from the female prison warden was so immense that I had a hard time working with the women prisoners, and thus cannot say that I fully comprehend what takes place in that prison. I was able to visit the death row section several times. On March 1, 2001, I saw two prisoners who were severely developmentally challenged awaiting execution. One sat naked in her cell in a trance, and the other knelt when she saw me and told me about her hallucinations and fears.

Women arrested and imprisoned outside Lagos State are held in male prisons in compartments built within the male prison yard for them. Upon visiting Makurdi prison on July 25, 2001, I asked the prison guards what happens when women get sick and are in need of medical attention. The clinic is located in the male section of the prison yard. The response I got was short and simple: "Women are hygienically cleaner than men and do not need to go to the clinic to heal; they can stay in their cells and heal there."

Women also become pregnant in these prisons, and it was unofficially reported that these pregnancies are the result of rapes by prison guards or male prisoners for whom the prison guards were doing favours. This prison held twenty women, eighteen of whom were awaiting trial. Of the two who were convicted one talked about the "insurance system" that resulted in her conviction.

After leaving Makurdi prison, and before heading back to Lagos to further investigate the "insurance" policy, we stopped at a new model prison, built just outside the boundaries of Makurdi in Benue State. It was an eerie sight for me; this building resembled North American prisons, right down to the type of bricks used for outdoor hallways and the colour of the paint inside the reception area. Apparently a blueprint of modern Western prisons had been sold to Nigeria, I assume, along with the building supplies. I was not able to confirm if this was done through private prison industry or government means. I was able to confirm that the prison was not in use, though construction was complete, due to a conflict between the building contractors and the Nigerian government. Our tour guide, a Nigerian guard, stated that the government did not pay the contractor in full, so in retaliation the contractor kept the keys. In this one instance I could say that government corruption served the people.

Whenever I had access to the Kirikiri female prison, I inquired about the reasons for women's imprisonment and eventually came to learn more about the "insurance" policy as it gets implemented by the Nigerian police force. I consulted with several lawyers for more details and learned that, if a male crime suspect cannot be located by the police during an investigation, the police arrest the first woman they find who has connections to him (mother, wife, girlfriend, daughter, niece, or other) and proceed to take her into custody for "insurance" purposes. If the man does not present himself to the police within a certain period of time, the woman gets sent to prison to await trial for his crime.

Many of the women I spoke to in Nigerian prisons were being held under such circumstances; some had been sentenced on conspiracy charges as a result of these "insurance" policies. Other women I spoke to who had been imprisoned for crimes not related to the "insurance" policy were serving time for crimes (mainly drug-trafficking offences) that they had committed for their husbands. Many spoke about the financial situations they were in and the reasons behind their decisions to help their husbands support their families.

CONCLUSION: FEAR, POVERTY, AND CONTROL

The awaiting-trial situation in Nigeria puts people in fear of the police. For those who are not well-connected or who do not have money, it is an everyday reality that they can be picked up by the police and can disappear into a prison for years or forever. Many prisoners gave me notes to pass on to their families; many prisoners had been missing for years, and their families presumed they had died. The amount of power the police command through these imposed fears is immense. It puts the penal system in a position of power that is not only unquestionable to the average citizen but also almost undeniable to the homeless population in Nigeria. Because they have no homes to sleep in at night, they are easier targets for the police. This level of power, so openly displayed against the poorest people in the country, is publicly acknowledged by most citizens. In Nigeria, the connections between poverty and crime are clear, and so are the connections between poverty and vulnerability to penal brutality.

NOTES

1   PRAWA is a Nigerian non-governmental human rights organization with headquarters in Lagos, and branch offices in Enugu, Nigeria, and Accra, Ghana. I was placed to work with PRAWA through the Canadian Voluntary Service Overseas [VSO] office. VSO is a non-governmental organization that places individuals from Canada,

India, Uganda, France, the Philippines, the Netherlands, Britain, and the United States in the global south to promote "development" while strengthening cross-national global experiences and connectivity. VSO volunteers are paid salaries in currencies and sums that are average to the general public residing in the host nation. As a VSO, I was encouraged to affiliate with the Lagosian community as my primary source of support, understanding, and security.

2   They were dangerous because of armed robbers but also because of the infamous police check points.
3   I specify Nigerian because I did meet Europeans and Americans who are in Nigeria as expatriots and businessmen/women. They flew into the country and were whisked away in air-conditioned SUVs with tinted windows to their American or European living compounds and only emerged to go back to the airport to visit their "home nations." Those people did not have to face the realities of oppression in Nigeria. The Chevron compound in Lekki, Lagos, for example, has its own school, movie theatre, grocery store, swimming pools, tennis courts, offices, and homes. People are paid in foreign currency and only interact with those Nigerians who have been hired to serve them.
4   NEPA stands for Nigerian Electric Power Authority, better known among Nigerians as "never expect power always."
5   Civilians against police officers, police officers against prison guards, prison guards against court magistrates, those who can pay the demanded bribes against those who cannot.
6   *Moimoi* is a dish of ground beans, steamed and often eaten with porridge or rice.
7   The dispersion of responsibility through colonial bureaucracies is in plain view in Nigeria. The inefficiency of colonial nation-state bureaucracies is also highly visible.
8   Women on the police force are not allowed to carry guns.
9   There are many fake pills in the markets in Nigeria that are sold as medicine to the people.
10 As far as I know, official funding for that home was not available. It was sustained through various donations and efforts by the PRAWA staff reaching out to the community for help. The home has closed since my departure.
11 Department For International Development, the development and foreign aid branch of the British government.
12 Olusegun Obasanjo was the president of Nigeria while I was there.
13 Many of the malnourished and half-starved prisoners die inside Nigerian prisons.

REFERENCE

Rosenberg, Matt T. (2004). "The Berlin Conference of 1884: The Colonization of the African Continent by European Powers." Interview. http://www.freemaninstitute.com/RTGcolony.htm.

CHAPTER 14

WOMEN'S RIGHTS BEHIND WALLS

Mechthild Nagel

INTRODUCTION

In the 1990s a global political consensus emerged that "women's rights" are also "human rights." In particular, the Beijing Women's Conference set forth an ambitious agenda, and activist-scholars in the global South began circulating ideas and papers on "putting women in the centre of analysis." I believe this focus is necessary, especially when it comes to critiquing the current prison system worldwide. Globalization has altered family relations and consumer behaviours, further marginalizing women in caste and class societies. There has been little research done on the impact of globalization on incarcerated women in Africa, with perhaps the notable exception of sex work and trafficking of girls and women from West Africa. This chapter offers a comparative approach to issues faced by criminalized and imprisoned women in several African countries. It also highlights the voices of resistance, especially women political prisoners of South Africa.

AFRICAN WOMEN AND THE GLOBAL HUMAN RIGHTS AGENDA

When feminists in the global North talk about women's rights in Africa, inevitably the first thing that comes to mind is the topic of female circumcision or, in feminist-charged speak, female genital mutilation.[1] This discussion may be followed by other discussions of sexualized violence, such as trafficking, AIDS, and, occasionally, customary practices such as polygamy and land tenure. On the bright side, the UN Millennium Goals have broader and more explicit gender perspectives affecting women in Africa, including economic and educational rights. Yet, overall, despite the important shift of the human rights agenda to do more than lip service to women's rights, African women get short shrift.

Feminist writer and educator Abena Busia tries to shift the discourse about women in Africa through a new academic endeavour, Women Writing Africa, sponsored by Rutgers University. She shares the following insight in an interview with WHR.net:

> In Women Writing Africa we collect women's cultural production—oral and written, formal and informal, sacred and profane. We try to collect whatever we can lay our hands on, as far back as we can get. We are looking at things that we know were written or spoken in female-centered spaces, about things that only women could say or in circumstances that women can control. What we are trying to do is get a sense of the way women have agency and control over their lives and negotiate their lives differently.
>
> We just got so tired of our non-existence as women of power and agency in Western discourse where we are predominantly viewed as *perpetual victims*—a barefoot pregnant woman holding a baby in our hands, or a barefoot pregnant woman with a baby on our back and hoe in our hand. We are labeled endlessly. That sense of missing many things—such as no agency, no affective space, no human negotiation—all those things, which in fact, everybody knows are profoundly central to our existence and shape our lives. (WHR.net 2003; emphasis added)

Given the colonizing lens that Busia describes so well, the outsider expert continues to label and exoticize the hapless African woman, and knows which remedies work best for African women and children (Mohanty 1990; Nagel 2001). This patronizing "speaking for" attitude has come under criticism, in particular with respect to vociferous attacks on female genital mutilation by non-African feminists (Butegwa 2002; Welch 1995).

In the decade of emerging women's rights, which culminated in the Beijing Women's Conference, it turned out that the African regional committee provided much food for thought for the conference. The final platform for action drew much of its content from the preparatory African meetings. No longer would African women be silent bystanders who have to be represented by "well-meaning" northerners; rather, under the leadership of Gertrude Mongella, dubbed in Africa as "Mama Beijing," they have joined the centre of discussions and shaped the platform for women decisively.

Now, having argued that one should take care not to "speak for" but to "speak with" African women, this chapter suffers from a particular epistemological and political dilemma. How does one address human rights violations concerning non-elite women without falling into the patronizing trap? How do women, who are walled in either in their families' compounds or in the state's carceral structures, participate when they do not get the chance to speak? Florence Butegwa (2002) argues sensibly that outsiders may speak on behalf of the oppressed only if it is impossible for the inside group to agitate: "I can see a role for capacity-building, including skills in problem analysis, organizing and advocacy. The content of their advocacy efforts, including definition of issues and possible solutions, should remain entirely for those working from within" (126). In describing women's imprisoned or "walled-in" experiences this chapter attempts to stay clear of normative claims that find little basis in lived experiences. Yet it is difficult, admittedly, to write about women prisoners and not thematize their enormous victimization.

In human rights campaigns almost invariably pure and deserving victims become the poster children. Similarly, in the prison literature about women one tends to find fervent appeals to the women's virtual innocence and rationalizations of a woman's particular offence. I do not claim to do anything different from that paradigm, but I also note that men's criminal acts could easily be justified by drawing on the environmental hypothesis: most violent offenders tend to have been victimized in their childhood by family members or others. Vivien Stern (1998) points out that there is a major difference for women's and men's imprisonment. Unlike men, few women resort to violence, and most commit property offences due to poverty. The world over, women's rate of imprisonment is about five percent (or less) of the total rate of imprisonment of a country (the exception is the United States, due to its "war on drugs" policy, which has targeted women).

I argue that there are two types of women prisoners: "imprisoned intellectuals," borrowing a term from Joy James (2003), and social prisoners. On the one hand, there are women who politically organize and oppose family and/or state power, of the stature of a Winnie Mandela (South Africa) or Wangari Maathai (Kenya), who may find political clout thanks to their international connections and even win prestigious prizes for their daring opposition to patriarchal, kleptocratic, and dictatorial regimes. On the other hand, there are invisible women who are criminalized and become social outcasts, women who have born children out of wedlock (Amina Lawal, Nigeria, one of the most prominent of castigated, fallen women) and who may turn their luck around thanks to energetic African lawyers (Hauwa Ibrahim, Nigeria) and local NGOs (e.g., Women Living under Muslim Laws). But most women who end up as social or common prisoners do not have high-end representation and face a number of challenges rarely addressed by human rights agencies.

AFRICAN HUMAN RIGHTS DISCOURSE: COLONIAL PARADIGM OR LIBERATORY PRACTICE?

In recent years several conferences and books have been devoted to the question of human rights in Africa. Does it make sense to focus on a "rights discourse," or is it more prudent to use "other languages of resistance" (An-Na'im 2002)? The human rights declarations that evolved from the global North focus almost exclusively on the negative rights of the individual against state power: from the British and American Bills of Rights to the Universal Declarations of Human Rights, these documents focus on individualized freedom to pursue self-interested ideals apart from community needs. Such ideology is alien (and therefore not universalizable) to most of the globe, where community interests trump individual interests, especially the possessive individual pursuit of happiness. Thus, John Mbiti (1970, 141) rearticulates the egocentric Cartesian *cogito* into a sociocentric variant: "I am because we are, and because we are therefore I am." Clearly, a Eurocentric "rights discourse" devoid of sensitivity toward cultural practices will not be applicable in an African context of sociality and responsibility toward one's community, customs, and elders. However, due to the colonial legacy, the rights discourse has firmly been instituted in the legal instruments of African countries.

The African Charter on Human and Peoples' Rights (1986) weaves together different traditions, and the outcome has been assailed as a contradictory mix of rights and duties of the individual and groups (Mutua 2002). However, as Makau Mutua emphasizes, Western human rights experts have underestimated the reality of individual rights of Africans before colonial conquest. Mutua's cursory view of precolonial practices of adjudication highlights the high respect for human life and the dignity of the person, the guarantee of equal protection of individuals (e.g., the Akamba of East Africa), the ability to dismiss a chief who rules oppressively (in the Akan society of West Africa), the presumption of innocence, and dedication to the juridical process (e.g., the Amhara of East Africa). Mutua is careful not to romanticize the historical record of precolonial Africa and points to cases where human rights of individuals, especially the rights of women, were not safeguarded. So in what ways can individual and group rights coexist in harmony, as the African charter imagines? The new South African Constitution (1994) also commits itself to this ideal of coexistence. However, the past decade witnessed serious tensions, particularly in customary family law (Chanock 2002). In 2005 the South African Supreme Court ended some aspects of the debate by ruling that customs that discriminate on the basis of gender have to be abolished. The debate is still going on in the northern states of Nigeria, which ushered in sharia law in 2000.

When it comes to the adjudication of rights, whether as group/culturally based rights or as individual rights, one has to look at individual cases for which the ideological position might be most advantageous and representative of women's needs. This is especially important for women who have transgressed against a person or against social standards. Here I would like to contrast practices in two different parts of West Africa: Mali[2] and northern Nigeria.

A woman in Mali killed her husband because he had married a second wife. The first wife poisoned the husband on the day of the naming ceremony of the second wife's child. The family's *jeli* (bard who engages in informal conflict resolution) intervened, and it was agreed to banish the offender from the village; she went into exile at her paternal home. Nobody proposed turning her in to the police, despite the severity of the crime (Kone 2003). The police, too, when called to arrest an offender, will ask whether people have tried to resolve the conflict in the customary way. This may be a bewildering gesture if one is accustomed to the Western worldview that an offence is done against the state, first and foremost, which then intervenes on behalf of the victim, and it may seem that victims' rights are disregarded in communally based adjudication. However, one ought to see the other side too.

When British colonialists started to prosecute persons for crimes against the Crown, such as property theft or murder (of another African), victims were bewildered when they did not receive the customary restitution from the offender's clan. "Doing time" in a penitentiary serves no purpose from the point of view of the aggrieved. Mali is a predominantly Muslim country that does not condone sharia law, but allows indigenous practices of mediation by the *jeli* caste and joking relatives to restore peace in the community and to solve conflicts between persons and clans. "Cultural justice" may not have to clash with secular "criminal justice" (Comaroff and Comaroff 2004), but the next case shows that it certainly can.

The Zamfara State government of Nigeria adopted the Islamic legal system, sharia law, in January 2000, in disregard of the secular nature of the Nigerian Constitution and of other religious minorities living in this state. Sharia law was declared by the governor as "not just a penal code but a way of life" (Abdullah 2002). All women were soon banned from sports activities, and single women received an ultimatum: get married within three months or lose your job! The controversy about the law heated up when the first penal sanctions were delivered: limb amputation for theft and public flogging of prostitutes and a male procurer. International attention came along with the conviction and flogging of seventeen-year-old Bariya Ibrahim for the offence of fornication. Proof of the offence was based on the fact of her pregnancy and her unmarried status. Such proof, however, is quite spurious, given that sharia law stipulates third-party eyewitnesses of the transgression of fornication, which did not occur (Abdullah 2002). Amina Lawal's case of adultery followed two years later, but her conviction and death sentence were overturned by the Sharia Court of Appeal.

These two cases show that it is impossible to differentiate between (pure) customs and traditional practices, on the one hand, and politically expedient customs, on the other. Customs are always open to contestation and interpretation; they can be read in a progressive way or in a reactionary way. This is meant as a caveat to liberal feminist human rights experts who jump to the defence of a woman cast as a victim of customary practices. I simply wish to point out that a human rights adjudication that relies on imprisonment as its main instrument may also be harmful to women.

A BRIEF HISTORY OF PRISONS IN AFRICA

Prisons in Africa are an un-African institution. In precolonial African societies one of the harshest sentences faced by an offender was expulsion; exile equated to social death. When the European colonialists arrived, in the "scramble for Africa," they converted slave forts along the Atlantic coast into jails or *cachots* (Bernault 2003). Chinua Achebe's (1954) anti-colonial novel *Things Fall Apart* describes well the trauma incurred by political leaders of the community who faced incarceration by the colonial power. For the African psyche it was simply unimaginable to utilize prisons as a form of punishment. West Africa's measures for crime control tended to be restorative and retributive justice; collective punishment, rather than individual punishment, was also common. Where an individual defrauded a member of another clan the offender's entire clan may have had to pay restitution, as is still commonly practised in Mali (Kone 2003).

During colonial times sexual assault and gang rape were particularly prevalent because women were not given separate quarters from men in prison. In Senegal African women were expected to cook for the entire prison population and sleep in the kitchen or on the porch of the fort or prison compound (Konate 2003). Colonial prisons enforced racial segregation, and European prisoners were housed in the vicinity of the warden's office or compound (Goerg 2003).

In postcolonial Africa several notorious prisons were shut down, and some serve as memorials for a haunted past, such as Robben Island, where South Africa's anti-apartheid activists were imprisoned. Due to the international pressures of the United Nations and human rights organizations, a few countries have opened separate prisons for women and adolescent men. However, most African prisons house men, women, and children, and may merely provide separate sleeping quarters for men and women.

Since the 1990s a few African governments have also invited an intergovernmental, regional agency to inspect their prisons. The African Commission on Human and Peoples' Rights appointed a Special Rapporteur on Prisons and Conditions of Detention in Africa. "This [appointment] provides a unique opportunity to take a more holistic approach to the problems in prisons which an individual appointed to consider torture or inhuman treatment, for example, may not" (Murray 2002). The rapporteur has noted in published reports that many African prisons face the following challenging conditions: severe overcrowding, unsanitary living quarters, inadequate diet, mixed gender facilities, and a high percentage of prisoners on remand.[3] The rapporteur visited Malian prisons several times and acknowledged improvements made after his recommendations. This, however, is a rare case of encouraging news. Most African countries prefer to take the walls behind which their citizens disappear to stand for "walls of silence" rather than offering their prisons to inspection and critique by an outside rapporteur. Given enormous budgetary constraints, governments are also under pressure by the public to invest in schools and health care before ameliorating the conditions of the least desirable subjects: prisoners.

GENERAL ISSUES OF WOMEN'S HUMAN RIGHTS BEHIND CUSTOMARY WALLS OR PRISON WALLS

Demographics of Criminalized Women

Even in Africa, prisons have turned into "homes" for young, socially displaced, undereducated, and poor women, many of whom are also mothers. Social displacement is an effect in part of globalization and structural adjustment. More single women leave their rural homes and venture into the cities for gainful employment. Unlike their male counterparts, female convicts' crimes tend to be non-violent, such as theft. Certain occupations, such as sex work or domestic work and, to a lesser extent, drug-dealing, expose women to a higher risk of sexual abuse and criminalization. Domestic workers tend to be young, rural, unmarried women who may risk being assaulted or raped by their patrons, and in countries where abortion is illegal they may commit infanticide out of despair. In some women's prisons, such as in Bamako, Mali, the majority of prisoners and remanded women are accused — or convicted — of infanticide. Mali does not sanction legal medical procedures for the abortion of an unwanted child. The social sanctions of having a child out of wedlock are severe. Unfair and sexist trial procedures put women at further risk. A divorced woman whose baby was stillborn was charged with murder because her doctor's evidence was not introduced in court (Amnesty International 2004).

In several African countries the familial practice of polygamy seems to be an additional stress factor, but it affects more women who have never received formal education and those who dropped out of primary education. Polygamy seems to be losing widespread support due to westernization, urbanization, and Christianity. A recent Ugandan study (Tibatemwa-Ekirikubinza 1999) actually notes the higher prevalence of female criminality (targeting the husband, junior co-wife, or the co-wife's child) in rural regions where polygamy is prevalent. Prisoners, in particular those who were senior wives, note the disparities in asset-sharing by their husbands; many times these convicts rationalize their violent offences by accusing the husband of total economic and emotional abandonment of the senior wife and her children, and devoting all the jointly earned resources to the new co-wife (Tibatemwa-Ekirikubinza 1999). The majority of women who are convicted of violent crimes have been in abusive relationships (see Walker 1984 on battered woman syndrome), and it is only since the UN conference in Beijing (1996) that domestic violence has been taken seriously as a public health concern.[4] Yet women who kill their abusive partners in self-defence or in premeditation receive punitive sentences, including capital punishment, rather than leniency and compassion.

Custodial Conditions

The United Nations rule that only women should guard women is widely followed in Africa (unlike in the global North). Male guards or visitors may enter women's quarters only in the presence of other female guards, or, as in Nigeria, men can only enter in exceptional circumstances, such as medical personnel providing health care (Stern 1998). Male prisoners can be a threat to women's well-being, which makes it necessary to insist not only on separate sleeping quarters but also on separate institutions, which was implemented in the capital of Mali in the late 1990s. The women's prison at Bolle (near Bamako) now serves as a model prison, not only in Mali but also on the continent. Few countries run separate women's prisons because of economics. Women's sections tend to be merely cordoned off by a high wall or housed in makeshift buildings. They are treated as an afterthought (Stern 1998).

In many countries unsentenced detainees held for more than five years comprise over seventy percent of the prison population. What is often deemed "death by natural causes" by prison officials is actually caused by lack of sanitation and clean drinking water, dietary deficiency, lack of adequate health care, and overcrowding. Mortality rates increase dramatically during the rainy season (Agomoh 2000). Often prisoners' families have to supply food, soap, hygienic products, and blankets for the prisoners. African governments are loath to spend the national budget on prisoners' amenities in part because of the public's outcry of undue favouritism toward criminals. In Kenya warders also live in prisons with their families in squalid conditions, which may well turn them into brutes who torture or kill prisoners (Muiruri 2005).

A recent Zimbabwean study (Musengezi and Staunton 2003) problematizes the lack of gender-specific consideration. Men's prisons are the standard according to which women are housed in sections of men's prisons or—more infrequently—in separate facilities. Therefore, women do not receive items that are not allocated to male convicts (e.g., basic sanitary items).

South African women common law prisoners were particularly denigrated by being denied panties and cotton from the prison system in the 1970s (Kuzwayo 1985). The lack of basic health and dietary needs is particularly grave for pregnant women. In most prisons in Africa pregnant convicts get minimal or no pre- or perinatal care; child mortality, as a result, is higher in prisons than in civil society.

Most female prisoners are mothers, and young children often stay with them in part because the father has abandoned the mother upon her incarceration or because the mother's family is ashamed of her convict status and refuses to take the child. In some prisons no extra clothing is provided for the child, and children suffer from the same poor diet as their mothers, so that the children are literally punished along with their mothers (Taylor 2004; Tibatemwa-Ekirikubinza 1999). "Women with babies in prison seem to carry a double punishment of coping themselves and fending for their children" (Musengezi and Staunton 2003). Measures of rehabilitation are minimal, and prison chores are overwhelmingly domestic — reinforcing the gendered division of labour. Many women are illiterate and have minimal formal education. Linguistic difficulties may adversely impact ethnic minorities and immigrants, who do not understand the lingua franca of the courts and the prison staff (de Klerk and Barkhuizen 2001).

In South Africa, where there is now an active prisoners' rights association (South African Prisoners' Organization for Human Rights) that even won the right to vote for convicts in the 1990s, rules seem to be selectively enforced with respect to illicit sexual practices. Since 1996, in male prisons, condom dispensers are ubiquitous, and condom use is encouraged to curb the spread of AIDS. On the other hand, in women's prisons, perceived lesbian convicts are reported to prison staff, and lesbians may also fear reprisals by other convicts (Dirsuweit 1999). This is not to say that relationships in men's prisons are of a consensual nature, and adolescents housed in adult prisons are vulnerable to assaults and sexual exploitation.

Political Prisoners

From the onset of the colonial conquest the carceral compound was used for political control of Africans. However, after decolonization many governments continued with the practice of incarcerating political opponents (Bernault 2003); even leaders who were political prisoners under colonial rule enthusiastically locked up their political opponents (Asumah 2001). Much of women's political imprisonment is predicated on their participation in liberation struggles during the colonial and apartheid era. Women instigated revolts against poll taxes (Nigeria) and fought alongside men for national liberation (e.g., Mau Mau members in Kenya, pass law resisters in South Africa). Many women faced sexual assault, rape, and other forms of torture and murder in detention camps and prisons cells (Harlow 1992; Kuzwayo 1985; Tesfagiorgis 1992; wa Wamwere 2002). Women political leaders also faced house arrest and banishment, which turned the banned person into a self-policing docile body (Ramphele 1995). Winnie Mandela, banned during apartheid, was so acutely aware of her exceptional status under the apartheid regime that she was always prepared to return to prison, having a suitcase ready at all times (Mandela 1985). Similarly, Gambo Sawaba readied her loin clothes because she was incarcerated more than a dozen times for her defiant stance (Shawalu 1990).

Political detainees and prisoners differentiate themselves from common or social detainees and convicts. They report serving their sentences with pride and determination. They instigate hunger strikes and launch grievances, never coming to terms with the label of prisoner; some refuse to work, and all refuse to be "rehabilitated." Some women are erroneously detained for participating in illegal political movements, yet upon release they actually join the liberation movement that they were falsely accused of belonging to (Tesfagiorgis 1992). In South Africa under apartheid political prisoners attempted to make common cause with common prisoners, who were condemned to hard labour (Meer 2001). Sometimes the warden placed common prisoners with political prisoners to press them into service to inform on the latter (Makhoere 1988). However, political prisoners were often able to educate common prisoners about their lot and the oppressive situation. Northern Nigerian political prisoner and Muslim Gambo Sawaba counselled other Muslim women to say that they were practising Christians to evade harsh sanctions of the sharia court (Shawalu 1990).

But at times political prisoners distance themselves from the "unfortunate drunks" and outcasts (First 1989). This hierarchy is reinforced by the warden's "fear of infectious belief": political detainees and political prisoners tend to be totally segregated so that they cannot incite the mass of social prisoners to rise up and organize for better prison conditions or, worse, to "conscientize" (to use South African vernacular) them about party politics. Almost all political prisoners who have written memoirs have participated in or organized a hunger strike to protest prison conditions. Caesarina Kona Makhoere (1988) reports that her cohort instigated the first strike in South Africa's women's prisons in 1976 — a time of mass arrests and deaths in detention of schoolchildren in the aftermath of the Soweto uprising. After 1976 the isolation of detainees increased. Being segregated for only a short time attacks the soul of the political prisoner; once the sense of time breaks down, sensory deprivation creates psychopathic and somatic responses; one ages faster and may have long-term health problems as a result of isolation (First 1989; Makhoere 1988; Mashinini 1989; Mandela 1985).

Sometimes political prisoners are allowed no other literature than the Bible or the Qur'an; they use the scriptures to shed light of their situations (Makhoere 1988; Meer 2001), in particular when they face psychological torture, such as interrogation (First 1989). Makhoere (1988) discovered the subversive messages of the Bible when she adorned a letter of complaint to prison authorities with pithy quotations from it. The letter was torn up by the apartheid prison officials. One political prisoner reports that male activists considered women's imprisonment to be lighter than what men experienced (Middleton 1998). While it was the case, as First

(1989) and others admit, that white women had much better conditions (especially regarding hygiene and food) than black women, it cannot be said in general that women suffered less than men from imprisonment and especially from isolation.

Release

There are long-term negative physical and psychological effects associated with incarceration. Many former political prisoners complain of heart problems, tumours, and other diseases affecting their long-term health. Emma Mashinini's account (1989) of her six-month solitary detention reveals an intense level of post-traumatic stress disorder (PTSD). Her isolation was only interrupted by extended interrogations by her tormentors. For social prisoners the return to civil society also involves an inordinate ordeal of shame, another form of social death. In the Bolle prison in Mali women who are going through an apprenticeship programme (e.g., learning soapmaking or typewriting) are told that they can return after their release to complete the programme. Few do so because society would judge them to be imprisoned again (Nagel 2007).

On the other hand, in Kenya some prisoners refuse to leave after their official release dates because prison has become a home after the vice president in charge of prisons instituted a series of reforms since 2003 (Obonyo 2005). Release may not necessarily be associated with freedom, for ex-convicts face "hostility, rejection and disdain from their families and society" (Ayieko 2005). Elizabeth Mwita, released in June 2005 after sixteen months of jail time, was served with divorce papers from her husband, who did not want to consort with somebody convicted of a criminal charge. He never visited her once in prison, which is a fairly typical experience for married women prisoners. In Bolle women's prison, Mali, women are allowed family visits, but rarely do family members come, whereas the men's prison in downtown Bamako bustles every day with wives visiting and bringing food to their incarcerated husbands. In addition, children of convicts and ex-convicts find themselves stigmatized and have difficulty finding work in Kenya (as elsewhere) (Ayieko 2005).

Clearly, the stigma of incarceration has huge repercussions for extended family networks. While the shame of imprisonment is felt by men and women alike across the continent, women and their children bear the brunt of a jail sentence—many studies the world over have shown the psychological, social, and economic costs associated with the incarceration of women who carry the main responsibility not only for parenting but also for subsistence living for their (extended) families (Taylor 2004).

For imprisoned intellectuals return to the community is experienced differently. Many such prisoners note with pride that they endured persecution, banishment, and prison life, and at times even "confess" to their interrogators that "everything I had done I would willingly do again" (First 1989, 90). Fatima Meer (2001), a former president of the Black Women's Federation of South Africa, reports that she did not want to miss the experience of five months of detention, even though she was already a banned person by the time she was detained. But she enjoyed great spiritual and material support from her family during her prison stint, and thus she did not endure the social ostracism with which common prisoners have to deal.

Women who are politicized because of group membership and subsequently tortured, and who have to adhere to an honour code, find it difficult to talk about their experiences, especially with their spouses. They often suffer from severe PTSD (Wenk-Ansohn 2002). According to psychologist Mechthild Wenk-Ansohn, men who have gone into prison due to participation in liberation movements tend to have less severe PTSD problems, even though they may have been severely tortured too. Their conviction about the cause tends to help them adjust to new circumstances, such as being refugees in a foreign country and culture, and their healing and social readjustment are more easily assured. Ex-prisoners who write about their detention experiences may find writing about them therapeutic (Pross 2002). Rarely do we find accounts by social prisoners. South

African Pumla Mkhize (1992), who was forewarned by her mother about prisons being "a snake with ice water," clearly is exceptional in discussing frankly not only the reasons for her incarceration but also how she gained favours inside (and early release) by snitching on other convicts. Snitching is considered to be one of the worst forms of transgression within the prison and violates the prisoners' own moral code.

CONCLUSION

This chapter has discussed in broad strokes human rights issues of African women, in particular those who are "walled in" by "culture" or by "criminal law" statutes. Let me return to the un-African custom of incarceration by the state.

Without question, women who enter the criminal justice system have experienced serious victimization prior to arrest and incarceration. While the reasons for their incarceration may be country-specific, victimization coupled with poverty comprises a major factor in pushing a woman into a difficult situation. It is then quite easy to argue for more lenient sentences for women victims-turned-perpetrators. One can argue that women should not face incarceration because it aggravates their already poor social status and gives them fewer choices when they return to civil society. Furthermore, the sentence often disconnects a mother from her children, who in turn are likely to become felons and prisoners too. However, it is quite another matter to argue for leniency toward other perpetrators, say men. Nevertheless, this is what some feminist prison activists are prepared to do. From the classic *Instead of Prisons* (Knopp et al. 1976) to the manifesto *Prisons and Social Control* (Kinesis 1987) activists have argued for the abolition of the criminal justice system, in particular curtailing the sentencing of people to prisons and making them into "slaves of the state" (Muntaquim 2003; Nagel 2003).

Human rights are safeguarded only when people are indeed treated with humanity, and 200 years of the experiment of caging people have shown us that prisons not only are "crime schools" but also prepare people for savagery and despair, not penitence and rehabilitation. Minimum standards for prisoners ought to be guaranteed, but this should not be the end of one's advocacy. It is merely the starting point of acknowledging that nobody forfeits rights, not even a prisoner on death row, and much more has to be done to encourage prison reform and eventual abolition.

ACKNOWLEDGEMENTS

For critical comments on an earlier draft, I thank Larry Ashley. I am grateful to Philip Rodi Otieno for providing research assistance on prison conditions in Kenya.

NOTES

1 The following is based in part on Nagel (2005).
2 Some of my discussion on prisons and restorative justice in Mali is based on Nagel (2007).
3 Prisons in Mozambique - Report of the Special Rapporteur on Prisons and Conditions of Detention in Africa, Series IV, 3; Prisons in Mali. Report of the Special Rapporteur on Prisons and Conditions of Detention to the 22nd Session of the African Commission on Human and Peoples' Rights, Series IV, 2.
4 Kenya, which has experienced a series of prison reforms since the NARC government took power in 2000, opened its first women-run police station in Nairobi in 2004. Kilimani Police Station deals exclusively with crimes and violence committed against women and children. In August 2004 a government report noted that more than half of the women in Kenya have experienced violence since the age of fifteen. Most of the violence is attributed to husbands, some sixty percent of beatings. Some of it leads to violent deaths of the women (Muiruri 2004).

REFERENCES

Abdullah, Hussaina J. (2002). "Religious Revivalism, Human Rights Activism, and the Struggle for Women's Rights in Nigeria." In *Cultural Transformation and Human Rights in Africa,* ed. Abdullahi An-Na'im. London: Zed Books, 151–191.

Achebe, Chinua. (1994) [1954]. *Things Fall Apart*. New York: Anchor Books.
Agamoh, Uju. (2000). "World Perspectives On What Is Wrong With The System: The African Criminal Justice System." Paper presented at ICOPA IX, Toronto, May.
Amnesty International. (2004). *Nigeria: The Death Penalty and Women under the Nigerian Penal Systems*. http://www.amnestyusa.org/document.php?lang=e&id=326565DE7A53C81580256E7E0041F90B. [Consulted October 12, 2007].
An-Na'im, Abdullahi A. (2002). "Introduction." In *Cultural Transformation and Human Rights in Africa,* ed. Abdullahi An-Na'im. London: Zed Books, 1–11.
Asumah, Seth N. (2001). "Development Crises, Predatory Regimes, and Prisons in Africa: An Impedance-Facilitation Perspective." Paper presented at the Thinking about Prisons Conference, State University of New York, Cortland, November.
Ayieko, Odindo. (2005, June 6). "The Chains of Freedom." *Daily Nation.* www.nationmedia.com/dailynation. [Consulted July 15, 2005].
Bernault, Florence. (2003). "The Politics of Enclosure in Colonial and Postcolonial Africa." In *History of Prison and Confinement in Africa,* trans. J. Roitman, ed. F. Bernault. Portsmouth: Heinemann, 1–53.
Butegwa, Florence. (2002). "Mediating Culture and Human Rights in Favour of Land Rights for Women in Africa: A Framework for Community-Level Action." In *Cultural Transformation and Human Rights in Africa,* ed. Abdullahi An-Na'im. London: Zed Books, 108–125.
Chanock, Martin. (2002). "Human Rights and Cultural Branding: Who Speaks and How." In *Cultural Transformation and Human Rights in Africa,* ed. Abdullahi An-Na'im. London: Zed Books, 38–67.
Comaroff, John, and Jean Comaroff. (2004). "Criminal Justice, Cultural Justice: The Limits of Liberalism and the Pragmatics of Difference in the New South Africa." *American Ethnologist, 31:2,* 188-204.
de Klerk, V., and G. Barkhuizen. (2001). "Language Usage and Attitudes in a South African Prison. Who Calls the Shots?" *International Journal of Social Language, 15,* 97-115.
Dirsuweit, T. (1999). "Carceral Spaces in South Africa: A Case of Institutional Power, Sexuality, and Transgression in Women's Prison." *Geoforum, 30:1,* 71-83.
First, Ruth. (1989) [1965]. *117 Days*. New York: Stein and Day.
Goerg, O. (2003). "Colonial Urbanism and Prisons in Africa: Reflections on Conakry and Freetown, 1903-1960." In *History of Prison and Confinement in Africa,* trans. J. Roitman, ed. F. Bernault. Portsmouth: Heinemann, 119–134.

Harlow, Barbara. (1992). *Barred: Women, Writing, and Political Detention.* Hanover, NH: Wesleyan University Press.

James, Joy, ed. (2003). *Imprisoned Intellectuals: America's Political Prisoners Write on Life, Liberation, and Rebellion.* Lanham, MD: Rowman and Littlefield.

Kinesis. (1987). "Prisons and Social Control: Vancouver Commission on the Status of Women." http://prisonactivist.org/women/prisons-and-social-control.html. [Consulted July 2, 2005].

Knopp, Fay Honey, et al. (1976). *Instead of Prisons.* Syracuse, NY: Prison Research Education Action Project.

Konate, Dior. (2003). "Ultimate Exclusion: Imprisoned Women in Senegal." In *History of Prison and Confinement in Africa,* trans. J. Roitman, ed. F. Bernault. Portsmouth: Heinemann, 155–164.

Kone, Kassim. (2003). Personal communication.

Kuzwayo, E. (1985). *Call Me Woman.* San Francisco: Spinsters Ink.

Makhoere, Caesarina K. (1988). *No Child's Play: In Prison under Apartheid.* London: Women's Press.

Mandela, Winnie. (1985). *Part of My Soul Went with Him.* New York: Norton.

Mashinini, Emma. (1989). *Strikes Have Followed Me All My Life: A South African Autobiography.* London: Routledge.

Mbiti, John. (1970). *African Religions and Philosophy.* New York: Praeger.

Meer, Fatima. (2001). *Prison Diary: One Hundred and Thirteen Days, 1976.* Cape Town: Kwela Books.

Middleton, J. (1998). *Convictions: A Woman Political Prisoner Remembers.* Randberg: Ravan Press.

Mkhize, Pumla. (1992). "A Snake with Ice Water." In *A Snake with Ice Water: Prison Writings by South African Women,* ed. Barbara Schreiner. Fordsburg: COSAW, 240–249.

Mohanty, Chandra. (1990). "Under Western Eyes: Feminist Scholarship and Colonial Discourses." In *Third World Women and the Politics of Feminism,* ed. C. Mohanty, A. Russo, and L. Torres. Bloomington: Indiana University Press, 51–80.

Muiruri, Stephen. (2004, October 2). "Women-Only Police Station Set Up." *Daily Nation.* www.nationmedia.com/dailynation. [Consulted July 15, 2005].

---. (2005, February 21). "Conditions in Jail Still Far from Rosy Despite Changes." *Daily Nation.* www.nationmedia.com/dailynation. [Consulted July 15, 2005].

Muntaquim, Jalil. (2003). *We Are Our Own Liberators.* Montreal: Abraham Guillen Press.

Murray, Rachel. (2002). "Application of International Standards to Prisons in Africa: Implementation and Enforcement." *Africa Newsletter,* 12.

http://www.penalreform.org/english/article_stafrica.htm. [Consulted July 3, 2005].

Musengezi, Chiedza, and Irene Staunton, eds. (2003). *A Tragedy of Lives: Women in Prison in Zimbabwe.* Harare: Weaver Press.

Mutua, Makau. (2002). "The Banjul Charter: The Case for an African Cultural Fingerprint." In *Cultural Transformation and Human Rights in Africa,* ed. Abdullahi An-Na'im. London: Zed Books, 68–107.

Nagel, Mechthild. (2001). "On the Limits of Feminist Cross-Cultural Analysis." In *Issues in Africa and the African Diaspora in the 21st Century,* ed. Seth Asumah and Ibipo Johnston-Anumonwo. Binghamton, NY: Institute of Global Cultural Studies Press, Binghamton University, 53-69.

---. (2003). "Prison Intellectuals and the Struggle for Abolition." In *Community and the World: Participating in Social Change,* ed. Torry Dickinson. New York: Nova Science, 165-175.

---. (2005). "Women Prisoners" and "Political Prisoners in Africa, South of the Sahara." In *Encyclopedia on Women in Islamic Cultures.* Vol. 2. Leiden: Brill Publishers, 436–439.

---. (2007). "Gender, Incarceration, and Peacemaking: Lessons from Germany and Mali." In *Prisons and Punishment: Reconsidering Global Penality,* ed. Mechthild Nagel and Seth Asumah. Trenton, NJ: Africa World Press, 43-51.

Obonyo, Oscar. (2005, June 26). "Prison Reforms and the Plight of Warders." *Daily Nation.* www.nationmedia.com/dailynation/printpage.asp?newsid=51875. [Consulted July 11, 2005].

Pross, Christian. (2002). "'Zersetzung': Psychologische Techniken der Staatssicherheit und ihre Folgen. Ein Blick in das zukünftige Instrumentarium von Diktaturen?" In *Das Unsagbare: Die Arbeit mit Traumatisierten im Behandlungszentrum für Folteropfer Berlin,* ed. A. Birk, C. Pross, and J. Lansen. Berlin: Springer, 271–287.

Ramphele, Mamphele. (1995). *A Life.* Cape Town: David Phillips.

Shawalu, Rima. (1990). *The Story of Gambo Sawaba.* Jos: Echo Press.

Stern, Vivien. (1998). *A Sin against the Future.* London: Penguin.

Taylor, Rachel. (2004). "Women in Prison and Children of Imprisoned Mothers." Geneva: Quaker United Nations Office. [Draft document].

Tesfagiorgis, Abeba. (1992). *A Painful Season and a Stubborn Hope: The Odyssey of an Eritrean Mother.* Trenton, NJ: Red Sea Press.

Tibatemwa-Ekirikubinza, Lilian. (1999). *Women's Violent Crime in Uganda.* Kampala: Fountain Publishers.

Walker, Leonore. (1984). *The Battered Women Syndrome.* New York: Springer.

Wamwere, Koigi wa. (2002). *I Refuse to Die: My Journey for Freedom*. New York: Seven Stories Press.
Welch, Claude. (1995). *Protecting Human Rights in Africa: Roles and Strategies of Non-Governmental Organizations.* Philadelphia: University of Pennsylvania Press.
Wenk-Ansohn, Mechthild. (2002). "Folgen sexualisierter Folter: Therapeutische Arbeit mit kurdischen Patientinnen." In *Das Unsagbare: Die Arbeit mit Traumatisierten im Behandlungszentrum für Folteropfer Berlin,* ed. A. Birk, C. Pross, and J. Lansen. Berlin: Springer, 57–77.
WHR.net. (2003). "Women Writing Africa: Women Negotiating Spaces and Lives, Women Telling the Story: An Interview with Abena P. A. Busia." http://www.whrnet.org/docs/interview-busia-0309.html. [Consulted July 2, 2005].

CHAPTER 15

NIGERIAN WOMEN IN PRISON: HOSTAGES IN LAW

Biko Agozino

INTRODUCTION

As I was writing this chapter, news reached me that a Nigerian female journalist, Isioma Daniel, had been sentenced to death by a deputy governor of a self-proclaimed Islamic state in Nigeria for writing an article that Muslims consider blasphemous. The article, published by *This Day* newspaper, suggested that the Prophet Mohammed would have liked to marry some of the beauty queens who were in Nigeria to contest for the Miss World crown. In the protest that ensued over 200 innocent Nigerians were slaughtered, and the organizers were forced to shift the venue for the finals of the competition to London. The staging of the contest in Nigeria had earlier been controversial because such contests encourage what most Muslims see as indecent appearance by women (although beauty pageants have been organized annually in Nigeria for a long time without similar incidents). On the other hand, many beauty queens boycotted the contest to protest the sentence of death by stoning for adultery of Amina Lawal, and some Nigerians now suspect that the campaign by the foreign press against the staging of Miss World in Nigeria was part of what made Muslims more sensitive to the contest. The president of the country, retired general Olusegun Obasanjo, regretted that efforts to attract foreign investors to the country would suffer due to the riots, but he promised that the journalist who wrote the offending article would not be arrested. The journalist had reportedly fled to the United States, but many Nigerians were demanding that the politician who tried to incite people to kill her should himself be arrested.

The Daniel case problematizes the common-sense equation between crime and punishment, and demonstrates that what is considered "criminal" is situational and culturally specific. In this chapter I suggest that this rupture does not exist in Nigeria as an outcome of a punitive version of Islamic fundamentalism alone. The arbitrary and unjust punishment of Nigerian women does not occur only under sharia law. Rather, the entire colonial system of criminal justice is based on the criminalization of innocent black women. The chapter starts by reviewing the theory of "victimization as mere punishment," which I developed in my study of black women and the British criminal justice system (Agozino 1997). This theory is illustrated with recent empirical evidence from Nigeria. Finally, the implications of the problems confronting Nigerian women for the struggle to decolonize Africa are outlined in the conclusion.

Jean Baudrillard (1983, 25) famously asserted that Disneyland is there to conceal the fact that it is the whole of America that is the real Disneyland, just as the prison is there to conceal the fact that it is the social in its entirety that is the prison. The implication of Baudrillard's statement is that you do not have to go to Disneyland to have fun in America. The whole country is one elaborate amusement park. Similarly, Americans do not need to enter the prison gate to become subjected to state surveillance and social control; rather, the entire population is controlled as inmates of the global lockdown. Nigeria is no America. The land mass is only a fraction of that of America, possibly the size of Texas alone. The population is dense in comparison: almost half the population of the United States. Of course, what Baudrillard was saying here was already said by Malcolm X, who told people who laughed when he referred to the time he was in prison that they were still in prison themselves, the prison without walls. Fela Kuti made similar remarks in his song "Beast of No Nation," in which he complained that people wanted him to sing about life inside prison as if life outside prison is much different in Nigeria.

More to the point, American prisons and jails hold more than two million citizens, compared to the fewer than 50,000 prisoners held in Nigeria. The surprising thing is that Americans believe they can teach Nigerians better ways of running the criminal justice system when it seems that what Nigerians can learn from the United States is how to avoid the high costs of what Reiman (1979) calls the theory of the pyrrhic defeat: the fact that, after spending about four times the national budget of Nigeria on the criminal justice system alone, Americans continue to name "crime" as one of their top concerns. Indeed, while Nigeria has just budgeted approximately $7 billion to run the entire country for 2003, the new US Department of Homeland Security alone has been allocated more than $30 billion.

Of course, the low number of prisoners in Nigeria compared with the number in America can be used as evidence that Nigerian law enforcement agents are inefficient. They have failed to arrest the criminals who roam the streets and intimidate ordinary citizens, while American mayors such as Rudy Giuliani of New York can claim that zero tolerance means that the "bad guys" are all locked up. However, even the greatest enthusiasts of law-and-order policies cannot claim that much success, since their law enforcement budgets rely on the continuing existence of criminals on the loose.[1] When people complain that Nigerian criminals are allowed to roam the streets, they more often mean the criminals in the corridors of power who cannot be touched, while many of the prisoners happen to be innocent poor people who lack the resources with which to bribe or influence their way out of the prison preindustrial complex.

HISTORIOGRAPHY OF AFRICAN WOMEN AND CRIMINAL INJUSTICE

In my earlier work on black women in the British criminal justice system (1997) I made a surprising discovery—that many of the black women who were placed under lockdown were completely innocent of the offences for which they had been convicted. I searched in vain for criminological perspectives that could help me to explain the unexpected finding, but I was frustrated because criminology focuses almost exclusively on the punishment of individual offenders. Jurisprudence uses the term "punishment of the innocent" to describe the imprisonment of those who have been falsely convicted (Lacey 1988). However, this concept tends to view the incarceration of "the innocent" as an unfortunate error in an otherwise just and efficient criminal justice system. As such, it fails to challenge the criminological concern with the individual and minimizes the disruptive potential of miscarriages of justice. In addition, the term "punishment" hides the fact that what is done to the innocent prisoner is a form of victimization, for which redress is required. Stuart Hall's (1980) analysis of the articulation of social relations in societies structured in dominance provides a more useful theoretical framework to understand the victimization of the innocent. Hall argues that the experience of black women must be viewed through the lens of the race, class, and gender oppression to which they are subjected. These three major social relations cannot be analyzed separately; rather, they are articulated, disarticulated, and rearticulated. Thus, the central point of "victimization as mere punishment" is that the criminal justice system institutionally violates the rights of certain groups of people because of the ways in which power relations are structured within society.

Historically, we can look at the African holocaust, otherwise known as European slavery, for an early example of victimization as mere punishment. The works of Angela Davis (1981), C. L. R. James (1980), and Walter Rodney (1972) alert us to the fact that our African ancestors did not have to commit any crime in order to be hunted down, chained (if not killed), and transported to a hostile world to be brutally exploited. Race-class-gender relations were articulated in the victimization of Africans during slavery, and African women suffered gender-specific inhumanities that are too well known to be recounted here. Contemporary African women and men continue to be locked down even when we have done nothing wrong. For example, the wives, mothers, sisters, or girlfriends of army officers are often arrested and detained with their children when their male relations are suspected of plotting unsuccessful coups and when they either flee or commit suicide. Sometimes these women are harassed, maimed, killed, or detained for years without being suspected of having committed any crime themselves. Such cases attract immense publicity because of the prominence of the individuals involved, but research indicates that what such hostages suffer is part of the daily experience of poor men and women in Africa.

Winnie Mandela (1984) had a "barometer" theory for this: she said that she was a social barometer because anything that the apartheid regime tried on her was later generalized to the oppressed in South Africa. Some scholars have tried to explain the oppressive treatment of black people by analyzing the prison system as the new slave plantation or the new ghetto (Wacquant 2001). What they have overlooked is the fact that African Americans did not have to break any law to end up in the slave plantation or in the ghetto. Rather, as Box (1983) and Reiman (1979) argue, the poor end up in prison not because they are more criminal but because they lack the resources with which to free themselves even when they are falsely accused. Meanwhile, the rich routinely get away with murder.

The concept of victimization as mere punishment requires us to rethink the purpose of the prison. The history of prison construction in Nigeria is intricately entwined with the history of attempts to repress the popular aspirations of Nigerian masses. The *African Concord* of August 6, 1990, reports that many "of Nigeria's prisons are more than one hundred years old. Records show that four prisons were built between 1800 and 1850, 11 prisons were built between 1851 and 1900, 83 were built between 1900 and 1950, and 33 prisons between 1951 to date" (Ehonwa 1996). As this article demonstrates, there was no prison in the place called Nigeria before 1800. European trading companies were the first to construct prisons in Nigeria for holding kidnapped Africans prior to the Middle Passage or for detaining Africans who resisted the banditry of Europeans in Africa.

Prisons were thus first built as part of the machinery of the brutal slave economy and are closely related to the African holocaust. In other words, the prison emerged in Nigeria not as an agency of the criminal justice system but as a tool for organized crimes against humanity. The Africans who were kidnapped and detained before being sold into slavery had committed no offences. The biological fiction of racial inferiority, not criminality, was used to justify their loss of liberty. The period 1850–1900 covers the first few decades of the official colonization of Nigeria after the 1860 Berlin conference for the partition of Africa. In this short period the number of prisons in Nigeria nearly trebled, reflecting increasing resistance to European penetration of the interior regions. The geometrical progression in the development of the prison preindustrial complex in Nigeria continued; the period 1900–1950 represents nationalist struggles when the gunboat criminology of imperialism failed to silence the call for independence and when many patriots were thrown into jail. Following independence in 1960, the rate of growth of the prison establishments slowed somewhat, reflecting the relative legitimacy of neocolonial regimes, but the rate remained high enough to reflect their continuing reliance on the colonial methodology for stifling popular protests in Nigeria.

I am not suggesting that all prisoners are freedom fighters. Some of the prisoners may have committed violent or unsocial acts. However, I am convinced that this correlation between the history of repression in Nigeria and the history of the expansion of penal institutions needs to be studied more closely. As Michel Foucault (1977) informs us, there were hardly any prisons in Europe until the late eighteenth century. Prior to that, punishment in Europe took the form of public display of torture. Foucault's genealogy of the prison implies that the prison is not an enduring feature of human society but a repressive technology of modernity. In the Nigerian context the birth of the prison cannot be separated from the histories of slavery, colonialism, and neocolonialism.

Political independence from the British has not ushered in a golden era of postcolonial justice. M. K. O. Abiola, who established *African Concord*, was one of the few rich and powerful people to suffer victimization as mere punishment in Nigeria. After claiming victory in the June 1992 presidential elections, which were annulled by the military, he was jailed and ultimately murdered in prison. While he was in detention one of his wives, Kudirat Abiola, was executed by an assassination squad set up by the bloody dictator General Sani Abacha, who also hanged Kenule Saro-Wiwa and eight other Ogoni environmental activists after framing them for the murder of four chiefs in Ogoniland. Abacha also sentenced to death several past military rulers of Nigeria, including the present president, General Obasanjo, following a trumped-up charge of complicity in a coup plot against him. Luckily for many of them, but too late for General Shehu Yaradua, who was killed in detention, General Abacha died suddenly, and they were released by his successor, General Abubakar. This close shave with death made Obasanjo pledge to support the campaign for the abolition of the death penalty worldwide.[2]

The first time that rich and powerful people found themselves behind bars in Nigeria was when Chief Obafemi Awolowo and leaders of the opposition were framed and convicted of plotting to overthrow the government by force in the first republic. Following his imprisonment a group of army officers attempted a coup with the aim of handing over power to Chief Awolowo, but they failed and were also detained in prison. A countercoup followed and facilitated a genocidal pogrom in the north against easterners. This led to attempted secession by the east, and the release of Chief Awolowo and the military officers from prison, before the onset of the Nigeria–Biafra war of 1967–1970. The second time large numbers of the elite saw themselves in prison was after the abortive military coup against the government of General Murtala Muhammad, which saw dozens of top army officers and several civilians executed for their roles in the coup attempt under General Obasanjo as the succeeding head of state. Again, following the overthrow of the second republic government of Shehu Shagari in 1983 the military rulers prosecuted and convicted many of the second republic politicians of high levels of corruption and embezzlement. They were given prison sentences ranging from twenty-five years to life. However, in 1985 the military government was overthrown, and all the rogue politicians jailed by Generals Idiagbon and Buhari were released by General Babangida. Babangida did not hesitate later to execute dozens of top military officers suspected of involvement in several abortive coups against his own military regime.

RECENT EMPIRICAL REPORTS ON NIGERIAN WOMEN IN PRISON

In the fall of 1998 I collaborated on a study of the militarization of Nigerian civil society (Agozino and Idem 2001). During the fieldwork we learned that social institutions such as the family, educational facilities, religious establishments, trade and commerce, the justice system, and community relations were permeated by the militaristic ethos of a society that had experienced long terms of military rule. Husbands assumed the roles of commanders-in-chief of their families, beating wives and children; educational institutions witnessed authoritarian styles of administration, while students formed secret cults with which to commit murder or gang-rape female students; religious and ethnic violence was the order of the day; and due process was almost non-existent. Militarism promoted violent means for settling quarrels in civil society: for example, traders would hire armed soldiers to murder their rivals. The militarism of Nigerian society is also reflected in policing and the prisons, which are feared as institutions imbued with violence, including sexual violence, corruption, and the rule of force.

Police Violence and Detention
The economic desperation of most families due to the Structural Adjustment Programmes decreed by the World Bank and the

International Monetary Fund means that families are forced to choose which children should be educated and which should be left in ignorance. This choice leads to the continued undereducation of girls, who are then more vulnerable to injustice and exploitation as young women. Moreover, the crushing poverty imposed on Nigerians as part of this "global lockdown" has led to popular protests by the masses, resulting in the widespread arrest of women either for participation in such protests or for being family members of suspected men. In 2001 Nigerian women stripped naked to intimidate oil workers and seize control of the facilities of Chevron Texaco, to press home their demand that the company that polluted the environment from which they could no longer earn their living as peasants should pay reparations to the community and provide jobs for their sons (not surprisingly, given patriarchy, the women did not also demand jobs for the daughters, wives, and mothers of the community). The women decided to lead the protest after the young men who had previously engaged in direct action were arrested and jailed. Although the women were not arrested, the disdainful response of the politicians was to ignore them and punish them with the bitter cold air of the open sea, where some of them reportedly caught pneumonia. Thus, the women did not have to go to prison to experience the cruelty of the global lockdown.

In 1984 Maroko slum was demolished on the order of the governor of Lagos State, and 300,000 ghetto dwellers instantly became homeless. Some were forced to sleep under bridges, but a few found refuge in some uncompleted housing estates that the government was developing. Again, the state military governor ordered armed police to eject the refugees, and in the process as many as seventeen women and girls were raped by the officers.

On the topic of arrest and detention, Akumadu (1995) reports that women are treated in a crude and unconstitutional manner. Many women are not told they are under arrest until they are lured to the police station under the pretext of helping police with investigations, and some are not told of the charge against them until they appear in court. To make matters worse, the police are given wide discretion by the law to make arrests without warrants under various circumstances. A prostitute, Adizat Mohammed, detained at the Kano police post, reported that the police raid prostitutes only when they are broke, and that those who pay the N300 "fine" or bribe demanded by the police are released immediately. Another woman who was a trader reported that she displayed her wares in front of her house once during a compulsory national environmental sanitation exercise when police officers arrested her and confiscated her wares. She was released on bail after two days in detention, but her wares were never returned to her. Another woman, Kemi (surname withheld), had a quarrel with her neighbour and was arrested with her baby. Both were held in detention for a week without any provision for child care. She suspected that the police officers must have been "settled" or bribed by her neighbour to torture her and her baby. The result of the overzealous use of detention by the police is that their tiny cells are always overcrowded, and the only toilet facility in such crowded cells is usually a bucket.

In the cells older inmates extort "state money" or taxes from new inmates, and refusal to pay can result in physical abuse. This practice is more common among male detainees, but they also extend their demands to female detainees, and any resistance is met with threats to throw the woman into a cell occupied by men. Such psychological torture is usually enough to make women acquiesce to extortion. In addition, food is rarely served to the detainees, and when served it is often not fit for human consumption. Thus, the detainees are expected to bribe police officers to be allowed to buy their own food from vendors at the police station. Women reported being tortured during interrogation by having a candlestick or the neck of a bottle inserted into their private parts by male police officers in an attempt to get them to confess to crimes they did not commit. The suspects are usually not allowed access to an attorney, and the illiterate ones are not even read their rights; police officers write up statements for them to sign with a thumbprint, and they do not even realize they are signing confessions.

One woman, Esther Ayorinde, went to a police station to complain that, by moving her husband from that station to another one far away, it was difficult for her to visit him. Her husband had been arrested following a quarrel with his elder brother over the sale of their father's land by the brother. The police officers arrested the wife for complaining and detained her in the same cell where suspected male armed robbers were held. She was gang-raped. Women rarely report cases of rape in custody out of a feeling of shame. Theresa Akumadu (1995), in *Patterns of Abuse of Women's Rights in Employment and Police Custody in Nigeria,* reports that women seeking redress for sexual harassment at work are often subjected to further violence by the police. She gives the example of a typist, Uzoma Okorie, who was maliciously accused of theft by her boss after rebuffing his advances. During her interrogation police officers gave her what they called the "VIP treatment" by stripping her naked, cuffing her hands behind a pillar, and inserting the neck of a bottle into her vagina while flogging her bare buttocks until she bled so much that she fainted, only to recover in the police hospital days later.

PRISONS

Recent research on Nigerian prisons focuses on overcrowding and concerns about a growing population. Agomoh, Adeyemi, and Ogbebor (2001, 6) reported that there are currently "148 prisons and about 83 satellite prisons or lock-ups (where few prisoners are held in court buildings), 10 prison farms and 9 cottage industries for the training of inmates." In 1999 the prison population was 40,899, and out of this number 21,579 or 52.8 percent were prisoners awaiting trial. While these figures appear much fewer than the two million Americans behind bars, we should note that Nigerian prisons have a combined capacity of 25,000, and are therefore significantly overcrowded. If the number of people awaiting trial were given bail, then more than half of the prisoners would be released, and the prisons would be nearer their full capacity. If the innocent people who are wrongly convicted were also released from prison, then the Nigerian prison population would be much lower still. And if non-violent offenders were corrected in the community, then Nigeria would not be in need of many prisons at all. Moreover, some of the prisoners are too young to be in prison. For example, in 1991, out of a total of 52,129 prisoners, 1,204 were below the age of sixteen. These youths were housed with adult prisoners, and they were thereby exposed to sexual and physical abuse by the older male prisoners and guards. Agomoh, Adeyemi, and Ogbebor (2001, 18) give the sex distribution of the population of Nigerian prisons by state as follows in Table 15.1 (note that Bayelsa did not record any prisoners, probably because it was a newly created state that was yet to construct its own prison facility).

Table 15.1
Distribution of Prisoners by Sex and State, June 1999

State	Males	Females	Total
Abia	1,117	27	1,144
Adamawa	1,527	20	1,547
Akwa-Ibom	1,323	28	1,351
Anambra	1,720	22	1,742
Bauchi	1,048	4	1,052
Bayelsa	-	-	-
Benue	603	3	606
Borno	1,609	9	1,618
Cross River	875	18	893
Delta	1,535	58	1,593
Ebonyi	709	16	725
Edo	1,744	67	1,811
Ekiti	273	6	279
Enugu	1,278	27	1,305

Gombe	586	7	593
Imo	1,401	40	1,441
Jigawa	647	5	652
Kaduna	2,016	22	2,038
Kano	1,431	40	1,471
Katsina	1,063	12	1,075
Kebbi	946	11	957
Kogi	286	3	289
Kwara	309	5	314
Lagos	5,442	92	5,534
Nasarawa	567	4	571
Niger	970	5	975
Ogun	689	11	700
Ondo	725	1	726
Osun	305	10	315
Oyo	745	16	761
Plateau	1,012	16	1,028
Rivers	2,064	67	2,131
Sokoto	854	19	873
Taraba	1,149	19	1,168
Yobe	631	2	633
Zamfara	681	6	687
Abuja	356	8	425
Total	40,260	726	40,986

From the above statistics we can see that Nigerian prisons reflect the global phenomenon whereby incarcerated populations are mainly male. The major difference between these findings and my study of black women and the British criminal justice system (Agozino 1997) is that in Nigeria social relations of race are almost irrelevant, given the relative homogeneity of the population.

In the place of race the politics of ethnicity is articulated with gender and class to explain the preponderance of women from certain parts of the country in women's prisons. The fact that the prisons in the predominantly Muslim north and those in the predominantly Christian south of the country are not remarkably different in the gender composition of prisoners is an indication that religion and ethnicity are not significant variables for the explanation of the prison population. Whether the prisoners are male or female, young or old, they are more likely to be poor, uneducated, and unemployed. However, more recent reports of the use of sharia law to oppress Nigerian women in the northern parts of the country indicate that women do not have to be in prison to qualify as inmates of the global lockdown.

Similar oppressive gender social control is also found in the south, where inhumane treatment is reserved for poor widows, while the practice of female genital mutilation remains widespread. The high populations of women in the prisons of Rivers State, Lagos State, and Kaduna State may be a reflection of the fact that these are trouble spots of recent ethnic/religious conflict that law enforcement agents try to repress through mass arrests and detentions without trial. Women do not have to riot to become suspects and be detained, since the police use the practice of holding women as hostages when they cannot find a son, husband, brother, or boyfriend who is wanted as a suspect.

In 1993 the Civil Liberties Organization (CLO) published a report written by Osaze Lanre Ehonwa. The report documented the cruel conditions of Nigerian men in prison, but hardly commented on the plight of women and children. The focus on men is common in "mainstream" criminology, where women remain invisible. To its credit, the CLO saw the shortcomings of its first edition and decided to issue a revised edition, in which women and children were mentioned, and a second volume (1996) was dedicated exclusively to women and children who are hidden in the shadows of prison walls. The report quotes Nigerian State High Court Judge Alhassan Idoko, who describes Nigerian prisons as ghettos and shanty towns where inmates are forced to live on top of one another due to congestion.[3] The use of mass release or amnesty by politicians trying to save money or seeking cheap popularity makes it difficult to assess congestion or to predict future trends. For example, the total prison population was 25,622 in 1979 and 31,000 in 1990, but the average monthly prison population grew from 32,000 in 1979 to 60,000 in 1990. The fact that the average monthly prison population was nearly twice the annual prison population in 1990 is indicative of the practice of mass arrests and mass releases by the military government, which was facing a crisis of hegemony from a people who refused to be intimidated. Overall prison congestion in male and female prisons is illustrated by Ehonwa (1993) in Table 15.2. The rate of congestion appears in parentheses.

Table 15.2
Selected Prison Capacities and Actual Prison Populations in Nigeria

Prison	Kirikiri Maximum	Ikoyi	Kirikiri Women's
Capacity	956	800	105
Population	2,596 (171.55%)	2,861 (257.63%)	137 (30.47%)

Other prisons are even more congested than the few examples from Lagos State shown above. For instance, Ado-Ekiti prison is overpopulated at a rate of 557.58 percent; Ogwashi-Uku prison at 456.86 percent; Auchi at 398.75 percent; Benin at 349.55 percent; Lafiagi at 318.18 percent; Sapele at 285.31 percent; Biu at 285.00 percent; Potiskum at 274.67 percent; Ilorin at 238.84 percent; Kirikiri medium security at 236.36 percent; Kwale at 222.73 percent; Enugu at 221.16 percent; Nguru at 213.98 percent; Warri at 202.69 percent; Okene at 183.33 percent; and Owo at 179.33 percent (Ehonwa 1993). Most of these highly congested prisons are in the southern part of the country.

It is evident that the female prison in Kirikiri is much less congested than the male prisons. The temptation here is for mainstream criminologists to deny that the women are undergoing repressive and inhumane conditions in prison. As Pat Carlen (1983) argues with reference to female prisons in the United Kingdom, the fact that they are relatively less overcrowded than the male ones often leads to the claim that female prisons function less for punishment, and they are inaccurately likened to colleges and motels. Such claims are grossly incorrect, because there is evidence that women are more likely to end up in prison as hostages of the law when men close to them are suspected of doing something wrong. The patriarchal assumption that conditions in female prisons are good derives from the use of male imprisonment as the false standard with which to measure how women should be treated. The consequence is that, even when innocent women are being unlawfully held as hostages in prison, there is little outrage because the difference between the capacity of the only women's prison in the country and the actual prison population is seen to be "so marginal that it is practically of no consequence" (Ehonwa 1996, 19).

The report goes on to indicate that women make up 3.4 percent of the prison population in Nigeria, but adds that, when women were kept in rooms within male prisons, their rooms were "reasonably spacious" even when thirty-one women were forced to share two rooms. However, the report warns that, if there are no plans to tackle congestion, the female prison and the female wings in male prisons might soon become as overcrowded as the male ones. The report tends to consider women only as an afterthought, but Table 15.3 and Figure 15.1 indicate the reasons for overcrowding in Nigerian prisons.

Table 15.3
Categories of Prisoners in Nigeria: 1988-1995

	1988	1989	1990	1991	1992	1995
Remand	19,745	21,063	19,219	21,615	19,985	35,750
Convict	31,871	31,193	28,448	30,511	21,767	17,902
Others	1,592	1,640	6,412	7,874	8,210	1,348

Figure 15.1
Bar Chart of Categories of Nigerian Prisoners: 1988–1995

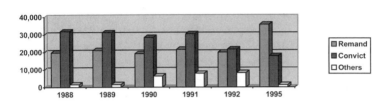

The figures suggest that, if the prisoners awaiting trial were given bail, the prison population would be nearer its normal capacity. Moreover, if children who are illegally detained in prison and non-violent offenders were corrected in the community rather than being held in prison, Nigerian prisons would be almost entirely empty. The category of "Others" in prison is not explained in the report, but they could include those who were detained without being charged with any offence, so they can be said to be neither convicts nor remand prisoners. From all the discussions above, we can predict that the proportion of women awaiting trial or those convicted of non-violent offences or those simply held as hostages or as "Others" will be extremely high.

In 1993 the CLO published a report on "prisoners in the shadows." These children and women are hidden behind the walls of the prison and are hidden from public curiosity about prison conditions, partly because prison authorities restrict access to women in prison even by researchers. This report shows that, although women prisoners are fewer in number, the rate of increase in the female population far outstrips that of the male population in prison. This is partly due to a media panic in Nigeria suggesting that women's liberation is leading to women committing as much crime as men.

That was part of the reason why the military government introduced the double jeopardy decree in the early 1990s to seek the retrial of Nigerians who had served prison sentences for drug offences abroad and to sentence them to fresh terms of imprisonment in Nigeria (Agozino 1997). Apparently, the inhumane conditions of the prison industrial complexes in Europe and North America were regarded by brutal dictators in Nigeria as child's play and not proper punishment. However, Oloruntimehin and Ogedengbe (1992) reported that patriarchal oppression of women is responsible for increasing substance abuse among women in Nigeria. The same patriarchal and imperialist oppression is also noticeable in the huge number of women being trafficked to Europe to work as prostitutes to earn money with which to support their families at home.

CONCLUSION: TOWARD COUNTERCOLONIAL CRIMINOLOGY

This chapter has demonstrated that Nigerian women do not have to commit any crime in order to fall under the repressive gaze of the global lockdown. While Nigeria has a relatively low rate of incarceration, its prisons are significantly overcrowded. In part this is due to the large numbers of imprisoned men and women who have not been convicted of any offence, as well as children and significant numbers of women held as hostages for men wanted as suspects. The crisis of Nigerian prisons reflects the larger crisis of underdevelopment in Nigeria. I therefore conclude with a discussion of policies that African leaders are touting as solutions to the problems of underdevelopment, including mass poverty and preventable death, mass illiteracy, and political repression. According to the African heads of state who met in Abuja, Nigeria, in 2001 to adopt the New Economic Plan for African Development (NEPAD), these problems are due to a lack of foreign investment in Africa. They argue that NEPAD will be the African equivalent of the Marshall Plan that helped to stabilize Europe after World War II.

I suspect that those who drafted NEPAD were making a practical joke on the suffering African masses. For a start, the acronym is notoriously close to NEPA or Nigerian Electric Power Authority, which is popularly known in Nigeria as "never expect power always" (or even at all).[4] NEPAD could equally be translated as "never expect progress, African democrats." This would be a fitting translation of NEPAD, given that the African leaders promote it as an original African initiative that will involve the masses in the development of the continent, yet the masses were not consulted when NEPAD was drafted. In addition, leaders promise that NEPAD will be to Africa what Marshall was to Europe, but they forgot that Marshall was a government grant given to Europe by the United States, whereas NEPAD involves begging for private foreign investment. Also, NEPAD is promoted as being gender-sensitive when it is based on the same economic policies of structural adjustment that the World Bank and IMF have been imposing on African countries to the detriment of women (Mikell 1997). Contrary to these predictions, NEPAD will lock African people more tightly into the cells of the imperialist global lockdown.

A more viable policy for Africa is that championed by Kwame Nkrumah (1968). A People's Republic of Africa would immediately eliminate the conditions of neocolonialism and halt the multiplication of military budgets in Africa. This alone would free up enormous resources for education, health care, and social security planning. A People's Republic of Africa United Democratically (PRAUD) would achieve more than the beggars' lobby that is called NEPAD or the empty promises of African Union. Such a powerful republic would effectively lead the struggle to obtain reparations for the African holocaust instead of the current situation, whereby President Obasanjo begs for foreign investment while dismissing the call for reparations as unrealistic.

While the crafters of NEPAD view the integration of Africa into the global economy as a panacea for social and economic underdevelopment, critics of neoliberal globalization have developed a different analysis. Fidel Castro in his address to the United Nations conference on the financing of development in Mexico, 2002, proposed that global economic integration was in fact a key reason for underdevelopment. According to him,

> the existing world economic order constitutes a system of plundering and exploitation like no other in history.... [In 2001] more than 826 million people were actually starving; there were 854 million illiterate adults; 325 million children do not attend school, 2 billion people have no access to low cost medications and 2.4 billion people lack the basic sanitation conditions. Not less than 11 million children under age 5 perish every year from preventable causes, while half a million go blind for lack of vitamin A; the life span of the population in the developed world is 30 years higher than that of the people living in Sub-Saharan Africa.... In the face of the present deep crisis, a still worse future is offered where the economic, social and ecological tragedy of an increasingly ungovernable world would never be resolved, and where the number of the poor and the starving would grow higher, as if a larger part of humanity were doomed.

While most criminologists busy themselves theorizing the punishment of offenders (as if everyone who is "punished" is necessarily an offender), Castro has proved himself a better criminologist by highlighting crimes of genocidal proportions that result from the global economic lockdown. The silence of criminologists on such massive criminal policies around the world is actually underdeveloping criminology as a discipline.

Criminal injustice systems worldwide have contributed to the inhumane treatment of people of colour, especially people of African descent. The battle of ideas has been a critical component of the criminal justice apparatus. This is why criminology is a common discipline in universities located in Europe and North America, while the discipline is hardly existent in Africa (apart from South Africa), Asia, and South America, for criminology was developed to serve imperialism as a tool for the repression of others.[5]

An old African proverb says that, if you hold someone on the ground, you too will not be able to rise until you let that person go. The prison officer is also a prisoner of some sort. This

saying provides insight into the nature of the global lockdown—
we are all inmates of the global prison whether we are behind
bars or in front of bars or branded with bar codes. Our collective
responsibility for imperialism (as the workers, investors, and
consumers who oil its machines and the teachers who train its
troops) means that we need to ask ourselves what we can do to
reverse the process of decolonization perpetrated by free-trade
agreements and IMF-led socioeconomic policies. Criminologists
need to study the history of the solidarity between their discipline
and imperialism, to learn from global struggles for decolonization,
and to develop a new methodology. Only in this way can we
use what Amilcar Cabral (1979) called the weapon of theory to
strengthen anti-imperialist struggles around the world.

NOTES

1   Increasingly, those "criminals" include police officers such as the killers of Amadou Diallo and the brutal attackers of Abner Louima and the corporate cowboys who fraudulently wreck the economy.
2   Close to the end of his first term in office as an executive president in Nigeria, he had yet to sign a bill for the abolition of capital punishment in Nigeria; such a bill was introduced only during the campaign for Obasanjo's re-election in 2003.
3   In Nigeria the term "congestion" is used rather than the term "overcrowding."
4   Despite national production of billions of dollars of oil every year, the Nigerian electricity infrastructure is so poor that a personal generator is a prerequisite for many businesses and middle-class homeowners.
5   For a more detailed discussion of this point, see Agozino (2003).

REFERENCES

Agomoh, U., A. Adeyemi, and V. Ogbebor. (2001). *The Prison Service and Penal Reform in Nigeria: A Synthesis Study*. Lagos: PRAWA.
Agozino, B. (1997). *Black Women and the Criminal Justice System: Towards the Decolonisation of Victimisation*. Aldershot: Ashgate.
---. (2003). *Counter Colonial Criminology: A Critique of Imperialist Reason*. London: Pluto.

Agozino, B., and U. Idem. (2001). *Nigeria: Democratising a Militarised Civil Society*. London: CDD [Center for Democratic Development].

Akumadu, T. (1995). *Patterns of Abuse of Women's Rights in Employment and Police Custody in Nigeria*. Lagos: Civil Liberties Organization.

Baudrillard, J. (1983). *Simulations*. New York: Semiotext(e).

Box, S. (1983). *Power, Crime, and Mystification*. London: Tavistock.

Cabral, A. (1979). *Unity and Struggle*. New York: Monthly Review Press.

Carlen, P. (1983). *Women's Imprisonment*. London: Routledge and Kegan Paul.

Castro, F. (2002). Address to the International Conference on Financing for Development, Monterry, Mexico, March 21.

Davis, A. (1981). *Women, Race, and Class*. London: Women's Press.

Ehonwa, O. L. (1993). *Prisoners in the Shadows: A Report on Women and Children in Five Nigerian Prisons*. Lagos: Civil Liberties Organization.

---. (1996). *Behind the Wall: A Report on Prison Conditions in Nigeria and the Nigerian Prison System*. Lagos: Civil Liberties Organization.

Foucault, M. (1977). *Discipline and Punish: The Birth of the Prison*. London: Allen Lane.

Hall, S. (1980). "Race, Articulation, and Societies Structured in Dominance." In *Sociological Theories: Race and Colonialism*, ed. UNESCO. Paris: UNESCO.

James, C. L. R. (1980). *The Black Jacobins: Toussaint l'Ouverture and the San Diego Revolution*. London: Allison and Busby.

Lacey, N. (1988). *State Punishment: Political Principles and Community Values*. London: Routledge.

Mandela, W. (1984). *Part of My Soul*, ed. A. Benjamin. Harmondsworth: Penguin.

Mikell, Gwendolyn, ed. (1997). *African Feminism: The Politics of Survival for Sub-Saharan Africa*. Philadelphia: University of Pennsylvania Press.

Nkrumah, K. (1968). *Neo-Colonialism: The Last Stage of Imperialism*. London: Heinemann.

Oloruntimehin, O., and R. O. Ogedengbe. (1992). "Women and Substance Abuse in Nigeria." In *Women and Substance Abuse*, ed. H. L-N. WHO/PSA/92.9. Geneva: World Health Organization, 30-41.

Reiman, J. (1979). *The Rich Get Richer and the Poor Get Prison*. New York: Wiley.

Rodney, W. (1972). *How Europe Underdeveloped Africa*. London: Bogle l'Ouverture.

Wacquant, L. (2001). "Deadly Symbiosis: When Ghetto and Prison Meet and Merge." *Punishment and Society*, 3:1, 95-134.

CHAPTER 16

PROTECTING THE HUMAN RIGHTS OF PEOPLE WITH MENTAL HEALTH DISABILITIES IN AFRICAN PRISONS

Uju Agomoh

INTRODUCTION

Persons with mental illnesses often face unique difficulties in ensuring respect for their basic human rights, both in the community and in mental institutions. There is growing international recognition of this fact and a consensus across the criminal justice spectrum that something has gone painfully wrong: "the nation's [US] jails and prisons have become mental health facilities—a role for which they are singularly ill-equipped" (Fellner and Abramsky 2004). It has been argued that the mentally ill are victims of two failed public policies: the failure of public officials to ensure an effective mental health system, and an overly ambitious criminal justice system that tends to send people to prison even for low-level, non-violent crimes.

This chapter addresses some of the human rights issues related to having mentally ill persons in prisons. This topic covers three broad areas in which people are categorized:

(1) mentally disabled persons who have been convicted of a criminal offence;
(2) mentally disabled persons on remand who have been charged with a criminal offence; and
(3) mentally disabled persons on remand who have not been charged with any criminal offence.

Here I am concerned primarily with the third category, though I also make brief references to the other two categories when necessary. People grouped in the third category are commonly referred to as "civil lunatics," while the others are referred to as "criminal lunatics."[1]

The practice of imprisoning mentally disabled persons raises critical questions. The rationale for imprisonment comes into question. Such practices also challenge both the human rights posture and the quality of health care delivery of the state in question. Our main focus here is the former, but the issue itself calls into question the "right of everyone to the enjoyment of the highest attainable standard of physical and mental health."[2] Aside from questioning the macrolevel concept of imprisonment, the practice of imprisoning mentally ill people also raises microlevel administrative issues, such as access to fair trials,[3] and protection against torture, inhumane or degrading treatment,[4] and arbitrary detention.[5]

When considering the question of criminal lunatics we are mainly concerned with the issue of a fair trial and the fairness/effectiveness of the review procedure(s) where applicable. With civil lunatics the key issue is arbitrary detention. The issue of torture or inhumane and degrading treatment becomes relevant when we consider the conditions of treatment in detention.

MENTALLY DISABLED PERSONS AND THE CRIMINAL JUSTICE SYSTEM

In most African countries mentally disabled people are detained in or commuted to prisons.[6] This section highlights the cases of Nigeria and The Gambia, and compares them with the system in the United Kingdom. The fact that the legal systems of these African countries[7] are modelled on the English common-law system presents the opportunity for a structural comparison of conditions in each context. European human rights case law on this issue may also provide some guidance for our look at this issue within the African human rights system. In Nigeria civil lunatics are often detained at the insistence of family members, with the support of the police. It has been alleged that these families are unable to pay for the treatment of these persons in psychiatric hospitals or, for other reasons, do not wish to send their family members to a psychiatric hospital. There are several issues here about the treatment of mentally disabled persons within the criminal justice system.

Procedures for Detention

The first issue relates to the procedure for detaining mentally disabled people in prisons. The process seems to be plagued by arbitrariness and a lack of due process. For instance, one of the prisoners detained as a civil lunatic in Enugu prison in Nigeria informed me that her husband had requested her detention in the prison because he wanted to marry another woman. The prison officers confirmed that the husband did marry another woman and that his first wife clearly suffered from postpartum disorder, which occurs usually after childbirth. She had suffered three previous episodes, which had been treated in a psychiatric hospital, and during the most recent episode her husband had decided to have her detained in prison instead. She was in prison with her newly born child when I met her. Prison staff noted that her husband had never visited her in prison. Another prisoner, a young man, reported that he was detained in prison only because his uncle wanted to sell the land of his deceased father and clearly wanted him out of the way. While these reports have not been fully investigated, they raise serious issues regarding the unlawfulness and arbitrariness of the arrest and detention process.

Article 9 of the ICCPR provides that no one shall be subjected to arbitrary arrest or detention. Section 32(1) of the Constitution of Nigeria reads thus: "Every person shall be entitled to his personal liberty and no person shall be deprived of such liberty save in the following cases and in accordance with the procedure permitted by law.... In the case of a person suffering from infection or contagious disease, persons of unsound mind, persons addicted to drugs or alcohol or vagrants, for the purpose of their care or treatment or the protection of the community." In justifying its position on the imprisonment of mentally ill persons the government argues that this exception should apply to "people of unsound mind who are categorized as threats to the peace and coexistence of society." It also argues that there are safeguards against abuse of the process, because, as was held in *Obolo v. Commission of Police*, it is the duty of the person arresting or exercising public authority to restrict the liberty of the citizen to show that his actions are in accordance with the laws of the land.[8] This has proven to be an inadequate safeguard. There seems to be wide discretion in police practice and there is no external oversight mechanism to supervise these powers. Also, what is the implication of the phrase "in accordance with the procedure permitted by law"? Does the fact that there is a provision in legislation or regulations against such practices make the detention of mentally ill persons in prisons "lawful"? How difficult is it to establish that arrest and detention were arbitrary? As established in the European case of *Winterwerp v. Netherlands* (1979), the deprivation of liberty must not only be described as "lawful" if it is prescribed by the municipal law but also must be lawful in a conventional sense. Detention may be "arbitrary" even if properly motivated *if* it is not proportionate to the attainment of the purpose of Article 5.1, which is similar in substance to Article 9 of the ICCPR stated above. The African Commission seems to echo this. Article 6 of the African Charter, which prohibits arbitrary arrest and detention, states that "every individual shall have the right to liberty and security of his person. No one may be deprived of his freedom except for reasons and conditions previously laid down by law. In particular, no one may be arbitrarily arrested or detained." The position of the African Commission is that mere mention of the phrase "except for reasons and conditions previously laid down" in Article 6 does not imply that any domestic law may justify the deprivation of such persons' freedom, and neither can a state party to the African Charter shelve this responsibility by recourse to this limitation.

Domestic laws must conform to internationally established norms and standards.[9] On the issue of whether the detention of persons believed to be mentally ill or disabled falls within the ambit of Article 6 of the African Charter, the commission stated that there are no violations of human rights in cases where mentally ill persons are detained in prisons. This, it argued, is because Article 6 was not intended to cater to situations where persons in need of medical assistance become institutionalized. This position is highly contestable. First, if the persons are detained in prison, how can such an institution aid in progressing their best interests or the best interests of society? Second, this position is too simple in its assumption that the process of institutionalizing persons in need of help is sufficiently met through criminal justice institutions. The persons responsible for such acts and the place/procedure of such institutionalization should be subject to the test of "arbitrariness," much as they are subject to such tests in cases where the prisoner is not mentally disabled.

Conditions of Detention

The second issue relates to the conditions of detention/ imprisonment of mentally disabled persons. Most of them sleep on bare floors in the prison or on torn mattresses and blankets, a situation also common to other prisoners, especially those on remand, because of overcrowding and lack of adequate resources. There is also no clear segregation[10] between the civil lunatics and the criminal lunatics, or between juveniles and adults, or between convicted and remanded. Those with babies have no special units. The guiding principles that decide where a prisoner is warehoused seem to be manageability and availability of cells. These principles clearly violate the international human rights provisions relating to the treatment of prisoners and persons in detention. Article 8 of the ICCPR states that "the different categories of prisoners shall be kept in separate institutions or parts of institutions taking account of their sex, age, criminal record, the legal reason for their detention and the necessities of their treatment."

The conditions of detention above raise concerns about violations of the rights to protection of every person from torture and cruel, inhumane, and degrading treatment. Article 7 of the Nigerian Constitution provides that "every individual is entitled to respect for the dignity of his person and accordingly... no person shall be subjected to torture or to inhuman or degrading treatment." In addition, Nigeria recently ratified the Convention against Torture.[11] The African Charter prohibits torture and cruel, inhumane, or degrading punishment and treatment. Article 5 states that "every individual shall have the right to the respect of the dignity inherent in human being and to the recognition of his legal status. All forms of exploitation and degradation of man, particularly slavery, slave trade, torture, cruel, inhuman or degrading punishment and treatment, shall be prohibited."

In *Media Rights Agenda v. Nigeria*[12] the African Commission held that the phrase "cruel, inhuman or degrading punishment and treatment" is to be interpreted to extend to the widest possible protection against abuses, whether physical or mental. Also, the commission held that exposing victims to "personal suffering and indignity" can take many forms.[13] In *Purohit and Moore v. The Gambia,* a recent case on the Lunacy Detention Act (LDA) of The Gambia, the commission drew inspiration from Principle 1(2) of the United Nations Principles for the Protection of Persons with Mental Illness and the Improvement of Mental Care, which requires that "all persons with mental illness, or who are being treated as such, shall be treated with humanity and respect for the inherent dignity of the human person."

The Review Process

The third issue relates to the lack of independent review procedures for assessing cases in which mentally ill persons are being detained in prisons. This lack of external review leads to a violation of the fair trial procedures and the principles of natural justice. There is no Mental Health Review Tribunal or a similar body with powers to release patients detained in the African countries under study. There is also no effective statutory instrument(s) for ensuring due process and fair trial procedures in the handling of these cases. Therefore, there are no national safeguards for protecting these persons against unjust and arbitrary detention.

In the United Kingdom there are some safeguards. An application can be made to detain a person in hospital for up to six months upon the written recommendation of two registered medical practitioners.[14] Restricted patients are entitled to apply for a review of their cases once every twelve months, and the home secretary has the discretion to refer a case of a restricted patient for hearing at any time he or she thinks fit.[15] He or she is also obliged to do this if the patient has not requested a review for three consecutive years.[16] Mandatory up-to-date medical reports from the patient's responsible medical officer, and other reports from sources such as social workers, psychologists, and independent psychiatrists, as well as the home secretary's statement, are required for every case under review.[17] Patients are also entitled to receive a copy of every document relevant to their applications.[18] In assessing eligibility for discharge for non-restricted and civil patients consideration is given to presence/lack of continuing mental disorder of a degree requiring detention in hospital for medical treatment or detention for their own health/safety or the protection of others.[19] In these cases the tribunal also has the general discretion to discharge the patients in any case, unlike with restricted patients, for whom there is the lack of such general discretion to discharge.

While the above can arguably be described as "safeguards," some of the provisions and practices have been criticized. In a general sense the independent tribunals in the United Kingdom continue to place mentally disabled persons in disempowered positions. While in Nigeria mentally disabled prisoners are at the total mercy of the prison service, mentally disabled persons in the United Kingdom are subject to the total discretion of mental health institutions.

In *X v. United Kingdom*[20] the tribunals' inability to authorize the discharge of restricted patients (as was the case under the

1959 Mental Health Act) was challenged. It was found that such practices were in violation of the European Convention on Human Rights (ECHR). In attempting to address such restrictions and unethical practices the United Kingdom implemented the 1983 Act. Another case worth noting is *R. v. (1) Mental Health Review Tribunal, North and East London Region, (2) Secretary of State ex parte H*,[21] where the Court of Appeal made a declaration of incompatibility with the ECHR in respect of sections 72 and 73 of the 1983 Act. The decision of the court stated that the compulsory detention of a patient cannot be implemented unless it can reliably be shown that the patient was suffering from mental disorder(s) unwarranted and contrary to Articles 5(1) and 5(4) of the ECHR. These articles relate to provisions on arbitrary detention. In 1998 an expert committee was commissioned to assess how the mental health legislation can reflect a balance between the protection of the rights of individual patients and the need to ensure public safety (Department of Health 1999a, 1999b, 2000; also see the Dangerous Severe Personality Disorder [DSPD] Order). Some of the new proposals include the extension of the tribunals' function to confirm compulsory treatment orders, and the renewal and review of such orders (Holloway and Grounds 2003).

Regarding the quality and procedural content of the review by a court, the Strasbourg jurisprudence has established that a court-like body sitting in quasi-judicial capacity will satisfy the requirement of Article 5.4 of the ECHR (Padfield, Liebling, and Arnold 1990, 105). The key requirements are as follows.

1. An oral hearing must be provided.
2. The detainee has the right to call witnesses, examine them, and cross-examine them.
3. The detainee must have adequate time and facilities to prepare his or her case.
4. The review of remedy should be exercised at reasonable intervals, and the decision must be taken speedily by the reviewer.

The hearings do not necessarily have to be conducted in public. The entitlement of persons with mental illness to be treated as such and to be heard and represented by counsel in determinations affecting their lives, livelihood, liberty, property, or status, is particularly recognized in Principles 16, 17, and 18 of the UN Principles for the Protection of Persons with Mental Illness and Improvement of Mental Care.

Following provisions in the UK system of institutionalization of persons with mental illnesses, the African Commission implemented *Purohit,* Article 7(1) of the African Charter. This article necessitates that, in circumstances where persons are to be detained, they should be presented at the least with the opportunity to challenge the matter of their detention before the competent jurisdictions that should have ruled on their detention. On this basis the commission held that The Gambia Lunacy Detention Act violates Article 7(1)(a) and (c). This is because the Act does not contain any provisions for the review or appeal of an order of detention, for any remedy for detention made in error, for any wrong diagnosis or treatment, or for the legal right to challenge the two separate medical certificates that constitute the legal basis of detention. While such revisions and policies attempt to deal with the unethical detention of mentally ill persons inside prisons, the problems in Nigeria and the United Kingdom illustrate that this human rights violation is not being addressed in either the bureaucratic systems of the United Kingdom or the criminal justice procedures of Nigeria.

Treatment of Mentally Ill Persons in Prison

The fourth issue is the quality of treatment received by mentally ill patients in prison. In Nigeria, often these patients receive no psychiatric treatment. Sometimes they are locked up in solitary cells and in chains if violent. Even when medications are prescribed, few or no funds are made available to purchase the medications.[22] There are often no psychiatrists working inside the prisons.[23] In Enugu prison two psychiatric nurses from the Federal Neuropsychiatric Hospital Enugu are usually posted to the female prison unit (to attend to the female prisoners) and the male asylum section respectively. At the federal neuropsychiatric hospital in Calabar staff sometimes arranged community outreach programmes to the prisons. These arrangements were made at the discretion of the hospitals. While these efforts are highly innovative and commendable, such ad hoc arrangements are far from satisfactory.[24] The government needs to take more positive steps in providing a comprehensive system that guarantees due process, as well as access to high standards of both physical and mental health, in line with its international human rights obligations. The United Nations has affirmed that all incarcerated persons with mental illness "should receive the best available mental health care."[25] It has been rightly argued that "society has no right to detain patients for the purposes of treatment if the resources for that treatment are inadequate" (Holloway and Grounds 2003, 146).[26]

It is important to note that in the case of *Estelle v. Gamble*[27] the US Supreme Court ruled that medical care or the lack thereof is unconstitutional (under the Eighth Amendment) when it involves the "unnecessary and wanton infliction of pain," and extends to the "deliberate indifference to serious medical needs of prisoners, including the treatment of mental illness." However, substandard quality of care, negligence, or malpractice does not suffice to establish a violation under the Eighth Amendment.

As held in *Farmer v. Brennan*,[28] officials can be found to be deliberately indifferent based not on what they should have known but on what they actually know. This preference for subjective criteria rather than an objective test (constructive knowledge) is certainly very limiting. It does not provide adequate safeguards for addressing violations of the rights of the mentally ill. Interestingly, Article 16(1) of the African Charter also provides for the right to enjoy the "best attainable state of physical and mental health," and Article 16(2) calls for state parties to take necessary measures to protect the health of their people and ensure that they receive medical attention when they are sick. Article 18(4) of the African Charter stipulates that the aged and disabled have the right to special measures of protection in keeping with their physical or moral needs.

The questions therefore are, first, why should the state keep mentally disabled persons in prison and, second, why does the state continually fail to provide adequate treatment for these persons? Such actions violate UNSMR Rule 62, which states that medical services of the institution shall seek to detect and treat any physical or mental illnesses or defects that may hamper a prisoner's rehabilitation as well as provide all necessary medical, surgical, and psychiatric services to achieve this end. It cannot be argued that the restrictive wording of this rule offers justification for the problems faced by mentally ill persons in prisons. The provision of such services cannot be hinged on only the ability to lead to "rehabilitation" of the prisoners. This could not have been the intention of the drafters of such legislation, especially when we consider other provisions of the UNSMR.

Sections 22(1), 82(1), and 82(2) of the UNSMR are worth noting. Section 22(1) states that there should be in every prison at least one qualified medical officer who is knowledgeable in psychiatry and that the institution's medical services should be organized in close relationship to the general health administration of the community or nation. Section 82 reads:

(1) Persons who are found to be insane shall not be detained in prisons and arrangements shall be made to remove them to mental institutions as soon as possible.
(2) Prisoners who suffer from other mental diseases or abnormalities shall be observed and treated in specialized institutions under medical management.

Will the argument of lack of resources suffice? The African Commission has this to say:

It is aware that millions of people in Africa are not enjoying the right to health maximally because African countries are generally faced with the problem of poverty which renders them incapable to provide the necessary amenities, infrastructure and resources that facilitate the full enjoyment of their rights. Therefore, having due regard to this depressing but real state of affairs, the African Commission would like to read into Article 16 the obligation on the part of the State party to the African Charter to take concrete and targeted steps, while taking full advantage of its available resources, to ensure that the right to health is fully realized in all its aspects without discrimination of any kind.[29]

In a recent publication by Human Rights Watch (Fellner and Abramsky 2004, 1) on the treatment of mentally ill persons it was reported that at least one in six prisoners in the United States is mentally ill—well over 300,000 men and women. The report also stated that there are three times as many mentally ill persons in US prisons as in the country's mental hospitals. American prisoners include people suffering from schizophrenia, bipolar disorder, and major depression, among other illnesses.

This situation in the United States suggests that the problem of imprisoning mentally ill people is influenced more by policy-related matters and societal attitudes than by economic or resource considerations. In addition, it becomes clear that the unethical practice of imprisoning mentally ill persons is not limited to Africa, but is an international issue linked to the use of imprisonment as a means of dealing with social problems and the lack of adequate resources made available to the general populations of many countries. While the assessment of policies and amendments to policies, and the presentation of institutional structural arrangements that imprison mentally ill persons, have been highlighted in this chapter, the use of institutionalization of mentally ill persons (whether in prison or psychiatric hospital) must cease to be the only response available for dealing with the problems mentally ill persons face.

REMEDIES FOR REDRESS OF VIOLATIONS

Domestic Remedies: National Courts

The ability to exhaust all local remedies is a primary consideration in accessing admissibility of cases before regional and international human rights mechanisms. Article 56(5) of the African Charter states that communications received by the commission shall be considered if they "are sent after exhausting local remedies, if any, unless it is obvious that this procedure is unduly prolonged." Article 2 of the First Optional Protocol to the ICCPR[30] restates a similar position. What if the domestic remedies are inadequate, ineffective, inaccessible, unfair, biased, or unduly prolonged? On this issue the African Commission rejected The Gambia government's argument that complainants could seek remedies by bringing actions in tort for false imprisonment or negligence.[31] The commission also questioned the fact that no legal assistance[32] is available to vulnerable groups in prison to enable them to access the legal procedures of the country. It therefore submits that the remedies should be both realistic and effective for the category of people[33] under consideration.

Article 1 of the ICCPR First Optional Protocol states that no communication shall be received by the UN Human Rights Committee (HRC) if it concerns a state party to the ICCPR that is not a party to the protocol. The status of ratification on principal UN human rights treaties indicates that thirty-three out of fifty-four African countries have ratified this protocol, while fifty-two countries have signed/ratified the ICCPR. Those that have ratified both the ICCPR and the Optional Protocol are Algeria, Angola, Benin, Burkina Faso, Cameroon, the Central African Republic, Chad, Congo, Cote d'Ivoire, the Democratic Republic of Congo, Equatorial Guinea, Guinea-Bissau, The Gambia, Ghana, Guinea, Lesotho, Libya, Madagascar, Malawi, Mali, Mauritius, Niger, Senegal, Sierra Leone, Somalia, Togo, Uganda, and Zambia. Four countries—Djibouti, Cape Verde, Namibia, and South Africa—have ratified both the ICCPR and Protocols 1 and 2. Sixteen countries have ratified the ICCPR but not the protocols. They are Botswana, Burundi, Egypt, Eritrea, Ethiopia, Gabon, Kenya, Liberia, Morocco, Mozambique, Nigeria, Rwanda, Sudan, Tunisia, Tanzania, and Zimbabwe. Two countries, Mauritania and Swaziland, have not ratified even the ICCPR. Therefore, in total about eighteen African countries are not able to access the

HRC. This number includes Nigeria, one of the countries under review in this chapter.

Although most African countries have ratified the major UN and regional human rights treaties, very few have taken further steps by domesticating the provisions of these treaties (Heyns and Vijloen 2001, 483). It is thus more difficult to rely on rights guaranteed in treaties before national courts. In a review of nineteen national court cases from seven African countries (South Africa, Zimbabwe, Namibia, Tanzania, Mauritius, Uganda, and Nigeria) it was observed that reference was made to the work of only three UN human rights treaty bodies: the Human Rights Committee, the Committee on Economic, Social, and Cultural Rights, and the Committee on Rights of the Child.[34] While most of these countries are within the southern region of the continent and mainly of Commonwealth jurisdiction, caution should be exercised in not overgeneralizing these observations. Some national courts may refer to the findings of the HRC but reach different conclusions.[35] At other times they rely on a dissenting opinion of one of the HRC members to give a ruling.[36] Sometimes different outcomes are reached even while relying on the same HRC findings.[37] Sometimes a worse outcome is reached. An example is *Mbushuu*,[38] in which the High Court of Tanzania, relying on the HRC in *Randolph Barrett and Clyde Sutcliffe v. Jamaica*,[39] not only ruled that the death penalty was constitutional, but also went ahead to quash the sentences of life imprisonment imposed by the High Court in favour of death sentences.[40] Judging from the above, one can conclude that the outcome of national courts relying on international human rights jurisprudence is unpredictable.

The illusion of institutionalized human rights as universal and objective is apparent in these cases. One national court stated that, while "they can derive assistance from public international law and foreign case law, [they] are in no way bound to follow it."[41] In these cases it becomes clear that a colonial approach to dealing with human rights violations in colonial institutions in Africa is not only problematic but also ineffective. While prisons were brought to Nigeria by the British, and while Nigeria continues to be influenced by UK policies in the treatment of prisoners and the implementation of policies to address problems with the detention of mentally ill persons, it is apparent from the study of outcomes of international policy implementations that the bureaucratic and institutional systems of control are not functioning in Africa. In addition, a comparative assessment of the imprisonment of mentally ill persons in the United States suggests that the human rights issues that mentally ill persons face in Africa are not a problem of "African governance" but a problem of imprisonment institutions and the overreliance on such institutions for social control.

African Regional Human Rights Protection Mechanisms

The African Charter on Human and Peoples' Rights (the African Charter)[42] has been ratified by fifty-four member states of the African Union (AU).[43] Article 6 of the charter is similar in substance to Article 9 of the UDHR and Article 9(1) of the ICCPR,[44] which prohibit arbitrary arrest and detention. Article 7(1) of the African Charter provides for fair hearings in line with Articles 9(2), 9(3), and 9(4) of the ICCPR.[45] However, there is no comparable provision in the African Charter to Article 9(5) of the ICCPR,[46] which provides for enforceable rights to compensation for victims of unlawful arrest or detention. Article 2(3a) of the ICCPR requires the state to ensure that any person whose rights protected under the covenant are violated has an effective remedy, notwithstanding that the violation has been committed by persons acting in an official capacity. What, then, is the effect of the lack of provision for compensation? No doubt it limits the scope of remedies available to those whose rights have been violated in the manner highlighted above.

In the most recent case involving the rights of mentally ill persons decided by the African Commission (*Purohit*) three recommendations were made by the commission after it found The Gambia in violation of Articles 2, 3, 5, 7(1)(a) and (c), 13(1), 16, and 18(4) of the African Charter. These recommendations are listed below.

1. The government of The Gambia should repeal as soon as possible the Lunacy Detention Act (LDA), and replace it with a new legislative regime for mental health that is compatible with the African Charter on Human and Peoples' Rights and international standards and norms for the protection of mentally ill or disabled persons.
2. Pending (1), the government of The Gambia should create an expert body to review the cases of all persons detained under the LDA, and make appropriate recommendations for their treatment and release.
3. The government of The Gambia should provide adequate medical and material care for persons suffering from mental health problems in the territory of The Gambia.

Is it possible that in the future the commission will expand its recommendations in this area to include compensation for victims? There is evidence that the African Commission tends to rely to some extent on the provisions of treaties from both the United Nations and regional jurisdictions. In *Media Rights Agenda v. Nigeria* the commission stated that, "notwithstanding the fact that neither the African Charter nor the Commission's Resolution on the Right to Recourse Procedure and Fair Trial contain[s] any express provision for the right to public trial, the Commission is empowered by articles 60 and 61 *to draw inspiration from international law on human rights to take into consideration as subsidiary measures other general or special international conventions,* customs generally accepted as law, general principles of law recognized by African States as well as legal precedents and doctrine" (emphasis added).[47] For example, in the above case the commission referred to General Comment No. 13 of the UN Human Rights Committee on the right to a fair trial and to Article 14 of the convention in the interpretation of the phrase "fair hearing." In *Legal Resources Foundation v. Zambia*[48] Comment No. 18 of the HRC was relied upon in defining what constitutes "non-discrimination."

Beyond the issue of treatment of complaints, another mechanism available to the commission is a fact-finding mission.

Article 58 of the charter empowers the commission to draw special cases relating to serious or massive violations of human and peoples' rights to the attention of the Assembly of Heads of State and Government of the OAU (now the AU), which "may then request the Commission to undertake an in-depth study of these cases and make a factual report, accompanied by its findings and recommendation." Some have criticized this article on the basis that the ability of the commission to act on complaints from non-state actors is dependent on prior authorization by the Assembly of Heads of State and Government of the AU. Also, critics of these policies argue that, even when the commission acts, its actions are limited only to carrying out in-depth studies. While policies and bureaucratic practices in Africa are expanding to implement an external body to examine human rights violations, the capacity to act on such violations is trumped by the power that the state affords to its institutions of control. This situation is similar to what occurs in Europe and the United States. Following in the footsteps of colonial governance, African states are working to implement international laws and tribunals that are "accepted" by the West, and in doing so are falling into similar traps and bureaucratic failings.

International Mechanisms for Addressing Issues

Beyond the treaty provisions and instances mentioned above, other mechanisms are available within the international human rights sphere: fact-finding missions,[49] a special rapporteur, and the establishment of the UN Working Group on Arbitrary Detention. On the issue of acts being in compliance with national/domestic laws, the working group has clearly stated that its mandate covers every case of deprivation of liberty if it is inconsistent with both domestic legislation and international standards. These include the UDHR and other relevant international instruments accepted by the state in question. The working group also emphatically stated that it is necessary that the act is inconsistent with one of these criteria for it to fall within its jurisdiction. Thus, even if the act is in compliance with domestic legislation, the working group can still address it if it is in violation of an international standard.[50] The working group's classification of cases under arbitrary detention is also worth noting, especially in view of the decision of the African Commission in *Purohit*. The challenge is how these efforts can be coordinated to complement each other in order to provide greater safeguards for mentally disabled persons. The African Commission is working to provide a working environment in which powers external to specific state institutions are able, not only to assess and study human rights violations of mentally ill persons held in prisons, but also to address the problem in manners that significantly and positively impact the lives of vulnerable populations in prison.

CONCLUSION

The international and regional human rights mechanisms dealing with the issue of mentally disabled persons in prison are comprehensive. Case law jurisprudence is quite progressive too. However, there is a need to provide more avenues for accessing and effectively utilizing the regional and international human rights mechanisms by national courts. These provisions will go a long way toward providing "effective domestic remedies" as well as internal oversight mechanisms of the process.

Provisions for compensation should be seen as a viable remedy for survivors of such violations. Other domestic human rights protection and promotional mechanisms should be utilized in addressing the problem of mentally disabled persons held by the justice system. These protections should fall within the jurisdiction of national human rights institutions, non-governmental organizations, and professional bodies such as the bar associations and the medical associations. The conditions of detention should be seen as raising, not just the question of the right to health, and the prohibition of torture or cruel and inhumane treatment, but also the right to a fair trial or a fair hearing, and the prohibition of arbitrary arrest and detention. A collaborative effort between the different sectors of the human rights community needs to be implemented in an African manner, one that shares responsibilities for violations and the power to ratify these problems.

As a first step there is a need to carry out a pilot project aimed at decongesting Nigerian prisons (and other African prisons) of mentally disabled persons: the civil lunatic and the criminal lunatic. The project should involve a multisectoral/dimensional approach, including the following:

(1) the release of prisoners labelled "civil lunatics" and "criminal lunatics";
(2) the transfer/management of such persons to proper treatment centres (psychiatric hospitals, African NGO houses that implement communal care of mentally ill people);
(3) raising the awareness of criminal justice agents, policy-makers, and the general public to help address the stigma that mentally ill persons face; and
(4) legislative advocacy to ensure that such violations cease and to prohibit them from occurring in the future.

All projects and amendments should work with and for the families and communities of mentally disabled people. Rehabilitation techniques, campaigns for human rights and equal access to liberty and high quality of life, and general resource management that provides for people with special needs are all natural components of many African societies. In a continent where community and governance are intimately linked, the problems that mentally ill persons face today can be dealt with in a manner that is relevant to our society and thus effective for those involved. While this chapter has focused heavily on the international legal components associated with the problems that mentally ill persons face in African prisons, it is essential to emphasize that, while knowledge of the international regulations that deal with human rights violations of mentally ill persons is essential to understanding the policy-related methods needed to deal with existing problems, this knowledge in itself is not sufficient to address the problems that institutions of control impose upon vulnerable populations. The legal knowledge presented in this chapter is meant to provide a resource upon which those interested in fighting for the rights of mentally ill persons held in prisons can build. The real struggle does not exist in policy development. It exists in the implementation of human rights and in the abolition of circumstances that place mentally ill people in prison.

NOTES

1   This is the categorization noted in prison records and statistics in Nigeria.
2   Article 12(1) of the International Covenant on Economic, Social, and Cultural Rights (ICESCR), Article 24(1) of the Convention on the Rights of the Child (CRC), and Article 14(2)(b) of the Convention on the Elimination of All Forms of Discrimination against Women (CEDAW). See also Article 16 of the African Charter.
3   Article 10 of the Universal Declaration of Human Rights (UDHR).
4   Article 5 of UDHR; Article 7 of the International Covenant on Civil and Political Rights (ICCPR).
5   Article 9 of ICCPR and Article 9 of UDHR.
6   Which holds all people who are not mentally disabled and are charged with or convicted of criminal offences.
7   Along with those of a large number of other African countries that are former colonies of the United Kingdom.
8   CCPR/C/92/Add.1, Nigerian State Party Report on ICCPR paras 61-63.
9   Communication No. 241/2001 para 64.
10 See Article 8 of the United Nations Standard Minimum Rule for the Treatment of Prisoners (UNSMR).
11 It was ratified on June 28, 2001, and came into force on July 28, 2001.
12 Communication No. 224/98.
13 See *John K. Modise v. Botswana*. Communication No. 97/93 (decision reached at the Twenty-Seventh Ordinary Session, 2000).
14 Section 3(3) of the Mental Health Act, 1983.
15 Section 71(1), ibid.
16 Section 71(2), ibid.

Protecting the Human Rights of People | 287

17 Rule 6, Mental Health Review Tribunal Rules, 1963.
18 Rule 12, ibid.
19 Section 72(1)(b) of the Mental Health Act, 1983.
20 [1982] 4 EHRR 88.
21 [2001] 3 WLR 512.
22 This is in complete violation of Principle 24 of the Body of Principles for the Protection of All Persons under Any Form of Detention or Imprisonment, which provides that medical care and treatment shall be provided free of charge.
23 See Rule 49(1) of UNSMR.
24 Prison Standing Order of the Federal Republic of Nigeria No. 423 provides for the removal of insane prisoners to mental hospitals. Unfortunately this provision is rarely used.
25 Principles for the Protection of Persons with Mental Illness and the Improvement of Mental Health Care (MI Principles), adopted by the UN General Assembly in 1991 (see Principle 20).
26 In the case of the United Kingdom, see section 72(1)(b)(i) of the Mental Health Act, 1983, which obliges mental health review tribunals to discharge patients who are no longer suffering from a mental disorder of a nature or degree warranting detention in hospital for treatment, even if they remain "dangerous."
27 429 US 97, 104 (1976).
28 511 US 825 (1994).
29 Communication No. 241/2001 para 84.
30 See also Article 35 of the ECHR, which gives a time limit of six months from the date on which the final decision was reached in domestic court within which communication should be sent to the European Court of Human Rights.
31 Communication No. 241/2001 para 28.
32 The Gambia has the Poor Persons Defence (Capital Charge) Act, which provides legal aid only to persons charged with capital offences.
33 Poor people mainly picked up from the streets.
34 See www.abo.fi/instut/imr/ILA-files/louw.doc.
35 See the Supreme Court of Zimbabwe and the Constitutional Court of South Africa on the crime of sodomy as decided by the HRC in *Toonen v. Australia,* Communication No. 488/1992.
36 See the Zimbabwean court in *S. v. Banana,* 2000(3) SA 885 (ZS).
37 See the South African court in *S. v. Makwanyane,* 1995(3) SA 391 (CC), and the Supreme Court of Nigeria in *Onuoha Kalu v. The State,* SCc.24/1996 [1998] 13 NWLR 531, on the constitutionality of the death penalty; both relied on the decision of the HRC in *Ng v. Canada,* Communication No. 469/1991 (November 5, 1993).

38 *Mbushuu and Another v. Republic of Tanzania,* [1995] 1 LRC 216.
39 Communication No. 270/271/1988 (March 30, 1992), 264.
40 *Mbushuu,* op cit., paras (e-f), 223.
41 Communication No. 470 (July 30, 1993) para 39, 687.
42 Adopted by the Assembly of Heads of State and Government of the member states on June 27, 1991; it came into force on October 21, 1996.
43 Formerly the Organization of African Unity (OAU).
44 Article 5(1) of ECHR, Article 7(1-3) of the American Convention on Human Rights.
45 Article 5(2-4) of the ECHR, and Articles 7(4-6) and 8(1) of the American Convention on Human Rights.
46 See also Article 5(5) of the ECHR. Article 10 of the American Convention on Human Rights only provides for the right to compensation where there is a miscarriage of justice in sentencing.
47 Communication No. 224/98.
48 Communication No. 211/98.
49 In 1999 such a mission was carried out by the Special Rapporteur on Violence against Women (Radhika Coomaraswamy) to the United States. She recommended, among other things, a study of national mental health policy and the imprisonment of women with mental health problems.
50 UN doc E/CN.4/1999/63 para 60.

REFERENCES

Department of Health. (1999a). *Report of the Expert Committee: Review of the Mental Health Act 1983.* London: Department of Health.

---. (1999b). *Reform of the Mental Health Act 1983: Proposals for Consultation, Cmnd. 448999.* London: Stationery Office.

. (2000). *Reforming the Mental Health Act, CM 5016-I and II.* London: Stationery Office.

Fellner, Jamie, and Sasha Abramsky. (2004). "Prisons No Place for the Mentally Ill." www.hrw.org/english/docs/2004/02/13/13/usdom7467.htm.

Heyns, C., and F. Vijloen. (2001). "The Impact of the United Nations Human Rights Treaties on the Domestic Level." *Human Rights Quarterly,* 23, 483.

Holloway, K., and A. Grounds. (2003). "Discretion and the Release of Mentally Disordered Offenders." In *Exercising Discretion: Decision-Making in the Criminal Justice System and Beyond,* ed. Loraine

Gelsthorpe and Nicola Padfield. Portland, OR: Willan Publishing, 139–163.

Padfield, Nicola, Alison Liebling, and Helen Arnold. (2003). "Discretion and the Release of Life Sentences Prisoners." In *Exercising Discretion: Decision-Making in the Criminal Justice System and Beyond,* ed. Loraine Gelsthorpe and Nicola Padfield. Portland, OR: Willan Publishing, 97–124.

SECTION IV

RESISTANCE

In addressing issues of colonialism and the continued implementation of colonial institutions in "former" European colonies in Africa, it is important to recognize that Africans have resisted these oppressions and continue to resist them. This section presents two main types of resistance: the first is political, and the second is academic.

Colonialism functioned on both these levels. During their occupation of African territories Europeans utilized a sociopolitical level of oppression. Entire social structures, government policies, and racist policies were imported into Africa from Europe in exchange for the export of African economic and material resources. Fela Kuti was a Nigerian political musician who recognized the absurdity of such an "exchange" and challenged the illusions of European superiority that colonialism proposed. Fela's resistance was a political one implemented through social and educational activism.

As colonialists invaded African territories, they relied on academic institutions to provide scientific and legitimate propaganda to justify and facilitate such crimes. Although the process through which such "knowledge" was produced was socially legitimate and politically empowered through allegiances to academic institutions it was not accurate. In contemporary academic institutions, the scientism that empowered colonialists lingers in the social sciences. Within the specific context of penal colonialism the study of academic legal pluralisms provides an avenue through which the process of producing faulty knowledge about Africa can be reviewed; in addition, the proposed use of non-essentialism presents an opportunity to implement academic resistance. This type of resistance provides an opportunity to dissociate from a form of knowledge production that not only facilitated atrocities in the past, but also continues to facilitate and justify contemporary oppressions.

CHAPTER 17

WOMEN, LAW, AND RESISTANCE IN NORTHERN NIGERIA: UNDERSTANDING THE INADEQUACIES OF WESTERN SCHOLARSHIP

Viviane Saleh-Hanna

INTRODUCTION

Colonialism in West Africa imposed foreign legal systems upon ethnically and structurally diverse regions that functioned in complex, precolonial, non-Western contexts. Colonial *legal systems* played a key role in the process of colonization because they defined and *(il)legalized* business transactions and codes of conduct among colonizers and colonized, and eventually came to *(il)legalize* interactions among colonized populations (Bentsi-Enchill 1969); this recent colonial era has left West Africa functioning in complex sociolegal settings. This chapter focuses on women in the contemporary northern Nigerian context: their interactions with pluralities of law in northern Nigeria, and the modes of resistance[1] they employ in facing colonial and patriarchal oppressions.

Legal centralism and legal pluralism have emerged as the two main paradigms[2] through which legal theories are constructed (Manji 2000). Each paradigm indoctrinates a foundation of assumptions about law and society, forming frameworks of ideological assumptions and guidelines for methodological activities that establish a "code of conduct" in which theorists who assess law and society construct sociolegal theories.

The legal centralist paradigm encompasses those theories that implement an "authoritative conception of law," *insisting* that the label of "law" must be confined exclusively to the laws of the state:[3] "that there is no distinction between law and positive morality, and that there is no ultimate unifying source of norms in a legal system" (Manji 2000, 631). In assuming that the "norms" of the powerful are also the "norms" of the oppressed, legal centralists impose a form of thinking that is elitist and inaccurate. They are predominantly a group of scholars trained in legal positivism, and tend to assume that "the state and the system of lawyers, courts, and prisons is the only form of ordering," and thus study "law" by studying legal institutions (Merry 1988, 874).

The legal pluralist paradigm encompasses those legal theories recognizing that "two or more legal systems coexist in the same social field" (Merry 1988, 870), and add that there exists a "large range of normative orders which, although they enjoy no connection to the state, are nonetheless described as law" (Manji 2000, 632). This school of thought is open to recognizing that "norms" are differentially created and rejects the oversimplifications imposed by legal centralists. Based on the categorizations of these two "paradigms," Manji (2000, 631) concludes that legal pluralism is most relevant to studying and appropriately representing women, specifically women in Africa. In general, *post*colonial settings imply an inherently legal pluralistic context (Bentsi-Enchill 1969) due to the colonial experiences that transported foreign European legal systems into Africa. In assessing the specific circumstances through which women interact with law in northern Nigeria, that generalization *appears* to be applicable. The monolithic and simplified assumptions of the legal centralist paradigm not only are inapplicable to women in northern Nigeria, but also seem to be inappropriate for addressing the complexities within which societies in that region interact with law and society.

Legal Pluralism in Nigeria: Historical Context

On October 1, 1960, Nigeria gained independence from the occupation of the United Kingdom's colonial government. After decades of military dictatorships, and a plethora of military coups, a new Constitution was adopted in 1999, marking the appearance of structural transition to civilian government. Nigeria is the most populous nation in Africa. With a population exceeding 140 million, the controversial 2006 census[4] reported that 71.7 million males and 68.3 million females live in the country. The Nigerian government's official statement on ethnic populations affirms that Nigeria is home to more than 250 ethnic groups: "Three of them, the Hausa [predominantly living in the north], Igbo [predominantly living in the east], and Yoruba [predominantly living in the south], are the major groups, and constitute over 40 per cent of the population."[5] In relation to religious affiliations, fifty percent of the nation identify as Muslim, forty percent identify as Christian, and ten percent identify with traditional African religions (*World Fact Book* 2007).[6] The legal system in Nigeria is "officially" implemented within a pluralistic framework based on English common law, Islamic sharia law (in some northern states), and traditional law modelled after precolonial African systems of justice.

The plurality of state legal institutions in Nigeria is a function not only of the colonial imposition of "new legal systems" but also of how colonial systems institutionalized traditional law. As the British began to colonize northern Nigeria in the early twentieth century, Hausa states underwent sharp changes through which the "Protectorate of Northern Nigeria" was adopted in 1903. This protectorate implemented an "indirect rule" policy that indoctrinated the philosophy that, "whenever possible, the metropolitan power should seek to recognize rule through traditional authorities in accordance with the indigenous social and political institutions and mores" (Callaway and Creevey 1994, 14). As a result Christian missionaries were denied access to northern Nigeria, and as a political function Islam became more entrenched in Hausa society. Islam became the avenue through which traditional autonomy could be maintained. "Thus," as Callaway and Creevey note, "the colonial state provided the stable conditions necessary for African Islamic cultures to grow and deepen. Under Hausa/Fulani rule and British protection, the Islamic (*sharia*) courts were at the heart of that culture" (14). As customary/local law in West Africa (including Islamic law) became institutionalized into Western structures and conceptions of what "law" should look like and do, a residual rule was formed. This policy stated that, in legal situations in which no expressed rule is applicable, the colonial court would have the jurisprudence to govern the situation according to the principles of "justice, equity, and good conscience" (Bentsi-Enchill 1969, 30). Since Nigeria was "created" as a colonial nation-state, this residual rule disappeared in western/eastern Nigeria, but was kept in the north with the specific purpose of regulating sharia laws. Through this context emerged contemporary sharia courts and the state-endorsed formality of legal pluralism in northern Nigeria.

Nigerian Population Demographics

The Nigerian population is young, with only 2.9 percent of the population reaching the age of sixty-five and 43.4 percent of the population being below the age of fourteen. In 2004 the average age for males in the country was 18.2 years, while the average age for females was 17.9 years. Males in Nigeria comprise a slight majority of the population; they also experience a slightly higher infant mortality rate and a slightly lower life expectancy rate (44.7 years) compared with females (45.8 years). The fertility rate is high in Nigeria, with the average woman in 2004 giving birth to about five children. In 2003 the majority of the Nigerian population was recorded as being literate (68 percent), with 60.6 percent of women and 75.7 percent of men in the nation knowing how to read and write.[7] In 2003 the Nigerian government announced the privatization of all oil refineries, resulting in economic structural growth in 2004, headed by increased oil and natural gas exports. Despite such growth, 60 percent of the population continues to live below the poverty line. With a labour force exceeding fifty million people, 70 percent of whom rely on agriculture, 10 percent on industry, and 20 percent on services, the push to expand oil and natural gas exports while continuing to neglect agricultural resources is problematic.[8]

Aside from such problems, and more specifically in relation to gender dynamics in northern Nigeria, women have a unique and strained relationship with law; nonetheless, they have managed to work against these obstacles by establishing networks and regulations through which they can achieve some autonomy. I will use legal pluralism, an academic framework that recognizes different levels of control and law in society, to illustrate these networks and to contextualize the laws used by/against women in northern Nigeria. Upon reviewing the literature on women in northern Nigeria and the three main frameworks of legal pluralism, I will offer an assessment of legal pluralism to identify which framework is best equipped to understand and properly represent women and their relationships to law in northern Nigeria.

WOMEN OF NORTHERN NIGERIA AND THE STATE: TRENDS IN ETHNOGRAPHIC RESEARCH

Since colonialism Western researchers have gained more access to conduct research in northern Nigerian societies. This intimate link between research and colonialism had a significant impact on the type of research produced by Western researchers. Whereas early works researched the relationships between colonizer and colonized, in the 1970s research began to focus more specifically on women in the north and their relationship to the state. Three topics of research have become prominent: sharia courts (what Westerners would call family and employment law), purdah (the practice of secluding women from public life), and prostitution. Western researchers tend to draw attention to the negative, gendered impacts of purdah and sharia, and have recently begun to work toward achieving an understanding of women's efforts to resist both; in so doing, they have come to emphasize female agency, and have begun to identify "law" as existing among women and not "law" as emerging only through state institutions.

Ayua (1998), Wall (1998), and Werthmann (2002) have conducted ethnographic research assessing women's experiences and struggles with sharia law. Relying on family planning and land ownership issues, they bring forth concerns about sociolegal status, emphasizing that the struggles of women are related to patriarchal legal structures and cultural attitudes. The foundations of such structures are closely related to the implantation and institutionalization of colonialism. While scholars have written about purdah for decades, recent work conducted by Callaway and Creevey (1994, 2003), Coles (1988), and Pittin (2002) emphasizes informal networks created by women to expand their access to opportunities in the socioeconomic realm. Emerging is a body of work on women's labour, focusing on both "formal" legal prohibitions and "informal" yet engrained networks, created by women to regulate prostitution and other forms of work. As these researchers conduct interviews and surveys, they present a literature emphasizing legal and cultural contexts that have been shown to influence interactions (or lack thereof) between women and the state.

According to Garland (2001), formal social control includes state-run institutions and state-set definitions of deviance. In addition, formal social control includes state-prescribed reactions to deviance (punishments, sanctions, regulations, and so on). In contrast, informal social control includes "the learned, unreflexive, habitual practices of mutual supervision, scolding, sanctioning, and shaming carried out, as a matter of course, by community members" (159).

The categorization of law and social control into formal and informal is a function of the dichotomized frameworks in which the majority of Western legal scholars conduct research. Although accepted as the "norm" in Western academic contexts, these divisions do not always reflect accurately the social and legal realities that Western researchers are attempting to assess. For women in northern Nigeria cultural behaviours (informal?) combine with sharia laws (formal?) to construct their living conditions. Women have created networks of interaction and female-established opportunity to combat obstacles and achieve some autonomy in their lives. Although defined as informal in most Western research, the accuracy of this category is questionable. What a Western scholar might define as informal in his or her textbook or published article can be formal for a woman in northern Nigeria.

In this presentation of women in northern Nigeria I have chosen to focus on socioeconomic circumstances because it is in this realm that women's empowerment and interactions with law are most visible; in addition, sharia cases involving women often include a dispute over socioeconomic/financial issues. With the implementation of purdah, economic activities by women, though formally limited, appear to function informally in highly organized networks. In contrasting and interrelating what Western scholars refer to as formal and informal in this specific context, a more comprehensive understanding of women, law, and resistance in northern Nigeria can be achieved. Whereas Cohen (2004) explains that the status of Nigerian women accountable to sharia courts is almost always defined through their relationships to men, Werthmann (2002) illustrates how these formal networks are challenged and transformed through informal applications by women in the region. At the root of much of this analysis is an understanding of the cultural and religious contexts within which women live.

Women in northern Nigeria are predominantly of Hausa[9] descent, and, though not all Hausa people are Muslim, most are. As a result much of Hausa society is deeply influenced by Islam and the ways in which it is interpreted: since the introduction of Islam in Nigeria, in the early fourteenth century, "Islam has been deeply intertwined with pre-Islamic Hausa cultural and religious tradition" (Robson 2002, 183). Thus, structures and institutions that are predominantly defined by Islam have come to form major tenets in Hausa culture and practice. On a 'formal' level of social control, Bentsi-Enchill (1969) explains that, when the British colonized West Africa, traditional systems of law functioned alongside colonial ones. At this time a reliance on Islam was constructed in Hausa societies to keep a distance from the colonial occupiers. Islam became the preferred "traditional, customary" law through which autonomy from the British invaders could be established. As this institutionalization of tradition and culture occurred, informal networks came to function alongside the newly formed colonial ones, and in combination these elements continue to structure women's interactions with the law.

On a formal level, sharia laws exist and are implemented through sharia courts. On cultural, social, and, at times, religious levels purdah is used to regulate women's living conditions. While purdah is not a stipulation under sharia to be used by all women in the region, the cultural tenets of Hausa society place many women within purdah. The interactions between purdah practices and sharia laws create an atmosphere in which women's relationships with the law are created and guided through an interaction of formal (legal) and informal (cultural, social, religious) interactions.

An example of these formal-informal interactions exists in marriage and divorce regulations. According to sharia laws, a man is able to legally have up to four wives at the same time. In conjunction, divorce is legally made easily available to men. Wall (1998, 349) implies that in Hausa society divorce is not only differentially available to men through sharia but also culturally encouraged: "A Hausa proverb bluntly states: *Zamanka kai kadai ya fi zama da mugunyar mace* ('Living by yourself is better than living with an evil woman').... Although a man could never live alone and retain any status in Hausa society, this contempt for an 'evil woman' is reflected in the ease with which men... can divorce a woman." Furthermore, sharia laws emphasize women's status through reproduction: if a child is not produced in marriage, the man may demand a partial refund of the dowry provided to his ex-wife's father at the time of marriage. These are examples of how the informal cultural practices and attitudes reinforce formal sharia laws in regard to divorce.

Despite the lack of formal access to divorce, women have informal methods to initiate it. Some move out of the husband's home and back into the father's home in an act of defiance known as *yaji* ("hot pepper"): "The embarrassment that such an act of defiance causes the husband" may force him to resolve the dispute in the woman's favour, or it may force him to divorce her (Wall 1998, 349). In this instance formal laws of divorce are either initiated or regulated by women through actions not defined or regulated by law: even though the law does not empower women to initiate divorce, through action and understanding of cultural dynamics they empower themselves when necessary. In such instances it becomes clear that the formal/informal dichotomies imposed by scholars to aid in their production of knowledge consist of an oversimplification that distorts social realities.

In attempts to comprehend such complex contexts, issues of power become important.[10] Instead of focusing on a methodology that attempts to understand these issues through the implementation of predetermined formal and informal categories, I turn to a methodology that aims to understand them through an assessment of context. The context I have chosen to study is the socioeconomic one, for through an understanding of social and material wealth one can begin to understand power.

A specific area of focus has been on ownership of land and possession titles on homes. In northern Nigeria women are limited in their access to ownership. Robson (2002, 184) reports that, "while women dominate domestic spaces, they rarely own the homes they live in.... Few women become wealthy enough to invest in land and/or property and some inherit property/land, but Islamic (*maliki*) inheritance laws, practiced in Hausaland, generally discriminate against women." Although Islamic laws preserve women's formal rights to ownership of land, these rights are often ignored through informal mechanisms of social control, encouraging discrimination against women. Ayua (1998, 237-238) states that "this pattern of behavior has tended to make women as second-class citizens. Most... have resigned themselves to their fate and have accepted the humiliating status accorded them by society. The few others... who would want to assert their rights or fight for them are discouraged for fear of being branded social deviants or rebels."

As a result of these dynamics women in Hausaland have created their own means of attaining wealth. Many of these are what Western scholars might refer to as informal mechanisms of conduct and control. Under sharia laws the socioeconomic standing of women is recorded through their fathers' or husbands' status, but women's controlled networks allow women to recognize "each other's abilities, skills, and economic successes, but this recognition does not translate into [formal] socioeconomic status" (Callaway and Creevey 1994, 95). Nonetheless, this lack of formal status does not translate into total disregard or disempowerment. In fact, a closer analysis of the issues illustrates that the lack of formal status accords more control to women, due to their distance from the state and the "under the radar" freedoms that such distance can provide.

In addition to sharia laws and cultural ideologies about gender that impact how these laws become implemented, women are further impacted through the practice of purdah. The US Bureau of Democracy, Human Rights, and Labor reported that "purdah, the practice of keeping girls and women in seclusion from men outside the family, continued in parts of the country [far north], which restricted the freedom of movement of women" (US Department of State 2005, section 1.f). Barkow (1972, 322) further explains that, in the context of contemporary Hausa societies, seclusion also "means that women are expected to be indoors during the daylight hours and to obscure their faces if they venture outside the compound. Few men refuse their wives permission to visit other compounds freely each evening, or to travel long distances to attend the ceremonies of kin."

The historical roots of purdah are well documented. The practice was introduced in the latter part of the fifteenth century "by the Sarkin Kano (the chief of Kano). At the time only wealthy rulers secluded their wives, and seclusion was not so much for Islamic religious reasons but for the social status attained by virtue of displaying their economic ability to dispense with their wives' productive labor" (Robson 2002, 184). An increase in the seclusion of women occurred at the beginning of colonial rule

(Werthmann 2002, 120). Much as sharia was used to implement legal distance from colonialists, purdah appears to be a practice implemented in the north to maintain physical distance from colonialists and missionaries. In addition to limitations on physical activity, Robson (2002, 183) offers an analysis of the symbolic implications of purdah: "Seclusion can be thought of as a spatial boundary defining gender," explaining that the physical setting is a manifestation of attitudes in Hausaland about the natures of men and women. Women are segregated from the public sphere during their reproductive years, and, while this practice can produce Eurocentric stereotypes and assessments of gender relations in Hausaland, my analysis of purdah focuses on its physical implications. I provide information about women in purdah and do not delve into an assessment of symbolism, not because symbolic elements are not important, but because such elements should be provided by women in purdah, not by researchers who are trained in Western academic institutions.

Out of the political and cultural stances that implement purdah emerges the physical construction of homes. The architectural designs of living compounds in the north make possible the implementation of purdah. Large walls surrounding each living complex are one element of the physical realms of seclusion. Within each living compound separate buildings (usually small huts) are arranged as rooms around a centralized open space known as the courtyard. Huts in which married women reside are designated no-entry spaces. The compound is accessed through an entrance hut with slanted pathways preventing direct vision into the courtyard or the huts that surround it (Robson 2002, 184). Yet secluded women in northern Nigeria have established "their own networks to regulate women's tasks and to arbitrate conflicts over the decisions they make and the goods they control" (Callaway and Creevey 1994, 38). Through these networks women achieve some autonomy.

Coles (1988) conducted an ethnographic study in Kaduna (a large state in northern Nigeria), and found that between 1981 and 1985 all the women she spoke to (125 in total) participated in economic activities providing for their families; she recorded an increase in the amounts of money women were contributing to family maintenance, coinciding with depletions[11] in the Nigerian economy at the time. These activities were never recorded in official statistics, due to their separateness from the public sector. Werthmann (2002) conducted a qualitative study of Hausa women living in Kano[12] in a modern housing estate referred to as the bariki ("barracks"), provided for police officers by the state. She spoke to the wives and female family members of police officers. Women who live in the bariki are segregated in their respective living compounds and emerge only to participate in all female celebrations or for specific social events that their husbands have given them permission to attend. Upon receiving this permission women are allowed to leave their living quarters, unescorted by their husbands, to visit close kin, attend naming ceremonies and weddings, visit relatives who are in dire health, attend funerals, and visit the hospital if they or their children are in need of medical attention (120). When a new woman moves into the bariki she is "successfully integrated into local networks such as the mutual borrowing of goods and money,... the exchange of gifts on ceremonial occasions,... and rotating credit associations" (115).

First contact for a newcomer is usually with her immediate neighbours, who greet her over the wall or send their children to welcome her to the neighbourhood. Werthmann (2002) also reports that polygamy is common and that many girls are married at a young age.[13] It is not expected that such marriages will last long; it is common and void of stigma to believe that "it is only the second, third or fourth marriage that may develop into a permanent bond between a man and a woman" (116). Upon divorce legal custody is most often given to the father; thus, many children are raised by female relatives of the father. Divorced women return to their fathers' homes and spend at least three months in seclusion before they can legally get married again (Barkow 1972, 320). This time span is decided and implemented through sharia law (Wall 1998, 349).

When a woman gets married she enters seclusion under purdah. It is the job of unmarried prepubescent girls to help run the household and to hawk products (foods or crafts) prepared by married women in purdah (Barkow 1972, 319). In this context custody issues enter the economic realm. For segregated women losing custody of a child brings forth great financial restraints, since only young girls and postmenopausal women are able to participate in public spaces. Robson (2002, 183-184) suggests that this enforced "invisibility" of women during their "reproductive years" brings to light an oppressive gender ideology. While she outlines the importance of an independent income, and shows that women are frustrated by the lack of access to job opportunities, other researchers focus on details of economic activities undertaken by women to combat these conditions.

Quantitative research in Zaria State in northern Nigeria records that the food-processing industries, run primarily by women, function through small-scale enterprises, with simple technology and a consumer-friendly orientation. Husbands and children provide women with necessary materials (readily available in village markets) for food grain production. While many women lack access to formal educational institutions, Simmons (1975, 156) identifies cooking as an educational skill taught to all females in this region, adding that "the amount of equipment and capital needed to take up employment in the [food-processing] industry is minimal. While weaving or trading... may demand relatively large investments... food processing can be profitably done in fairly small amounts with normal household utensils." She found that, "in hundreds of villages, hamlets, towns and cities of northern Nigeria, many tons of grains, grain legumes, and starchy roots are processed for sale as convenient ready-to-eat foods" (147). These factors illustrate that Hausa women do participate in income-generating activities. In relation to starting up, Cohen (2004, 66) explains that a woman is "given initial capital in the form of her marriage payment, to which she is entitled by the Shari'a and with which she can start business." Many of these businesses, as Simmons (1975) described, include household activities: "preparing and selling cooked food, doing laundry, sewing, hairdressing, taking care of children, weaving straw floor mats, pounding grain, chopping up ingredients for each other, or making charcoal or incense. Older women may develop a small-scale trade in such items as soap, kola nuts, or cloth; a few will be midwives. Wealthier women may engage in the trade of jewelry, shoes or imported wax prints. In all cases, though, the activity is essentially carried on from behind the walls of seclusion" (Callaway and Creevey 1994, 102). In addition to participating in income-generating activities, Callaway and Creevey note, custom stipulates that women regulate expenditures for all household incomes; thus, capital is accumulated through "the small amounts of money which she 'cuts' for herself from the household money, which her husband hands over daily" (1994, 66-67). In polygamous households co-wives establish agreements defining how much money each will receive when it is her turn to control household incomes. In accumulating these reserves of cash women establish or expand their businesses. Often considered extensions of "common household activities," they can be classified as informal, but in relation to the accumulation of wealth the monetary gain remains unrecorded in formal statistics.

In addressing dominant methods of income generation in Hausaland, it is essential to present those areas of revenue in which women do participate in the public space. One such area is prostitution. In this realm there exist networks through which prostitution can be implemented in female-controlled settings known as *karuwai* ("courtesan") in Katsina State in northern Nigeria. *Karuwai* networks developed historically among Hausa women in northern Nigeria, and continue to incorporate an autonomous setting in which houses owned and occupied by women are used to ensure their physical and financial safety in their work. "With the loss of women's state-wide political power, control over women became fragmented, but was generally allocated to husbands, fathers and other senior male kin. The *karuwai*, however, lived away from these authority figures," and functioned in a formal realm only in their active avoidance of confrontations with authorities (Pittin 2002, 178-179). In this instance resistance to domination by one system is found through the implementation and use of another.

Despite establishing autonomy from patriarchal figures, prostitutes cannot accumulate great wealth. Thus, while a housewife's ability to accumulate wealth surpasses that of a prostitute, housewives cannot invest or expand wealth by entering into competition with men in public places. Prostitutes, with access to public spaces, can compete with men and invest earnings, but are not given opportunities to accumulate great wealth (Cohen 2004, 67). Despite these difficulties, women have established networks of function to produce significant socioeconomic power.

In light of these conditions legal pluralism arises as a relevant framework in which women's relationship (or lack thereof) to the state can be studied because it incorporates recognition of different levels of sociolegal functions. Focusing only on formal "law" and "status" is misrepresentative, because women do not live within those realms: "I did not vote during the last elections because I saw no need for it. My success in life depends on what I do with my hands and not what anybody promises me, so I prefer to be left alone. Politics is not for women. It is for men—men who can lie and those who have the time" (quoted in Callaway and Creevey 2003, 595). In this context it becomes essential to incorporate a level of analysis that recognizes law as it functions in what Western scholars have named the informal realm (purdah, informal business networks), and how that functioning interacts with laws in what Western scholars have named the formal realm (sharia).

While studies of informal networks have been conducted to assess the socioeconomic activities that women participate in throughout Hausaland, further analysis of the relationships they develop between "law" and "society" needs to be implemented.

In this social field it appears that the plurality of systems of governance and the layers of normative orders that exist for women are all relevant. The elimination of formal or informal categories in conducting research in the region would produce more accurate information, due to the inherently fluid and plural nature of life and law for women in Hausaland.

LEGAL PLURALISM: THREE FRAMEWORKS

A presentation and assessment of three legal pluralist frameworks will help us to ascertain which approach is most appropriate for achieving a comprehensive understanding of women and their relationships to law in northern Nigeria. In presenting legal pluralist frameworks it is necessary to define them according to their emerging academic contexts, methodological assumptions, and definitions of law. Within the paradigm of legal pluralism I present three main ideological frameworks. In 1988 Merry identified two: classical legal pluralists and new legal pluralists. More recently Tamanaha (2000) presented a third framework: non-essentialist legal pluralism. Each framework incorporates varied practices in presenting and assessing legal pluralism, based on respective assumptions about law and methodological approaches to studying law and/in society. I will use their different approaches to identify the pluralistic applicability of both the *definitions* of law in the theoretical sphere and the *methods* available to researchers working to identify boundaries of research, while attaining access to the circumstances that function in social fields in relation to law.

Classical Legal Pluralism

The emergence of legal pluralism as an academic field of study is intimately linked with colonialism. It was through the process of colonialism that a more visible form of legal pluralism was produced for Western legal scholars. This occurred through the implantation of colonial laws in African societies with pre-existing laws, increasing the visibility of plurality, and producing an academic opportunity and awareness through which the plurality of legal systems in one society could be studied. In addition, it was during the process of colonialism that the study of legal pluralism became established academically. While it was accepted that Western law is law, one of the main goals of classical legal pluralism was to identify and differentially recognize (or not recognize) non-Western legal systems.

In this chapter I focus solely on British colonialism in West Africa to assess the emergence of legal pluralism; in doing so I will briefly present the "logistics" of pluralism. It is important to note first that British colonies established before the middle of the seventeenth century in Africa implemented a form of legality quite different from those established after the American Revolution; these new legal policies indicate that, within classical legal pluralism, there are several forms of legality to be assessed.

According to Bentsi-Enchill (1969, 3), British colonies established in Africa early in the seventeenth century used British-based international law to legalize "matters of general Imperial concern covering such matters as shipping, nationality, aliens, coinage, bankruptcy, and matters requiring legislation outside the powers of the local legislature." Colonies acquired by settlement at this time began through business ventures that resulted in the establishment of large expatriate populations, which implemented British laws to legalize and facilitate business transactions. After the American Revolution laws granting British subjects rights to gain "representation" in African governments and powers to pass legislation were enacted; as Bentsi-Enchill notes (3), these laws were facilitated by the fact that "African aboriginal inhabitants" of colonial settlements were not recognized under international law as having any rights. Under this legislation occupied African territories came under "absolute disposition of the Crown," but there was no presumption that private laws extended to the "aboriginal inhabitants" of these colonies. The assumption at the time was that local laws functioned in a manner that related well to local populations, but were unsuitable in meeting the "needs" of European settlers.

Consequently *Freeman v. Fairlie* (1828) concluded that British or Christian settlers were to adhere to British laws, while "locals" could continue to adhere to customary laws, "with some particular exceptions that were called for by commercial policy, or the convenience of mutual intercourse" (Bentsi-Enchill 1969, 4). Further legislation stated that locals could continue to rely on precolonial laws "until 'the Sovereign' through her judges" enacted laws to replace them (5). During this process legal pluralism began to be formally established, whereby British law was enacted to differentially institutionalize and recognize (or not recognize) different systems of local law. Merry (1988) documents the literature that addresses "customary law" and highlights the fact that "custom" became "law" as a function of colonialism.

In attempts to colonize Africa, the British transformed social control mechanisms in Africa societies into words and structures that mirrored Western notions of "systems" of law; thus, as colonialists "communicated" with African populations, they created "customary laws" according to those "versions of customary law which meshed best with their own ideology of land ownership as well as other legal relations" (Merry 1988, 875). Not recognizing such contexts, Western legal scholars who studied classical legal pluralism in Africa relied on an established colonial "vision of a traditional, unchanging African past ruled by long-established customs" (876). Such visions are distorted and resulted in the inaccurate production of knowledge about legal pluralism in West Africa.

In his assessment of colonialism from an African perspective Bentsi-Enchill (1969) states that British invasions of West Africa marked the establishment of British colonial endeavours on the continent. In Nigeria local or customary laws were mirrored after a court ordinance entitled "Application of Native Law and Custom," outlining the boundaries within which these laws could function:

1. Nothing in this Ordinance shall deprive the Courts [British courts] of the right to observe and enforce the observance, or shall deprive any person of the benefit, of any native law or custom existing in The Gambia,[14] such law or custom not being repugnant to natural justice, equity and good conscience, not incompatible whether directly or by necessary implication with any law for the time being in force.
2. Such laws and customs shall be deemed applicable in causes and matters where the parties thereto are natives and also in cases and matters between natives and non-natives [Europeans] where it may appear[15] to the Court that substantial injustice would be done to either party by a strict adherence to the rules of English law. (quoted in Bentsi-Enchill 1969, 7)

Bentsi-Enchill makes three key observations in relation to this law. First, he states that it gave the British courts supremacy in deciding when customary laws would or would not be applied. Second, since the overwhelming majority of the population (the "natives") was being ruled by customary laws, British courts were able to expand the jurisdiction within which their control applied through this recognition of "customary" in their laws. And third, the British government used this recognition of customary laws to grant itself the power to decide what was, and what was not, law according to African customs and social structures.

These laws eventually came to create what was referred to as the "West African formulation," which was implanted in the rest of the continent as colonialism expanded. The manner in which legal pluralism became recognized legally occurred within the above-described politically motivated, Eurosupremacist, imperialist, colonial dimensions, and from within this context grew the academic study of legal pluralism.

Assumptions and Ideological Framework

Bohannon (1967), Gluckman (1973), Hoebel (1954), and Malinowski (1959) have been identified as key scholars in classical legal pluralism, a framework receiving its "classical" title in the 1970s. Prior to this researchers did not identify with different schools of thought in the study of legal pluralism. Legal pluralism initially was the study of colonized societies, and of the legal interactions between colonial and non-colonial legal systems. Merry (1988, 872) defines classical legal pluralism as "the analysis of the intersection of indigenous and European law," which prior to the 1970s was applied only to colonial and *post*colonial societies. Much of what has become defined as classical legal pluralism was deemed so by new legal pluralists. In their separation from classical legal pluralism they worked to critically define classical assumptions and methodologies. That process of separation included an identification of the "classical" to distinguish it from the "new" legal pluralism. A lack of understanding of this "definitional" process created a lack of understanding of "classical" legal pluralists as they are viewed in contemporary legal pluralist literature, mainly because those defined as "classical legal pluralists" never named themselves as such. In recognizing this dilemma I present the works of classical legal pluralists from the initial Western academic realizations that legality exists in plurality in society. I present classical legal pluralism as conducted prior to the emergence of new legal pluralism to address the imposition of definitions employed by new legal pluralists.

Defining Law

Classical legal pluralism is the first framework of sociolegal studies that endeavoured to study several legal systems as they exist in the same society at the same time. Classical legal pluralists were the first Western scholars who employed a framework assuming that a variety of legal systems can and do exist in the same society at the same time. Gluckman's (1973) conception of pluralism represents the framework within which classical legal pluralists worked. Gluckman identified the "most crucial concepts of law" as "elastic or of multiple meaning" and concluded that the essence of law "can absorb a variety of different presumptions" (393).

This variety is the legal pluralism that classical legal pluralists worked to identify. Hoebel (1940) added that law can only emerge from formal "politically organized societies."[16] Within the classical legal pluralist framework scholars worked to identify what "politically organized societies" looked like and what types of laws they produced. In addition, Bohannon (1967) and Gluckman (1965) were in constant discussion about the linguistic approach to presenting customary laws in the English language.[17]

Their debate over linguistics[18] is indicative of the dichotomized framework within which the classical legal pluralists functioned: they relied heavily on the process of categorization in forming knowledge. Their disagreements were over how those categories should be approached and defined. Bohannon and Gluckman often disagreed over the boundaries within which definitions for customary law should fall (Nader 1969). The details of the debate were elaborate and based on lengthy ethnographic experiences throughout Africa, but those details are not the central focus of this analysis. The presentation of their debate illustrates the commonalities that tie Bohannon (1967) and Gluckman (1965) together, within the classical legal pluralist framework: the implicit assumptions that both held were related to the "essence" of law as a categorical entity; while the specifics of the categories may be disputable (as in their debate), a preconceived notion of law that is dependent on two categories (state law and customary law) was not. The classical legal pluralist framework relies on the existence of categories and in doing so employs a dichotomized approach to understanding legal pluralism: customary versus state law, native versus Western societal organization, and so on. This framework requires that more than one "legal system" fit into one of its *preidentified categories* of "law" for legal pluralism to exist.

Classical legal pluralists rely on categories to identify plurality in legal systems; two levels of analysis exist in this process. On one level classical legal pluralists relied on a consensus model whereby "law" in all societies could be defined according to generalizable components; on a second level law could be described as manifesting in society through two main categories, customary (relating to non-Western legal systems) or colonial (state) structures (relating to Western legal systems). A representative definition of the requirements that are necessary in defining "law" as it was viewed by classical legal pluralists was presented by Gulliver (1963, 1): "In any society, there must, by definition, exist regularized procedures... to deal with alleged breaches of norms and injuries.... There must be ways by which it can be established whether in fact a breach occurred, and what is the extent of the injuries; and there must be means of determining and enforcing decisions which provide a settlement of the dispute, and perhaps also means which tend to prevent recurrence of the matter." This definition emphasizes procedural elements of law, while relying on the unproven assumption that social norms exist. Associations of "formality" with Western structures of organization and of "informality" with non-Western structures of organization are a resounding theme in the classical legal pluralist definitions of law.

Malinowski's (1959, 15) work on "savage justice" presented a definition of customary law widely used in classical legal pluralist theories. Malinowski emphasized a view of non-Western laws as based on "obligation" (informal) and of Western laws as based on "authority" (formal). These formal/informal dichotomies continue to influence many aspects of contemporary legal pluralist scholarship. Implicit in these categorizations are a supremacist attitude toward formal (Western), and a primitivist attitude toward informal (African) social structures and legal organizations.

African legal scholars at the time presented a very different picture of law than the one presented by Western classical legal pluralists: "The African peoples are... at varying degrees of political, cultural, and economic development. Since law is inevitably interlocked with all these phases of social life, it naturally manifests itself in different ways and conditions, and so we sometimes get variation in details, if not in essentials, as we pass from one society to another" (Elias 1956, 8). Elias also emphasized (293) that some African societies function through non-centralized political authority (as kinships), some function through strong centralized political authorities (with military, administrative, and judicial branches), while some function as "loosely knit confederations" (with semi-independent chiefdoms with one "supreme" king presiding over them). From this perspective it becomes difficult to classify law within Western legal pluralist assumptions about formal Western categories and informal non-Western categories. Despite these contradictions, the strongly dichotomized nature of the classical framework prevailed, and aided in keeping its theorists functioning in a categorical mindset that aimed to classify law into predefined categories and proceeded to compare/contrast these categories.

Llewellyn and Hoebel (1941, 39-40) state that the only differences between modern (Western) and primitive (non-Western) laws are the "technicalities" through which normative orders are enforced: "The only thing about technical law which is different in the sense of comparable is that it has a technical field of discourse," and, if those technical and institutional tools were to be put aside, then the essence of "law" that transcends all manifestations of "law" would "become at once familiar instead of different." This view presents the basic approach to defining law in classical legal pluralism. It is a categorical definition that relies on the existence and positive attributes of consensus (similarities), and de facto[19] assumes that conflicts or differences are "problematic."

Bohannon (1967, 27) insisted that the "essence of law" can be found in "four legal attributes: authority, obligation, intent for universal application, and sanction." He further claimed that these attributes are present in both "Western/state" and "tribal/customary" legal systems. From these categorizations emerged a definition of law focusing on consensus, assumed generalizability, and official states and/or political organization to produce and implement law.

Methodological Framework

The methodological framework of classical legal pluralism relies on an "unbiased observer" role for researchers. Hoebel (1954, 17) states that "in the study of a social system and its law by the specialist it is his job to abstract the postulates from the behavior he sees and from what he hears." Hoebel (29) and Malinowski (1959, 15) both stress that the multifaceted nature of law requires an eclectic and elastic approach to researching law and society. Hoebel (36) placed great emphasis on "phonetic training" (learning the language of the society under study) and "notetaking." He also presented the "case method" through which specific cases are gathered, followed by a search for thematic and generalizable illustrations of "facts," leading to realistic jurisprudence. Implicit to the case method is the assumption that what cannot be generalized within the predetermined thematic categories of law does not qualify as law.

Malinowski (1959, 14), in line with Hoebel's (1954) methodological procedures, stressed the need to conduct research with goals to "arrive at a satisfactory classification of norms and rules of a primitive community," and, in doing so, to draw distinctions between customary laws and other customs that do not translate to law in "primitive" societies. The categorical view of law in this framework impacts the manner in which one can assess law: first, in assuming that separate categories of types of law exist and, second, in assuming that researchers can observe/record these categories.

Gender Analyses

Classical legal pluralists relied heavily on the *formal status* of women in assessing the roles of women in relation to law in colonized regions; the majority of the work conducted within this framework studied women as wives, widows, or slaves when slavery was legal (Hill[20] 1972). This placed the understanding of women's interactions with law within these rigid and unrepresentative boundaries. Gluckman (1965, 223-225) presents the role of women in "primitive" African societies as relating mainly to rituals and bewitching. In addition, he presents the role of women as "manipulated" in the political realm to solve political conflicts through the presentation of opportunities for men to rule and gain kinship. In another study Gluckman (1973, 216) presents the stereotypical view of African gender roles as he tells a story in which an African man claims, "like all Whites, I [Gluckman] spoil women." This attitude is not problematic from *within* the "formal" superior and "informal" inferior categories of law, for if the African legal systems of governance are assumed to be inferior, then it would only be natural for scholars who adhere to such ideology to assume their own personal and cultural "superiorities" in relation to the "other" men and societies they are studying.

Gulliver (1963) presents a highly submissive image of African women in his account of customary courts in Tanzania. Hoebel (1954) and Malinowski (1959) made no specific mention of women in their presentations of methodological assessments in classical legal pluralism. In contrast to these negative stereotypes presented by Western scholars, Elias (1956, 101), upon presenting specific examples in diverse contexts, asserts that an African "woman's life is passed differently from that of men and has its own sphere, but the woman's position amongst most tribes cannot be regarded as depressed or slavish." Despite such attempts at destabilizing the Western conceptions of Africa and Africans, Western scholars continued to present information that portrayed their biases and racisms toward the continent.

The negative views of African women presented in classical legal pluralist literature contrast with the views of Cheyenne married women presented by Llewellyn and Hoebel (1941). Women in these contexts are shown to function within the sociolegal capacities of respect and honour, though oppressed in the social realm. These categorizations of women from different 'non-white' societies fall neatly within the racial hierarchies created by European colonialists: these racist hierarchies placed "white" people at the top, "black" people at the bottom, and "red" people slightly above "black" people. In accordance with such categorizations Western scholars present images of African women as the "most oppressed" in their "black societies," "red women" as slightly better off, and "white women" as the least oppressed because their "white men" spoil them. Although contemporary scholars do not refer to racial categories in such obvious and obviously racist manners, they continue to adhere to a hierarchical ideology assuming that "white" structures and values are less oppressive than "non-white" structures and values. The stereotypes associated with gender inequality continue to be perpetuated in contemporary frameworks that assess women and the law in Africa, as shown in the presentation of Western assessments of what occurs in northern Nigeria today.

In making this point I am not stating that women are not oppressed in Nigeria; I am pointing out that, although women struggle against patriarchal conditions in both Western and non-Western societies, the prevailing assumption is that women in Africa suffer more serious types of oppression and subjugation. I assert that such normative judgments are based on Western standards of gender equality. They are also based on the Western need to categorize *everything,* including oppressions. Included in the need to categorize is the need to implement hierarchical understandings: one type of oppression is better or worse than another. The very nature of the methodology employed by Western scholars, specifically those who practised classical legal pluralism, relies on both predetermined categories and hierarchies. Ironically, it is assumed that reliance on such methodologies allows researchers to be "unbiased" in their approaches to scholarship.

New Legal Pluralism
Merry (1988), Nader (1969), and Pospisil (1967), starting in the 1960s and continuing until the present, represent some of the

most influential new legal pluralist scholarship. Much of their work is based on dissatisfaction with classical definitions of law and methodological approaches. New legal pluralists recognize that the imposition of European colonial law in Africa created "a plurality of legal orders[21] but [assert that classical legal pluralists] overlooked, to a large extent, the complexity of previous legal orders" (Merry 1988, 870). In addition, new legal pluralists state that the literature that addresses "customary law" in Africa is problematic because "custom" became "law" as a function of colonialism (875). New legal pluralists assert that, in attempts to colonize Africa, the British transformed social control mechanisms in African societies into words and structures that mirrored Western notions of "systems" of law; thus, as colonialists "communicated" with indigenous populations, they created "customary laws" according to those "versions of customary law which meshed best with their own ideology of land ownership as well as other legal relations" (875). New legal pluralists reject these impositions, urging scholars to recognize that these classical constructions of law create knowledge about legal pluralism that is not accurate.

The main ideological shift that spurred the emergence of new legal pluralism occurred when legal pluralism "expanded from a concept that refers to the relations between colonized and colonizer to relationships between dominant and subordinate groups" (Merry 1988, 872). Nader (1969, 2) asserts that the shift from classical to new legal pluralism was based on a shift from a focus on legal theory as pursued through an anthropology of law to a focus on "law in culture and society as it is affected by and affects the individuals who make the law both similar and different." Implementation of these shifts in academic approaches to legal pluralism also included the emergence of a postmodern conception of law: the deconstruction of law is one of the main contributions arising through the new legal pluralist framework (Santos 1987). In addition, new legal pluralism presented inequality and power relations as central elements in the study of law and legal pluralism (Greenhouse 1994).

Assumptions and Ideological Framework

Emerging in a framework that expands definitions and boundaries for research, new legal pluralists incorporated a basic assumption that the deconstruction of "law" is integral to this framework. The deconstruction of law begins with an understanding that law emerges both through the state and through "nonlegal forms of normative ordering" (Merry 1988, 870). In this recognition lies the implicit understanding that "law" is not always what the state defines as such. Santos (1987, 297), in deconstructing law from a postmodern standpoint, states that the limitations that plagued classical legal pluralism can be addressed through an assessment of legal pluralism that rejects the dichotomization of formal/informal elements of law: he asserts that "it is time to see the formal in the informal and the informal in the formal."

Greenhouse (1994, 12) places these deconstructionist notions of studying law within a politics of equality that she views as transcending all sociolegal analyses. She states that classical legal pluralists were "optimistic... of law's ability to deliver justice and community to divided nations," and contrasts them with new legal pluralists in the 1960s and 1970s who "drew fundamentally on tacit emotional understandings of equality as integral to the process of sociolegal research itself." Greenhouse also states that new legal pluralists have begun to pursue a study of equality outside the traditional realm of state-defined laws. This expansion in focus is due to a recognition that state legal systems function to disenfranchise and silence; in challenging the unitary power of states in defining law, new legal pluralists began to set new boundaries in defining law, stating that laws emerge from the state and a plurality of social-cultural foundations.

In attempts to truly grasp the essence of law new legal pluralists incorporated a framework of study that made cultures central to the study of law, thereby reinforcing the notion that the state is not the only producer of "normative thinking and power" (Weisbrod 2002, 5). The study of culture as it relates to the production and implementation of law incorporates a power-related context. It assumes that "culture always involves power, and so is partly responsible for the differences in individuals' and groups' abilities to define and meet their needs" (Valdes 2004, 272). In studying culture and forms of law that emerge outside the realm of the state new legal pluralism began to incorporate a study of resistance as a function of understanding law. In essence this framework emphasizes the "role of law in furthering cultural transformations," and in the *post*colonial context has come to study how colonialism "transformed and controlled these subjects [dominated groups] and how these subjects have mobilized the imposed legal system in resistance" (Merry 2000, 18).

In addition to extending definitions/foundations of law, new legal pluralists implemented an extension in geographical locations of legal pluralist societies. They began to recognize so-called "noncolonized societies, particularly to the advanced and industrial countries of Europe and the United States," as legally pluralist societies (Merry 1988, 872). Such recognition, while considered progressive in its shift in focus, bringing Western societies under the pluralist microscope, is problematic in its definitions of colonialism. The United States, defined as a "noncolonized" society by new legal pluralists, was established as a land mass upon which several Western European nations created "colonies." As these colonies began to war with each other, the British established an expansion in colonies. When the members of these colonies "separated" themselves from England they proceeded to impose a Eurocentric and predominantly white social structure upon North America. Their separation in government from the British did not end colonialism in North America, but merely transformed it. Such transformations continue to manifest themselves physically in the occupation of these lands, which, unlike occupation in Africa, in North America have become "homelands." Nonetheless, there are new legal pluralists who study colonialism of the Americas.

As new legal pluralism expanded, an awareness of the different types of colonialism was incorporated into analyses:

"The instance of American colonialism differs from many of the British examples by its emphasis on incorporation rather than exclusion" (Merry 2000, 258). While British colonialism included the incorporation of "dual" legal systems that "sought to construct boundaries between colonizer and colonized," American colonialism worked to *incorporate* and thus *civilize* colonized populations. This "incorporation" framework was key in laying foundations upon which Europeans can continue their control over North American land and peoples. While the British imposed legal pluralism in a manner that eventually resulted in the withdrawal of occupation, the Americans found a form of colonialism that did not require eventual withdrawal from colonized lands.

Much of the framework of analysis for new legal pluralism involves *expansion.* That expansion included for some a study of colonialism in the Americas. In addition to expanding the geographical location of the social field,[22] new legal pluralists expanded the framework for understanding law to include the "informal" sector. This framework also expanded research on legal systems, recognizing that colonialism is an invasive manner in which legal systems are used to define, dominate, and control lands foreign to Europe. These expansions have aided in incorporating an understanding recognizing that the study of legal pluralism includes research into a diverse set of structures and practices.

Defining Law
The definition of law in new legal pluralist scholarship, in accordance with the expansion themes, states that "not all law takes place in courts.... The concern is to document other forms of social regulation, that draw on symbols of law, to a greater or lesser extent, but operate in its shadows, its parking lots, and even down the street in mediation offices"; it also emphasizes that "other forms of regulation outside law constitute law" (Merry 1988, 874). This definition relies heavily on culture as central to defining law. Culture in this school of thought is viewed as a

fluid, changing, interrelated phenomenon, emerging through an intermixing of tradition and everyday interactions among people living in the same social setting (Comaroff and Comaroff 1993). These interactions (defined as culture) create and implement law.

New legal pluralists rely on a definition of law that has a predetermined essence, emerging in formal and informal elements. Pospisil (1967, 24) defines legal systems as capable of existing mainly through interactions among subgroups who live at all levels in society and who, combined, make up society: "Every such subgroup owes its existence in a large degree to a legal system that is its own and that regulates the behavior of its members." He challenges centralist notions of law that place law solely within the context of the state, because they present a definition of law without incorporating the role of social interactions in defining and implementing law.

In composing new and broader definitions of "law," new legal pluralists present a broader and more flexible conception of customary law as compared with classical legal pluralists. Engel (1980, 429) defines customary law as emerging "wherever patterns of repeated interaction among people necessarily lead to mutual expectations and interdependencies that serve to regulate conduct," and emphasizes that this occurs in both non-Western and Western settings.

This definition is heavily reliant on the role of culture in defining law, and, while the definition of culture is disputed, there appears to be a definition of legal cultures that is widely accepted: the legal culture of a society is produced through a "synthesis of formal and customary elements," continually changing and evolving "in response to changing circumstances," concluding that "the totality of norms and behavior of the local citizenry" comprises the legal culture of that community (Engel 1980, 431). Still existing in this definition of law are categorical constructions of law. New legal pluralists, while challenging the construction of these categories and deeming them "too narrow," proceeded to expand the number of categories in which law can be defined.

They did not challenge the categorical nature through which classical legal pluralists produced knowledge about "law"; they challenged only the relevance of the categories used.

Working specifically within the African context, Hellum (2002) presents an understanding of law that emphasizes new legal pluralist works to deconstruct law. She observes the construction of a tension between the implementation of "international standards of human rights" and the "inequalities" imposed through African customary laws, and she adds that, while it is often assumed that legal pluralism in contemporary Africa is an attempt to revive or preserve traditional African legal structures, it is seldom recognized that "in many countries a number of the discriminatory customary rules *that were created by the colonial courts* have been upheld" (637; emphasis added). Merry (1988) and Nader and Grande (2002) provide a foundation for this deconstruction, expanding the boundaries through which law can emerge and be defined. While new legal pluralists deconstruct the assumed "nature" of law that tends to place the centrality of law in the state,[23] they also examine what has been referred to as "customary" law, and study the colonial roots that named and shaped it. The categories used in new legal pluralist work place the centrality of law in society, not the state.

Methodological Framework

Based on the increased number of categories in which law can exist, a new methodological framework was implemented by new legal pluralists. The goal of this new methodology was to access informal mechanisms of social control and creations of law. Pospisil (1967, 8) proposed that, if the point of reference of law and society shifted from "society as a whole" to "the individual subgroups that exist within society," researchers would discover "radically different bodies of 'law' prevailing among these small units." Collier's work (1968) operationalized this proposition with an ethnography conducted in Chiapas, Mexico. In studying the rituals of marriage Collier documented the courtship, dowry, and ceremonial elements of the process (six categories in total leading up to the wedding ceremony), and thus illustrated that the cultural meanings and practices associated with each ritual contribute to and facilitate the final contractual union of marriage.

In bringing forth the subgroups of associated actors and actions Collier (1968) was able to better explain the process through which marriage laws are practised in Zinacantan, Chiapas, Mexico. Her work emphasized the informality of law as it emerged in diverse contexts and exemplified the interrelational, subgroup emphasis in this framework that centralized culture to assess law. In the methodological framework of new legal pluralism the researcher must enter a social field in search of both the formal and the informal elements of law, looking to discover and record a wide array of elements that merge to create law.

Gender Analyses
It is important to note that the rise of new legal pluralism coincided with the increased participation of female scholars in the field: as women came to study law and society from a legal pluralist perspective gender analyses in social fields became more prominent, as the roles of women and their relationships with law came under consideration. In Merry's (2000) ethnographic work women encompass a much different role than what was offered in the classical legal pluralist paradigm. Merry places gender as one element[24] of understanding colonial processes. She assesses gender relations to illuminate the types of transitions occurring in law and culture through colonialism (111). Merry illustrates how in precolonial Hawaii women had leadership/ decision-making roles, and explains how the transitions that made male power dominant in Hawaii's sociolegal structures were linked to the emergence of capitalism (property ownership as wealth) and the secularization of the state: "This meant a shift from the sovereignty of the chiefs [many of them women] to the sovereignty of men of property," with the result that "only men were viewed as entitled to govern themselves" (110-111).

In this contextual framework gender relations are not viewed as markers for civilization in societies, as was done in classical legal pluralism. In new legal pluralist frameworks gender is used as a variable through which the processes that guide cultural and legal relations can be better understood and identified. In addition, the recognition of normative orders and informal methods of social control as law in this paradigm allows new legal pluralists to access a more relevant understanding of the role of women as members of patriarchal societies run by patriarchal, colonialist laws.

This gendered approach to legal pluralism is linked to the new legal pluralist assessment of "inequality" as central to an understanding of law (Greenhouse 1994). In expanding on definitions of law, and in implementing a methodological framework that used "subgroups" for access to social fields, new legal pluralists expanded on the understanding that "law" is experienced differently by different subgroups. In this methodological framework there is room to present and understand the experiences of women with law, culture, and society.

Contemporary Applications of the Classical Legal Pluralist Framework

In contemporary legal pluralist scholarship new legal pluralism is dominant, yet several strands of classical legal pluralism continue to function. Despite the racist and sexist foundations of classical legal pluralism, and despite the problematic associations between classical legal pluralism and colonialism in Africa, this form of scholarship continues to influence contemporary scholars. Normative legal pluralism presents one such field of study. Assessing the significance of the ideological advancements of new legal pluralism within an "operational context," La Torre (1999, 193) states that "normative legal pluralism can be operative only *within certain limits*. Otherwise it will be transformed into *descriptive* pluralism, interesting perhaps for the sociologist but useless for the lawyer and the citizen who are called to orient their conduct in a specific situation."

Normative legal pluralism, according to La Torre (1999), functions within a form of legal monism that studies and utilizes pluralities as they exist within "the rule of law." This approach prefers to place pluralism within the realm of the state and to keep the definitions of law within a hierarchical realm. The methodological framework in this type of pluralism incorporates Moore's (1973) semi-autonomous social fields. Moore states that "'law' is a short term for a very complex aggregation of principles, norms, ideas, rules, practices, and the activities of agencies of legislation, administration, adjudication and enforcement, backed by political power and legitimacy" (719). In the complexity of the state and its interactions with society this form of legal scholarship defines legal plurality.

Whereas La Torre (1999) presents a contemporary assessment of how classical legal pluralism is applied in contemporary conceptions of the state, Moore (1973) advocates a return to Malinowski's focus not only on "rules" but also on how rules are made valid and implemented in society, reaffirming the customary elements of law. In relation to methodological frameworks, Moore disagrees with the new legal pluralist definitions of law in her assertion that the "semi-autonomous field" in which law can be studied encompasses a relationship between the state and society, and does not place the emergence of law in that relationship. The social field functions in a semi-autonomous context: "It can generate rules and customs and symbols internally, but... it is also vulnerable to rules and decisions and other forces emanating from the larger world by which it is surrounded" (720).

Moore (1973) recognizes the threat of force and fear associated with the punitive structures of state law, and emphasizes the legitimacy and power of other forms of law (not imposed or defined by legal institutions) as having impact on the people functioning within a semi-autonomous field. In this sense she rejects Pospisil's concept of law as emerging from the relationships and interactions among subgroups, and, in line with much of the criticism of new legal pluralists, asserts that they "see law everywhere" and, in their deconstructions of law, confuse definitions of what law is with functions of social control.

In addition to presenting a critique of new legal pluralism this form of contemporary classical legal pluralism illustrates, in a more familiar setting, the ideological assumptions of classical legal pluralism. It is a framework that functions in a highly dichotomized and categorical manner (mirroring how colonialists defined and addressed African social structures), presenting information about "colonial state law" as separate from "customary tribal laws," "formal" (state) laws as separate from "informal" (community-oriented) laws, and, as La Torre (1999) points out, "sociological" and "legal" scholars as encompassing separate, not interrelated, functions.

Despite such attempts to emphasize the dichotomies used by academia to produce knowledge, the emphasis within normative legal pluralism on state law as "plural" creates a scholarly link between legal centralists and legal pluralists, illustrating the existence within academia of the interrelations between paradigmatic affiliations and highlighting that, when these categories pre-exist, one (state laws in La Torre's case) will inherently be perceived as more relevant or more powerful than the other (community laws in La Torre's case). The function of dichotomy is to implement a predetermined and academically constructed hierarchy. In attempts to deconstruct "law" new legal pluralists redefined dichotomies and expanded the realm within which such categories can exist, but they, like past and contemporary classical legal pluralists, did not challenge the methodological structures that reinforce and continue to assume the existence of generalizable dichotomies in the emergence of law in society.

In acknowledging and understanding the dichotomized and categorical structure within which classical and new legal pluralists function, one can achieve a greater understanding of the theoretical approaches and conclusions reached in relation to legal pluralist scholarship. One can also begin to achieve an understanding of the academic institution's tools, which "professionalize" the definitions of law and keep them within a framework that mirrors the state's dichotomizing processes of social control.

The same academic frameworks that professionalized the processes of colonialism through the dichotomization of people into races continue to dichotomize the definition of "law," and thereby to aid in justifying past and present brutalities. The explanations employed by classical and normative legal scholars present an academic opportunity for Western scholars to continue to speak about Africa in manners that are racist and white supremacist. While new legal pluralists appear to have "better intentions," they too aid in the implementation of a hierarchy that places African social structures in an inferior position that is "informal,"[25] and colonial, European, American structures in a constructed superior one that incorporates both the "informal" and the "formal" elements of civilization. It is generally assumed in Western scholarship that the formal elements of African societies either have never existed or, if they did exist, were permanently destroyed by colonialism.

Non-Essentialist Legal Pluralism

Much as the emergence of new legal pluralism was rooted in dissatisfaction with classical legal pluralism, non-essentialist legal pluralism is now emerging due to dissatisfaction with new legal pluralism. Tamanaha (2000) is prominent in the presentation of a non-essentialist legal pluralist framework. Building on Teubner's (1997) critique of how the deconstruction of law was pursued in new legal pluralism, Tamanaha presents a non-essentialist approach to legal pluralism that focuses on implementing a more successful deconstruction of law. The main component is a mode of analysis that rejects the assumption that law has any predetermined "essence."

Teubner (1997b, 773) states that the methods through which law has been deconstructed have been unsuccessful and claims that the deconstruction of law manifests itself like a dance, caught in a "performative contradiction" that critiques law on stage but fails to challenge it behind the scenes. Tamanaha (2000) associates this failure with the new legal pluralist assumption that law has an "essence" that can be predetermined in academic institutions and then sought out in the social field.

A non-essentialist framework presents a legal pluralism that places law within the minds and actions of people: law is what the people define as such. Non-essentialists, like new legal pluralists, reject the assumption that law is created, controlled, and implemented by the state alone. Furthermore, non-essentialism challenges the very assumption that "law" has an essence that can be *predetermined* by researchers. Non-essentialist researchers assume "nothing" before communicating with people in the social field under research.

Teubner's (1992) assessment of legal pluralism was identified by Tamanaha (2000, 306) as "the point of departure for the non-essentialist approach to law." Teubner (1997a, 15) identifies two problems with the new legal pluralists' approach to law. The first is their *broad* approach to law, which renders them incapable of distinguishing between law and other forms of social control, and the second is their *narrow* approach to law, which limits its functions to social control and maintenance of order. In these criticisms non-essentialists begin to question how legal pluralists have produced knowledge and make notes of the reoccurring inadequacies. From these notes emerges the non-essentialist legal pluralist paradigm.

Assumptions and Ideological Framework

A non-essentialist version of legal pluralism defines plurality in manifestations of institutional or non-institutional, systemic or or non-systemic, seen-through or not-seen-through patterns of behaviour, sometimes implemented through force, sometimes not implemented through force. Thus, non-essentialist legal plurality "involves different phenomena going by the label Law, whereas [new or classical] legal pluralism usually involves a multiplicity of one basic phenomenon, Law (as defined)" (Tamanaha 2000, 315). One of the main criticisms of new legal pluralists is that they "find law everywhere." This critique results from the expanded essence by which new legal pluralists define law. Non-essentialism implements an ideological framework that does not prioritize assumed (expanded/depleted) essences of law, but works to build a fluid, flexible, and changing definition of law.

Nader (1969) presents a discussion that took place during a Law and Society Association meeting on whether "law *and* society" should be changed to "law *in* society." In this debate the definition of "law" was challenged as scholars disputed the point of departure for law: does law emerge apart from society, or does law emerge from within society? Nader explains that the suggestion to shift from *and* to *in* was met with defensive retorts. The resulting discussion brought out implicit assumptions that new legal pluralists hold about law: "Somehow, law is conceived of as in reality being a system independent of society and culture" (8). This may be a point of overlap from classical to new legal pluralists, with theorists working within both frameworks insisting that law has essence and thus is studied along with, and not in, society.

A non-essentialist approach to legal pluralism would incorporate a law-*in*-society perspective. Tamanaha (2001, 120) challenges essentialist legal pluralisms by challenging "the mirror thesis." The mirror thesis asserts that law is a reflection of society and implies that, while law "reflects" a society's morals and values, it exists separately from society through its institutions, which implement an agreed-upon social contract. The mirror thesis assumes that, first, society is governed by the social contract (emerging through law) and that, second, there exists a moral consensus that can be identified and implemented through law. Tamanaha deconstructs the mirror thesis by challenging the *existence* of a moral consensus in society, while illustrating the "law" as an institution that has yet to be proven *dominant* in governing social interactions. He does so by presenting an awareness of the contextualized diversities within and between societies, and how these differences manifest in diverse reactions to legal systems. He concludes that, "extensive as the consequent changes to society and law might be, the result of these changes is not necessarily that law and society move entirely in sync; often mismatch, rather than mirror, remains" (120).

Classical and new legal pluralists provided a foundation for the emergence of the "mismatch" hypothesis, as was clear in the observation that the concrete "lived law" is different from the abstract "written law" expressed in legal texts (Ehrlich 1936, 501). The distinction between the "real" and the "ideal" elements of law is said to have created a foundation upon which the emergence of "a socially oriented legal pluralism" could emerge (Melissaris 2004, 59). Yet with this foundation Ehrlich (1936, 57) established an essentialist view of law within the legal pluralism framework, asserting that the essence of law is its dispute-resolving functions. Tamanaha (2001) found these foundations of legal pluralism inaccurate, adding that these foundations have been limited through an essentialism that skews pluralist approaches to studying law.

Defining Law

In non-essentialist legal pluralism "law" is viewed as a socially, politically, and culturally constructed phenomenon, and, outside the actions and beliefs of people, does not essentially exist. Thus, to study "law" one must study the behaviours and interactions of people in specific social settings: law is what behaviours/interactions prescribe as such. Legal plurality in this framework is recognized as occurring when more than one form of "law" is recognized and is seen in the social practices of a group. What makes this non-essentialist approach to studying legal pluralism different from that of new legal pluralists is rejection of the notion of law as "fundamentally functional in nature" (Tamanaha 2000, 308).

While the functions and functionality of law are central to essentialist legal pluralisms, a non-essentialist view of law does not assume that "law" is essential to the functions and survival of society. Parnell (2003, 1) provides an approach to studying law that is representative of the non-essentialist framework: "Both crime and law are created in culture as people negotiate social change. At the same time, crime and law may arise as separate culture-making processes and become linked to each other in a wide array of associations." He also explains that there are circumstances in which an official law may not have been broken yet the perception of the occurrence of a crime may be prevalent. In addition, rule implementations may occur outside the realm of the state, and may or may not include the use of force.

A non-essentialist framework incorporates the ability to identify these complexities as a central element of understanding law in its various contexts, manifestations, and implications. Non-essentialism asserts that, "despite the shared label 'Law,' these are diverse phenomena, not variations of a single phenomenon, and each one of these does many different things and/or is used to do many things" (Tamanaha 2000, 313).

"Law" is not the "rules" that guide society; "law" is the interactions that take place to create, implement, and guide social interactions. In light of these complexities non-essentialist legal pluralism concludes that functionality is not central[26] to all "law." Failing to understand this complexity is a failure to define law, not because researchers are not searching well, but because law has no essence: the "essence" they are searching for does not exist.

Non-essentialism suggests that legal pluralists have "made up" law in academic institutions and have proceeded to try to locate it in society. Furthermore, the constructions of law in essentialist legal pluralism tend to mirror the assumptions about law that the state has presented: that it is functional, that it is necessary, that it always plays a social control function, that it can exist outside the realm of social interactions, that it is defined by institutions and codes, that it exists only in categorical, rigid entities, and that it is most powerful (power defined in formality) when backed by the state because state power trumps all other forms of organization in a society. Non-essentialists challenge all these assumptions and assert that the only way to "define" or "find" law in society is to assume that "law" has no essence.

Methodological Framework

In light of the realization that law has no essence, how does one go about "defining law"? The process is laid out in the emergence of a non-essentialist methodological framework. First, non-essentialist legal pluralists employ a methodological framework that *rejects* the implementation by researchers of *predetermined* categories of law in society. This framework incorporates Teubner's (1992) approach to "locating" law through an autopoietic approach: relying on linguistic foundations and suggesting that the use of a binary code that limits an assessment of law to verbalized "legal/illegal" entities are sufficient for defining law. Thus, law is what people define as "legal" and "illegal." Law in this context is different between groups in the same society, is different between societies, and is different over time.

Second, in addressing the nature of the relationship between law and society, this framework brings the study of law into society — not the study of society into law, as is done in essentialist legal pluralist frameworks. The use of this framework allows for the ability to locate law, not only by looking for it in society, but also by asking those 'under study' to define "law." *Law is what the people say is law* (Tamanaha 2000; Teubner 1997a).

Third, non-essentialists assume that the only essential feature of non-essentialism is the lack of essence. According to Tamanaha (2000), "essence" is the predetermined assumption(s) that researchers bring with them into the society they are studying. Thus, non-essentialists assume *only* that law has no essence. With this as a starting point Tamanaha urges researchers to start *without* a predetermined definition of law, proceed to look for areas in which social interactions occur and, on finding such areas, incorporate a research method that asks people to verbalize "law" in that setting. The key research questions posed to people in the social field would include what is law, and is that law? By implementing a strategy of cumulative observation and data-gathering, non-essentialism identifies law as researchers gather people's responses to such questions (Tamanaha 2000).

As conceptions of law begin to take shape within a society, it is important to recognize that these conceptions are fluid, interdependent, and not separate. Conceptions in this framework are not "dichotomized" entities, as categories are in essentialist frameworks (such as customary law or state law in the classical framework, or formal or informal social control in the new legal pluralist framework). Conceptions here overlap, are interdependent, and change through interactions among people in varying situations/settings. What is formal for a specific group may be informal for another group, and what is considered "law" by some may not be so considered by others.

Fourth, in relation to the technical application of non-essentialist research there is the issue of *who* identifies law and *how many people* need to view something as "law" before it becomes recognized as such. Tamanaha (2000, 319) sets a low threshold and never explicitly offers answers to these questions. In reference to "who," he does say "any group within the social arena," and adds that they would have to claim it as "law" for it to be defined as law, and that the definition would emerge through their actions/behaviours among other people in the (sub)group. In line with the ideological foundations of this framework, an answer to "how many" formed before entering the social field would transform the non-essentialist researcher into an essentialist one. One thing is clear: due to reliance on social interactions to identify law, a unitary source (such as a penal code) cannot create or implement law.

Fifth, Tamanaha (2000) states that sociolegal theorists should not "shrink away" from the possibility of identifying plural forms of law, explaining that fears that "too many" social practices become identified as law under this framework are unfounded, because people do not lightly or widely use the label "law."

A main obstacle recognized by non-essentialist legal pluralists includes the academic applicability of the proposed approach to identifying law. Tamanaha (2000) recognizes that, because the definition of law is contingent upon the social field, not upon academic discourse, non-essentialism may offend "conventional" social scientific expectations: in non-essentialist frameworks there occurs a shift in power from the academic researchers' professional identity and assumed expertise in defining law to the people in society through which law emerges. Thus, obstacles to the progression of non-essentialist research include the humbling of academic sources of knowledge and are not limited to non-essentialist methodological frameworks.

Gender Analyses

In the non-essentialist framework the role of gender would require an assessment of law as it is defined and used by women in the social setting. Manji (1999) presented an assessment of women and law in *post*colonial Africa that incorporated resistance as a central theme of study. In this incorporation Manji utilized a non-essentialist framework that defined law according to women's experiences, not according to preconceived notions of law. By doing so she was able to identify resistance as central to their relationships with law, and thus proceeded to represent gender in the study of law and society appropriately within the realm of a larger social structure that is patriarchal. A non-essentialist study of gender in law and society is able to incorporate legal pluralism as it is used by women, and does not place "law" or normative systems as defined in academia as central to theoretical goals.

Within the context of northern Nigeria non-essentialist researchers would *have* to ask women what they define as law: if normative orders emerge as law according to women, if communication methods emerge as law according to women, or if their socioeconomic dealings emerge as law according to women, then they are law. A non-essentialist analysis in northern Nigeria would allow women to inform the researcher of what is or is not law. Given the circumstances under which women live and the obstacles they face in achieving status/socioeconomic wealth in the international patriarchal order, non-essentialism appears most relevant in accessing knowledge and appropriately representing women's interactions with law.

ASSESSMENT OF LEGAL PLURALISM: APPLICABILITY TO NON-WESTERN CONTEXTS

In presenting the three main legal pluralist frameworks it becomes evident that their diverse approaches to law and society provide different opportunities for research; in addition, the relevance of each framework differs as different societies enter into the academic search for knowledge. The following is an analysis of the three frameworks in relation to the African context. Included is an assessment of the definition of law in each framework, and of the relevance of these definitions to women and law in northern Nigeria.

Based on the heavy reliance on formal definitions of law and social status in classical legal pluralism, it appears that this framework of analysis is not equipped to access the networks that women create and work within in northern Nigeria. This inability is evident in the deficient assessments of gender prevalent throughout classical legal pluralist work. While new legal pluralists emphasize the importance of accessing informal social control networks in the study of law and society, this framework does not implement an understanding of law that identifies the fluidity and interdependence of formal and informal networks of social control. In the northern Nigerian social setting formal social control mechanisms (sharia, colonial laws) have given rise to the informal (and at times formal from the women's perspectives) networks created by women. It is thus important to implement a legal pluralist framework capable of identifying that connection while allowing women in the region the opportunity to explain *their* social settings, *their* networks, *their* actions, and *their* laws.

Given these circumstances, it appears that non-essentialist legal pluralism provides a framework that allows researchers to place the definition of law within the methodological realm as well as the ideological realm of scholarly work. Through non-essentialist legal pluralism the definitions of law can be brought forth in the interactions that women in northern Nigeria experience, not through reliance on classical definitions of law or on a preconceived definition of what constitutes law, as is the case in new legal pluralist scholarship. A non-essentialist legal pluralist approach to studying law in society allows scholars to learn about law according to Hausa women in northern Nigeria and, in doing so, better represent Hausa society, and provide a more comprehensive and accurate assessment of women and law in the region.

In general this framework appears to be most relevant for understanding law in non-Western contexts, and for accessing knowledge that lies outside the boundaries of Western definitions, experiences, and academic assumptions. It implements an understanding of law that is complex and allows researchers to enter a social field that is radically different from their own with the preconceived understanding that "law" as they have known or experienced it may not be "law" as people in non-Western settings have known or experienced it. Masaji (1998, 232) suggests that a "non-Western legal pluralism may be seen in theory as one form of the dual structure of state law and minor law or coexistence of modern law with traditional law. Its reality is, however, never reduced to the simple structure or coexistence, but is built up with other systems of law." A non-essentialist approach to law may be able to further explain this coexistence: *listening* to women living with purdah/sharia will illuminate their perceptions of these contexts, bringing forth their definitions of law as it emerges through their experiences/ interactions. *Resisting* the urge to categorize and thus westernize their experiences may allow academia to present relevant and accurate understandings of their lives.

A macrolevel context of *post*colonial African social structures illustrates that legal pluralism in the African context is the study of legal systems as they interact with, are created by, and overlap with society and social interactions: it is not merely an interaction that occurs between African and non-African legal systems, but also an interaction between legal systems created by states and normative orders implemented by the people. In northern

Nigeria women appear to have implemented normative orders that contradict and, at times, defy both African and British legal expectations and definitions of status. An approach to studying law in these settings that does not incorporate an understanding of these interactions, due to a reliance on law as owning an essence separate from the perceptions and actions of women, is ill equipped to address the interrelationships that form law.

An understanding of legal pluralism must allow for an understanding that law for Hausa women in the north may have an essence that is different from, or even contradicts, the assumed essence that classical and new legal pluralists assign to law. I believe that women in northern Nigeria can be best understood within this context: their interactions with the law are more a function of colonialism than they are a function of the Nigerian state and sharia laws. It comes down to a function of survival that takes place daily on a continent that has seen much upheaval but has maintained its identities and cultures. A non-essentialist approach to women's interactions with law creates an academic opportunity whereby these complexities can be brought forth: in listening to *women's* definitions scholars will be able to identify "law" as it exists for women, and not law as it is expected to exist for Western scholars.

While elites in contemporary Africa define "modernization" and key elements for "nation-building" through "development" as important, and equate such progress to the implementation of a unified legal system (usually based on Western legal models) (Okoth-Ogendo 1979, 165), research on the socioeconomic actions of women in northern Nigeria has shown that "development" is not always capable of being recorded officially or defined through Western academic boundaries. While the "official" legal functions continue to westernize conceptions of women's lives, it is important to academically understand that these "official" manifestations are met with resistance through a rejection of law and the creation of new laws when necessary.

The shifts in academic discourse that non-essentialism provides are not "important" for the women in northern

Nigeria; they are important for scholars who need to keep their academic disciplines relevant. If social science academics are truly embracing the quest to produce relevant knowledge, then they must place the *social* above the *science*. They must learn to "let go" of the conceptions that academia has formed and begin to really look at the society they are trying to understand. They must work to create a science that is relevant to the social before they worry about using a science that their fellow misinformed scholars will accept or reject.

Fortunately, more scholars are beginning to discover that women in Africa rely on more than formal law for their day-to-day survival: "African norms and values are incompatible with the norms and values applying in the West" (Hellum 2002, 636). This realization should not only alter the way scholars understand law in Africa, but also alter their methodological approaches to research in Africa. In realizing the fundamental differences in experience, in history, in culture, and in social setting, academics must begin to approach research in the region from a non-essentialist perspective, not to deny the existence of "essence" in law, but to deny the Western assumption that law has a predetermined "essence" that they bring forth through their own constructions of law and society.

Academic attempts to essentialize law and to impose a preconceived definition of law that guides researchers have resulted in an academia that is not relevant or appropriate for accessing knowledge about women in northern Nigeria. The incorporation of a non-essentialist perspective is key to strengthening academic tools and abilities to address the *diversity* that is a function of *pluralism*. In recognizing that many systems of law exist a non-essentialist legal pluralism also recognizes that these many systems exist differently, according to different people in different settings, and elicit different reactions. These differences can best be understood through an abandonment of reliance on "essence" as existing in law. Sharia is not just codes and implementations of rules, but also an experience of law by women in northern Nigeria, and, although sharia codes remain constant, the experience of sharia for men and women creates a different law with different functions and implications. Non-essentialist legal pluralism, unlike other frameworks, allows for an understanding of these differences.

While non-essentialism is most relevant for research on women and law in northern Nigeria, obstacles do exist in its applicability and ideology. First, it is assumed in this framework that researchers can enter a social field without preconceived notions and biases. The "objective researcher" assumption is dangerous, because it does not take into account the impact of the presence of a researcher on a social setting, and because it posits that researchers can transcend the human element and relinquish bias while conducting research. Second, non-essentialism does not account for the transformations that take place when recording information: upon "defining law" according to people in the social field, how does a researcher avoid transforming these definitions in the process of presenting them in scholarly works? Does a researcher impose "essence" upon law when he or she translates social realities into academic materials?

These types of obstacles are not insurmountable. In my opinion non-essentialism adds complexity to academic endeavours and, in doing so, brings the complexity of law in society into a more appropriate arena for academic discussion. Non-essentialism may make research "more difficult" and may impose a level of self-reflexivity upon researchers that appears to be lacking in academia, but these impositions may expand the scope of knowledge available to academic disciplines.

A complex social reality that is unstable, fluid, and interchanging requires complex academic approaches that may not be "perfectly" definable, generalizable, or predictable. Above all, the production of knowledge in sociolegal disciplines needs to shift from unquestioned and taken-for-granted assumptions about "law" and "society," and to rely more heavily on the interactions in society without which law could never exist. I believe that more researchers need to confront the fact that without social interactions there would be no law, but that without law social interactions would continue; thus, social interactions take precedence in defining law and not vice versa.

Women and Resistance in Northern Nigeria

Some scholars have stated that the policies of colonial and contemporary African states toward women have ranged from mild lenience in instances where their activities contributed to the economic structures of the nation to forthright domination and attack when women proved themselves "uncontainable" (Jackson 1987). Manji (1999, 443) explains that "a corollary of the failure of the African ruling elites to achieve hegemony—and the consequent use of authoritarianism and force rather than consensus to achieve compliance—has been the search by subordinate groups within the state for means to resist its coercive tendencies." Such situations have been met with two main forms of resistance that are most relevant to women in Africa.

The first form of resistance is the practice of "exit," whereby withdrawal avoids confrontation with violent state policies and actions. This withdrawal is accomplished through the creation of a private[27] realm in which non-state systems of law are employed. Both Fatton (1989) and Hirschmann (1981) address "exit" as a mechanism of resistance employed in many contemporary African nation-states. Parpart and Straudt (1989) provide examples more specific to women's relationships with African nation-states. They record activities in which women participate that the state finds difficult to regulate. These activities include "illegal" trading, creation of cooperatives, participation in prostitution, and implementation of informal mechanisms of communication and networks of support that aid in maintaining autonomy from the state.

While the "exit" strategy appears to be easier to implement in urban settings, rural settings incorporate a second form of resistance: a "secrecy and concealment" strategy, whereby women are able to create and implement their own laws and governance techniques for economic and political survival (Manji 1999, 447). This form of resistance employs "exit," but does so in ways that are less accessible to the majority of those not included in the participating subgroups. In rural settings anonymity is not enjoyed as it is in urban settings; thus, this form of resistance involves arrangements and agreements that, at times, are unspoken yet, upon implementation, are clearly established.

In identifying these two main forms of resistance, it becomes clear that it would be difficult and potentially impossible to build a legal pluralistic theory relevant to women in contemporary Africa without the incorporation of an understanding of resistance. Legal pluralism in these settings is largely a function of resistance to oppressive state laws that continue to mirror colonial modes of governance: "To summarize, writing on women and the state in colonial and post-colonial Africa indicates that the relationship of women to the state has been at best ambivalent, and at worst characterized by actual and symbolic coercion," resulting in a distancing by women from the state, either through physical exit or through symbolic exit in secrecy and concealment (Manji 1999, 448). Thus, Manji concludes that the implementation of legal centralist theories would be highly problematic, due to their reliance on the state to define laws. I would add that the implementation of any "essentialist" conceptions of law in these social fields is just as problematic. Preconceived conceptions of "law," especially ones arising from Western academic standards and cultural contexts, might theoretically "appear different," compared with legal centralist theories, but would misrepresent situations and reach conclusions that are just as problematic.

Examples of such problematic conclusions are found in the contradictions reached through different forms of academic assessments. In discussing land rights and legal ownership of property in northern Nigeria, Ayua (1998, 237-238) reports that Islamic laws preserve women's rights to ownership of land, but notes that these rights are often ignored. She concludes that "this pattern of behavior has tended to make women second-class citizens. Most of the women have resigned themselves to their fate and have accepted the humiliating status accorded them by society. The few others... who would want to assert their rights or fight for them are discouraged for fear of being branded social deviants or rebels." These conclusions come in direct contradiction of assessments of women's roles, actions, and identities from a non-state-oriented form of legality. Examples of women's participation in the informal and "socially moral" socioeconomic sector have been presented in contradiction to such disempowered conclusions about women in northern Nigeria. Void of an understanding of resistance strategies, assessments of law in northern Nigeria present a highly disempowered picture.

In studying resistance and organizational strategies among factory workers in Kano, a state in northern Nigeria, it was found that female involvement in the formal labour process was sufficient to form a class consciousness, but it did not extend to a formal consciousness of gender discrimination. It was thus concluded that, "in order for this class consciousness to generate a gender dimension built into it, the women must also be able to understand that the additional disadvantages which they suffer have to do with their gender, an experience which sets them aside from their male colleagues" (Abdullah 1997, 65). On a formal level Abdullah asserts that a gendered understanding does not emerge into formal strategies of organization to fight patriarchal oppression.

On a more informal level Shebi (1997) identifies liberation for women in Nigeria as beginning with empowerment through identity, role, and development. As women work on developing their identities through autonomous networks and organizations, Shebi places a symbolic value on "the start of liberation for our women, liberation from the inhibiting identity and role of our culture, which men have imposed on them and which has enslaved them for ages" (133). It becomes apparent that the views held in relation to women, resistance, and their relationship to law are greatly influenced by the understanding (or lack of understanding) of resistance. It also becomes evident that in the formal realm women are viewed as largely oppressed and degraded, while in the informal realm they appear to be self-regulating and autonomous. These contradictory conclusions destabilize the academic approach to studying law in northern Nigeria, and illustrate that the conclusions reached rely heavily on the focus and orientation of the researchers.

Legal centralist and classical legal pluralist paradigms, with a heavy focus on formal law (state and customary), are not equipped to assess the "informal" lives that women lead. On the other hand, the new legal pluralist framework, while encompassing the ability to recognize and address the "informalities" and their relevance, may not be equipped to address the oppressions that do occur due to formal legal policies and implementations. In addition, the formal/informal dichotomies employed by legal centralists as well as by classical and new legal pluralists present academic frameworks so reliant on categories and divisions that they become unable to learn about the complexities of law in northern Nigerian societies.

A non-essentialist legal pluralist methodology works best in this setting, for it allows women in northern Nigeria to present the relevance of informality while addressing the elements of formal oppressions they face. In entering the social field without preconceived definitions of what constitutes "law," and what is "formal" or "informal," researchers in this framework are more able to portray representative understandings of the relationships between women and law.

CONCLUSION: THE RELEVANCE OF NON-ESSENTIALIST LEGAL PLURALISM FOR RESEARCH ON WOMEN IN NORTHERN NIGERIA

For women in northern Nigeria the boundaries between formal and informal social control are blurred. Sharia and the practice of purdah work in conjunction with cultural, social, and economic factors. It appears that all forms of social control/law in this setting are fluid and interchangeable: they do not exist as separate academic categories. In addition, women in northern Nigeria lead lives that are radically different from those of women elsewhere in the nation: Hausa women in the north live in social and at times formal political seclusion. In northern Nigeria women in rural settings face different circumstances than women in urban settings. In such differences lies a methodological dilemma only if an academic framework looks to dichotomize and generalize findings. Any attempt to understand women and law in Nigeria may require a specialized approach to producing knowledge, with an acceptance that diversity in social settings and experiences does not equate to "problems" in methodology.

The most appropriate ideological framework to address these issues appears to be a non-essentialist one. It rejects the need to rely on dichotomies between categories and does not work to generalize its findings. Non-essentialist researchers approaching this social field, with an understanding that law's essence exists solely in the experiences and beliefs held by women in the region, will be able to approach such overlapping "categories" more readily. Because non-essentialism encompasses a realm of goals focused on "identifying" (not defining) law, any generalizations beyond that have yet to be established by the people whom researchers are attempting to understand. In this framework of analysis women in northern Nigeria are able to present their experiences with law according to their specific social, cultural, political, and legal circumstances.

It has been shown that the assumption that generalizations and themes can aid in creating a better understanding of social realities and their intersections with law is based on a presupposition that there exist implied collective social realities, that there are "themes" that govern social life. These assumptions reduce an understanding of "society" to a monolithic as opposed to a complex and diverse entity. At times discussions about "law" seem to disconnect from social realities in society. Researchers become overridden by the "essence" of their ideological assumptions and lose touch with "law" as it is created in society. Discarding that "essence" may allow for more representative research and theories.

Classical, new, and non-essentialist legal pluralisms have been presented in this chapter according to the ideological foundations of their frameworks, the definitions of law they employ, the boundaries they set in defining their methodological expectations, and, finally, the applicability of their theories to women living in contemporary northern Nigeria. Tamanaha's (2000, 2001) non-essentialist version of legal pluralism provides a theoretical framework that is flexible enough to allow for research to define law, to attribute power appropriately to different forms of law (as is relevant to the specific social settings), and to create opportunities for understanding that are analytically and instrumentally sound within the legal pluralist paradigm.

Non-essentialist legal pluralism appears to be most relevant for research on women and law in northern Nigeria because of the flexibility it affords in definitions of law, and the power it relinquishes from academic professionalizations of law to the lived realities and experiences of Hausa women who produce and implement law in Hausaland. The applicability of non-essentialist methods has not been attempted on a wide academic scale, and, as the number of scholars who undertake non-essentialist research expands, the lack of structure in this framework may result in conclusions that are difficult to compare. This may result in the production of knowledge that is difficult for academic institutions to understand.

These problems clearly fall within the realm of academia and are not directly correlated to problems in "society"; thus, changes need to occur in academia, and perhaps, if those shifts are sufficient, social problems and social triumphs can begin to be better understood in the "social sciences." Until then the majority of scholarly works emerging in Western academic settings will continue to misrepresent, misunderstand, and wrongfully analyze African social settings.

NOTES

1. Resistance in this context is non-conforming responses to attempts to control, dominate, and subjugate.
2. Kuhn states that theorists "whose research is based on shared paradigms are committed to the same rules and standards of scientific practice. That commitment and the apparent consensus it produces are prerequisites for normal science, i.e., for the genesis and continuation of a particular tradition" (1962, 11).
3. "State" being a single structure with unifying institutional bureaucracies.
4. The census is controversial since many ethnic groups believe that their populations were not properly accounted for in the official population reports. The north/south divide has been increasing with the most recent assertions that Kaduna (in the north) has a larger population than Lagos (in the south).
5. See http://www.nigeria.gov.ng/NR/exeres/05758900-C8A9-4055-87C1-9A6766C59879.htm. [Consulted October 25, 2007].
6. See https://www.cia.gov/library/publications/the-world-factbook/geos/ni.html. [Consulted October 25, 2007.] Again, these "official" statistics are disputed in Nigeria: with both Christians and Muslims claiming a majority population, and more people adhering to "traditional" spiritual practices, but doing so in secrecy due to the stigma associated with missionary and colonial dehumanization of African spiritual practices.
7. These "official" figures have been disputed by the US Bureau of Democracy, Human Rights, and Labor, which found in its human rights report (2005) that 58 percent of women were literate (US Department of State 2005).
8. Population demographics are cited from http://www.odci.gov/cia/publications/factbook/geos/ni.html.
9. The Hausa are one of the three dominant ethnic groups in Nigeria. Historically, they resided in what is now Niger and the northern regions of Nigeria, Benin, Togo, and Ghana. The majority of Hausa people in Nigeria continue to live in the northern region, and thus the northern states are often referred to as Hausaland.
10. Power in this context is formal, and is measured through wealth and access to land/home ownership rights.
11. As the Nigerian naira became less valuable, prices were increased throughout the nation, and economic difficulties for families were on the rise.

12 Kano is one of Hausaland's largest urban centres. It is one of the oldest and most populated cities in Nigeria.
13 She did not report a specific age. Wall (1998) did report in her study of Hausa women that some girls who are premenstrual are married in some Hausa societies.
14 The same law was substituted word for word when Nigeria was created.
15 The onus of proof was on the party who wanted to use customary laws to prove that English law would result in substantial injustice (Bentsi-Enchill 1969, 28).
16 Classical legal pluralists (e.g., Hoebel and Gluckman) concluded that societies without political organization (as they recognized it) were societies lacking in law. Bohannon (1967) asserts that different categories, when implemented, would reveal law among tribal societies and organizations.
17 With Bohannon accusing Gluckman of distorting reality by relying too heavily on English in his work, and Gluckman responding that his audience is English and accusing Bohannon of alienating scholars (Gluckman 1973).
18 Gluckman insisted that the English language was sufficient for categorizing non-Western legal systems, while Bohannon insisted that much of the essence of non-Western legal systems is lost or transformed in translations into English. Bohannon encouraged researchers to learn the language used in the region of study and to use that language when presenting categories of law. Gluckman insisted that this was impractical and unnecessary.
19 As a function of the dichotomized framework in which it functions.
20 Hill is one of the very few women who participated in classical legal pluralist research.
21 As recognized by classical legal pluralists.
22 New legal pluralists expanded legal pluralist research to include Western nations. They concluded that colonialism in Africa may have provided "obvious" legal plurality, as colonial law came to exist alongside customary law, but they added that, with the expansion of the definition of law to be centralized in "culture," legal pluralism is a reality in all societies, including the North American ones.
23 This is done in both classical legal pluralism and legal centralism.
24 The three subgroups that she presents are property ownership, maleness, and race.
25 Few new legal pluralists present an understanding of African social structures as "formal," mainly because the term "formal"

has historically been associated with colonial structures. It was constructed as such by classical legal pluralists. While new legal pluralists have challenged these constructions by emphasizing the relevance of the "informal," they do not deconstruct the very existence of "formal" and "informal" categories.
26 Not all social interactions are "functional"; some are dysfunctional, some uneventful, some minor, some major, and so on.
27 Private here is identified as fields functioning outside the realm of public, state-defined and state-regulated social fields.

REFERENCES

Abdullah, Hussaina. (1997). "Multiple Identities and Multiple Organizing Strategies of Female Wage Workers in Kano's Manufacturing Sector." In *Transforming Female Identities: Women's Organizational Forms in West Africa,* ed. Ega Evers Rodander. Stockholm: Gotab, 54-66.

Ayua, M. (1998). "Land and Property Rights of Women in the Northern States of Nigeria." In *Women and Law in West Africa: Situational Analysis of Some Key Issues Affecting Women,* ed. Akua Kuenyehia. Accra: Faculty of Law, University of Ghana, 237-248.

Barkow, Jerome H. (1972). "Hausa Women and Islam." In *The Roles of African Women: Past, Present, and Future.* Special issue of *Canadian Journal of African Studies,* 6:2, 317-328.

Bentsi-Enchill, Kwamena. (1969). "The Colonial Heritage of Legal Pluralism." *Zambia Law Journal,* 1:2, 1-30.

Bohannon, Paul. (1967). *Law and Warfare.* Garden City, NY: Natural History Press.

Callaway, Barbara, and Lucy Creevey. (1994). *Islam, Women, Religion, and Politics in West Africa.* London: Lynne Rienner.

---. (2003). "The Heritage of Islam: Women, Religion, and Politics in West Africa." In *Women and Law in Sub-Saharan Africa,* ed. Cynthia Grant Bowman and Akua Kuenyehia. Accra: Sedco Publishing, 592-598.

Cohen, Abner. (2004). *Custom and Politics in Urban Africa.* New York: Routledge, Taylor, and Francis Group.

Coles, Catherine. (1988). "Urban Muslim Women and Social Change in Northern Nigeria." Working Papers on Women in International Development, Michigan State University.

Collier, Jane Fishburne. (1968). *Courtship and Marriage in Zinacantan, Chiapas, Mexico.* New Orleans: Middle American Research Institute.

Comaroff, John L., and Jean Comaroff. (1993). *Ethnography and the Historical Imagination*. Boulder, CO: Westview Press.

Ehrlich, E. (1936). *Fundamental Principles of the Sociology of Law*. Cambridge, MA: Harvard University Press.

Elias, Olawale T. (1956). *The Nature of African Customary Law*. Manchester: Manchester University Press.

Engel, David M. (1980). "Legal Pluralism in an American Community: Perspectives on a Civil Trial Court." *American Bar Foundation Research Journal*, 5:3, 425–454.

Fatton, R. (1989). "Gender, Class, and State in Africa." In *Women and the State in Africa*, ed. J. Parpart and K. Straudt. London: Lynne Rienner, 47–66.

Garland, David. (2001). *The Culture of Control: Crime and Social Order in Contemporary Society*. Chicago: University of Chicago Press.

Gluckman, Max. (1965). *Politics, Law, and Ritual in Tribal Society*. Oxford: A. R. Mowbray.

---. (1973) [1955]. *The Judicial Process among the Barotse of Northern Rhodesia (Zambia)*. 2nd ed. Manchester: Manchester University Press.

Greenhouse, Carol. (1994). "Constructive Approaches to Law, Culture, and Identity." *Law and Society Review*, 28:5, 1231–1242.

Gulliver, P. H. (1963). *Social Control in an African Society*. London: Routledge and Kegan Paul.

Hellum, Anne. (2002). "Human Rights and Gender Relations in Postcolonial Africa: Options and Limits for the Subjects of Legal Pluralism." *Law and Social Inquiry*, 25:2, 635–656.

Hill, Polly. (1972). *Rural Hausa: A Village and a Setting*. New York: Cambridge University Press.

Hirschmann, A. (1981). *Essays in Trespassing Economics to Politics and Beyond*. Cambridge, UK: Cambridge University Press.

Hoebel, E. Adamson. (1940). *The Political Organization and Law-Ways of the Comanche Indians: Memoirs of the American Anthropological Association 54*.

---. (1954). *The Law of Primitive Man: A Study in Comparative Legal Dynamics*. Cambridge, MA: Harvard University Press.

Jackson, M. (1987). "'Facts of Life' or the Eroticization of Women's Oppression? Sexology and the Social Construction of Heterosexuality." In *The Cultural Construction of Sexuality*, ed. P. Chaplan. London: Tavistock, 52–81.

Kuhn, Thomas. (1962). *The Structure of Scientific Revolutions*. 3rd ed. Chicago: University of Chicago Press.

La Torre, Massimo. (1999). "Legal Pluralism as Evolutionary Achievement of Community Law." *Ratio Juris*, 12:2, 182–196.

Llewellyn, Karl N., and E. A. Hoebel. (1941). *The Cheyenne Way: Conflict and Case Law in Criminal Jurisprudence.* Norman: University of Oklahoma Press.

Malinowski, Bronislaw. (1959). *Crime and Custom in Savage Society.* Paterson, NJ: Littlefield, Adams.

Manji, Ambreena S. (1999). "Imagining Women's 'Legal World': Towards a Feminist Theory of Legal Pluralism in Africa." *Social and Legal Studies, 8,* 435–456.

---. (2000). "Like a Mask Dancing: Law and Colonialism in Chinua Achebe's *Arrow of God.*" *Journal of Law and Society, 27:4,* 626–642.

Masaji, Chiba. (1998). "Other Phases of Legal Pluralism in the Contemporary World." *Ratio Juris, 11:3,* 228–245.

Melissaris, Emmanuel. (2004). "The More the Merrier? A New Take on Legal Pluralism." *Social and Legal Studies, 13,* 57–79.

Merry, Sally Engle. (1988). "Legal Pluralism." *Law and Society Review, 22:5,* 869–896.

---. (2000). *Colonizing Hawaii: The Cultural Power of Law.* Princeton, NJ: Princeton University Press.

Moore, Sally Falk. (1973). "Law and Social Change: The Semi-Autonomous Social Field as an Appropriate Subject of Study." *Law and Society Review, Summer 1973,* 719–746.

Nader, Laura, ed. (1969). *Law in Culture and Society.* Chicago: Aldine Publishing Company.

Nader, Laura, and Elisabetta Grande. (2002). "Current Illusions and Delusions about Conflict Management in Africa and Elsewhere." *Law and Social Inquiry, 27:3,* 573–594.

Okoth-Ogendo, H. W. O. (1979). "The Imposition of Property Law in Kenya." In *The Imposition of Law,* ed. Sandra B. Burman and Barbara E. Harrell-Bond. New York: Academic Press, 147–166.

Parnell, Philip. (2003). "Introduction: Crime's Power." In *Crime's Power: Anthropologists and the Ethnography of Crime,* ed. Philip C. Parnell and Stephanie C. Kane. New York: Palgrave Macmillan, 1–32.

Parpart, J., and K. Straudt. (1989). *Women and the State in Africa.* Cambridge, UK: Cambridge University Press.

Pittin, Renee Ilene. (2002). *Women and Work in Northern Nigeria: Transcending Boundaries.* New York: Institute of Social Studies; Palgrave Macmillan.

Pospisil, Leopold. (1967). "Legal Levels and Multiplicity of Legal Systems in Human Societies." *Journal of Conflict Resolution, 11:1,* 2–26.

Robson, Elsbeth. (2002). "Wife Seclusion and Spatial Praxis of Gender Ideology in Nigerian Hausaland." *Gender, Place, and Culture: A Journal of Feminist Geography, 72:1,* 179–199.

Santos, B. de Sousa. (1987). "*Law*: A Map of Misreading: Toward a *Postmodern Conception* of *Law*." *Journal of Law and Society, 14:3,* 279–302.

Shebi, Esther. (1997). "A Nigerian Sisterhood in the Transformation of Female Identity." In *Transforming Female Identities: Women's Organizational Forms in West Africa,* ed. Ega Evers Rodander. Stockholm: Gotab, 123–135.

Simmons, Emmy B. (1975). *The Small-Scale Rural Food-Processing Industry in Northern Nigeria.* Special issue of *Food Research Institute Studies,* 14:2.

Tamanaha, Brian Z. (2000). "A Non-Essentialist Version of Legal Pluralism." *Journal of Law and Society, 27:2,* 296–321.

---. (2001). *A General Jurisprudence of Law and Society.* New York: Oxford University Press.

Teubner, Gunther. (1992). "The Two Faces of Janus: Rethinking Legal Pluralism." *Cardozo Law Review, 13,* 1443–1458.

---. (1997a). "Global Bukowina: Legal Pluralism in the World Society." In *Global Law without a State,* ed. Gunther Teubner. Brookfield, NJ: Dartmouth, 3–28.

---. (1997b). "The King's Many Bodies: The Self-Deconstruction of Law's Hierarchy." *Law and Society Review, 13:4,* 763–788.

US Department of State. (2005). *Report on Human Rights Practices: Country Reports on Human Rights Practices, Nigeria.* Released by the Bureau of Democracy, Human Rights, and Labor. http://www.state.gov/g/drl/rls/hrrpt/2003/27738.htm.

Valdes, Francisco. (2004). "Culture, 'Kulturkampf,' and Beyond: The Antidiscrimination Principle under the Jurisprudence of Backlash." In *The Blackwell Companion to Law and Society,* ed. Austin Sarat. Malden: Blackwell Publishing, 271–291.

Wall, Lewis L. (1998). "Dead Mothers and Injured Wives: The Social Context of Maternal Morbidity and Mortality among the Hausa of Northern Nigeria." *Studies in Family Planning, 29:4,* 341–359.

Weisbrod, Carol. (2002). *Emblems of Pluralism: Cultural Differences and the State.* Princeton, NJ: Princeton University Press.

Werthmann, Katja. (2002). "*Matan Bariki,* 'Women of the Barracks': Muslim Hausa Women in an Urban Neighborhood in Northern Nigeria." *Africa, 72:1,* 112–130.

CHAPTER 18

FELA KUTI'S WAHALA MUSIC: POLITICAL RESISTANCE THROUGH SONG

Viviane Saleh-Hanna

Fela Kuti: 77 albums, 27 wives, over 200 court appearances. Harassed, beaten, tortured, jailed. Twice-born father of Afrobeat. Spiritualist, Pan-Africanist. Commune King. Composer, saxophonist, keyboardist, dancer. Would-be candidate for the Nigerian Presidency. There will never be another like him.
—Guralnick and Wolk (2002)

"BEAST OF NO NATION" (BY FELA)

Ahhhh
Let's get now into another underground spiritual game.
Just go dey help me dey answer you go dey say: aya kata

Oh yah
O fey shey loo
Aya kata
Mo fey shey 'gbon
Aya kata
O fey shey loo
Aya kata
Mo fey shey 'gbon
Aya kata
O fey shey wa'
Aya kata
Mo fey shey g'bein
Aya kata

Basket mouth wan' start to leak again-o
Basket mouth wan' open mouth again-o
Abis you don forget to say I sing-eo
Basket mouth wan' open mouth again-o
I sing you say
I go open my mouth like basket-eo
Malag be agbere
Basket mouth wan' open mouth again-o...

Fela weitin you go sing about-o
They go worry me...
They go worry me — Worry me worry...
They go worry me
They want to make I sing about prison

"BEAST OF NO NATION" (TRANSLATED)

Fela is getting ready to narrate...
Let's get down to another spiritual level: try to understand
   what I am saying
Just help me by answering: things are not good
Let's start...
They used a punch to beat me up
Things are not good — oh no...
They used a punch to finish me off
Things are not good — oh no...
They used a punch to beat me up
Things are not good — oh no...
They used a punch to finish me off
Things are not good — oh no...
They used a punch to shake me up
Things are not good — oh no...
They used a punch to finish me off
Things are not good — oh no...

My mouth wants to leak info again
Fela wants to speak again
Have you (gov't) forgotten that I sing
Fela will start to talk again
You (gov't) know that I sing
I will start to talk a lot in my songs again
And I don't care what people will think
Fela will start to talk again

Fela, what are you going to sing about
The people keep asking me
Fela what are you going to sing about
The people are bothering me
The people want me to sing about prison

... They want to know about prison life
They go worry me...

The time where I dey for prison
I call 'em inside world

The time where I dey outside prison
I call 'em outside world

Now craze world, no be outside world
Craze world

No be outside world the police dey
Craze world

No be outside the soldier dey
Craze world

No be outside the court them dey
Craze world

No be outside the bad street dey
Craze world

No be outside the judge them dey
Craze world

Now craze world be that
Craze world

No be outside Buhari dey
Craze world

Now craze man be that
Craze world

... They want to learn about prison life
They are asking him for information...

When I am inside the prison
I call it the inside world

When I am in Nigerian society
I call it the outside world

Nigerian society is the crazy world
Crazy world

Police are in the outside world, right?
Crazy world

Soldiers are in the outside world, right?
Crazy world

Courts are in the outside world, right?
Crazy world

Dangerous streets on the outside, right?
Crazy world

Judges are in the outside world, right?
Crazy world

Now that is the crazy world
Crazy world

Nigerian president is in outside world?
Crazy world

Now that is a crazy man.
Crazy world

Animal in craze man skin-e
Craze world
Now craze world be that
Craze world
No be outside Idiagbon dey
Craze world
Now craze man be that
Craze world
Animal in craze man skin-e
Craze world

MUSIC AS A TOOL FOR RESISTING STATE-IMPOSED OPPRESSIONS

Music was used as a culturally appropriate tool of political resistance by Fela Kuti in Nigeria during an era of military regimes. Within the historical and spiritual contexts of Fela's work, the power of this tool is understood both as empowering for the people and as threatening to the state. This is true in Nigeria, and in other nations where people continue to resist state authoritarianism, and the implementation of racist and colonial, structural and institutional, inequalities. In Nigeria cultural resistance to colonial structures thrives in music. Antonio Gramsci in his *Prison Notebooks* emphasized the power of cultural resistance and placed it as "central to political change, as it concerns the creation of alternative social meanings and values which challenge the dominant ideology of the ruling class" (Ghunna 1996–97, 7). In Nigeria, a land of extremes and immense diversity, music pulls people together, and creates avenues for connectivity and communication.

Artists who produce socially significant texts that critique authoritarian state regimes and structures in their lyrics play a key role in resisting state violence: "Cultural struggle is about raising the political awareness of the mass population, exposing the apologists for injustice and inequality, and creating an

> An animal hiding in a crazy man's skin
> *Crazy world*
> Outside is the crazy world
> *Crazy world*
> Tunde Idiagbon (chief of staff) is in the outside world, right?
> *Crazy world*
> That is a crazy man
> *Crazy world*
> An animal disguised in crazy man's skin
> *Crazy world*

---

alternative set of values and different perspectives of the world" (Ghunna 1996–97, 7). Fela's music represents such alternative values. His songs provide an avenue through which oppression can be both discussed and criticized, and thus destabilized.

HISTORICAL AND POLITICAL CONTEXT OF NIGERIA

Nigerian history is full of upheaval and turmoil. Two hundred years of commercial slave trading in West Africa yielded devastating results. Between 1500 and 1700 Africans went from being a minority in the world's slave population to being a majority. It has been estimated that "eleven or twelve million of the... eighteen million or more slaves exported from Africa... came from West and Central Africa," and this number is evident in the "continuing influence of West African culture in the Caribbean and North America" (Africa Policy 1996). In 1914 Nigeria became a country under British colonial rule, achieving independence in 1960 through political negotiations, not war (Nigerian Government 1999). The lack of a violent struggle brought about a peaceful transition, which legally is *post*colonial but economically is not. European and North American nations continue to have immense access to African resources. This access has resulted in much upheaval and unrest in Nigeria.

After legal independence approximately thirty years of military rule plagued the country, with dictatorships accompanied by flagrant human rights violations that instituted colonial economics and politics. Fela's life started during colonial times, spanned the era of military regimes, and ended two years before democracy was achieved with President Obasanjo (a former military dictator who ordered the 1977 raids on Fela's home and the murder of his mother) as Nigeria's president. It is from within this context that Fela's political stance was constructed and presented in his music.

MUSICAL CONTEXT: FELA'S AFRO-BEAT AS EMPOWERING AND ACCESSIBLE

Initially, Fela sang non-political songs in Yoruba and English, "but he soon started to sing anti-establishment songs, which very quickly brought him in collision with both imperialism and their local agents in power at home" (Ogunde 1998, 1). Fela coined the term "Afrobeat" and created a sound to define it. It was inspired by dissatisfaction with High Life, a form of music that dominated African recordings at the time. He was disturbed by the European emphasis on loping beats and singular guitars in High Life, as opposed to the rhythmic drums and brass-based beats of African sounds. He began using "jazz,... syncopated call and response vocals and brass," and a "raw and natural honesty and energy" that came to define Afrobeat, both as a form of music and as a political avenue for commentary (Connelly 1999).

Rader (2003, 185) explains that for political artists "forging their own artistic language is not simply an aesthetic, it is also an ethic." There is a sense of empowerment in the artistic creation of a voice, and through Afrobeat Fela empowered his voice and inspired African people who could relate to it to listen to his music. Through the re-emergence of African sounds in music Fela inspired people to relate more closely to African culture and African pride.

SPIRITUAL CONTEXT: EMPHASIZING AFRICAN CONCEPTIONS OF RECORDING HISTORY

The *abiku* in Yoruba traditions refers to ideas of reincarnation. More specifically, *abiku* refers to the concept of reincarnation as it emerges in Yoruba spirituality: "The Yoruba refer to the denizen, back from the chthonic region and born again, as a*biku*.... The metaphysical idea of Abiku... and the notion of rebirth serve as a master-narrative of the parent–child relationship in Pan-African socio-political contexts and literary texts" (Ogunyemi 2002, 663). Within the context of *abiku* social memory is passed down through generations in the spirits that reincarnate and inhabit the bodies of *abiku* children. Fela was identified as an *abiku* child by his family. It was believed that he possessed his grandfather's spirit. Through that possession he had the experiences and the wisdom that the spirit carried. This is important in relation to the oral culture of many West African traditions. "Since abiku/ogbanje [ogbanje is the Igbo concept of reincarnation] evokes the past, with its separations and instability, the concept can serve as a springboard for examining issues of memory" (Ogunyemi 2002, 663). Within the context of Fela's songs the assessment and denouncement of oppression exists in links between precolonial, colonial, and "post"colonial Africa. Being *abiku*, Fela had the ability to relay history as well as the impact of the past on present situations in Africa. He presented his songs on contemporary oppression as a connected continuation of the past.

LINGUISTIC CONTEXT: FELA'S LAGOSIAN ENGLISH

In Fela's songs language is crucial. "Apart from his musical progressiveness he mixed up elements of at least three languages... Standard Nigerian English,... Nigerian Pidgin English and... Yoruba" (Coester 1998, 1). Code-mixing or code-changing, as defined linguistically, includes the incorporation and intertwining of languages, something Fela did often in his lyrics. When addressing the elite he used Standard Nigerian English; when addressing civil society he used Nigerian Pidgin English;

when addressing Yoruba political issues he used Yoruba. Often, as he changed back and forth between dialects and languages, Fela mixed them and created new words that drew his three audiences together. These new words came to represent modes of expression distinct to Lagos State, and became associated primarily with Nigerian urban life and culture: *Aya kata, Aya kotu, Aya keetee* are words that Fela created, and they have come to be expressions of suffering, oppression, and struggle in Lagos.

Fela's songs continue to influence the way Lagosians speak and have come to illustrate Lagosian life. Maier (2000, 24) explains that Lagos is "a place full of frustration borne by millions of people who moved to the city in search of riches, but only found poverty, power cuts, water shortages, and breathtaking mounds of garbage. The city's heart literally beats to pulsating rhythms and angry lyrics against the thieves in power from the Afro-beat musician and political activist, Fela Kuti." On the national scale there are current political attempts to make pidgin English the official mode of communication in Nigeria because traditional English is viewed as elitist (mastered by those who are Euro-educated) and representative of the "slavery method of communication" in a manner that reimplants colonial structures in the country (Bala Habu 2004, 4). Fela's heavy reliance on pidgin to communicate through song expanded the boundaries of his audience while reinforcing the importance of identity through language. Instead of shunning pidgin and relying on British English to communicate, Fela used British English only to emphasize the elitist and oppressive elements of European relations with Africa. His politicization of language through songs has provided support for the movement to abolish British English as the official form of communication in Nigeria.

MUSIC IN AFRICAN SOCIETIES

Fela's native language, Yoruba, has been described as a "musical" one, with a "richness and rhythmic quality" that encompass a naturally musical feel to its sounds and expressions (Morales 2003, 151). In addition, as Morales notes, it has been stated that, within the African and Caribbean contexts, "the interdependence of music/dance/gesture to language is strong.... By listening carefully to the musician and writer from these cultures, one can discern this connectivity" (150). Also, "South African writer Mongane Wally Serote points out how pervasive music is in the African culture: 'one grew up, was brought up by music really. It... articulated one's dilemma, one's hopes'" (148).

Because music is such a key aspect of many African cultures and lifestyles, the use of music for sociopolitical commentary became a particularly powerful tool for Fela; it is within this understanding that the Nigerian state's reactions to Fela can be better contextualized. The state was threatened by him because his anti-state politics reached many people, and those who felt powerless could relate to his messages and analyses. Using music and song to communicate provided Fela with an avenue natural to the lifestyle, upbringing, and culture of many Africans. In addition, the history of song and music in many parts of Africa (South Africa being the most documented) illustrates that Africans have used music and lyrics to communicate during difficult times, to denounce oppressive leaders, and to encourage resistance to brutality.

ORAL HISTORY AS AN AFRICAN TRADITION

In the 1960s scholars began to use "local oral traditions as a source for reconstructing the pre-colonial African past.... Such sources placed emphasis on African perspectives, thus providing a much-needed balance to Euro-centric accounts then prevalent" (Lee 2004, 83-84). This emphasis on African voices reinforces the relevance of Fela's firsthand presentation of Nigerian experiences. The emphasis on oral traditions is relevant to his use of the narrative in presenting his stories, both by legitimizing his mode of expression and by emphasizing its necessity. In oral historical research methodological constraints are observed through the researchers' influence on the people they are interviewing (Lundberg 2003, 68). Issues relating to translation, expression, and researcher bias become pertinent. In Fela's case the songs are a form of oral history, recording the implications of military regimes from the perspective of the average citizen in Nigeria. Issues related to transcription and researcher bias become minimized in this form of oral history, since the information is already recorded in song. In her assessment of oral historical research methods Lundberg (2003) refers to a ceremonial song that recorded and passed down through generations a historic voyage that a First Nations people undertook in resistance to colonization. In this song it becomes evident that historical records, in Native American history (similar in Nigerian history), are not only based on events but also focused on recording the experiences associated with such events.

Fela's songs take people through specific experiences. The spiritual game Fela refers to in his songs invites his audiences to remove themselves from immediacy and to place themselves within the journeys he is narrating to them. As an *abiku* he represents both narrator and ancestor in his songs. As a musician he is able to invite large numbers of people to experience that journey.

FORMS OF POLITICAL RESISTANCE IN FELA'S SONGS

While many of Fela's songs illustrate his style and mode of resistance, I focus here on "Beast of No Nation" (see above for excerpts) to highlight his techniques and political messages. Most of his songs are presented in a narrative format, a style that engages his audience in a conversation about politics, colonialism, and oppression. "Beast of No Nation" illustrates his role as both political narrator and oppressed character. This is the first song Fela released after his imprisonment. In it he refers to himself, the oppressed character, as a basket mouth with the ability to leak words; this leaking makes him a target of the Nigerian military regime.

In this narrative Fela is conversing with his audience, using his voice to repeat the questions they ask him and then using his background singers to answer these questions. He says that the people keep asking him why he continues to spill words if the result continues to be beatings, arrests, and imprisonments by the military government. In response Fela explains that it is not he who speaks but politicians who speak lies to the people. The use of narratives in this song reveals how he uses music as a political tool of resistance. Fela mocks the state for its attempts to silence him, he dubs himself "basket mouth," and he reverses people's questions about his thoughts and experiences to bring their attention back to the state.

In response to questions about his experiences in prison Fela uses this song to explain that the outside world has the police, the courts, the corruption, and the lying politicians. Prison, he explains, is an inside world where that madness exists only as an extension of the madness in society. He urges Nigerians to see the madness of their own society, and to work to challenge and change it. Fela uses this song to present his strength despite imprisonment and to point fingers at political, social, and economic structures that oppress the people. His strength lies not only in refusing to be silenced, but also in exposing those who have tried to silence him.

By presenting narratives that mirror or address experiences specific to Nigerian society, Fela piques the interest of his audiences and captures their attention. He brings their own understandings of and experiences with oppression to a level of awareness that addresses global oppression and colonialist histories. In a political context these elements combined become threatening. Not only can Nigerian people relate to him, but also they can relate on a level that is interpersonal. His songs have the potential for what the Nigerian nation-state would consider disastrous, as Fela explains in "Beast of No Nation" — disastrous because his audience is large and, through his songs, is becoming more educated about and aware of the conditions that oppress them.

Rader (2003, 180) defines engaged resistance as having two necessary elements. One involves a "unified act of resistance," and the second involves acts of "expression and communication that are fundamentally linked to... histories, cultures and beliefs."

Fela's music often pulled people together in several formats. While Fela was alive people conversed with each other about his newest releases and his political messages. His concerts came to mirror organized rallies and always involved a large segment of spoken words in which he addressed the most recent political and economic scandals in Nigeria. After the military government killed his mother Fela wrote a song outlining their actions and organized a rally throughout the streets of Lagos, during which he presented this song for the first time to his fans. Included in this rally was a replica of his mother's coffin. The rally was alsoa re-enactment of his mother's funeral, which ended at the military barracks, where Fela left her coffin before the gates: you killed her, you bury her, was the message. This rally/funeral drew tens of thousands of protesters. After Fela died in 1997 his own funeral was attended by approximately one million people (Connelly 1999).

Fela's music provided a resonance that addressed Nigerian historical, cultural, and spiritual systems. In addition to education and political conversation through song, Fela used humour as a tool of resistance. "Humor remains one of the most successful and most frequent modes of... resistance. Laughing at the enemy is a way to make him less dangerous, more human" (Rader 2003, 183). Fela debased the authority of the military regimes by exposing them as people vulnerable to criticism and ridicule. He thus challenged their perceived invincible status.

ART AS POLITICAL EDUCATION AND EXPOSITION

In assessing Mona Hatoum's visual art as resistance to oppression of the Palestinian people Jabri (2001, 38) states that it "presents what Michel Foucault refers to as a 'critical ontology of the self.' It encompasses both a critique of the present and an awareness of the place of history in the constitution of the self." This presentation of the self within the context of the history that led up to the creation of that oppressed self is key in understanding Fela's themes and modes of resistance through song: Fela draws a macrolevel picture that enables his oppressed audiences to better understand their conditions. Within these modes of expression the power of resistance lies not only in exposing Nigerian sociopolitical, economic, and historical realities, but also in making the links between them.

In addressing resistance through political art forms Jabri (2001, 39) states that there is "a vulnerability associated with this space so the viewer is no longer a mere passive onlooker, but is deeply involved. The viewer enters a zone of questions and interrogations. The subject comes to bear witness, has to bear witness, and it is in this moment that the ethical emerges. It is in this moment of reflection that the subject acquires a critical attitude, an ethos built on creativity and critique." This analysis describes the power of the narrative and interactive style in Fela's songs and performances. Fela often engaged his audiences during live performances. In his recorded music he always relied on his backup singers to answer his questions and probe at his ideas. He engaged in conversations with them as he sang and recorded his music of resistance. This engagement drew those who listened to his music into a conversation, forcing them to communicate with him as he sang; listeners ceased to be passive and became deeply involved in the messages of the songs.

Jabri (2001, 40) also states that political art "represents a form of resistance that Foucault refers to as a permanent critique of the present... articulat[ing] a political subjectivity.... Each work contains a remembered past,... while in and through this history, the present in all its tensions, all its dangers, is opened out to the viewing public." Fela's sung narratives draw people into that space of political instability that forces them to address political problems. His stories about everyday life and struggle in Nigeria are personal and accurate. These details, in conjunction with the historical-political context, comprise a strong message that, when understood on the grander scale of oppression and within the context of *continued* exploitation of Africans, is angering, emotional, and personal, and constitutes the necessity of resistance.

CHINESE AND CUBAN STATE REACTIONS TO POLITICAL MUSIC

In assessing the Nigerian nation-state's reaction to Fela Kuti it is important to provide perspective through an analysis of other nation-states' reactions to dissident musicians. I present two main responses: one matches the reaction of the Nigerian nation-state (China), while the other counters it (Cuba).

On April 27, 1998, Wu Ruojjie, a Chinese rock musician, was sentenced to three years in a "'labor re-education' camp for disclosing the arrest of four poets in southwest China." He was sentenced for "divulging state secrets" in a song (Huang 2003, 183). Wu associated himself with the student democracy movement in China and sang about the Tiananmen Square massacres. He belongs to a community of political rock musicians who challenge the Chinese nation-state through their songs. Cui Jian, the father of this community, wrote songs in which he defined music as a weapon, stating in one song that his guitar is a knife. Out of this community and leadership emerged Wu's political use of music as resistance through exposure, education, and political dialogue and commentary. In China it is recognized that the promotion of political resistance is unsafe. As Huang notes, "the cruel lessons of the Tiananmen massacre have taught rockers that implementation of genuine political challenges is hazardous to one's health" (191).

In Nigeria the repercussions of musical rebellion were also apparent. Fela faced much opposition and attack from the Nigerian military regimes during his life. In resistance to such reactions, Fela established the Kala-kuta Republic: the land on which he lived and performed was transformed into a republic, which incorporated laws and social control mechanisms, and functioned as a political, musical community. In November 1975, the Kala-kuta Republic encountered an attack, which included a raid that destroyed much of the property, severe beatings, and the rape of women found inside the compound (Connelly 1999). Two years later a "ruthless invasion" of the rebuilt Kala-kuta

Republic was undertaken by "'unknown soldiers,' who maimed and raped its inhabitants, and looted and burned the place down" (Ogunde 1998, 2). One thousand soldiers were present that day (Connelly 1999). Regardless, Fela remained politically vocal and unrelenting until death. His attitude to music was framed as a responsibility: if one had the talent to produce song, then one had a responsibility to use that talent to promote social change and freedom. Fela did not allow the consequences of such resistance efforts, although dangerous and at times lethal, to deter him from using his musical talents to progress the fight for freedom.

As the hardships of political resistance come with responsibility, this responsibility is accompanied by status, making the entertainer also an intellectual. Huang addresses this status when he points out that in China "rockers enjoy the status of culture creators" (2003, 191). An important element of that status is not only access to an audience willing to listen to the music, and thus the messages presented through the music, but also the ability to stimulate awareness of key political issues. Thus, while resistance through song has been challenged and discouraged through nation-state attacks and violent attempts at silencing musical dissidents, this avenue also provides tremendous opportunities to reach great numbers of people and affords musicians much access to the intellectual realm through which culture can be formed.

Rebellion through music, with such immense opportunities, has been used to challenge many elements of contemporary social structures that contribute to oppressive living conditions. This is illustrated in the musical rebellion initiated in China against patriarchy. A female rocker band named Cobra uses music to politically challenge oppressive gender roles: "China's all-female band, Cobra,... transgresses conventional Chinese gender roles" both in appearance and in social orientation (Huang 2003, 198). While Fela Kuti and Wu Ruojjie used music to address state-imposed institutional and cultural oppressions, other bands may have a different focus, choosing to structure their music to address diverse elements of oppressive sociopolitical structures. As each band addresses issues specific to its experiences with oppression, it is hoped that collectively their work will address a large segment of social struggles against oppressive living conditions. As such movements begin to come together, music as a political tool for resistance and change becomes one of the more effective tools to challenge the comfortable status quo established in varying types of nation-states. This is a status quo that institutionalizes racism and classism, in manners that assume these oppressions are natural and necessary in all societies. Through the music the assumed naturalness of these oppressions is challenged and revealed as in*human*e, and thereby unnatural to *human* societies.

In Cuba political rap was inspired by African American activists who visited Cuba and spoke a language of "black militancy that was appealing to Cuban youth" (Fernandes 2003, 578). Rap music became a method of criticizing the Cuban state for ignoring and perpetuating racial inequalities in the country (580). Two forms of rap emerged: the underground and the commercial. Underground rappers use rap "as a vehicle to criticize the silencing of race issues in post-revolutionary society... [and to] challenge stereotypes of blacks as criminals... [while talking] about the repercussions of slavery in the contemporary period" (584). Commercial rappers promote "alternative strategies of survival such as consumerism and hustling, thereby challenging new regimes of labor discipline and standards of revolutionary morality" (584).

Initially, Cuban rap emerged at a local, grassroots level. In the 1990s the Cuban state provided institutional resources to promote it and allowed multinational recording companies access to Cuban talent (Fernandes 2003, 578). This was an "important avenue of transnational participation" for the Cuban state, providing access to the US economy (578). Knowing that the capitalist economy buys out challenges to the oppressive status quo, Castro opted to use capitalism to co-opt revolutionary music: "While hip-hop in the US started as an urban underground movement, it is now a major political product distributed by five of the largest multinational music labels" (578). Initially, the Cuban government attempted to implement this co-optation strategy, promoted "as a way of diluting the radical component of the genre" (585). While this worked for some rap artists in Cuba, a specific segment rejected such attempts at silence. Underground rap groups that rejected these changes were approached by Cuban state authorities, and in July 2001 they were provided with state-sponsored resources for the production of their music. "While initially the Cuban state attempted to sideline underground rappers by supporting the commercial element, the state is increasingly relating to the former, praising them for their rejection of commercialism" (585). "The image of Cuba as a mixed-race nation with African roots" is promoted, thus "inscribing the imagery of Africa into the revolutionary project, helping to construct internal unity," while criticizing the United States for its racial disparities and capitalist structures (585). In this instance capitalism was used to silence those whom it could buy out, and Cuban state resources were used to buy out those who could not be bought by American money. For underground artists their success in the Cuban music industry provided Cuba with an image of diversity, which promoted the revolutionary history of the country.

Co-optation and silencing strategies in relation to revolutionary music differ according to each nation-state's resources and cultures of control. In China and Nigeria silence is promoted through the military and imprisonment. In Nigeria these strategies are congruent with the militarization of Nigerian society, which occurred during colonialism. In Cuba strategies included access to commercialism to silence those who could be bought, while promoting anti-capitalist music to divert attention away from racial inequalities within the nation. In the United States the consumer culture and the heavy reliance on capitalism allow the nation-state to encourage those who do not promote revolution through music, while limiting resources for those who do promote resistance through music. The realities of life in a consumer economy prevail to silence those who do not have the resources to produce revolutionary music. Fela, coming from a rich and politically powerful family, chose to use his resources to promote resistance through song. His family was not powerful enough to immunize him from Nigerian military and criminal justice brutalities; nonetheless, he persevered and did not allow his messages or his songs to be co-opted.

THE POWER OF RESISTANCE

Music as a tool of political resistance has been used internationally and historically. Under apartheid in South Africa music was used as a means of communication about oppression during times when communication among black and "coloured" peoples was controlled and punishable. Under the official institution of slavery in the United States black people used music to pass on messages and to plan rebellions. During the implementation of the chain gang the continued extortion of labour from African Americans was resisted through song: men on the chain gang used song to regulate the rhythm of their work, and they were able to successfully slow down the pace of work in a manner that went unnoticed by prison guards. In more recent times music has emerged as a mode of communication among oppressed peoples, and has promoted resistance through education and political dialogue.

Music, when used politically, provides a method of peaceful resistance to violent oppression. The violent reactions to political music illustrate how threatening this form of resistance is to the status quo. The capitalist silencing of revolutionary music illustrates the effort afforded to silence or co-opt resistance. Despite such attempts to maintain the colonial status quo, music continues to be a relevant avenue to promote empowerment for the oppressed. On the national level one can see the relevance of such efforts. Fela's music was localized in a manner that drew in his Nigerian audiences and allowed them the opportunity to view their oppressive living conditions through an empowered lens. On the international level music as a form of resistance unites nations of oppressed peoples and creates international communities of artists who establish solidarity through song. Within the context of a group, and within the community-building elements of international musical revolutionaries, political artists are able to pursue resistance together. In the creation of international communities that transcend colonial and genocidal efforts to build contemporary nation-states, political musicians both promote resistance locally and challenge oppression globally.

REFERENCES

Africa Policy. (1996). "Nigeria Country Profile, Capsule History (pre-1960): Background Paper." http://www.africaaction.org/bp/niger2.html.

Bala Habu, Murtala III. (2004). *Nigeria at 43 Years Old: Did Nigeria Need Independence from Great Britain to Be Independent?* http://www.gamji.com/NEWS2858.htm.

Coester, Markus. (1998). *Language as a Product of Cultural Contact: A Linguistics Approach to Fela Kuti's Lyrics.* http://ietpdl1.sowi.uni-mainz.de/~ntama/main1/language_as_product/nod6.html.

Connelly, Chris. (1999). "Fela." *Roctober,* 25. http://www.roctober.com/roctober/greatness/fela.html.

Fernandes, Sujatha. (2003). "Fear of a Black Nation: Local Rappers, Transnational Crossings, and State Power in Contemporary Cuba." *Anthropological Quarterly,* 76:4, 575–609.

Ghunna, Michael Mac Golla. (1996–97). "Cultural Struggle and a Drama Project." *Journal of Prisoners on Prisons,* 7:1, 7–13.

Guralnick, P., and D. Wolk. (2002). *Da Capo Best Music Writing 2000: The Year's Finest Writing on Rock, Pop, Jazz, Country, and More.* Cambridge, MA: Da Capo Press.

Huang, Hao. (2003). "Voices from Chinese Rock, Past and Present Tense: Social Commentary and Construction of Identity in Yaogun Yinyue, from Tiananmen to the Present." *Popular Music and Society,* 26:2, 183–202.

Jabri, Vivienne. (2001). "Mona Hatoum: Exiled Art and the Politics of Resistance." *Social Alternatives,* 20:4, 37–40.

Lee, Christopher. (2004). Review of *African Words, African Voices: Critical Practices in Oral History,* ed. Luise White, Stephan F. Miescher, and David William Cohen. *Oral History Review,* 31:1, 83–86.

Lundberg, Anita. (2003). "Voyage of the Ancestors." *Cultural Geographies, 10,* 64–83.

Maier, Karl. (2000). *This House Has Fallen.* London: Penguin Books.

Morales, Donald. (2003). "The Pervasive Force of Music in African, Caribbean, and African American Drama." *Research in African American Literatures, 34:2,* 145–154.

Nigerian Government. Office of the Presidency, Federal Secretariat. (1999). *National Orientation and Public Affairs.* http://nopa.net/Useful_Information/clinton/nigeria-hist.htm.

Ogunde, Oke. (1998). "Nigeria: The Revolutionary Essence of Fela Kuti's Music." *Nigerian Marxist Journal, Workers Alternative,* http://www.marxist.com/Africa/fela_kuti.html. [Consulted October 25, 2007].

Ogunyemi, Chikwenye Okonjo. (2002). "An Abiku-Ogbanje Atlas: A Pre-Text for Rereading Soyinka's *Aké* and Morrison's *Beloved.*" *African American Review, 36:4,* 663–679.

Rader, Dean. (2003). "Engaged Resistance in American Indian Art, Literature, and Film." *Peace Review, 15:2,* 179–186.

SECTION V

STEPPING BEYOND THE COLONIAL PENAL BOX: AFRICAN JUSTICE MODELS AND PENAL ABOLITIONISM

This book presents information that illuminates the criminal and colonial foundations and structures of the penal system. In light of such information it is important to present information about African justice models, and bring forth efforts in African nations to rely less on penal colonial institutions and more on community-oriented methods of social control. In presenting this section it is necessary to address the obstacles that stand in the way of progress. The first obstacle is a psychological one: for generations global societies have been bombarded with the constant and inaccurate assumption that the penal system is the only option available for addressing conflict in society. The second obstacle is a structural one: the penal system has become an entrenched and powerful system of control. It is powerful not only in its ability to harm target populations, but also in the muscle it provides for the state in implementing a racist and classist status quo.

Despite such conditions, there are those who "emancipate themselves from mental slavery," and there are initiatives in the works to decrease reliance on penal institutions, and to search for ways to implement non-European and non-colonial methods of social function. Penal abolitionism is a movement that works to challenge both the psychological and the structural powers of the penal system. This section provides the Nigerian context in which African models of justice emerge. It also provides contemporary examples of alternatives to the penal system as they are being used in Africa—these are alternatives to a Eurocentric justice system, and are necessary for the restructuring and strengthening of African societies. In reverting to African social function mechanisms African societies are rejecting not only colonialism, but also the so-called superior and civilized identity that colonialists brought to Africa.

CHAPTER 19

ALTERNATIVES TO IMPRISONMENT: COMMUNITY SERVICE ORDERS IN AFRICA

Chukwuma Ume

Many developing countries are finding it very difficult to manage their prisons. Overpopulated penal institutions can often only provide inadequate conditions to inmates, both physically and psychologically. Prisoners have to be detained for long periods on remand, and prisons are frequently unable to carry out the task of training and rehabilitation, despite these being stated as aims in the national statutory texts which govern them. At the same time, rising crime rates, especially in large conurbations, make these inadequacies all the more worrying. Minor offenders are brought into close proximity with more hardened criminals without there being any real possibility for their rehabilitation into society and employment.

—Magistrate Odette Luce Bourvier,
Technical Adviser to the Senegalese Minister of Justice

INTRODUCTION

The observations above are apt to describe penal institutions in most developing countries, Nigeria included. Indeed, they categorically sum up the problems that have bedevilled imprisonment and, by extension, entire criminal justice administrations on the African continent, particularly in Nigeria. To this end one may ask the following questions.

- Does the status quo offer justice and security to the people?
- To what extent have the agents of the criminal justice system, particularly of the prisons, been able to administer justice and enhance social cohesion, as expected of them statutorily?

To unravel these questions and many other salient ones, this chapter presents a brief account of the prison service in Nigeria. The concept and implementation of community service orders are presented as a practical alternative to imprisonment. The chapter also puts forward the rationale for the call for more viable and functional alternatives to imprisonment (ATI). In addition, the chapter draws on lessons from African countries where such ATI measures have been implemented. The chapter ends with suggestions for the criminal justice system in Nigeria.

Details of the prison service in Nigeria have been provided in previous chapters (see also Agomoh, Adeyemi, and Ogbebor 2001; Ume and Saleh-Hanna 2005). Suffice it to say here that the institution of imprisonment, like most public institutions in Nigeria, is part of our colonial heritage, intended to pursue, promote, and protect the then colonial interests. Thus, it was not only punitive but also lacked any systematic and well-developed programmes for rehabilitation and reintegration of ex-prisoners into the larger society upon discharge. Remarkably, though regrettably, this ugly trend had a spillover effect into our "post"colonial era; hence, prison officers not amenable to change are often described by prisoners as "colonial warders," associating their current behaviours with the colonial militarized mentality in their dealings with prisoners.

Colonial warders are not an anomaly in Nigerian prison institutions but a function of them. When colonialists imposed their systems of justice upon Africa they recognized (minimally) that colonial justice systems existed alongside "native" ones. Upon so-called independence, policies were passed to "unify" colonial and native justice systems. This unification included the increasing formalization and superiority of colonial justice systems compared with African ones. In Nigeria this unification was facilitated through the Gobir reports, which concluded that there was a need to unify the various prison commands in Nigeria: the "federal" and "native" authorities were unified on April 1, 1968. Subsequent reorganizations in the prison administration led to the promulgation of Prison Decree No. 9 in 1972 (Agomoh, Adeyemi, and Ogbebor 2001). The decree ordered, among other things, the following cardinal functions of the prison service:

(1) to keep safe custody of persons legally interned;
(2) to identify the causes of their anti-social behaviour, treat, and reform them to become law-abiding citizens of a free society;
(3) to train them toward their rehabilitation on discharge; and
(4) to generate revenue for the government through prison farms and industries.

Achievement of these lofty ideals has been at all times poor and questionable. This is the case in societies that have used prisons for centuries, and it certainly is the case in African societies that have had prisons imposed upon them by European colonial occupations.

CONTEMPORARY INSTITUTIONS OF IMPRISONMENT

Imprisonment in Nigeria has become a haven for human rights abuses, with countless custody deaths and acts that degrade human dignity. With a prison population that has exceeded sixty-five percent in awaiting-trial prisoners, conditions have reached epic brutality. People who ordinarily would be productively engaged in contributing to the functions and development of a balanced and healthy society are languishing in prisons. These ugly prison conditions are not solely attributable to the prison department, but are also the result of various agencies and social institutions. Some of the problems of the prison service in Nigeria, especially those of overcrowding, inadequate facilities, and poor treatment of prisoners, suggest that the prison in Nigeria occupies the back burner and is the dumping ground for the larger problems with criminal justice administration in the country. Unfortunately, too, efforts toward eradicating some of these problems, or reducing the number of prisoners through "special arrangements" such as legal aid and presidential or state pardons, have made little or no impact.

Consequently the prison service lacks both deterrent and reformative values. Yet, at a National Conference on Alternatives to Imprisonment in Nigeria in 2000, it was asserted that the government spends a lot of money on food, clothing, shelter, and other needs of prisoners. It was stated that the government spends as much as N1,825,000,000 annually on feeding inmates. This figure does not include the costs of medication, clothing, and accommodation. This institution is not only unjust and brutal in its treatment of prisoners, but also expensive. Although this expense is immense in Nigeria, it does not come near the expenses incurred with the administration of justice in industrialized nations.

Julita Lemgruber (1998), the former director of prisons in Rio de Janeiro, presented an argument along these lines. She noted that industrialized nations "go on incarcerating many people who commit petty crimes." To illustrate the problematic nature of such practices, she pointed out that there were some "noteworthy" cases illustrating recklessness in the administration of criminal justice. These cases included a woman who served a sentence of two and a half years for stealing two packages of disposable diapers from a supermarket; a man who was sentenced to a prison term of more than four years for stealing a fighting cock (cock fights are illegal in Brazil); people who have served time for stealing twelve heads of lettuce or five heads of cabbage or twelve roof tiles; and so on. The items stolen do not justify, in terms of danger to the public or financial loss to the community, the use of imprisonment. Lemgruber explained that two packages of disposable diapers cost about US$ 14, while the woman who served time for these thefts ended up costing the taxpayer US$ 16,000. Many more thousands are spent to keep petty thieves behind bars who could well be dealt with differently. In her assessment of the financial restraints and conditions of penal systems Lemgruber explained that countries such as Brazil or other developing nations are not in a position where they can (or should want to) afford the maintenance of large numbers of their citizens in prisons.

This understanding is not arguable in the "developing" world. It is an understood fact that the prison system is financially unreasonable, ineffective, and problematically colonial. In assessing the colonial structures of control that prisons represent it has been observed that prisons are not community-oriented. The penal system is self-contained and looks inward. For instance, when people are put in prison they have left their world behind. This impact of imprisonment works to destabilize both the individual and the community, which has been dichotomized by these institutions of control. Within the institution overcrowding, lack of nutritional diets, boredom, and the internal pains experienced with the loss of freedom are major issues that destabilize the humanity of this form of social control. From an African perspective the real pains of imprisonment include separation from family and friends, the loss of jobs and homes, the fear of being forgotten, and the anxiety in thinking about whether one will fit into society upon eventual release. Thus, imprisonment is recognized as a physiologically, psychologically, and emotionally destructive institution; in addition, it is socially damaging, culturally abhorrent, and penologically disastrous. Buttressing this view, Adeyemi (2000) stated that, in addition to the apparent inefficiency of imprisonment as a deterrent and the increasing financial burden it imposes on African countries, there is a growing resurgence in the African region of its culturally aberrant and abhorrent disposition. Hence the compelling need to look for viable alternatives of social control.

ALTERNATIVES TO IMPRISONMENT

Alternatives to imprisonment, as construed in this chapter, are measures used in the administration of justice that are not penal, alternatives to addressing conflict that do not criminalize or ostracize individuals while working to build and strengthen, not dichotomize and weaken, the community. Although fledgling, these concepts are not alien to Africa; rather, they are autochthonous. To underscore this assertion, Elias (1969) explains that, "in the traditional African societies, imprisonment as a form of punishment was almost unknown.... There [was] no room for institutionalized forms of punishment such as imprisonment for preventive detention.... Offenders were often left in the care of their families or extended families once the appropriate penalty had been imposed" (Adeyemi 2000). It therefore follows logically and is safe to say that an African system of justice to a large extent abhors imprisonment, and is not "criminal" but restorative and transformative.

Upholding the argument, Adeyemi (2000) pointed out that the use of imprisonment imprints on the ex-prisoner and his family a social stigma; in addition, imprisonment closes avenues for employment, rented accommodation, marriage, and the establishment of a family, and it encompasses other forms of social ostracism that are not coherent in Nigeria or conducive to the development of our society. Quoting Meek's "Law and Authority in a Nigerian Tribe" and Gunn's "Pagan Peoples of the Central Area of Northern Nigeria," Adeyemi illustrated his argument with examples from the Ibo and Kagoro peoples, who never had any form of imprisonment prior to the arrival of the British. According to Adeyemi, the disdain of the Nigerian people was further epitomized by the attitude that colonialists and Western legal scholars held toward what they termed "native courts." This attitude is evident in the instruction issued to Nigerians by Lord Lugard: when he discovered that the natives continued to employ restitution for theft, instead of imprisonment, he is recorded as having "instructed" native courts that restitution for stolen property or an abducted person was not a sufficient penalty. According to Lugard, punishment should always be added to restitution. Remarkably, the native courts refused to comply with such instructions and resorted to compensation, compensatory fines, and fines as appropriate measures instead of imprisonment (Elias 1969).

This clear and emphatic rejection of imprisonment by the native courts, even in the face of instructions from the governor general of the Nigerian nation-state, indicates the odium toward imprisonment in Nigerian society—it was understood then, and on many levels is understood today, that the penal and criminal systems of control are seemingly incompatible with Nigerian traditional conceptions of justice.

Against this backdrop I now present an operational definition of alternatives to imprisonment as they exist in the African context. For the purpose of this chapter ATI measures to address conflicts include suspended sentencing, probation, fines, and community service. It is believed that an increase in the use of such sanctions by the criminal justice system would lead to a decrease in the use of imprisonment. While these measures continue to exist within the penal context, and are not necessarily congruent with all forms of community justice, it is advocated that an increase in these types of sanctions would aid in primarily decongesting the overcrowded prisons and restoring some semblance of balance to the communities that continue to lose their citizens to prisons.

Community Service Orders

Community service orders are a cardinal alternative to imprisonment. Recalling the Kampala Declaration of 1996, which takes into account the limited effectiveness of imprisonment, especially for those serving short sentences, and the cost of imprisonment to the whole society; noting the growing interest in measures that replace custodial sentences and recognizing the promising developments across the globe in this regard; appreciating the importance of the Kampala Declaration, which annexed a resolution on international cooperation for the improvement of prison conditions in developing countries (United Nations 1997); bearing in mind the United Nations Standard Minimum Rules for Non-Custodial Measures (Tokyo Rules 1990); considering that the level of overcrowding in any prison is inhumane; recalling the African Charter on reaffirming the dignity inherent in a human being, and the prohibition of inhumane and degrading treatment; recognizing that a "stronger," more bureaucratic, criminal justice system that does not prioritize community-based measures only leads to a growing prison population, as has been illustrated in the United States, I lend credence to these resolutions and observed facts, and accordingly state that there exists a strong platform on which we are calling for the adoption and establishment of alternative measures to imprisonment in all African countries.

In addition to the researched and policy-oriented support for the increased use of community service orders in Africa, the following are more administrative, justice-oriented, and ideological reasons to support an increase in the use of community service orders in all African nations.

- Our criminal justice system is comprised of agencies that work without coordination: African societies are not bureaucratically structured, and they should not strive to be.
- The court machinery is overloaded with cases, slow, and not readily accessible to all. Our options become to strengthen the system or dispense with our reliance on it.
- Prisoners are a low priority in Nigeria, as in many other African countries. Where three-quarters of the prison population is comprised of poor and powerless people, prisons are seen as not being worth the time, energy, or resources needed to improve them.
- Imprisonment is all too regularly used—even for minor offences and as punishment for first-time offenders. It

does not function in Africa or elsewhere as a means of last resort.
- Penal institutions have been shown to be overpowering in their dynamics within any society, and Africans need to decentralize and restructure their systems of justice before the penal system becomes as entrenched in our society as it for Western, industrialized nations.
- "Development" for Africa is not working to build societies and social structures that mirror colonial, European, or Western societies. Development in Africa is working to re-establish our own social structures. A reliance on penal institutions as social control continues to reinforce colonial social structures that have been destructive and decivilizing.

Community Service Orders in Africa

Efforts toward the implementation of alternatives to imprisonment in Nigeria, besides the statutory provision of fines and bail options, are still at embryonic stages (Penal Reform International 2000). However, in some African countries, such as Zimbabwe (despite much-touted human rights violations and political instability), Kenya, Uganda, Malawi, Mali, Senegal, and Burkina Faso, there are strong indications of the use of non-custodial measures on functional and legitimate levels. These countries have successfully established the use of community service orders, which are beginning to consolidate the accruable gains of less use of imprisonment as a means of administering justice. Community service orders are being used only for those people who have been sentenced to imprisonment. This regulation prohibits community service orders from being employed as an add-on to the criminal justice system and maintains them as an alternative to imprisonment. These orders are used for people who have been given short sentences and for first-time offenders.

It is worth noting that this innovative approach has hinged on two major areas: the first includes putting in place appropriate structures to implement these orders, while the second involves comprehensive community involvement that builds on the strength of societies and incorporates a holistic approach to the administration of justice. Following I present case studies of two countries — Zimbabwe and Kenya — that have employed and benefit from an increased use of community service orders.

Zimbabwean Experience

Since 1993 Zimbabwean law has provided that offenders may have options other than prison sentences: namely, community service has been made applicable to all offences that carry a maximum sentence of one year in prison.[1] Community service has come to be recognized as a system that ensures non-custodial measures, and generates unpaid labour for community building and empowerment projects — it has essentially become the default measure for short-term imprisonment. Accordingly, if a court must impose imprisonment, in any of the countries that have implemented community service, the sentencing court must state specific findings why imprisonment is justified. This requirement has led to a high level of involvement of the members of the judiciary, at both the local level and the national level, in a discussion of both if and when imprisonment is necessary, and in a continued understanding that alternatives to imprisonment are legitimate, relevant, and necessary in African societies.

In assessing the contributions and accomplishments of the community service programme in Zimbabwe I briefly list some indicators of the benefits that it has presented as an ATI since its inception in 1993.

- There is a high success rate: 120,000 offenders have been sentenced to community service since its inception (Stern 1999). A survey of 6,000 participants revealed that ninety-four percent have completed their placements successfully.
- There is a decline in recidivism: a survey of 6,000 offenders who participated in the community service programme

showed that only fifty percent had reoffended following completion of their sentences.
- There has been a decreased prison population since 1993: the prison population has declined from 22,000 to 18,000, notwithstanding an increase in the crime rate.
- There is a reduction in cost: it costs approximately US$ 120 per month to keep an individual in prison in Zimbabwe compared with approximately US$ 20 per month for participation in the community service programme.
- There is public approval/acceptance: being placed in the community service programme permitted offenders to keep their jobs and continue to support their families. This along with other visible results has helped the programme to gain public approval. Public support is currently at such a level that requests from placement agencies to participate in the community service programme exceed the number of offenders sentenced to community service.

Kenyan Experience

In Kenya lessons were learned from earlier efforts to introduce alternative measures. Planning for the community service project was elaborate and had a well-thought-through implementation plan (Wahl et al. 2002). In December 1995, following a seminar report on community service orders and the administration of criminal justice in Kenya, an interim committee on the subject was established. The committee looked at the existing penalty, extramural penal employment (EMPE), and found a number of problems that affected the performance of this programme. These problems included lack of clear guidelines, inexperienced staff, lack of information on offenders sentenced to EMPE, and poor record-keeping and documentation (Stern 1999). Against this backdrop the committee, under the auspices of the Ministry of Justice, devised plans for implementing the recommendations of the December 1995 seminar. This led to the drafting of a community service order bill.

Between August and September 1996 the committee visited all the prisons in Kenya on a fact-finding mission. Also during that period committee members made frequent television appearances to publicize the state of conditions in the prisons in Kenya. By the end of 1996 they had made study tours of other jurisdictions, including South Africa, Swaziland, and Zimbabwe. All of these efforts gave rise to the preparation of new legislation hinged on the already functional Kenyan probation service. The new bill envisages that the probation service will hold the administrative responsibility for implementing community service orders, while the judiciary will manage the programme.

In 1997 another international conference was convened to discuss the report of the interim committee and a proposed draft bill. In late 1997 the cabinet endorsed the bill, and it was passed by parliament in December 1998. This development marked the beginning of a renewed and much more purposeful alternative to custodial measures within the justice system in Kenya. The new programme encompasses establishing and implementing treatment programmes, restorative justice, mediation and reconciliation, probation, fines, parole, bail, and suspended sentences. All these options are presented and encouraged in opposition to a reliance on imprisonment in the administration of justice in Kenya.

Implementation in Nigeria

Given the benefits of community service orders as an ATI in other African countries, it remains imperative for Nigeria, along with other African nations, to begin implementing these alternatives. In doing so African nations are affording themselves the ability to functionally and legitimately address the many interrelated problems of the criminal justice system, particularly the prisons, with their overcrowded cells, infectious diseases, malnourished and traumatized inmates, and high death rates. Against this backdrop the following comprise a possible panacea to the current Nigerian justice system.

- There is the need to demonstrate enough political will to implement non-custodial approaches to criminal justice. Legislators need to have a clearer picture of the situation on the ground to help them make laws to initiate and back the implementation of ATIs. This could well be the way out for Nigeria's crisis in penal justice. As all previous efforts and campaigns toward implementation of ATIs have yet to receive legislative attention, the starting point is political support for such measures.
- The judiciary in Nigeria has to be in the vanguard of the implementation stage. In trying to implement alternatives to imprisonment those who imprison people in Nigeria need to be involved. Magistrates and judges need to be trained specifically in this regard. There is a need for basic guidelines to ensure a standard upon which magistrates and judges can rely to identify and treat cases that are apt for non-custodial measures.
- The involvement of the judiciary is equally vital for the social impact of the scheme. Members of the judiciary need to be involved, not only in sentencing, but also in appreciating the negative consequences that flow from imprisonment. By including the judiciary in the educational elements and philosophies of ATIs we ensure their commitment to making these programmes successful.
- Wherever possible, and for offences meticulously specified, community service orders can be built into Nigerian sentencing options. To assist in this process the dynamics of successful alternative measures in other countries should be studied, copied, improved upon, and applied in Nigeria to suit our socioeconomic, political, and cultural imperatives.
- A national monitoring committee needs to be set up to fully implement these recommendations. The committee should include members from the Ministry of Justice,

the Ministry of Internal Affairs, the police force, prisons, the Bar Association, the Law Reform Commission, and relevant non-governmental organizations, as well as academics/researchers.

CONCLUSION

The problems of imprisonment and the need to find alternative forms of social control in Nigeria have been highlighted in this chapter. Accordingly, a significant reduction in the use of imprisonment in dispensing justice has been adduced. It is hoped that the judiciary and other identified stakeholders will commence a much more purposeful and diligent effort in the administration of justice, without recourse to the use of imprisonment as the first port of call. A quick reference could be made to other African countries where such ATI mechanisms are being used. Consequently this would lead to the use of other means of justice that can begin to rely on restitution, compensation, bail, fines, and innovative community service orders. These alternatives provide an opportunity both for offenders to take responsibility for the harms they have caused and for empowerment rather than dichotomization of the community.

To get to the point of having community service orders in Nigeria political and non-governmental support is needed in expediting actions aimed at passing a bill that will in turn enable implementation of ATIs in Nigeria. While various models of justice may continue to receive immediate attention and review to strengthen their existence in African societies, Nigeria needs to begin seriously considering the benefits of such measures while working toward the viable and legitimate implementation of these options. This way we can take a step in the right direction, recognizing healing for offenders, victims, and the community at large, and employ mechanisms of social control that are not alien to Nigeria. The African society we strive to achieve will give everyone the opportunity for self-development.

NOTES

1   Implementation of community service orders as an alternative to imprisonment in Nigeria has not received any legislative motion, and no bill has been passed for their eventual takeoff.

REFERENCES

Adeyemi, Adedokun. (2000). "Alternatives to Imprisonment in Nigeria: Problems and Prospects." Paper presented at the National Conference on Alternatives to Imprisonment in Nigeria, Abuja.

Agomoh, U., A. Adeyemi, and V. Ogbebor. (2001). *The Prison Service and Penal Reform in Nigeria: A Synthesis Study.* Lagos: PRAWA.

Elias, T. O. (1969). "Traditional Forms of Public Participation in Social Defense." *International Review of Criminal Policy, 27.*

Lemgruber, Julita. (1998). "The True Cost of Prison." Paper presented at Prisons in South America: Which Way Out?, Kingston, ON.

Penal Reform International. (2000). *Abuja Declaration on Alternatives to Imprisonment.*

Stern, Vivien. (1999). "Alternatives to Imprisonment in Developing Countries." London: International Centre for Prison Studies; Penal Reform International.

United Nations. (1997). Sixth Session of the Commission on Crime Prevention and Criminal Justice, Vienna, April 28 to May 9.

Wahl, Hans et al. (2002). "International Standards, Good Prison Management, and Community-Based Sanctions: Training Workshop Materials on Advanced TOT, Kenya." Topic 11-A.2p5.

CHAPTER 20

THE IGBO INDIGENOUS JUSTICE SYSTEM

O. Oko Elechi

INTRODUCTION

This chapter examines the indigenous justice system of the Igbo of southeast Nigeria from restorative, transformative, and communitarian principles. The Igbo, like other societies in Africa, had a well-developed, efficient, and effective mechanism for maintaining law and order prior to colonialism. These social control practices and processes were rooted in the traditions, cultures, and customs of Igbo people. However, the Igbo system was relegated to the background by the British colonial authorities, who installed their own versions of "justice": the common, civil, and criminal legal institutions. The Nigerian postcolonial government has inherited this practice from the colonial era and continues to undermine the Igbo indigenous justice system.

Despite colonial and postcolonial state subjugation, the Igbo indigenous justice system holds sway, especially in rural areas, where the majority of the people reside. In line with Igbo egalitarian worldviews, crime is viewed as a conflict between community members. As primary stakeholders in the conflict, victims, offenders, and the community are actively involved in the definition of harm and the crafting of solutions acceptable to all stakeholders. The quality and effectiveness of justice are measured through the well-being of victims and the community.

Conflict creates opportunities for the education, socialization, and resocialization of offenders, victims, and all community members. Conflict also creates an opportunity for the reevaluation of community values and socioeconomic conditions.

IGBO PEOPLE AND IGBO SOCIETIES

The Igbo occupy the southeastern part of Nigeria and constitute one of the three dominant ethnic groups in Nigeria, with a population of about twenty-three million. The Igbo fall into two main groups: Riverine and Heartland Igbos. There are more than thirty dialects of the Igbo language, and there is great variance in their mutual intelligibility. However, to enhance communication a central Igbo language has been developed from the various dialects. This is the language taught in schools and used in commerce. Like many other Africans, the Igbo are a deeply spiritual people who believe in "one God, in lesser deities, spirits and in ancestors who are regarded as lesser deities and may be worshipped as such. This traditional religion is non-aggressive or evangelical but involves the use of propitiatory rites designed to appease the deities or to request their aid in times of need and crisis" (Awa 1985, 31).

Most Igbo societies are described as acephalous, in that they operate through a decentralized government. In this political and administrative arrangement authority is exercised through age grades, lineage heads, and pressure groups. There are also a few Igbo kingdoms, namely the Onitsha, Agbaja, Arochukwu, and Aboh. Despite the hierarchical social and political arrangement in Igbo societies that incorporate a constitutional monarchy, villages in these societies remain autonomous, and leadership is exercised through the Council of Elders. Furthermore, participatory democracy and the egalitarian outlook of the people are not affected. Awa (1985, 38) explains that

> the typical Igbo governmental system consists of: (1) the Chief and council of elders at the centre, (2) lineage groups, age

grades, secret societies, priestly groups, etc., who exercise a considerable amount of influence over the decision processes of the community, and (3) the town/village forum. From the well-known processes by which these institutions take decisions and exercise power, we know that Igbo people value participatory and consensus politics, along with checks and balances. We must note in particular that in consensus politics, the individual is entitled to express dissent on any issues that crop up in discussions and the leaders of the institution concerned must somehow explain away the problem raised so that all can go along together.

This political arrangement and process are not peculiar to the Igbo. According to Ayittey (1999, 86), in "virtually all the African tribes, political organization of both types began at the village level. The village was made up of various extended families or lineages. Each has its head [the patriarch], chosen according to its own rules."

It is important to note that, "at certain levels of political discourse, women and children were not allowed full participation" (Elechi (2004, 165). However, women have access to constitutionally enshrined sanctuary powers that can be brought into play to offset the dominance of men. In addition, women have analogous institutions where they adjudicate on conflicts among themselves. Furthermore, women are encouraged to bring their marital problems to the village courts for adjudication. It is also important to note that women do dominate the informal realms of social control (which in a communitarian model of justice hold more weight than the Western professionalized forms of justice), and are gaining more formal authority and rank in Igbo societies.

From the foregoing, I reiterate that the Igbo, like other societies in Africa, had a well-developed, efficient, and effective mechanism for maintaining law and order prior to colonialism. These social control practices and processes were rooted in the traditions, cultures, and customs of Igbo people. Deviance or conflict is a characteristic of any social group, and the method or instrument employed to realign recalcitrant individuals speaks volumes about the civilization of that society. The Igbo indigenous justice system is in the main restorative, transformative, and communitarian: strenuous efforts are made to restore social safety without resorting to punishment. This is because punishment is believed to undermine the goal of justice, which is primarily the restoration of social equilibrium. When punishment is employed in the maintenance of social safety it is as a last resort, used only after all other efforts have failed to achieve conformity, order, and community safety.

PRINCIPLES OF THE IGBO INDIGENOUS JUSTICE SYSTEM

The Igbo indigenous justice system is process-oriented, victim-centred, and humane, and it applies persuasive and reintegrative principles in adjudicating justice. A major component of the Igbo indigenous justice system is that it is participatory, and decisions are reached through consensus. Everybody has equal access to and participation in the justice system; furthermore, no one can arrogate to himself or herself the role of "professional" or "expert," thereby subjugating the voices of ordinary community members. Again, the goal of justice is the restoration of relationships and social harmony disrupted by the conflict. It is understood in Igbo justice models that all members of society are experts on their shared social realities and are thus qualified to participate in the quest for justice.

My own ethnographic research shows that the indigenous justice system is better and more effective in addressing issues of crime and justice in Nigeria. One reason the indigenous justice system is more effective is because it recognizes that crime is a violation of people and relationships, not just a violation of "law." From this perspective accountability should be to the victims and the community, not to an external system of legal codes and bureaucratic procedures. As a balanced justice system Igbo indigenous justice works to empower, not criminalize, victims, offenders, and the affected community. The focus of this system is to actively and meaningfully participate in the identification and definition of harm, and to have direct involvement in the search for restoration, healing, responsibility, and prevention. As a restorative justice system it emphasizes a move away from the law-and-order model of criminal justice, and encourages steps toward implementing a human rights model of social justice.

This system of justice has illustrated, first, that social sanctions, even when devoid of punishment, are sufficient to bring people to order, and to resolve conflicts and maintain social safety; second, that justice-making is more viable and effective when enmeshed in the daily life of local communities, as opposed to centralized and depersonalized institutions of criminal justice; third, that democracy is, after all, about the decentralization of power in governance and the involvement of all segments of society in decision-making. Thus, the principles and practices of the Igbo indigenous justice system further support the notion that crime is a local event, and that a centralized policy of governance is insufficient in bringing "justice" to the "crime" problem. These illustrations reinforce democratic principles of governance, emphasizing and practising within this very important principle that government, having obtained its mandate to rule from the people, should also be accountable to the people. As a democratic system of justice the Igbo indigenous justice system emphasizes the involvement and empowerment of the people in social control.

Law-Making in Igboland

The Igbo indigenous justice system views legal violations primarily as victimizations of an individual or groups of individuals, and secondarily as victimizations of the community and its social order. This approach is vastly different from that of the Western criminal legal system, which places the state as the primary victim and officially records the state as the only victim of crime in court cases. While victims of crime are treated as "witnesses" (at the most) in Western criminal justice systems, the Igbo social justice system views victims of crime as participants in the quest for justice, empowering them to be part of the process of justice and restoration, as opposed to categorizing them as bystanders, silent observers, or witnesses open for interrogation in the "justice" process.

The Igbo also distinguish between crime and tort. These concepts are therefore used here to describe such phenomena as they are conventionally understood. I disagree with Western criminological literature arguing that use of the terms "crime," "torts," and "laws" to describe such practices in precolonial Africa is inappropriate. Maine (1969) and Diamond (1973), pioneer Western researchers of the living habits and social customs of precolonial peoples in Asia and Africa, argue that the customary practices of Asians and Africans are erroneously described as indigenous "laws." The evidence often presented to support this line of thinking is that precolonial African societies lacked centralized governments essential to the formulation and enforcement of laws. The assumption here is that governmental structures that mirror those used in the West can enact and enforce laws.

The inability to understand diverse structures of governance led many Western researchers to erroneously conclude that societies not structured in a hierarchical and centralized Western manner were "less civilized," and thus settled conflicts through violence and blood feuds. They further assumed that, since there was no recognizable central authority, there was no authority at all, concluding that victims of crime took matters into their own hands, and that chaos, not civility, structured and guided non-Western societies.

Available records suggest that the contrary was the case. The very principles of Igbo justice models recognize the interrelationships between the victim, the offender, and the community, and thus cannot constitute a society that alienates its victims and does not participate with them in the quest for justice. In my view Western conclusions on precolonial African laws highlight the divergence between restorative and retributive justice systems. Whereas retributive systems of justice rely on centralized forms of social control and law-making, restorative systems of justice do not. Most African justice systems incorporate restorative and transformative systems of justice, and thus were not recognized by the Western scholars who were not versed in these frameworks. This lack of recognition led to the assumption that there was a lack of justice.

African societies had agencies, groups, and individuals with authority to make, apply, and enforce laws. Laws served the same purpose in Africa as in other societies, which Gluckman (cited in Aubert 1969, 163) notes is the "regulation of established and the creation of new relationships, the protection and maintenance of certain norms of behavior, the readjustment of disturbed social relationships, and punishing of offenders against certain rules." Eze (cited in Motala 1989, 379) further points out that "in most traditional African societies the law existed outside the framework of a state in the modern sense. Obedience to the law was maintained through custom and religion as well as established patterns of sanction. These pre-colonial African societies had a high level of organization in which political, economic, and social control was maintained."

Laws and regulations guiding behaviours and interpersonal relationships, and the procedures for seeking grievances, are defined by the appropriate authorities in Igboland. Actions that are prohibited are clearly defined and stated, and the procedures for enacting and enforcing laws are unambiguously stated by the institutions of society charged with such responsibilities. As Ayittey (1999, 91) rightly points out, the African "village meeting under a big tree" and the European "parliament" were simply different forms of the same institution of democracy. What Africans had was participatory democracy; Europeans introduced parliamentary democracy. A unique characteristic of Africa's indigenous system of government was that it was open and inclusive. No one was locked out of the decision-making process. One did not have to belong to one political party or family to participate in the process; even foreigners were allowed to participate.

Most Igbo societies are egalitarian, with decentralized political authority. The power and authority to make and enforce laws are vested in the Council of Elders. A few Igbo societies had a hierarchical political arrangement with the power to make and enforce laws located in the office of the constitutional monarchy and the elders' council. Laws are distinguishable by the types and seriousness of the acts they seek to regulate, such as serious crimes, social obligations, and duties imposed by custom. As Obi (1963, 27), as cited in Okereafoezeke (2001, 22), rightly observes, the Igbo, like other African societies, are able to distinguish among "purely *social obligations* (such as the duty to honor invitations), *duties imposed by custom only* (for example, a father's duty to provide his male children with their first wives in order of seniority), and *legal duties* which can be enforced against the will of the party on whom such a duty lies." Okereafoezeke further notes that a distinction can be made between crimes against public security, such as theft, assault, battery, public nuisance, and violation of rules and regulations governing masquerade displays. Others include crimes against public morality, such as incest, adultery, and the murder of a kinsman, and the defilement of sacred institutions, such as a shrine. Prior to colonialism and the advent of popular education, as Okereafoezeke observes (24), the laws and procedures for law creation and enforcement were mostly unwritten, so "the natives relied on their individual and collective memories to ascertain the controlling legal authority on an issue. Because of the high integrity and honesty among community members, the absence of written documents as objective statements of the laws was not a major handicap to ascertaining and applying laws."

The Igbo indigenous justice system respects and promotes the rights of litigants. This is because respect for and promotion of human rights are values deeply rooted in African cultural values. As Gyekye (1996) rightly observes, the African believes in the sanctity of human life and human dignity, which is an expression of the natural and moral rights of the individual. However, the individual's rights must be appreciated within a communal context, as Elechi (1999) notes. This is because the community's rights or interests override those of the individual. That the community right is supreme does not mean that the rights of individuals are in jeopardy or compromised as a result. The individual versus the community rights paradox is eloquently described by Achebe (2000, 14): "In the worldview of the Igbo the individual is unique; the town is unique. How do they bring the competing claims of these two into some kind of resolution? Their answer is a popular assembly that is small enough for everybody who wishes to be present to do so and to 'speak his own mouth,' as they like to phrase it." The African humane and communitarian values make the welfare of one the concern of all. The African humanitarian and communitarian values make it difficult to subjugate anyone or deny his or her rights. Ifemesia (1978), as cited in Iro (1985, 4), describes Igbo societies as communitarian and humane. According to Ifemesia, humane living conditions encompass a "way of life emphatically centered upon human interests and values, a mode of living evidently characterized by empathy, and by consideration and compassion for human beings.... Igbo humanness is deeply ingrained in the traditional belief that the human being is supreme in the creation, is the greatest asset one can possess, is the noblest cause one can live and die for."

The Victim in the Igbo Indigenous Justice System

The victim is central to the Igbo indigenous justice system. Victims take the lead in bringing offenders to justice, unless the crime victimized the entire community. Victims may be assisted by family members and others in the search for justice. Victims are empowered by being accorded a voice and a role in the judicial process. The justice system seeks to vindicate the victim, and protect his or her rights and interests. The restoration of victims is achieved through their empowerment and by addressing their needs. Opportunities are provided to victims to tell relevant others how the actions of the offenders affected them. This all occurs in a secure and respectful setting. Victims are further reassured of protection against further victimization. This approach leads to validation of the victims' hurts and losses. Furthermore, victims feel validated when afforded the opportunity to share their concerns with empathetic listeners. Victims are encouraged to openly vent their anger and frustration. Respectful and secure settings do not have to be emotionally sterile and controlled, as is assumed in Wesetern court settings. In the Igbo process of justice victim care is a priority because of strong social solidarity and the prevailing spirit of good neighbourliness in the society in which these justice models are implemented.

The Offender in the Igbo Indigenous Justice System

Offenders are actively involved in the definition of harm and the search for resolution to the problem. Ample opportunities are provided to offenders to feel the impacts of their actions on the victim and the community. They are also persuaded to be accountable to the victim and the community for their actions. Offenders are made to appreciate the fact that their actions harm more than the individual victims, for they also harm the community. Offenders are made to realize that they are also harmed by their own actions. Igbo societies view themselves as collectives responsible for the well-being of all members of the community. This responsibility includes offenders who have contributed to the destabilization of the community through the imposition of harm. Offenders are held accountable for their actions and are persuaded to pay compensation to the victims. This approach is different from that of Western criminal justice processes, in which offenders pay compensation for their crimes to the state by serving time in prison or by paying fines.

In Igbo justice processes holding offenders accountable is not tantamount to punishing them. The goal of justice is to restore, as much as possible, victims to the positions they were in before victimization occurred. Compensation to the victim, according to Nsereko (1992), goes beyond restitution. It also represents a form of apology and atonement by the offender to the victim and the community. Restitution to the victim is integral to the settlement of the disputes because of the understanding in the community that a victim whose needs are not addressed is a potential offender.

An offender's accountability includes restoring the victim to the position he or she was in prior to the offence, limited of course to the extent to which money or property can solve the problem. Offenders are further made to show remorse for their actions through apology and atonement to the victim and the community. The Igbo people believe that no offence is so serious that it cannot be atoned for with a commensurate sacrifice and reparation. It is generally believed in Igboland that human beings are inherently good, but may be driven to violate societal norms by evil forces or circumstances beyond their control. Conflict resolution therefore becomes an opportunity for the education, socialization, and resocialization of offenders, victims, and other community members. Conflict resolution becomes an opportunity to probe the underlying socioeconomic causes of the individual offender's actions.

Family members of offenders are held accountable for the actions of one of their own. They are either chastised or made to appreciate where they failed as parents or family members. In this inclusion of family also lies the distribution of responsibility necessary in properly addressing harm in a manner that will avoid future harms. The incident could not have occurred in an isolated context (because society is communitarian), and thus the solution cannot be found in isolation of responsibility. Where the offender is unable to pay restitution to the victim the family is held responsible. It is important to note that, in a system of justice that does not rely on revenge and harmful punishment to deal with conflict, the dispersion of responsibility is not problematic, as it is in a system of justice that chooses to hurt and violate those who have offended.

In holding the offender and his or her family responsible for the offender's actions strenuous effort is made not to sever the connection between the offender, the family, and other community members. The prevailing culture is such that the actions of the offender can be condemned while a message of love and respect is extended to the offender. The basis for this thinking is the belief in the community that justice-making is an opportunity to promote repair, reconciliation, and reassurance.

The mainstay of the people's economy is agriculture. Agrarian economy is labour-intensive, and as such no body is expendable. All efforts are made to reintegrate offenders into the community to remain productive members. Furthermore, violations indicate a failure of responsibility by the offender on the one hand and the community on the other. The reasoning is that it takes a village to raise a child. Community members also acknowledge and accept their responsibility for failing in raising a responsible and productive citizen. Justice-making therefore becomes an opportunity for the re-evaluation of community values, culture, and political, social, and economic conditions. Justice and fairness are enhanced as decision-makers become conscious of their own vulnerability, as they could be at the receiving end of justice in the future.

The Community in the Igbo Indigenous Justice System

The Igbo indigenous justice system recognizes the community as also affected by criminal behaviour. Since crime is a local event, and an intraethnic and intraclass affair, community peace and harmony are undermined when there is conflict between community members. Crime creates fear in the community. It can lead to isolation and distrust, which further weaken community bonds. The community response is therefore critical to bringing about desired restoration and reconciliation, failing which will further polarize the community. Due to these understandings the community is actively involved in the definition of harm and the search for a resolution acceptable to all stakeholders. The community's goal in intervening in a conflict is to reform the offender and reintegrate him or her into the community. There is an implicitly recognized need to restore order, stability, reassurance, and faith in the community.

As previously stated, the Igbo indigenous justice system can differentiate between individual victimization and offences where the entire community comes to be or feel victimized. When the matter is strictly between two people or groups of people the community becomes actively involved by assisting the litigants to find a quick resolution to their conflict. The understanding is that if the conflict is not quickly resolved it may escalate, and undermine societal order, peace, and harmony. If it is a matter where the entire community is a victim, the offender is prosecuted at the community's tribunal. In the following sections I review how the Igbo and other Africans handle cases of murder and theft to appreciate the principles and practices of the Igbo indigenous justice system.

Responding to Law Violations in Igboland
All behaviours that violate the society's laws and regulations attract one form of sanction or another. In the Western legal context sanctions are primarily structured to impose harm upon the offender, based mainly on the assumptions that people inherently want to harm others and thus that the law functions to deter such animalistic tendencies. In the Igbo model of justice sanctions are primarily a method through which harm can be addressed within the understanding that all people are inherently good, but at times make mistakes, lose control, or slip up. While not all sanctions in Igbo justice processes avoid harming an offender, harm (such as execution) is only imposed if the community, the victim, and the offender's family all agree that it is necessary. From within this context (and implicit difference in approach to humanity) the institutions of Igbo society charged with enforcing laws see it as their obligation to respond appropriately to behaviours that violate the norms of society. Failing to do that would be an open invitation to chaos in the community. As Dike (1986, 17) rightly observes, "control of the activities of individuals and groups within Igbo societies is therefore of paramount importance at all times, hence the existence of a multiplicity of institutions and organizations for enforcing compliance with Igbo societal

norms. Such institutions include the masquerade societies, age grades as well as the assemblies of lineage elders who hold the *Ofo* [the symbol of legitimate authority and justice] and perform important political roles."

Murder

Murder is a very serious crime in Igboland. Igbos distinguish between murder and manslaughter. Within these distinctions the nature of the crime determines the community's response. Murder is generally viewed as a crime against the victim and the victim's family, and thus murder cases are mediated between the victim's family and the offender's family within the normative framework of the community. An agreement can be reached whereby the offender's family is made to pay compensation to the victim's family. This payment is decided upon according to the contributions that the murdered victim made to the survival of his or her family. The cost of burying the victim is also the responsibility of the offender. These compensations are meant to address the logistical losses incurred by the murder. In addressing such losses Igbo justice is not undermining the emotional elements of harm involved with the violent taking of life, but working to address the situation in a manner that brings about the least suffering possible for surviving family members — by addressing immediate financial struggles that the murder has imposed, the surviving family members are better equipped to face other burdens (emotional, psychological, traumatic) imposed on them. In addition to restitution, murder evokes a diverse array of sanctions in Igbo justice models.

In Afikpo (Igbo) society, according to Elechi (1999), if the murder occurs in the course of a robbery, it is viewed as a crime against the Afikpo community as a whole. The circumstances of the act will determine the community's response. If the offender is a repeat offender and/or perceived as dangerous, and a major threat to life and property in the community, he or she could attract the community's harshest response. A conviction will result in capital punishment in which the offender is buried alive, with an iroko tree planted to mark the grave to act as a general deterrent to others. Before such sentences can be carried out the matrilineal relatives of the offender have to sanction it. In some cases murderers are expelled from the community.

The killing of a kinsman is viewed more seriously. It is an abomination, for which the remedy is cleansing and expiation rather than punishment. As Amadi (1982, 58) observes, "in many tribes the killing of a kinsman, the antithesis of caring for him, was not only a crime but also an abomination. After the murderer had been executed his family would perform sacrifices and rites to remove the stain of evil and ward off the anger of the gods." Amadi further notes that the murder victim's family and the murderer's family met to negotiate appropriate compensation. Reparation negotiations were always under the watchful eyes of the entire community. The bargaining was always supervised by the elders of the community to ensure that retribution was not excessive.

In some African societies the murderer was forced to commit suicide. In some cases the murderer's son, wife/husband, or other relation was executed in his or her place if he or she escaped the long arm of the law. Some African communities force the murderer to die the same way the victim died. In still others the murderer is persuaded to compensate the victim's family by providing a close relation as a replacement for the victim. Amadi (1982, 15-16) notes that

> The Kwale (Igbo) required a girl as replacement and twenty bags of cowries as compensation. The Kakkakari tribe required the murderer to substitute either two girls or a girl and a boy. The Gamawa required fourteen slaves as recompense. In some tribes, like the Gade, the Arago, the Burra and Ikwerre, bargaining was possible, and the death penalty could be commuted to a heavy fine, usually involving replacement by a slave or free-born. In tribes like the Ikwo (Igbo) the murderer was simply handed over to the family of the deceased, which was free to do whatever it liked with him.

As can be seen from the foregoing, the punishment for murder varied from one African community to another, from one era to the next. Even among the Igbo community responses for murder varied greatly from one town to the other. For example, the Orlu (Igbo) used execution by hanging if the murderer was apprehended immediately after the crime was committed. However, if the murderer was able to escape justice and stay away for three years, he or she could return to the community as a free person. Yet other societies, such as the Kadara, "treated murderers fairly lightly. They isolated them for a month or so, and that was the end of the affair" (Amadi 1982, 16).

The community's response to murder also varies depending on whether the offender and the victim are from the same place. In societies where bargaining between the victim's family and that of the offender is the norm the outcome might be different when the murderer is a stranger. In such a case the stranger will likely be killed or taken into slavery unless the victim's community and the murderer's community have some bilateral arrangement or understanding on how such cases can be handled. However, should the unknown murderer escape arrest, the communities of the offender and the victim can enter into arbitration, whereby compensation to the victim's family will be sufficient.

Sorcery and Magic

Most cases of murder in Africa originate from sorcery, magic, and witchcraft. It is not always easy to distinguish among them, notes Parrinder (1973, 113), as cited in Elechi (1999, 275), because in Africa it is difficult to distinguish between "material and spiritual.... Hence the distinction of magic and medicine is difficult to make, and the two words can both be used, provided that their wide connotation is borne in mind." Magic can have medicinal value and can be used for fortification purposes. It can also be used to both protect and harm people. Thus, crimes of sorcery, murder, incest, and bestiality are viewed very seriously in many African societies.

One explanation is that Africans are highly religious and blame every misfortune on either the gods or an enemy (Elechi

1999). Africans blame accidents, sudden deaths, delayed pregnancies, and prolonged labour or illness on the work of witches. Witches and wizards are thought to have supernatural powers, and can wreak havoc at will. Amadi (1982, 22) explains why witches are feared in Africa:

> Witches were believed to have the power of metamorphosis; that is, it was thought that they could change at will into non-human creatures like bats, leopards, mosquitoes, crocodiles. While in these guises, they could harm their neighbors. One method of killing that was widely attributed to witches was vampirism or blood-sucking. At night, using their mysterious powers, they were said to pass through closed doors to get to their sleeping victims, whose blood they drank. The victims became progressively weaker and might eventually die unless the aid of an experienced medicine man was sought. Sometimes witches left marks on the bodies of their victims.

The crime of sorcery is understood to be perpetuated through supernatural powers, and as such it is difficult to prove. This accounts for why it is not easy to convict anybody accused of sorcery, and for the resort to oath-taking as a way of establishing guilt or innocence. The punishment for sorcery is also left in the hands of the gods to avenge. In Afikpo, for example, according to Elechi (1999), the community will order someone suspected of sorcery to swear to an oath. But this is the case where the victim is still alive. Where the victim is dead the alleged offender is tried by ordeal, where he or she is persuaded to drink some of the water used to wash the corpse of the victim. The belief is that, if the accused is guilty, he or she will die within a year after drinking this water. If the alleged sorcerer survives after drinking the water, then he or she is presumed innocent. After the oath-taking is administered the case is washed off the hands of those mediating and is placed in the hands of the gods. The understanding is that the gods will vindicate the innocent and punish the guilty by killing them.

Theft

Theft is a very serious offence, and attracts the community's harshest punishment of fines and ridicule in Afikpo, according to Elechi (1999). Theft leaves a lasting stigma on the offender and his or her family. The victim of theft is not awarded any compensation beyond what he or she lost. This practice is not peculiar to Afikpo. According to Amadi (1982, 16), "for the people of Alanso, Okposi, Afikpo and parts of Owerri it was enough for a thief to return the stolen goods." It is important to point out, however, that it is not every act of acquiring someone else's possessions without the owner's consent that constitutes theft. Food and other commodities taken for sustenance are acceptable, provided the person taking them does not intend to sell them. Describing other Nigerian ethnic groups with similar behavioural ethics, Amadi states that "among the Nupe stealing food was not punishable if the offender consumed what he stole on the spot. The Jawara tribe pardoned an offender if he pleaded hunger as a reason for stealing. In Ikwerre and parts of Igbo it was quite normal for one person to take a few nuts from another's bunch of palm fruits heaped by the wayside. The quantity of nuts taken was not expected to exceed what could normally be consumed by an individual or, in the case of a woman, what was needed to yield enough oil for a pot of soup" (16).

Elechi (1999) and Amadi (1982) observe that the punishment for theft varied greatly from one African community to another. The penalty for theft in Igara, for example, entailed the offender paying restitution to the victim at double the value of the goods stolen. In Jawara the penalty for theft was five times the worth of the original commodity stolen. In Oratta it was sufficient for the thief to return the stolen goods to the owner, but the thief was also made to pay a fine to the community and to endure public disgrace. The public spectacle included forcing the thief to climb a palm tree where all members of the community could see him or her. The Ohaffia and Ibibio people painted the thief's face black and paraded him or her through the community. The thief was sometimes forced to dance to a song sung by children and women of the village.

For some communities the punishment meted out to a thief depended on where the theft took place. The Aro (Igbo) would execute an offender who stole in the market instead of imposing the customary penalty of a fine. One explanation of this discrepancy is that the market holds great value for the Aros, for whom trading is the most common vocation. In the same vein, people who stole yams at the farms and barns in Afikpo had one of their hands cut off. The mainstay of the Afikpo economy is agriculture, and the yam is the staple food of the people. Some repeat offenders who were considered a threat to life and property were sold as slaves. Amadi (1982, 17) states that "the people of Arago, Bassa, Awka, Ndoki, Western Ijaw, Ibibio, Igbira, to name but a few, routinely sold off thieves into slavery."

Secret Societies in Igboland

Not every dispute or violation of the norms and laws is amenable to easy resolution. Complex cases are referred to secret societies, which are believed to have supernatural powers, and so are able to tell who is telling the truth and who is lying. When a secret society is invoked it is believed that every litigant or witness will tell the truth, as failure to do so before the masquerade can attract the punishment of death. Umozurike (1981, 12), describing the secret society of the Aro, notes that "the ekpe hardly fails when it is invoked to intervene in a dispute. Its fairness is usually assured because of its mystical powers to inflict evil on lying witnesses as well as on corrupt judges." In this context spirituality ensures truth in African societies. This is similar to the use of the Bible to swear on in court for witnesses who take the stand. While some of the rituals of African societies and justice models may seem unusual to Western observers, it is important to recognize that all societies have rituals and processes in which members of those societies participate.

In Afikpo the *Okumkpo,* a masquerade organized through the men's secret society, is a major agent of social control. While its role may be entertainment, the goal is really to address disputes or cases of a complicated and delicate nature. These are cases that are not amenable to regular court processes, yet they need to be addressed in the interests of village peace and harmony. Cases that the masquerade dramatizes include murder in which the accused may have sworn to the oath and survived, yet public opinion is strong that he or she is guilty of the offence, but was able to escape death through either manipulating the system or possessing other charms (spiritual powers) that counteract the power of the oath. Other cases that the masquerades address include the abuse of power by elders in their administrative and judicial functions. The masquerade performance is a trial in the court of public opinion within a humorous setting. The acts and songs are loaded with moral rectitude. They also play the role of investigating cases, and their evidence cannot be challenged. Because the masquerade performers wear masks they enjoy certain immunity from prosecution in whatever they say or do during the masquerade.

CONCLUSION

This chapter reviewed the Igbo indigenous justice system from restorative, transformative, and communitarian principles. In line with Igbo worldviews, crime is viewed as a conflict between community members. As primary stakeholders in the conflict, victims, offenders, and the community are actively involved in the definition of harm, and the crafting of solutions acceptable to all stakeholders. The quality and effectiveness of justice are measured through the well-being of victims and the community. Conflict creates opportunities for the education, socialization, and resocialization of victims, offenders, and all community members. Conflict is also an opportunity for the re-evaluation of community values and socioeconomic conditions. The Igbo indigenous justice system is process-oriented, victim-centred, and humane, and it applies persuasive and reintegrative principles in adjudicating most cases brought to justice processes. The overall goal of justice is restoration, not only of the victim, but also of the community.

REFERENCES

Achebe, Chinna. (2000). *Home and Exile.* New York: Oxford University Press.

Amadi, E. (1982). *Ethics in Nigerian Culture.* Ibadan: Heinemann Educational Books.

Aubert, Vilhelm. (1989). *Continuity and Development – in Law and Society.* Oslo: Norwegian University Press.

Aubert, Vilhelm. (1969). *Sociology of Law (Selected Readings).* Harmondsworth: Penguin Books Ltd. (pp. 142–194).

Awa, E. O. (1985). "Igbo Political Culture." In *The Igbo Socio-Political System: Papers Presented at the 1985 Ahiajoku Lecture Colloquium.* Owerri: Ministry of Information, Culture, Youth, and Sports.

Ayittey, G. B. N. (1999). *Africa in Chaos.* New York: St. Martin's Press.

Diamond, S. (1973). "The Rule of Law versus the Order of Custom." In *The Social Organization of Law,* ed. Donald Black and Maureen Mileski. New York: Seminar Press, pp.318 – 341.

Dike, C. P. (1986). "Igbo Traditional Social Control and Sanctions." In *Igbo Jurisprudence: Law and order in Tradtional Igbo Society.* Ahiajoku Lecture (Onugaotu) Colloquium. Owerri: Ministry of Information and Culture.

Elechi, O. Oko. (1999a). "Doing Justice without the State: The Afikpo (Ehugbo) Nigeria Model." PhD diss., Simon Fraser University, Burnaby, BC.

---. (1999b). "Victims under Restorative Justice Systems: The Afikpo (Ehugbo) Nigeria Model." *International Review of Victimology,* 6, 359–375.

---. (2004). "Women and (African) Indigenous Justice Systems." In *Pan-African Issues in Crime and Justice,* ed. A. Kalunta-Crumpton and B. Agozino. London: Ashgate, pp. 157–179.

Gyekye, K. (1996). *African Cultural Values: An Introduction.* Accra, Ghana: Sankofa Publishing Company.

Iro, M. (1985). "Igbo Ethics and Discipline." In *The Igbo Socio-Political System: Papers Presented at the 1985 Ahiajoku Lecture Colloquium.* Owerri: Ministry of Information, Culture, Youth, and Sports.

Maine, H. (1969) [1917]. "From Status to Contract." In *Sociology of Law,* ed. Vilhelm Aubert.

Motala, Z. (1989). "Human Rights in Africa: A Cultural, Ideological, and Legal Examination." *Hastings International and Comparative Law Review,* 12, 373–410.

Nsereko, N. (1992). "Victims of Crime and Their Rights." In *Criminology in Africa,* ed. Tibamanya mwene Mushanga. Rome: United Nations Interregional Crime and Justice Research Institute.

Okereafoezeke, N. (2001). "Africa's Native versus Foreign Control Systems: A Critical Analysis." Paper presented at the Tenth Annual Pan-African Conference, California State University, Sacramento, May 1–5.

Umozurike, U. O. (1981). "Adjudication among the Igbo." In *Perspectives on Igbo Culture: The 1981 Ahiajoku Lectures Colloquium*. Owerri: Ministry of Information and Culture.

CHAPTER 21

PENAL ABOLITIONIST THEORIES AND IDEOLOGIES

Viviane Saleh-Hanna

PENAL ABOLITIONISM: A RADICAL CRIMINOLOGY

Penal abolitionist academic discourse emerges through the critical criminological academic context, with subparadigmatic affiliations to radical criminology. The emergence of radical criminology occurred when critical criminology could no longer fully satisfy all the theories that emerged as critical of the social order. Radical criminology builds upon critical criminological attempts to question mainstream criminological discourse. While critical criminologists work to expose the oppressive status quo that mainstream (mainly classical and positivist) criminology scientifically works to maintain, radical criminologists present a level of analysis that promotes a more accurate questioning of crime and the (dys)functions of law: "The groundbreaking argument for redefining crime from a radical perspective was made by Herman and Julia Schwendinger.... They argued that criminologists should be concerned with violations of human rights as well as with behaviors traditionally proscribed by the criminal law. Since then, radicals have compiled quite a list of socially injurious behaviors and would-be-crimes" (Lynch and Groves 1989, 32).

Penal abolitionism falls within the realm of the radical perspective because it promotes radical revisions to the social order, both in relation to the distribution of power and in relation to attitudinal social functioning. In addition, penal abolitionism problematizes the structures that promote crime while not recognizing harm. Most abolitionists advocate a mental as well as a social revolution that should not only result in the destroying of penal structures as the only form of justice, but also promote the rebuilding of a society that is able to function without resorting to revenge-oriented reactions to harm.

Penal abolitionists also fall within the realm of radical criminology because they are generally under the assumption that "with very few exceptions... the concept of crime as such, the ontological reality of crime, has not been challenged" (Hulsman 1986, 28). Two questions about the penal abolitionist perspective are whether it is a theory of crime and whether it can or does address the nature of crime. Here I will illustrate that penal abolitionism is a theory that radically addresses the nature of crime, but in that assessment rejects the categorization of its perspectives as a theory of crime. This rejection is based on *the abolitionist definition of crime:* "Crime does not exist. Only acts exist, acts often given different meanings within various social frameworks. Acts, and the meaning given to them, are our data. Our challenge is to follow the destiny of acts through the universe of meanings. Particularly, what are the social conditions that encourage or prevent giving the acts the meaning of being crime?" (Christie 2003, 3). From this perspective crime is a socially constructed category, and it is the nature of this construction that is assessed from the penal abolitionist perspective.

Reiman (1990, 81) explains the importance of addressing the process of criminalization in attempting to understand the nature of crime. His assessment of this process is that it "makes certain that the offender at the end of the road in prison is likely to be a member of the lowest social and economic groups in the country.... *For the same criminal behavior,* the poor are more likely to be arrested, they are more likely to be charged; if charged, more likely to be convicted; if convicted, more likely to be sentenced to prison; and if sentenced to prison, more likely to be given longer terms than members of the middle and upper classes." This definition of crime illustrates that the abolitionist assessment of crime is rooted, not in the individual, but in the state and social structures that criminalize oppressed groups. In addition to addressing class-based issues, radical scholars (predominantly African, African American, and other academics of colour) also work to establish the links between criminalization and racialization of criminal justice.

THE PENAL SYSTEM: SLAVERY, IMPRISONMENT, AND THE JUSTIFICATION OF RACIST INSTITUTIONS

The overrepresentation of people of colour in prisons in the United States, and around the world, is blatant proof of the racism that exists within and is perpetuated through the criminal justice system. A brief historical analysis of the penal system in relation to Euro-American slavery of African people aids in both the historical and the economic contextualization of the racist structures of penal systems. In 1850 the US penal system incarcerated nearly 6,700 people, almost none of whom were black. At the time black people were more valuable economically outside the prison walls—they were "already imprisoned for life on plantations as chattel slaves" (Acoli 1995, 5). As Acoli notes, following the Civil War and at the so-called end of slavery "vast numbers of black males were imprisoned for everything from not signing slave-like labor contracts with plantation owners to looking the wrong way at some White person, or for some similar petty crime" (6). Five years after the formal institution of slavery was abolished black representation in the prison population rose from almost zero to thirty-three percent: "Many of these prisoners were hired out to Whites at less than slave wages" (6). Eventually, "convict leasing" was phased out, and it came to be replaced by "one of the most brutal forms of convict forced labor in the United States, the chain gang" (Browne 1996,

64). Control of unpaid black labour shifted from the official institution of slavery to the official institution of imprisonment, initially used to maintain private and white family-owned business enterprises. Eventually, the US government came to recognize that in building a nation black labour could be used through the chain gang at no expense to the state. Convict labour became profitable and politically popular in many southern states, as Browne notes: "The fundamental 'reform' in abolishing convict leasing and replacing this system with chain gangs was that the state now owned the convicts and their labor" (64). This form of exploitation and economic manipulation continues to exist, and grow, through prison industries in the contemporary US economy. The chain gang has been revived in Alabama, and since 1995 "several other states have responded positively to the idea.... Arizona has already begun modeling the program in their own prisons" (69).

The economic value of prisoners used as workers expands beyond chain gangs, though, and all sorts of intense labour and forced work exist today. "The Prison Industry Authority (PIA) is a multi-million dollar industry that is dependent on the productivity of prisoners in California. As inmates are classified for placement in an institution, they are surveyed for almost 50 different work skills, from appliance repair to x-ray technician, to determine which institution they should be placed in" (Browne 1996, 65). A close analysis of prison labour illustrates that convict labour plans are not about job training and education, but about profit and industry. While the Department of Corrections in California maintains that prisoners work on a voluntary basis, it is clear, according to Browne, that those who refuse to work serve sentences that are twice as long as those who do work because "each day worked reduces a prisoner's sentence by one day" (65). Those who refuse to work, or work less, receive no privileges or fewer privileges through a classification process called the Work/Privilege Group. Under this programme, prisoners who refuse to work are not entitled to family visits, are given smaller limits for canteen withdrawals, can make telephone calls only in cases of emergency (at prison staff discretion), and are not allowed access to recreational or entertainment segments of the prison: "These extreme coercive tactics contradict the claim that labor is voluntary" (65). These conditions bring forth the expanding role the economics of penality plays in the implantation of criminal justice in the United States. One Canadian lifer summarizes the economic and inhumane aspects of the conditions of the "prison industrial complex" effectively in one sentence. He states that "they [corrections] count you like diamonds and treat you like shit" ("John" 1997, 29).

THE CRIME CONTROL INDUSTRY: FINANCIAL AND ACADEMIC PROFITS

Some scholars link "the rise of the penitentiary to the economic concerns. In this view, not only was the penitentiary an economically effective and self-sustaining institution, but the practice of institutionalization was thought to have economic benefits for society as well" (Welch 1995, 252). The financial domain within penality is seldom discussed in popular discourse; it is well documented, though, in the critical and radical criminological realm.

In his discussion of power and punishment Foucault asserts that the success of the prison lies in its reproduction of delinquents, who serve as raw material and provide the necessary energy that keeps the prisons running (1972, 39). Christie develops this argument in relation to the industrial aspect of crime control: "Societies of the Western type face two major problems: Wealth is everywhere unequally distributed. So is access to paid work.... The crime control industry is suited for coping with both. This industry provides profit for work while at the same time producing control of those who otherwise might have disturbed the social process" (1993, 13).

Christie further outlines the profit-making aspect of crime control and presents an alternative view of the functions of penal systems. In his analysis the profit-driven system is vastly different from a security-focused system that works to provide safety within communities. In politicizing crime control and discussing the industrial aspect of penology Christie lays out one of the largest obstacles in the path of penal abolition. He points out that an "urge for expansion is built into industrial thinking" and that this mentality is similar to the penal system's policy implications (1993, 13).

Within the North American context Cayley points out that "levels of crime and levels of imprisonment show no regular or predictable relationship.... In both Canada and the United States, [crime] has gone down for a number of years without any abatement in the growth of [the] prison population" (1998, 5). One can conclude that a large section of the prison population is dependent on political decisions and economic growth. Comparing crime control to other industries, Christie concludes that "the crime control industry is in the most privileged position. There is no lack of raw material—crime seems to be endless in supply. Endless also are the demands for the service, as well as the willingness to pay for what is seen as security" (1993, 13). Looking at the bigger picture, it becomes harder to accept the failure of the penal system as a consequence of bad people behaving in bad ways. It becomes clear that Western industrialized nations rely on a 'criminal' class to build their economies, and that penal systems function to maintain a status quo that keeps some people rich and the majority poor. These class-based structures are defined through race, both within the boundaries of Western industrialized nation-states and globally, as nations ruled by white people interact with nations ruled by people of colour.

CONTEMPORARY PENAL SYSTEMS: UPHOLDING HISTORICAL SLAVE LABOUR AND COLONIAL LEGACIES

The penitentiary is the ultimate penal structure as society knows it today. Supposedly the prison functions to punish, to protect, to rehabilitate, and to transform, among other things. In terms of the everyday functions of the prison, ironically enough, it is maintained by the same people whom it oppresses. In the prison "inmates have produced all of the work that supports the prison system, such as making the clothes, washing the clothes, and building the cell equipment, day room furniture, lockers, and mess hall tables" (Browne 1996, 66). Browne also notes that, aside from building and maintaining the prison's physical structure, prisoners have also made "shoes, bedding, clothing, detergents, stationery products, license plates and furniture for all state agencies. In addition, convict laborers have provided 'special services' such as dental lab work, micro graphics, and printing" (66). All of these tasks are generally assigned to male prisoners.

In line with patriarchal gender stereotypes "the women's prison industries have generally been in the areas of re-upholstery, fabric production, laundry, and data entry. In men's prisons all of this work is done, as well as metal production, wood production, and the operation of farms, dairies, and slaughterhouses" (Browne 1996, 66). These processes and tasks add up to a multi-million-dollar industry. The prison is not only saving money when prisoners build, maintain, and clean the prison, but also making money when labour outside the realm of the prison is brought into the oppressive, unequal power dynamics of the penitentiary. Browne mentions that "this enormous, multi-million-dollar industry was purportedly created to address the problem of 'inmate idleness'... by helping in rehabilitation, building effective work habits, and providing job training. Yet a prisoner who spends a ten-year sentence processing stationery products on an assembly line or washing laundry has not learned any highly employable skill [outside the prison industry], nor has been mentally or emotionally challenged through this service to the state" (66).

In essence prisoners are taught skills that will provide them with experience to work in prison, for prison, and only within the conditions that are prescribed and enforced by prison. Such realities illustrate that the penal system in the

United States functions through a racist and capitalist agenda. Based on a history that relied on the slave labour of Africans, the contemporary criminal justice system in the United States upholds its own legacy. In relation to penal systems in Africa history is more closely linked to colonialism and European invasions that worked to control and destabilize African societies. Contemporary implementations of penal systems in Africa uphold those European modes of social control that work to divide and conquer populations. They uphold the legacy of colonialism that worked to destabilize and delegitimize African social structures and cultures.

ABOLITIONIST MOVEMENTS: EXTENSIONS OF RACIST HISTORIES

The assessment of crime and penal systems of control has a long history in academic disciplines. As a starting point "abolitionists raise questions like: What logic, and ethic, makes it so certain that punishment has priority over peacemaking?" (Christie 2003, 80). This line of assessment touches on not only the administration of justice, but also the nature of society, the nature of human behaviour, and the nature of crime. Abolitionist literature in the Western academic realm can be traced back to 1919, to a Dutch penal scholar, Clara Wichmann, who wrote about "the class interests that guide the process of criminalization" (van Swaaningen 1997, 57).[1] Her views mirrored Bonger's (1967) rejection of the notion of deterrence, arguing that the implementation of penal punishments in attempts to control social behaviour is irrational and counterproductive. Bonger's work delegitimized the very concept of social control through fear, emphasizing that human behaviour is not and cannot be controlled through a system that threatens to punish those who do not follow the so-called social contract that the state assumes relevant to society. Wichmann's assessment of Bonger's work was critical of his omission of "the selectivity of criminalization in the legislative process" and the fact that Bonger had not "argued against apparent cases of class justice" (van Swaaningen 1997, 57). Her perspectives were rooted in the early critical paradigmatic affiliations that incorporated a Marxist- and Engels-oriented promotion of socialism.

Wichmann considered the classical scholars' concepts of crime and punishment to be "far too limited. With the unfounded suggestion of a direct causal relation between crime and punishment, the political character of criminality is obscured: poverty and repression do not receive the label 'crime,' but the consequences of poverty and repression" do (van Swaaningen 1997, 57). This analysis provided a foundation for the abolitionist perspective, which views crime as an oppressive categorization of the powerless, and punishment as an oppressive method of social control.[2] It is assumed here that penal-oriented methods of social control that rely on punishment and revenge ideological frameworks work to maintain the status quo, not to maintain (or even create) social order.

In 1919 Wichmann connected her political ideas with her criminal law profession to form the CMS (which translates as the Action Committee against the Prevailing Opinions on Crime and Punishment). "The CMS was a political platform which found its basis in various revolutionary groups, and strove for penal abolition. Opposition to the state's right to punish is as old as the state itself" (van Swaaningen 1997, 54). The premise of the CMS manifesto, as it related to the nature of crime and crime control, is very much rooted in an analysis of state power dynamics and social control of the powerless classes.

Emerging directly after World War I, the CMS saw links between penal and military systems, "and regarded both as man-created institutions of pointless and repressive cruelty" (van Swaaningen 1997, 55). Quinney's assessment of the penal justice model falls in line with that assessment. Quinney states that, "when we recognize that the criminal justice system is the moral equivalent of the war machine, we realize that resistance to one goes hand in hand with resistance to the other" (1991,

12). Within such assertions lie concepts about society and social control that are the foundations of radical criminology.

The concept (not just the application) of penal punishment was viewed by Wichmann as both counterproductive and inhumane: "By retaliating against the evil of crime with the evil of punishment, the threshold of answering violence with violence is continually lowered. Punishment is a form of unresponsive violence, and CMS rejected, following Tolstoy, its legitimacy — both as retribution and as rehabilitation" (van Swaaningen 1997, 55). Morris further defines those "evils" of punishment as unjust (racist and classist), and concludes that in the US version of criminal justice "money talks and everybody else does time" (1995, 7).

These conclusions arise from a general critique of capitalist social structures that rely heavily on the existence of a surplus labour population that can be exploited to build capital for profit. The recognition that the penal system is a function of those structures is a central tenet of penal abolitionist ideologies. Penal abolitionism focuses on the function of the criminalization process as maintaining a status quo of oppression for the majority and profit for the minority. The influence of Wichmann's CMS and the ideology presented in it can be seen in contemporary penal abolitionist literature, both in the assessments of punishment and systems of social control, and in the role that the process of criminalization plays in the production of an ideology that legitimizes and normalizes oppression.

In 1912 Wichmann's dissertation, entitled "Reflections on the Historical Foundations of the Present-Day Transformation of Penality," emphasized the "current manifestations of crime" as "inherent in the capitalist structure of society" (van Swaaningen 1997, 55). This emphasis on the correlation between capitalist structures and crime is presented clearly in Christie's (1993) assessment of crime as functionally relevant to capitalist structures.

In her dissertation Wichmann reached the conclusion that "the socioeconomic conditions under which crime emerges, as well as the treatment of delinquents, need a better solution than repression" (van Swaaningen 1997, 55). This conclusion has academically evolved into the contemporary penal abolitionist view of the nature of crime as a process of criminalization that continues to repress the most powerless populations in each society: the poor in Nigeria, African Americans in the United States, and First Nations people in Canada.

In understanding these components of the criminalization process penal abolitionists today assert that "there is no such thing as crime: not just the contents of what is at a given time and place defined into that category, but the category of crime itself does not exist outside the context of 'criminalization.' 'Crime' as a category is reliant upon historical 'inventions' to criminalize what the capitalist economy identifies as the 'surplus population'" (Steinert 1986, 26). The definition of acts as criminal is based not on harmful acts, or on dangerous people, or even on acts that break the social contract. Crime is in fact a social construction, to be analyzed as myth presented as reality in everyday life (Hess 1986).

"As a myth, crime serves to maintain political power relations and lends legitimacy to the expansion of the crime control apparatus and the intensification of surveillance and control. It justifies inequality and relative injustices. Thus, the bigger the social problems are, the greater the need for the crime myth" (De Haan 1996, 357–358). From within this assessment emerges the functional element of crime as perpetuating and legitimizing the social structures that Wichmann found so problematic. In this context harmful behaviours are not all recognized as criminal. Harmful acts committed by corporations and nation-states are not crimes. Crime, criminalization, and penal sanctions are saved for those people whom the state sees fit to punish, for those populations that the capitalist structures can oppress in order to maintain a white and dominant status quo. Whereas some criminalized acts are violent, much of what has been deemed criminal is not. From an abolitionist perspective *criminal* justice is violent in structure, in ideology, in institutions, and in implementation.

Nineteenth-century European scholars (Nietzsche, Guyau, Tolstoy, Kropotkin) put forth penal abolitionist arguments that continue to inspire "the rejection of criminal law as an expression of violence" (van Swaaningen 1997, 54–55). The term "abolition" has come to be viewed in more contemporary times to describe those people who are opposed to the use of the death penalty. In addition, the prison abolitionist movement in the United States and Canada has come to be viewed as an extension of the movement to abolish slavery. This extension is well documented and, on the most basic level, best illustrated in the Thirteenth Amendment to the US Constitution:

> *Amendment 13 Abolition Of Slavery Ratified Dec. 6, 1865:*
> *Section 1.* Neither Slavery, nor involuntary servitude, *except as a punishment for crime* whereof the party shall have been duly convicted, shall exist within the United States, or any place subject to their jurisdiction.
> *Section 2.* Congress shall have power to enforce this article *by appropriate legislation.* (emphases added)

The penal system was able to step up and take responsibility for the extension of slavery from historical into contemporary times: mass incarceration of such large numbers of *the direct descendants* of slaves by such large numbers of *the direct descendants of slave-owners and other people of European descent* visibly and economically mirrors historical slavery. These obvious facts and extensions are lost in the contemporary criminal justice system's shift in language. Where black used to mean "slave," it now means "criminal." However, as white people shift the language they use to refer to black people, and the institutions they employ to control and exploit them, little else changes. In both eras justifications and explanations presented to implement the continued exploitation of black people have been accepted by the vast majority of Europeans and people of European descent living in Western, so-called civilized societies.

In the "developing" world the abolitionist movements came to represent the move to physically remove European governments from African soil. In more recent times penal abolitionist movements in Africa can be viewed as an extension of the movement to abolish colonization: in fighting to remove colonial institutions of control one continues to fight colonialism in Africa.

In light of these social realities, and against the overwhelming opposition that abolitionists face in all areas of society, Scheerer (1986, 7) presented an analysis of the history of abolitionist movements and concluded that "the great victories of abolitionism are slowly passing into oblivion, and with them goes the experience that there has never been a major social transformation in the history of mankind that had not been looked upon as unrealistic, idiotic, or utopian by the large majority of experts even a few years before the unthinkable became a reality." The standard criticism that can be heard all through the history of abolitionism relates to abolitionist goals comprising merely a moral position of little theoretical value and material foundation, much less policy impact.

A discussion on the abolition of slavery with the average white American in the 1700s would have included a diatribe accusing abolitionists of being unrealistic, idealistic, and crazy. "The same is being said today in view of penal abolitionist activists and academics. It is a standard reply to theoretical works of abolitionists such as Nils Christie, Louk Hulsman, Thomas Mathiesen, and Heinz Steinart" (Scheerer 1986, 8), and it is a standard and well-rehearsed reply to any activist or community organizer who engages in discussion with mainstream society about penal abolitionism. "But there is a blind spot in this criticism, as it fails to give an explanation for the sudden popularity of abolitionist positions in some European countries. Abolitionist books find a receptive audience; the basic ideas of abolishing prisons and/or even the criminal justice system, utterly utopian as they seem to the majority, seem to be quite stimulating to a sizeable minority not only in the university class rooms" (8).

A PENAL ABOLITIONIST'S DEFINITION OF CRIME

This section provides a presentation and assessment of contemporary penal abolitionist discussions and discourses on crime. According to De Haan (1996, 355), "the term 'abolitionism' stands for a social movement, a theoretical perspective and a political strategy." In this assessment of abolitionism I will put aside the penal abolitionist political strategies and social movements to allow for an in-depth presentation of the penal abolitionist theoretical perspective.

Emerging from the critical paradigm, penal abolitionists embrace a constructionist view of "crime":[3] "Abolitionists regard crime primarily as a result of the social order and are convinced that punishment is not the appropriate reaction" (De Haan 1996, 355). That social order is defined within the context of power and conflict. It is assumed within the abolitionist perspective that conflict is related to power: both interpersonal conflicts that result in harm and structurally imposed conflicts that result in crime.

The study of crime from a penal abolitionist perspective does not necessarily address violence or deviance or delinquency. According to abolitionist discourse, these issues are important, need to be addressed, and do get addressed by abolitionists (peacemaking criminologists, transformative justice theorists, restorative justice theorists, and others), but the importance of these issues does not automatically qualify them all as criminal. Crime does not and cannot represent social and interpersonal harms, because crime is a construction of the state's reality. Crime is defined by state laws and relies heavily on the implementation of those laws: an understanding and assessment of state behaviour leads to an understanding and assessment of crime. To properly represent and illustrate the penal abolitionist theoretical model of crime, we must first address the terms being used, and the need to differentiate between crime and violence.

Abolitionists are firm in the conviction that violent acts are not necessarily criminal acts (consider acts of violence in self-defence, victimless crimes, state executions), but the fact that they are not criminal does not preclude them from being violent. Thus, violence and harm do not define crime. Pepinsky and Jesilow (1992, 28) confirm this view by explaining that "crime is not purely and simply harmful behavior. To begin with, the law is rather arbitrary about what kinds of harm are regarded as crime. It can be considered criminal to refuse to kill, as conscientious objectors have discovered during wartime. It can legally be tolerated to kill, in self-defense or in defense of property." As a result of these observations, and in line with this logic, abolitionists conclude that crime is defined through the process of criminalization, and that this process is not immersed in morality or safety. It is immersed in the maintenance of a racist, classist, and oppressive status quo.

Chambliss (1996, 227) states that "there is little evidence to support the view that the criminal law is a body of rules which reflect strongly held moral dictates of the society. Occasionally we find a study on the creation of criminal law which traces legal innovations to the 'moral indignation' of a particular social class." Pepinsky and Jesilow (1992, 28) further explain that "common sense and compassion are often missing in the law's definition of what is permissible"; thus, one begins to question and assess the role of criminalization. If it is not found in the professed role of social safety or in the implementation of a non-existing moral consensus, abolitionists conclude, it is found in the unprofessed goal of state-imposed social and economic controls.

Criminalization is found in the attempts to institutionalize and exploit powerless populations for the progression of capitalist economic structures. Abolitionists also conclude that the *true* nature of crime does not lie in prediction and risk assessment of future criminals. Abolitionists assert that the predictive process is fruitless because it has been shown time and time again that future criminals are those whom the future will oppress. Whether that oppression comes by means of the classism, racism, sexism, ageism, or any other "ism" of the social structure is not focal: what is focal and necessary in understanding the true nature of crime, according to abolitionists, is a proper understanding of criminalization.

Abolitionists hold the view that violence is much more complex and much more widespread than the simple and mythical concept of "crime" can define or address. Thus, violence cannot be appropriately defined or dealt with from within the confines of the penal frameworks and/or institutions. In other words, violence cannot be defined or represented within the poorly constructed concept of crime. Violence is better defined and more appropriately represented from within the experiences of those involved with and affected by violence. Based on this line of reasoning, *crime* represents the state's functional conceptualization of harm and thus is best understood within the confines of these conceptualizations. These confines lie within the state's interests, and the socioeconomic and racist structures that the state imposes to advance those interests. "One advantage of this definition is its affirmation that criminality is not an intrinsic quality or an inherent character of the behavior; it is a label that is attached to the behavior. It also emphasizes the roles of authority and coercion in defining certain acts as criminal" (Fattah 1997, 35).

In presenting the penal abolitionist definition of crime it is not representative to state that crime does not encompass a violent element, but it is representative to say that the violent or harmful elements in crime are not the defining components in categorizing certain acts as criminal. Instead, the unequal distribution of power in society is the key element in defining crime (as illustrated by Reiman 1990, 80–85).

Within this view of crime the abolitionist perspective, as the conscientious objector in criminological literature, puts "into question the validity of the guilt-and-punishment frame of reference as well as hitherto well-accepted beliefs about the relevance of terms like crime, dangerousness, and many others. In this respect... abolitionism much resembles the labeling perspective, which in its refusal to accept the traditional biases of criminology did much to reveal the inadequacy of usual questions and answers" (Scheerer 1986, 10).

The assumptions held by penal abolitionists in relation to the state point "to the basic problem as one of non-useful-ness.... There is no longer any reason to trust that the welfare state will provide work for all. Society is gradually changing from having a shared—common—rationality into one of individual rationality" (Christie 1993, 63). Individual rationality cannot hold a consensus view of social order because with individuality comes diversity, and with diversity comes the inherent potential for conflict. The penal structure denies society the ability to deal with the existence of diversity in its monopoly, both in the administration of justice and in the conceptualization of crime as representative of social conflict: "the essence of state power is not just the particular way it deploys its forces of criminalization and punishment but its initial normalizing power, that is, its radical monopoly to define what is right" (Cohen 1992, 229). This monopoly defines the power of penal systems more so than the actual relevance of penal structures and institutions of control.

Abolitionists recognize that actions deemed criminal function to advance the interests of the state (as illustrated by Pepinsky and Jesilow 1992). The same actions undertaken by an individual and carried out on behalf of that individual's interests, not the interests of the state (or corporate agencies that progress the state's capitalist structures), are criminal. The few exceptions to this differential application of legality in regard to violent behaviour, those few times that corporate or state-affiliated individuals are criminalized for their actions, serve only to legitimize the grander structure by providing a few scapegoats to present an illusion of equality under the law. In doing so the state is able to legitimize its power, and continue the unequal and racist distribution of criminality. In line with Christie's perspective, crime thus functions to provide the raw material that fuels the crime control industry; it is an industry with stocks in power and control, and it fits well within the framework of economic advancement in the social structures of white capitalism.

To summarize the penal abolitionist theoretical model of crime: the state uses the law to define acts as criminal, and it is the state, not the individual, that has a direct correlation to crime, for without laws to break there would be no crimes to assess. Within this perspective a study of deviant individual human behaviour cannot be related to the study of crime, because crime does not wholly and unconditionally define human-perpetrated violence, and human-perpetrated violence does not wholly and unconditionally define crime; therefore, in studying crime from a behavioural perspective, the focus of abolitionists is the behaviour of the state, not the behaviour of the individual. In studying violence (as separate from studying crime) abolitionists assess and address human behaviour. It is within that realm that alternative forms of social control and microlevel analyses of harm are utilized. The term "crime" is not functional within this assessment because it is a state-perpetrated act, not an individually perpetrated act. Crime is not necessarily violent. The process of criminalization is.

HOW DOES SOCIETY CREATE CRIME?

In adopting a constructionist view of crime penal abolitionists assume that society creates crime. According to Cohen (1992, 46), before society can create crime it must first be structured in a manner that allows for the existence of certain segments of the population "that are more likely to contribute to the crime rate than others. There is no need to make any sweeping deterministic claims about 'poverty causing crime.'... No amount of sophisticated research and theory can hide the fact that in Western industrial society, the bulk of officially *recorded* crime is committed by those at the bottom of the socioeconomic ladder." In capitalist societies, where money dictates power, it is logical to conclude that the economic variable is present in the determination of power, and thus it is confirmed that those with the least amount of power are those who will become criminalized.

Quinney (2001, 207) further explains this concept, which links societal organization with criminalization: "All behavior may be understood in reference to the organization of society.... Basic to such a perspective are the assumptions that, first, behavior becomes structured in a segmented society and that, second, some segments impose their order on others by formulating and applying criminal definitions." An application of the context of power to this logic affirms that the criminalization process is not about safety but about maintenance of the status quo.

Within the assertion that society produces crime the penal abolitionist perspective does not deny that crime "has something to do with differences in opportunity" and the relative vulnerability of the criminalizable group "to the machinery of social control: arrest, sentencing, punishment" (Cohen 1992, 47). Furthermore, as Cohen notes, society will continue to generate crime by problematizing specific segments of its population, while promoting the very values that generate it: "individualism, masculinity, [and] competitiveness" are highly encouraged traits in contemporary social structures, and are essential for the building of wealth and power, but they are also "the same ones that generate crime" (47).

Last but not least, society creates crime by creating law: "By definition, true of all societies,... we make the rules whose infraction constitutes crime. Crime is simply a behavior that violates the criminal law. It is a category that is not fixed or immutable. By definition a major cause of crime is the law itself" (Cohen 1992, 47). Caulfield (1991, 232-233) suggests that the role of the criminologist in this element of crime production in societies is not neutral. It is not just the legislators who create laws that are involved with the creation of crime, but also the criminologists who promote theories of crime that lack a problematization of the criminalization process. Criminologists aid in defining criminals as an enemy population, and in doing so criminologists serve to divert attention away from what the state is doing, away from the state's harmful behaviours; thus, criminologists serve to legitimize and maintain society's ability to create crime.

THREE TYPES OF ABOLITIONISTS

Within the criminological[4] realm there are three types of abolitionists: the prison abolitionists, the gradual penal abolitionists, and the immediate penal abolitionists. Prison abolitionists focus on the institution of imprisonment. Gradual penal abolitionists assert that legitimate alternatives to penal systems of control and conflict resolution (prisons, courts, police, parole) will result in the eventual delegitimization of the penal system, leading to penal abolition. Absolute abolitionists assert that the immediate and unconditional removal of penal structures is essential in the progression of freedom, and in the fight against racism and classism. These competing and conflicting forms of abolition exist together within the abolitionist movement.

As each type of ideology and opinion works to advance its visions, what at times appears as conflicting represents a continuum of understanding within which people work and conduct research. Morris explains that "being an abolitionist is not a finished state.... Abolitionists can be gradualists, or believe in immediate abolition. Some... began as prison abolitionists and have moved to penal abolition: realizing that bad as prisons are, as long as the goal of the system is revenge, prisons or something equally bad must follow" (1995, 52).

The difference between prison and penal abolitionists lies in ideological frameworks. The former focus on the administrative failures and oppressive elements of the prison as an institution. The latter extend the notion of abolition to include structures that have implemented and allowed the prison to exist for as long as it has. Penal structures and mentalities have kept the prison going, and if it is to be abolished, and the structures are not abolished with it, the rise of newer, more oppressive, and potentially more inhumane institutions will likely occur. This likelihood was evident in the abolition of slavery followed by racialized mass incarceration in the United States. The abolition of the institution of slavery was not sufficient.

Within the capitalist and racist structures of Western societies institutional abolitions do not challenge the grander structures that benefit from oppression and brutality. The shift from prison to penal abolitionism (in the 1980s) gave rise to the opportunity for a more thorough analysis of social structures, the concept of penality, criminalization processes, and the assumptions made about human nature and society within these processes. A focus on institutional abolition (prison abolition) is relevant, but it is not enough. Abolitionist movements in contemporary times must begin to address grander structural issues in order to succeed in abolishing oppression, not just abolishing specific institutions that oppress. In addressing the grander structures of oppression, the abolition of institutions of oppression (such as slavery) cannot result in their replacement by transformed oppressive institutions (such as prisons).

Mathiesen (1974, 212) explains abolition as a process with both short-term and long-term goals: "Not only is it necessary, in order to attain a long-term goal of abolition, that you stubbornly insist on abolition on a short-term basis and in the immediate present; conversely it is just as important, in order to insist on abolitions in the immediate present, that you have a more long-term goal of abolition to work for." According to this perspective, absolutist and gradualist abolitionists play their own roles in the progression of a vision. While gradualist abolitionists tend to focus on the long-term vision, promoting the inclusion of legitimate and separate models of justice and conflict resolution, immediate abolitionists focus on the short-term perspective, and assert that there is no room for alternatives within the present oppressive penal structure. Absolute abolitionists insist that any alternatives erected at this time will only be co-opted because the present social order, the present justice model, has claimed a monopoly on harm. Many of these long- and short-term visions are rooted in a process that defies the mainstream, and promotes underrepresented questions about the distribution of power, the nature of humanity, and the social order within which we (criminals, academics, state bureaucrats, frontline workers, victims of violence) all live.

PENAL ABOLITION: A MINORITY POSITION

Within the realm of critical criminology, and its role as conscientious objector in the discipline of studying crime, the penal abolitionist perspective puts forth questions about crime and penality that are challenging, not only in questioning the status quo, but also in problematizing it. Cohen (1992, 47) states that "the *behavioral* questions, the ones criminologists are obsessed with — 'Why did they do it?' — might be dead-end ones when compared with the *definitional* questions: Why is that rule there? How is it enforced? What are the consequences of this enforcement?" Christie adds that,

> with a perspective on crime as an endless natural resource, we can raise the questions which are rarely made explicit. We can ask: When is enough, enough or, eventually, when is it too little crime? And following that, what is the suitable amount of control through the penal apparatus — eventually, what is the suitable number of officially stigmatized sinners? How large can we let the penal system grow, or conversely, how small can we have it, if we need it at all? Is it possible to establish upper, and eventually lower, limits to the amount of punishment that ought to be applied in modern society? And lastly, for those of us working close to this field, is it possible for us to influence what happens? (2003, 101)

In light of these challenges and proposed questions, the role and contribution of penal abolitionism in the criminological field become clearer. Although it is a perspective that most find obscure or idealistic, or not academic, to mention a few of the reactions that penal abolitionism has elicited, and although it is a perspective that few take the time to study and fewer take the time to research, it is also a perspective that thrives in its marginality and embraces the role of a 'minority position' in academia. It is the diversity in this field that makes it relevant, for if there was a total monopoly on the production of knowledge, mainstream academia would become an *official* branch of the state's social control apparatus. It is in the power games that seem to inherently infuse the politics of diversity that the penal abolitionist perspective, much like disenfranchised populations in society, finds itself.

CRITIQUES OF PENAL ABOLITIONISM

Given its disenfranchised position in the field, penal abolitionism is often held up to criticism and, when referred to at all, referred to within the context of *explain yourself* more than within the context of *who are you and what do you stand for?* It is also a position that is lumped into the crazy radicals stereotype, often perceived as holding a uniform identity, because through a mainstream lens 'minorities' all look the same and do the same things. The power games that oppress exploited populations in society do not oppress the 'minority' populations in academia; they may briefly silence them, but it is during those moments of silence (to mainstream ears, not among the minority) that observation of the mainstream is exercised, and true contemplation of a strategy to implement change is done.

Within this context, I address the issues that arise when a critique of penal abolitionism is presented. Christie explains that "the most radical among them [abolitionists] want to eliminate penal law and formal punishment altogether. But there are several major problems with that position" (2003, 80). He explains that absolute abolitionists, those whom Morris referred to as immediate abolitionists, those who advocate for the eradication of the penal system in its entirety, are in essence taking away the opportunity of retributive justice (revenge) for victims of harm who may want to use it. Absolute abolitionists tend to address this critique through a presentation of victims' needs that outlines the need for revenge as occurring early in the stages of surviving victimization. In most cases those who seek to address the harms they have encountered are encouraged to address violence in non-violent manners.

It is only through the criminal justice system that violence is encouraged and revenge offered as a solution to harm. The answer to this question that some victims may want revenge is different for gradual abolitionists: the value of retaining options is essential. The gradual abolitionist would suggest that other models for achieving justice be implemented as totally separate from the penal structure but just as legitimate. It is hypothesized that, if the general population can come to realize that there are "other less painful and more productive ways" of dealing with harm, they will turn to these options. It is also hypothesized that the penal system, set up alongside other legitimate options for conflict resolution, and thus opening itself up to comparison, would eventually prove itself obsolete.

Absolute abolitionists criticize this assertion, claiming that penal structures work to legitimize penality and co-opt any other legitimate options for conflict resolution—alternatives cannot exist alongside the penal structure. In response gradualist abolitionism asserts that the power of resistance is infinite, and turn to non-Western nations for examples of societies that do not rely heavily on an oppressive penal regime. A study of legal pluralism aids in addressing these questions and working toward solutions to these debates.

Christie also put forth the critique that, "in enthusiasm for mediation, it is important not to forget that rituals and arrangements in penal courts might have important protective functions. When tensions run high, maybe even immediate violence threatens, the solemn and often utterly tedious and dull rituals in the penal apparatus might have a calming effect" (2003, 81). While this argument may hold true within classical and positivist assumptions about the nature of society, it is important to emphasize again the principles of peacemaking and a reaction to conflict that understands that, "if violence is admitted and addressed, it is less likely to be destructive than if it is repressed" (Mindell 1995, 223); thus, the numbing of volatile situations through the implementation of dull and tedious proceedings does not diffuse the flame, but only represses it, creating a greater chance for larger explosions later.

An often misunderstood feature of penal abolitionism relates to the perceived goal of achieving an idealistic society void of violence and harm. Van Swaaningen (1997, 25) explains that "Wichmann and Bonger both rejected the notion of an ideal society or the idea that crime will ever disappear. They concluded that 'truly educational reactions cannot be of a punitive nature, but should indeed offer positive stimuli to the individual's personal development'"; to do this properly, peacemaking principles need to be pursued. According to Kohn (1996, 55, 58), effective discipline has been associated with conformity and obedience, while rewards and punishments have been associated with control, not order. Also, it is the predictability of rules that invokes comfort in knowing what to do — it is the categorization of reactions to conflict that provides safety in rule-setting, not the actual existence or implementation of the rules themselves (70). Utopian expectations lie in the categorical definition of conflict and categorical response to it. Conflict is seldom rational, seldom organized, and seldom predictable; it is the opposite of these principles that makes it conflict, so *a response that is categorical and rule-oriented is utopian*; the promotion of more flexible options to deal with conflict and the realization that we cannot continue to believe that, "if you scare people enough, they will comply" are not.

It is important to note that penal abolitionism is not a rejection of the existence of violence, but a rejection of the counterproductive nature of punishment. In that rejection abolitionists recognize that punishment is more than an administrative principle; it is an ideology. That ideology is elemental in contemporary social structures and their oppressive status quos: those structures that legitimize classism, racism, sexism, heterosexism, and ageism also legitimize the penal mentality, which in turn allows the penal system to exist. The enforcement of penality as a method of social control imposes a *criminal form of justice* that is oppressive, idealistic in its expectations of deterrence, and unrealistic in its expectations of creating safety.

Wichmann emphasized what later came to be Mathiesen's (1974) notion of the "unfinished," a rejection of the notion of completeness. Wichmann stated that "crime has always been and will always remain. Its massive character is, however, not self-evident and can be limited by social measures. The realization of socialism will first of all change the nature of crime, and perhaps also diminish the level of crime as a whole" (van Swaaningen 1997, 58). In this respect Wichmann's analysis and propositions are much like Bonger's and Engel's, rooted in a critique of capitalist structures. In this analysis conflict does not disappear; instead it appears in a manner that avoids demonization, stigmatization, and fear, while promoting the values of taking responsibility and maintaining social balance.

The most verbalized concern about penal abolitionism is the basic: so what do you propose to do instead? Knopp (1991, 181) explains that "the pressure is always excessive for abolitionists to produce a *plan,* a plan that solves every problem and deals with every criminal act before abolition can be considered. But it is not necessary to have a finished blueprint; it is not necessary to know the last step before taking the first step. The first step toward abolition is to break with the old system and help conceptualize the new."

Within the penal abolitionist framework the finished, the determined, and the predictable tenets hold elements of repression and inflexibility; thus, when a plan is called for, abolitionists respond from within the ideology of Mathiesen's unfinished. Pepinsky (1991, 315) presents a response to this concern that explains the logic behind such responses. He explains that "peacemaking means being ever open to surprise and discovery of good and bad, successes and failures.... There are, as Ms. Knopp notes, no final solutions for a peacemaker. To act on a 'solution' is to stop listening and responding to one's impact on others. It is a tip-off that warmaking entrepreneurs typically promise to solve 'all your problems.'"

The lack of an absolute answer does not justify the unnecessary evils of penal repression. In attempts to delegitimize abolitionism the mainstream and the privileged rely on a silencing of the questions, putting forth a demand for a solution. That very demand for a solution, while admitting a problem with penal justice, refocuses the discussion from an understanding of these problems to an answer to the unasked critical questions of penality.

As Mathiesen (1974, 13) points out, "abolition is a point of departure." Abolitionism is not absolutism. Absolutism is a tenet of the positivist, classical, and mainstream criminological disciplines. Absolutism promotes a dichotomized, right-and-wrong assessment of social reality and social problems. In the critical and radical criminological paradigms these tenets are not prioritized; thus, according to abolitionism, "there is no reason to expect any terminated condition of final abolition; for example, no country can count on attaining a terminated condition of final revolution; a retrospective consolidation of abolition which has been attained — for example a revolution in a country — is the same as finishing the abolition and in large measure returning to the old. The maintenance of abolition implies that there is *constantly more to abolish,* that one looks ahead towards a *new and still more long-term objective of abolition*" (Mathiesen 1974, 211–212).

The most recognized principles among academics who are not abolitionists are those related to the policy implications and suggestions made by abolitionist researchers. The least recognized but most fundamental aspects of the abolitionist perspective lie in a recognition of crime as a legal, not a social, concept, and in the assessment of the power dynamics involved in state politics and oppressive social structures. Based on these *theoretical* foundations, the emergence of a penal abolitionist *administrative* policy occurs. Penal abolitionists do not just call for the abolition of the penal system. The perspective provides a logic, a mode of reasoning, a theoretical model concluding that abolition of penality is imperative in the quest to deal with violence and inequality.

How do penal abolitionists use scientific data to support theoretical foundations and conclusions? Abolitionists hesitate to glorify and follow in the footsteps of Western philosophical traditions. "They are suspicious of the, both legal and sociological, custom not to be satisfied with anything before all particular events have been neatly arranged in mental drawers of classification schemes," and the cause of these suspicions "is the experience that classifications are treated as if they were realities.... Hence if there is such a thing as crime it can only exist as something one can immediately see, i.e. a very specific act" (Scheerer 1986, 11). In relation to notions of empiricism theoretical abolitionists identify well with what Takeyoshi Kawashima once called empirical immediacy. "To the Japanese," as Scheerer notes, "each thing has its own characteristics which differentiate it from other things. So it cannot be seen as falling within a class. The reflexive approach to crime and criminal justice evident in abolitionist thinking might reveal a structure quite similar to this kind of Eastern thinking. Both distrust and abstract general classifications... stress a limited social nexus, thus preventing the rise of universals" (11).

Abolitionists recognize that there is a sense of comfort that comes with predictability and categorization, but they also recognize that the process of generalization, while convenient for the scientific production of knowledge, is not convenient when the quest is to properly represent the society one is attempting to assess. This radically different perspective, which is not popular among or understandable to most Western researchers, results in a criticism of the abolitionist perspective by "numerous scholars who find it rather strange to their own way of perceiving things" (Scheerer 1986, 11). Aside from a conceptual gap between penal abolitionist and classical/positivist methodological boundaries, a functional gap also exists. The functional gap is illustrated through a presentation of Mathiesen's action research proposal.

Mathiesen explains that, "since all research involves influencing of the system which is being investigated, and since all information which is disclosed constitutes a 'response' to such influence, all research may be said to be 'action research'" (1974, 29). The influences that he is referring to are not limited to crime policy: they may result in that (ideally), but in addition research on crime impacts and influences the social construction of crime as a category, and sometimes impacts public attitudes toward the criminalized population. These realizations about the functions of research extend well beyond discussions among academics and enter the realm of social existence. The transition from traditional research to action research provides the researcher with the opportunity to engage in resistance. As Mathiesen points out, "the bases for resistance... are among the many which contribute to the maintenance of a relationship between research and politics through which both activities are exposed to internal binding, internal strangulation. The conscious breaking down of the boundary between them may possibly create the foundation for research and politics being more of a liberated field for all the people; research being liberated by politics, and politics by research. At least, this may be an ideal goal" (36). It is this direct and implied abolitionist link between theory, research, and politics that causes many scholars to dismiss the academic nature of the abolitionist perspective. But within the rejection of the ability to achieve objectivity in research the link is legitimate and necessary from a radical criminological approach.

While the majority of the literature on abolitionism focuses on destructuring the present oppressive social order, there is also a focus on the dehumanization of individuals in both the academic- and the state-oriented categorizations and assessments of the 'criminal' or at-risk-of-becoming-criminal populations. The scientific process, as implemented through positivism and mainstream criminology, aims to advance knowledge with little consideration of the dehumanized elements it brings upon the subjects of their research. This may not be done consciously, but is implemented through a miscalculation of the amount of power that academia possesses in its role as a producer of knowledge.

While the policy implications for criminal justice administrative sanctions are not always clear, it is important to realize that the academic criminological culture has claimed expertise in crime, and with that expertise comes responsibility. According to penal abolitionism, that responsibility is not primarily to science but to society. Science is regarded as a tool to be used in the progression of knowledge and ultimately in the progression of quality of life. When science is used to legitimize oppression through an unquestioned acceptance and justification of the criminalization process, especially within the contemporary context of the criminalized population's demographics (race, age, and class seem to be the most crucial determinants of inclusion in the criminal population), the typical abolitionist cannot help but cringe.

Scientific studies that undertake analysis of the criminal population, but do not incorporate the context of power and social order, or do not incorporate a critical assessment of the criminalization process, are, in the view of abolitionists, participating in the legitimization of oppression through a scientification of the dehumanization of the powerless. Objectivity in research, according to abolitionism, is rejected as not only unrealistic but also unnecessary. In addition, the professionalization of justice is problematic because it disempowers the people directly involved in conflict and sends the message that people cannot properly define or deal with their own problems. Likewise, the professionalization of knowledge is problematic because it loses touch with the people who are being used to produce this knowledge. Following these assumptions, abolitionists undertake research in a manner very different from traditional positivist and classical criminological paradigms.

Abolitionist Use of Quantitative Data
In rejecting the notion of objectivity abolitionists recognize that official crime statistics used in positivist and (neo)classical

research studies can tell a very different story when viewed through an abolitionist lens. Through this lens official statistics represent the behaviour of the state, not the behaviour of individuals. The number of arrests made each year, the number of people in prison, and the number of cases a court processes do not represent social behaviour: they are records of the state's behaviour, and are relied on as clear, accurate descriptions of what the state did, whom it criminalized, and how it dealt with them. Chambliss and Nagasawa's concluding remarks in a 1969 study affirm penal abolitionist views of the roles and functions of official crime data: "The findings of this study... lend support to the argument that official statistics may tell us a good deal about the activities of agencies responsible for generating statistics, but they tell us very little about the distribution of criminal or delinquent activities in the population" (77).

Self-reported data, according to abolitionism, are not necessarily different from officially reported data in their implications and validity, because self-reported data rely heavily on state definitions of harm—if anything, self-reported data illustrate how much crime the state did or did not detect, and serve as a measure of effectiveness for the state's penal institutions: how much crime the state detected compared with how much crime the general population participated in.

Christie provides a good example of how quantitative data are used within the penal abolitionist perspective. He explains that the United States currently has 2.1 million prisoners, 730 prisoners per 100,000 inhabitants. "The increase [in the prison population] has been unbelievable since 1975. The growth has slowed down recently, but has not come to a complete stop" (2003, 53). He adds that, with 4.7 million people on bail, probation, and parole, "6.8 million of the US population in 2003 is under some sort of control of the institution of penal law" (53).

In this context the use of official statistics has little to do with measuring or representing violence in society, and has a lot to do with measuring the amount of control a state exercises over people through its use of criminal justice. Christie (1993) points out that 2.4 percent of the entire US population, and 3.1 percent of the population over the age of fifteen, are under some form of control by the penal system. He also provides cross-national statistics that illustrate the disproportionately high number of people in prison in the United States compared with other countries on a per-capita population basis. His conclusion is not that citizens of the United States are more violent but that the US government participates in imprisoning its citizens more than other nation-states. This shift in focus is instrumental in the abolitionist framework. Instead of relying on government statistics to assess the behaviours of the people, abolitionists more appropriately use government statistics to assess the behaviours of the government.

Abolitionist Use of Qualitative Data

Because crime is a socially constructed notion, and because society's behaviour cannot be assessed through a study of state-gathered evidence, quantitative data sets produced by the state represent state behaviour; while official data are used to reveal the flaws of the state (racism, classism, and so on), ethnography is used to put forth a firsthand presentation of experiences with violence, harm, and/or criminalization. A widely used quantitative tool in the penal abolitionist perspective is the use of writing by prisoners when attempting to discuss or assess the processes of criminalization and, more specifically, portray the experience of imprisonment. The *Journal of Prisoners on Prisons* gathers articles written by prisoners from all over the world, and publishes them for use in university classrooms, distribution to imprisoned peoples all over the world and sale in bookstores. It is an underlying philosophy in the abolitionist methodological realm that, to portray criminal experiences, it is best to hear about them from the sources.

Ethnographies in the penal abolitionist perspective are best presented as biographies or autobiographies. Davies explains that "it is important to recognize the existence of a philosophy of incarceration which is specifically located in the experience of having been in prison" (1990, 21). He further divulges that in his presentation of prison writings "my interest is not with how we rationalize having prisons, nor how prisons fit into a general conception of social order, but how, being prisoners, we come to terms with our own incarceration" (21). He contextualizes his intentions by stating that, "if we are to be more than reflectively impotent... the writings must be placed within our own communities, with a connectedness that is able to deal with social structures not simply as alien impositions, but as human creations that must be remade, transformed. And to do that we have to rethink our entire sense of human relationships" (240). In his assessment he is referring specifically to the role of prison writing; I extend this philosophy beyond prisoners' work and into how qualitative data are used in the penal abolitionist realm. The intention is to capture the experiences of criminalization, victimization, and marginalization, as opposed to using these experiences to explain any specific theory of crime.

Maintaining the penal abolitionists' emphasis on firsthand experience as the most reliable voice, Ruth Morris's (2000) book *Stories of Transformative Justice* is an example of an abolitionist work that captures stories and experiences in a manner that is personal. Morris presents firsthand accounts of her experiences with transformative justice, and combines these experiences with records of actions taken and successes achieved on the road to abolition. She presents stories of transformative justice as told by the people who experienced them, and she places herself within this ethnography, including her experiences with transformative justice alongside the experiences of those whom she interviewed. This method of placing the researcher within the research not only deprofessionalizes the role of the researcher, but also humanizes the people interviewed. It also equalizes the power balance between researcher and researched, and relates well with Mathiesen's conceptualization of action research.

The role and function of ethnographic research in penal abolitionist methodological works is well articulated in Gaucher's (2002) analysis of the task of the *Journal of Prisoners on Prisons*. Gaucher states that "the analysis and commentary of prisoners in this anthology represent a counter-inscription to these developments [expansion in prison populations and the crime control industry] and the arguments that legitimize them. Located firmly within the long-established tradition of prison literature... , they collectively represent the prisoner-intellectual's responses to the current conjecture, *as informed by the experience of criminalization and incarceration* in the 1990s" (5; emphasis added). It is in this philosophy that the humanization of the *criminalized* population as pursued in penal abolitionist methodological works is presented, in the hope of contradicting the dehumanization of 'the criminal population' enforced through positivist and (neo)classical assumptions of objectivity and deluded conceptions of the researcher as apolitical.

CONTRADICTIONS IN PARADIGMATIC METHODOLOGIES

Mathiesen's assessment of the role of research in abolitionism incorporates a bottom-up, unfinished perspective, as opposed to a top-down, completed framework. Mathiesen states that "it is assumed that the refined theory will, through new hypotheses, lead to a new and refined disclosure of information, in a feedback process with theory. In this way, research is in principle an *unfinished* process.... It is this character of being in principle unfinished that may give vitality to research. In this respect, research perhaps resembles art, and is not unlike a series of other activities in society—in the world of labor and leisure—which are not in principle finished" (1974, 29).

Within this paradigm's theoretical models "theory and practice should always be reciprocal, and the incentive for innovation is formed by social movements" (van Swaaningen 1997, 54). In essence the penal abolitionist perspective emerged out of dissatisfaction with the penal system. It incorporated (and continues to incorporate) a mode of knowledge production that is in direct contradiction with the very structures it opposes: individual determinism, generalization of individual experiences, and the inherent dehumanization processes involved with such structures.

It has been shown how the acceptance of an unfinished philosophy in abolitionism is incorporated into the methodological tools used within the perspective. It is through the presentation of personal experience within a framework that highlights the scale to which penal repression can rise (as illustrated in Christie's assessment of quantitative crime data) that the penal abolitionist methodologies function. It is with the *expressed* goal of humanization and empowerment that this perspective carries out research.

THE PRODUCTION OF KNOWLEDGE: ACHIEVING CONCLUSIONS

In this chapter I have presented a definition of the penal abolitionist perspective as a theory of the nature of crime, embracing a social constructionist definition of crime and encompassing a peacemaking definition of the view of human nature. I have illustrated through the form of analysis chosen here that contextualization of knowledge is as relevant to the production of knowledge as is the contextualization of socially constructed categories to the production of crime. My presentation of knowledge production in the penal abolitionist perspective illustrates how penal abolitionism uses data to support both its theoretical conclusion and its ideological framework. Penal abolitionism encompasses a destructuring impulse. I have illustrated how a starting point for destructuring the concept of crime may well be within the structuralized nature of knowledge.

Cohen (1992, 89) states that one may wonder why the study of crime, "a subject so obviously grounded in the real world," should put effort into

> mapping out the histories and present contexts in which knowledge is produced rather than in getting along with the

real business. The answer is paradoxical: some measure of self-consciousness about how knowledge is produced and diffused is needed to assess what proportion of this knowledge speaks only to itself. This is true even for the natural world; as Sir Arthur Eddington, an astronomer, once told his colleagues, "we have found a strange footprint on the shores of the unknown. We have devised profound theories, one after another, to account for its origins. At last, we have succeeded in reconstructing the creation that made the footprint. And lo! It is our own."

Penal abolitionism assumes that, a realization that the footprint is "our own," the notion of crime as a social construction will be emphasized in the academic field of criminal justice. Only then will the conceptualization of crime shift from understanding it as a phenomenon of human behaviour to understanding it as a process of criminalization imposed by the state.

For that to happen the grander social structures need radical revamping, and in some cases abolition, as is the case for penal structures. Abolition in this structural sense extends beyond the institutions of penal control and into the mental structures that allow these institutions to exist. These mental structures are currently grounded in a categorical, deterministic, and completed framework that is both oppressive and counterproductive. Unfortunately the academic structures associated with the study of crime are themselves dichotomized. A move away from paradigmatic divisions would be ideal, even though their present positions are contradictory and volatile, presenting an atmosphere for the study of crime that is at least structurally representative of the contradictory and volatile nature of the subject at hand. Kuhn presents an assessment of the paradigmatic trap that is relevant to these observations:

> Without commitment to a paradigm there could be no normal science. Furthermore, that commitment must extend to areas and to degrees of precision for which there is no full precedent. If it did not, the paradigm could provide no puzzles that had not

already been solved. Besides, it is not only normal science that depends upon commitment to a paradigm. If existing theory binds the scientist only with respect to existing applications, then there can be no surprises, anomalies or crises. But these are just the signposts that point the way to extraordinary science. If positivistic restrictions on the range of a theory's legitimate applicability are taken literally, the mechanism that tells the scientific community what problems may lead to fundamental change must cease to function. And when that occurs, the community will inevitably return to something much like its pre-paradigm state, a condition in which all members practice science but in which their gross product scarcely resembles science at all. Is it really any wonder that the price of significant scientific advance is a commitment that runs the risk of being wrong? (1996, 100–101)

Fortunately (or unfortunately), in the social sciences, the risk of being wrong is minimized. The subject that we study, the *complete* nature of crime, is so complex, so ambiguous, and so susceptible to myriad influences and explanations that the possibilities are endless yet relevant. The key to grasping these possibilities lies in the ability to assess theories of crime according to their contextualized paradigmatic cultural affiliations, and the relevant conflicting basic assumptions held in relation to humanity and society. The key to advancing knowledge on crime lies not in proving or disproving theory, but in *abolishing* the perceived ability to unify the nature of crime.

NOTES

1 In presenting Wichmann's ideology I rely on van Swaaningen's translation of her works.
2 Much of Wichmann's work was heavily influenced by Marx's notions of revolution, both in the social realm and in the scientific realm, as well as his view of socialism (Marx 1956, 25).
3 "Crime" is presented in many abolitionist texts with quotation marks to emphasize its constructed nature.

4   The term is meant to encompass both criminology and criminal justice disciplines.

REFERENCES

Acoli, Sundita. (1995). "A Brief History of the New Afrikan Prison Struggle." In *The Black Prison Movements USA: Free Our Political Prisoners,* ed. Muntu Matsimela et al. Trenton, NJ: African World Press, 4–26.

Bonger, W. A. (1967). *Criminality and Economic Conditions.* New York: Agathon Press.

Browne, Julie. (1996). "The Labor of Doing Time." In *Criminal Injustice: Confronting the Prison Crisis,* ed. Elihu Rosenblatt. Boston, MA: South End Press, 61–72.

Caulfield, Susan L. (1991). "The Perpetuation of Violence through Criminological Theory." In *Criminology as Peacemaking,* ed. Harold Pepinsky and Richard Quinney. Bloomington: Indiana University Press, 228–238.

Cayley, David. (1998). *The Expanding Prison: The Crisis in Crime and Punishment and the Search for Alternatives.* Toronto: House of Anansi Press.

Chambliss, William J. (1996). "Toward a Political Economy of Crime." In *Criminological Perspectives,* ed. John Muncie, Eugene McLaughlin, and Mary Langan. London: Sage Publications, 224–231.

Chambliss, William, and Richard D. Nagasawa. (1969). "On the Validity of Official Statistics: A Comparison of White, Black, and Japanese High School Boys." *Crime and Delinquency, 6,* 71–77.

Christie, Nils. (1993). *Crime Control as Industry: Towards Gulags Western Style.* 2nd and enlarged ed. London: Routledge.

---. (2003). *A Suitable Amount of Crime.* London: Routledge.

Cohen, Stanley. (1992). *Against Criminology.* Piscataway, NJ: Transaction Publishers.

Davies, Ioan. (1990). *Writers in Prison.* Toronto: Between the Lines.

De Haan, Willem. (1996). "Abolitionism and Crime Control." In *Criminological Perspectives,* ed. John Muncie, Eugene McLaughlin, and Mary Langan. London: Sage Publications, 355–366.

Fattah, Ezzat. (1997). *Criminology: Past, Present, and Future: A Critical Overview.* New York: St. Martin's Press.

Foucault, Michel. (1972). *Power/Knowledge.* New York: Pantheon Books.

Gaucher, Bob. (2002). *Writing as Resistance: The* Journal of Prisoners on Prisons *Anthology (1988–2002).* Toronto: Canadian Scholars Press.

Hess, H. (1986). "Kriminalität als Alltagsmythos: Ein Plädoyer dafür, Kriminologie als Ideologiekritik zu betreiben." *Kriminologisches Journal, 18:1,* 22-44.

Hulsman, Louk. (1986). "Critical Criminology and the Concept of Crime." In *Abolitionism: Towards a Non-Repressive Approach to Crime,* ed. Herman Bianchi and René van Swaaningen. Amsterdam: Free University Press, 25–41.

"John." (1997). "They Count Us like Diamonds and Treat Us like Shit." In *Life 25: Interviews with Prisoners Serving Life Sentences,* ed. P. J. Murphy and Lloyd Johnson. Vancouver: New Star Books, 29–44.

Knopp, Fay Honey. (1991). "Community Solutions to Sexual Violence: Feminist/Abolitionist Perspective." In *Criminology as Peacemaking,* ed. Harold Pepinsky and Richard Quinney. Bloomington: Indiana University Press, 181–193.

Kohn, Alfie. (1996). *Beyond Discipline: From Compliance to Community.* Alexandria, VA: ASCD Publications.

Kuhn, T. (1996) [1962]. *The Structure of Scientific Revolutions.* 3rd ed. Chicago: University of Chicago Press.

Lynch, Michael J., and Byron W. Groves. (1989). *A Primer in Radical Criminology.* 2nd ed. Albany, NY: Harrow and Heston Publishers.

Marx, Karl. (1956). *Selected Writings in Sociology and Social Philosophy.* New York: McGraw-Hill Book Company.

Mathiesen, Thomas. (1974). *The Politics of Abolition.* Oslo: Scandinavian University Books.

Mindell, Arnold. (1995). *Sitting in the Fire: Large Group Transformation Using Conflict and Diversity.* Portland, OR: Lao Tse Press.

Morris, Ruth. (1995). *Penal Abolition: The Practical Choice.* Toronto: Canadian Scholars Press.

---. (2000). *Stories of Transformative Justice.* Toronto: Canadian Scholars Press.

Pepinsky, Harold E. (1991). "Peacemaking in Criminology and Criminal Justice." In *Criminology as Peacemaking,* ed. Harold Pepinsky and Richard Quinney. Bloomington: Indiana University Press, 229–327.

Pepinsky, Harold E., and Paul Jesilow. (1992). *Myths that Cause Crime.* Santa Ana, CA: Seven Locks Press.

Quinney, Richard. (1991). "The Way of Peace: On Crime, Suffering, and Service." In *Criminology as Peacemaking,* ed. Harold Pepinsky and Richard Quinney. Bloomington: Indiana University Press, 3–13.

---. (2001). *The Social Reality of Crime.* Piscataway, NJ: Transaction Publishers.

Reiman, Jeffery. (1990). *The Rich Get Richer and the Poor Get Prison.* 3rd ed. New York: Macmillan Publishing Company.

Scheerer, Sebastian. (1986). "Towards Abolitionism." *Contemporary Crises, 10*, 5–20.

Steinert H. (1986). "Beyond Crime and Punishment." *Contemporary Crises, 10*, 21-38.

van Swaaningen, René. (1997). *Critical Criminology: Visions from Europe.* London: Sage Publications.

Welch, Michael. (1995). "A Sociopolitical Approach to the Reproduction of Violence in Canadian Prisons." In *Violence in Canada: Sociopolitical Perspectives,* ed. Jeffery Ian Ross. Oxford: Oxford University Press, 252–285.

CHAPTER 22

THE TENTH INTERNATIONAL CONFERENCE ON PENAL ABOLITION (ICOPA X)

Viviane Saleh-Hanna

INTRODUCTION

This book has presented the ideological and practical problems of criminal justice in Nigeria. Colonial impositions prevail in Africa, and will continue to do so as long as British colonial criminal justice systems continue to exist there. Having outlined the problems associated with the penal system in Nigeria, and having illustrated the structural and ideological issues that exist along with the penal system in general, I find it necessary to provide an ideological and activist context within which such issues can be addressed. This is best accomplished through penal abolitionism, *penal* being a representation of all institutions legally yet violently used to convict and imprison oppressed people all around the globe (prisons, courts, police, probation, parole), and *abolitionism* being a movement that questions the relevance of these institutions and calls for the destructuring of such violent structures, while working to implement methods of conflict resolution that are socially relevant and non-violent.

Following a long line of academic literature, and growing through activist affiliations, this chapter outlines penal abolitionism as it was presented to the Nigerian community in efforts to organize the Tenth International Conference on Penal Abolition in Nigeria. While in the previous chapter I presented the scholarly history of penal abolition, in this chapter I present penal abolitionism in my own words, through my own understanding of the abolitionist movement, highlighting the questions and issues associated with the current penal crises that Nigeria and other nations, all over the "developed" and "developing" world, are facing.

WHAT IS PENAL ABOLITION?

Penal abolition is the name given to the social/political activist movement, theory, and lifestyle that rejects the use of penal sanctions to deal with human conflict. It is a complex phenomenon that not only redefines reality as many know it, but also rejects the assumptions we make about conflict, social safety, and crime control. Using penal punishment as a solution to harm is viewed as oppressive and counterproductive; in addition, penal sanctions are rejected as the only and necessary reaction to crime. Deterrence is recognized as a failed attempt to scare people into not breaking rules, and isolation is recognized as a creator of greater problems—community safety is not promoted through either penal structures or ideologies. Penal abolitionists work to define problems in a manner more relevant to the community and to reach more realistic forms of conflict resolution.

Penal abolitionist ideologies recognize that societies have existed and were able to function without penal sanctions in the past, and thus contemporary society, though mentally and structurally reliant on the penal system, is capable of functioning without such a violent system. The challenge lies in finding a non-penal, anti-violent, non-oppressive structure that is compatible with contemporary social needs. This challenge is far from impossible to meet, and at this point, during times of overcrowded, inhumane, dehumanized penal institutions and policies, it is a necessity.

Penal abolitionists recognize that the penal mindset is ingrained in many factors of everyday existence and functioning, and thus realize that the battle is both concrete (fighting against human rights violations) and abstract (revolutionizing thoughts and challenging assumptions). In working to change the way human beings have been conditioned and socialized to think and react, penal abolitionists believe that an essential starting point is a new awareness of the words we use to communicate with each other.

A PENAL ABOLITIONIST DICTIONARY

Crime

This word is not used in penal abolitionist discourse; it is rejected based on the social stigma it imposes on all those labelled criminal. Instead of focusing on crime penal abolitionists focus on harms; they attempt to empower the community in defining its own problems and thus dealing with them on its own terms. In addition, "crime" is a term that is state-imposed; it is a word that defines thousands of very different acts and somehow implies that all these acts are connected enough to elicit one solution. Abolitionists reject this notion, reinforcing the belief that there is no single solution to the diverse social problems resulting from and elicited through what we today refer to as crime.

Harms

Harms are actions that intentionally cause pain (physical, emotional, sexual, mental, financial or other) for another person. These acts are the primary focus for penal abolitionists who work to deconstruct the notion of crime. All other acts that do not implicitly and directly result in harm should not be defined as criminal; such acts should be decriminalized and dealt with in their appropriate spheres. For example, drug use: a person who chooses to use drugs is free to do so as long as he or she is not harming anyone in the process; if a user develops an addiction needing formal attention, then that person needs medical or social attention (whatever the specific situation defines as necessary), not justice-oriented intervention. It is important to highlight the separation of moral judgements from justice judgements in this redefinition of harm.

Community
The concept of community is all-inclusive and interconnected. One cannot separate the community by building a wall and involuntarily placing people behind it. Prisoners continue to be part of our community, despite their physical separation; they become a feared and very mysterious segment, but still remain a segment of the community. Under this definition the prison can be compared to an ostrich sticking its head in the sand and assuming that its problems will disappear because it can no longer see them. Of course, if the ostrich leaves its head in the sand for too long, it will inevitably suffocate.

Safety
"Safety" is a term that can be defined in two main spheres: individual and social safety. Individual safety involves personal, private issues, while collective individual safeties lead to social safety. A key word associated with safety is *cohesiveness*. Abolitionists emphasize that all members of the human race have a right to a safe, cohesive, and empowered existence. This belief does not justify the imposition of institutional violence (prison, death penalty, corporal punishment) in the name of safety. Safety is the responsibility of the individual, the community, and the overall social structure — it is a responsibility, not a legitimization. It is about social interactions rather than state interventions. In allowing a community to establish agency one empowers that community to be safe. While the criminal justice system promotes security, penal abolitionists identify security as a false sense of safety that does not provide communities with opportunities to coexist. A security perspective relies heavily on the demonization of "other" populations, while a safety perspective relies heavily on the democratization of society in a manner that promotes coexistence and equal access to opportunities and resources.

Violence
Penal abolitionists have a broad view of violence. Violence involves acts of harm and is not limited to individuals.

According to penal abolitionists, violence is much more prevalent than most people like to admit. Violence from a penal abolitionist standpoint is expanded to include actions of the state, corporations, institutions, and social structures (such as capitalism). Penal abolitionists recognize that violence at state, corporate, and institutional levels (war, genocide, embezzlement, imposed poverty) affects far more lives than do individual acts of violence (armed robbery, homicide, assault). Abolitionists also recognize that the same organizations that harm the community at the highest levels of human cost are defining individual-level harms as the most problematic. This redirection of fear and focus allows state and economic institutions to maintain a status quo that redirects attention away from their own acts of violence. When violence perpetrated and funded by the state through its institutions (death penalty, war, corporate violence) is brought forth it is often presented to the public as a necessary evil. Penal abolitionists recognize that all harms and evils are unnecessary at all levels—no justifications (with the exception of self-defence in extreme circumstances) are accepted for the imposition of violence.

Responsibility

This is a very important concept for penal abolitionists. The abolitionist notion of responsibility expects that all persons who partake in violent, harmful behaviours should accept direct responsibility for their actions in non-violent, non-harmful ways. The penal system as it exists today does not allow people who have committed wrongs to take responsibility for them. Instead the penal system claims ownership of their actions and takes responsibility for their lives. Penal abolitionists are vehement in their pursuit of social justice and believe that it begins with the proper recognition of all harms, followed by properly represented, relevant, necessary actions, as defined by the voiced needs of all affected victims, offenders, and other community members.

Victim

This term is not meant to disempower people or relegate them to a helpless position, but it is important in the recognition of harms imposed and violations experienced. Like "crime," the term "victim" encompasses too many experiences, and thus its use loses the true essence of a harm suffered. Abolitionists rely more on the term "survivor" because of the negative connotations the penal mindset has imposed on the term "victim." "Survivor" implies progress and gives the person credit for overcoming to whatever degree the violation(s). Much as the penal system has stigmatized criminals, that stigmatization has been extended to disempower victims. In resistance to such implications abolitionists seek to use different terms that may elicit an awareness of the diversity available for defining, dealing with, and addressing harm and conflict.

Offender

An offender is a person who directly or indirectly, through action or inaction, has harmed another person. Penal abolitionists believe that those who have hurt others need to take full responsibility and can only do so if they come to understand the consequences of their behaviours for those they have hurt. In the pursuit of social justice penal abolitionists focus on restitution, reconciliation, and social coexistence. It is important to stress that all of those things do not necessarily imply forgiveness — such expectations are not imposed upon survivors of harm. At the same time abolitionists stress that, once a harm has occurred, the person harmed as well as the person who has harmed are now connected at least through that event (if not through many more events that led up to the harm); thus, in addressing the harm imposed and endured, a proper recognition of that act and its context must be achieved. Thereafter direct action toward resolving/reimbursing/restituting the harm may be pursued. When the harm is irreversible (murder, rape) penal abolitionists focus on the needs of those who have survived the harm. Such needs can only be identified by those directly involved and should not be assumed identifiable by the state or its criminal justice apparatuses. In recognition of individuality and diversity among people's needs and reactions to harm, penal abolitionists take a situation-by-situation approach, and thus call for the creation of a response system that is flexible and empowering enough to allow the humans within it to achieve justice.

Social Stability

Social stability is the ultimate goal. Abolitionists assume that human nature thrives with a sense of acceptance, a sense of belonging and self-worth, and the opportunity to be comfortable and safe. Most human actions (positive, negative, violent, non-violent) are the results of attempts to achieve those goals based on personal and social perceptions of happiness (by acquiring power, money, status, trophies, education, family, possessions and so on). Realizing and accepting that all humans have *needs* may lead to a greater, more positive understanding of the nature of human behaviour and eventually may lead to communities that *can* coexist. In assuming that all people have needs the common ground of a society is based on the building of a structure that functions to provide for the needs of all its citizens. The present social and cultural assumptions do not rely on a need-based understanding of human behaviour. The present social order assumes that human nature is hedonistic, or selfish, or determined by negative influences surrounding us. Such negative assumptions, while accepted by most to describe "others," we do not hold to be true about ourselves. If more people begin to understand that "others" are not that different from "us," then the fractured state of contemporary society might begin to heal. The anger, hatred and fears that communities of privilege hold toward those who are oppressed may begin to dissolve, and the call for state-sanctioned revenge in addressing conflicts and inequalities may begin to be revealed as unreasonable and violent.

IDEOLOGIES OF PENAL ABOLITIONISM

What Penal Abolition Is Not

Penal abolition is often perceived as an easy way out for 'criminals'. It is not. If anything, penal abolitionists demand that people who have hurt other people need to take proper responsibility for their actions. In facing the realities of their actions (and not in disappearing behind prison walls), and in understanding what they have done, offenders need to actively participate in transforming, restituting, or resolving each specific situation. At the same time abolitionists are not revenge-oriented and do not advocate harming those who have harmed others in order to teach them not to harm.

Penal abolitionism is not a movement to solve the problems of the world by coming up with an easy solution. Problems cannot be solved without collaboration, and all those involved in the problem should be included in the solution. The present penal system works in an exclusive, not an inclusive, framework. Often people say, "Abolition sounds like a good idea, we know the penal system is not helping society deal with violence, but what do you propose to do in its place?" The abolitionist response to this expectation is "Work with me, and we will figure it out together." There are no easy solutions, and there is no one answer, structure, or alternative that can replace the penal structure. To ask for one solution is to ask for a structure that is just as counterproductive and inhumane as the penal system is now.

Penal abolition is not an impossible dream—to believe something is impossible is to render it impossible. Penal abolition is relevant not only in small communities, but also in large cities. People often argue that in a small town or village it is easier to create and maintain the type of community that can work without penal sanctions, but in a large city the environment is too impersonal, too disconnected, and too big to really have any sense of true community. Penal abolitionists recognize that with more people the challenge of establishing community spirit is bigger, but they also recognize that with more people around there are more resources for support and network-building. It is about celebrating diversity and personalizing human interactions. It is about breaking down capitalist barriers and fighting the depersonalized state of many large cities. In a way abolitionists view community as a non-concrete phenomenon that can exist anywhere people really want it to exist. Geography does not limit community. Communities are made up of people who share similar interests, goals, ideals, and visions. With this concept of community penal abolitionism can thrive in all settings.

Penal abolition is not about the removal of all social controls, but about the implantation of a social system that is not violent or based on fear. It is about unity, equality, and coexistence. Penal abolitionism is about destructuring oppressive penal regimes/structures, and creating a cohesive, safe society that accepts *all*, belongs to *all*, and functions to serve *all*.

Abolition versus Reform

Only reforms that work toward abolition are considered productive within the penal abolitionist movement. It has been a trend in penal reform that all attempts to humanize the penal system have been co-opted into its inhumane structure, and only work to strengthen its existence and expand its power. Thus only reforms that exist outside the realm of the penal structure are pursued by penal abolitionists. They work to advance the vision of an empowered, enlightened community, and only when sections of power are handed over is a reform truly an alternative, and not a simple add-on to the already too powerful, revenge-oriented penal system.

Restoration versus Transformation

Penal abolitionists do not generally support notions of restoration, mainly because to restore is not necessarily to change. If harm occurs and the community works to restore the survivors to the state they were in before the harm occurred, and they succeed in this restoration, then all they have really done is restored them to a situation that allowed the harm to happen in the first place. Transformation looks at why the harm occurred and deals with the poisons that allowed it to grow into harm (social alienation, capitalist greed, poverty, racism, classism, sexism, heterosexism, ageism, and so on). In addition, penal abolitionists do not always believe that restoration is realistic. When a harm occurs the survivor of that harm will never again be the person s(he) was before the harm occurred. Penal abolitionists look at the processes of transformation that are necessary in dealing with the harm, and work to integrate its consequences into the person's life in a way that is tolerable, livable, and, if possible, positive and productive.

Prison versus Penal Abolition
Penal abolitionists recognize that abolishing the prison is not necessarily sufficient in abolishing penal oppression. The real problem is the penal mindset that allows the prison to exist: abolishing the prison without abolishing this mentality and structure would only open society up to the possibility of different yet still brutal penal oppressions. Because the prison is so concrete and so open about its oppressive elements, it is an easy target. The goal is to understand how the prison and other penal institutions (police, courts, probation, parole) are legitimized: the prison is the end result of what really needs to be questioned, revealed, and abolished.

It is primarily a revolution of the mind taking place in the current consciousness of the people. This revolution must occur if productive structural changes are to be properly implemented. Penal abolitionists do recognize that the society we live in today has created a situation in which people, and the socioeconomic and political power structures they live within, are constantly hurting and violating each other. Change needs to start within the mind, the soul, and the essence of each human being before it can take any real shape on a larger structural level. Without a revolution of the mind any and all penal reforms will continue to be co-opted by a legitimate and legal yet violent penal system.

Penal abolitionism does recognize a dire need for structural reforms: too many people languish within the claws of a violent penal system, and too many people suffer from violence in the community. Penal abolition is about the creation of real alternatives to revenge, institutionalized violence, and penal powers. The community needs to be empowered to create and choose its own versions of justice, and only then will the reliance on criminal justice be truly recognized for its brutal, counterproductive, dehumanizing elements.

THE INTERNATIONAL CONFERENCE ON PENAL ABOLITION

The International Conference on Penal Abolition (ICOPA) represents one of the most visible elements of the penal abolitionist movement. Initially ICOPA was the International Conference on Prison Abolition. In 1987 ICOPA in Montreal resolved to change the name to the International Conference on Penal Abolition, incorporating an understanding that the abolition of prison does not deal with the penal system's revenge-oriented, violent structures. To abolish the prison is not to address the problematic nature of the penal system's framework of *criminal* justice. The ICOPA movement has travelled the world, starting in Montreal in 1983 and returning several times to Canada over the years. ICOPA was also held in the Netherlands, Poland, the United States, Spain, Costa Rica, and New Zealand before finding its way to West Africa. In presenting how ICOPA X was organized in Nigeria an example of the methods used by abolitionists to work toward achieving penal abolition can be analyzed.

ICOPA X Struggles and Triumphs

The Tenth International Conference on Penal Abolition (ICOPA X) was held in Nigeria, breaking new ground as the first ICOPA to be hosted by an African nation. The decision to host ICOPA in Nigeria was controversial. Racism is a violent and silenced topic, even in the penal abolitionist movement. Up until ICOPA IX, in Toronto in 2000, the penal abolitionist movement lacked African or African American representation. Participants in ICOPA IX included members from Critical Resistance, an anti-racist activist organization from the United States. In bringing forth issues of racism within ICOPA and emphasizing ICOPA's lack of representation of people of African descent these participants challenged the contemporary abolitionist movement, and worked to expand its parameters and membership. They also brought in a more emphatic awareness of the links between the movement to abolish slavery and the contemporary penal abolitionist movement. From this perspective racism is central to oppression.

The efforts to bring in stronger African and African American representation resulted in the decision to hand ICOPA over to Nigerian representatives. This decision was met with much resistance and fear, and resulted in the initiation of a discussion (which continues) about splitting up ICOPA into different meetings that would accommodate its diversity. Despite such difficult conversations and conflicts, the vast majority of ICOPA founders and organizers were in support of ICOPA in Nigeria. Although racism did arise, they were loudly voiced by a small number of people, and unfortunately countered and silenced by the majority of ICOPA's participants and organizers.

The main issue, as I have come to understand it, is this: the social structures within which we all live are dichotomized and divisive; in addition, the penal system is vast and exploits many different populations in many different ways. As we work to build a strong penal abolitionist movement, strong emotions are bound to be felt and voiced. The need to represent *all* voices and experiences in a manner that does not compete (who is being oppressed the most or the least) will be a challenge because the contemporary order demands a quantification of results and a comparative paradigm that generalizes conclusions.

In working to build a stronger and more effective abolitionist movement ICOPA must provide a space that represents *all* peoples affected by the penal system, in a manner that allows them to voice their opinions of and frustrations with the penal system. Furthermore, ICOPA participants must learn to accept the fact that, despite their radical positions, and their battles against oppression and penal colonialism, they too are impacted by the negative structures of contemporary racist societies. In accepting that we cannot all do the same thing, or have the same experience with the penal system, we might be able to move forward in a manner that is strengthened, and not weakened, by our diversities. What ties us together in the end is the abolitionist goal.

While I work to bring into ICOPA African and African American voices, I also work to respect those who bring in the voices of the poor and/or imprisoned, the young, and women. To begin competing with each other for space in ICOPA would be to fall into a social control trap. Avoiding this trap in the future will include a conscious effort to respect, as opposed to feeling threatened by, each other's differences and knowledges. In the end most people in the world are affected negatively by penal colonialism. If ICOPA is able to focus more on this fact it may be more open to learning about penal abolition from colonized peoples. The underrepresentation of black voices in ICOPA is an issue that must be more readily changed.

Despite all these obstacles, the abolitionist movement has strengths. ICOPA in Nigeria was attended by people who are long-time supporters of the conference and the movement. In addition, many who could not attend due to financial restraints remained in touch and provided support. Some long-time supporters of ICOPA chose not to attend the Nigerian conference; those who were unable to resolve their own issues with racism stopped communicating with ICOPA participants during the time ICOPA spent in Africa.

This experience of racism within ICOPA in Toronto made it clear to me that the abolitionist movement is not immune to the social ills that plague the society it is attempting to change. Racism continues to challenge and destabilize communities all over the world. In my opinion, and from my experiences, racism is at the root of many issues of oppression and inequality, and ICOPA participants were forced to face these realities; some learned from the experience, and some became defensive. Despite such issues with racism and internal struggles, ICOPA did prevail in Nigeria, and the message of abolition was brought at a critical time into an African context. ICOPA had much to learn from West Africa: hosting ICOPA on the land with a long history of European slave trading and colonialism was an excellent way, not only to expand the understanding of abolition, but also to address the racisms that ICOPA was and still is struggling against.

Organizing ICOPA X

Prior to ICOPA X public awareness and community mobilization were pursued nationally in Nigeria. The goal was to make Nigerians more aware of the penal abolitionist movement and the journey that ICOPA had taken through the years. Public awareness was pursued through a media campaign that involved several local and national television broadcasts, a nationwide radio programme that allowed for call-in discussions, and print media promotions in Nigerian newspapers and one African magazine. In addition, ICOPA X was announced and discussed at many Human Rights Network meetings.[1] One non-governmental organization, the Nigerian Youth Leadership Movement led by Ezekiel Ogundare, took an interest in the central issues and the ideas surrounding ICOPA, and, on its own initiative, held a penal abolitionist workshop to raise awareness in its own community in April 2001.

ICOPA X participants comprised a diverse and dynamic group. Participants came from Ghana, The Gambia, Liberia, New Zealand, the United States, Canada, and the United Kingdom. In addition, Nigerians representing the three major ethnic groups and many of the minority groups from different regions in the country were in attendance. Nigerian participants for ICOPA X included University of Lagos students from the law, psychology, and sociology departments; several representatives from non-governmental human rights organizations; academics; activists; lawyers; high- and low-ranking prison officers; high-ranking police officers; National (Nigerian) Human Rights Commission representatives; representatives from the National House of Assembly; ex-prisoners; Nigerian military personnel; poets; musicians; and interested Nigerian youths. The international participants were mainly academics and activists, while continental participants included high-ranking prison officers from neighbouring West African countries, ex-prisoners, human rights NGO representatives, and musicians. The Local Organizing Committee was comprised of PRAWA staff, student volunteers, and youths from the local community in Lagos. The entire participant list for ICOPA X was approximately 100 people: about 65 University of Lagos students and community members, about 15 international participants, and about 20 Nigerian non-governmental and governmental representatives.

ICOPA X: Abuja Panel

On August 23, 2002, ICOPA X was launched in Abuja, the capital of Nigeria, with a Policy Makers Panel in the Nigerian National Assembly. The purpose of the panel was to raise awareness about ICOPA and the notion of penal abolition among Nigerian governmental officials, while bringing forth issues surrounding the death penalty and the need for its removal from the criminal code in Nigeria. This panel was booked weeks in advance, yet there was a slight and unexpected problem in scheduling that day: a week before the panel took place the Nigerian government called a meeting on the day of the panel to discuss the impeachment of the president of Nigeria on charges of corruption and embezzlement. This resulted in a few hours of delay, and participants in the panel did not know whether the panel would take place at all. Upon finishing the meeting, which directly addressed corruption in Nigeria, government officials who had committed to participating in the ICOPA panel did come to it. The panel commenced with several members, including the chairperson, from the House of Representatives Committee on Human Rights and Legal Matters, high-ranking police and prison officials, human rights activists, university professors, and representatives from the British Embassy. Following presentations about the concepts of penal abolition, African justice models as they existed prior to, during, and after colonialism, and a critical outlook on the current colonial penal system in Nigeria, discussions, questions, and debates began.

A debate about the relevance of the death penalty in Nigeria ensued, and a pinnacle was reached when the question of statistics on executions in the country was brought up. Sitting on the panel as a PRAWA representative, I asked "when was the last time an execution was carried out in the country." Professor Adeyemi, dean of law at the University of Lagos, suggested that the Nigerian Prison Service representatives were likely in the best position to answer the question. In response a high-ranking representative of the prison service explained that all over the country state governors refused to sign execution warrants and that this refusal resulted in life sentences on death row for many prisoners. He added that inevitably ending in prisoners' deaths, this form of the death penalty is prolonged and indirect. As for when the last execution *actually* took place, he stated that "There are a lot of silent executions in Nigeria, as my friend who is present will tell you," and he pointed at the police officer sitting beside him. The officer confirmed that "silent executions" do take place and stated his belief that they are a necessary measure in Nigerian society. These executions are carried out in police cells after arrests and prior to court appearances. This debate led to a discussion on deterrence and how ineffective it is. Hal Pepinsky, a professor of criminal justice at Indiana University and one of the international participants at ICOPA X, responded that deterrence in the United States, with its structured and well-funded criminal justice system, does not work either, and he pointed out that the harsher a punishment is, the less people relate to it and follow the law it is trying to implement.

Adeyemi gave a detailed presentation on penal policies and African alternatives. He spoke about the researched public opinion of criminal justice in Nigeria and the widespread distrust of criminal justice in Nigeria, which results in "jungle justice" on many of Nigeria's streets. He defined jungle justice as being comprised of vigilante groups who literally hunt down armed robbers and kill them publicly. An issue that arises in these situations, aside from the gross inhumanity of these public and graphic killings, is that tribalism and politics are usually in control of such vigilante groups. Adeyemi proceeded to give an in-depth analysis of traditional (precolonial) Nigerian justice and stressed that it did not rely on the death penalty or other violent means of resolving conflict or dealing with harm: "It was restorative in terms of social equilibrium: it recognized that you can't solve conflict with conflict, and reconciliation was widely used."

Adeyemi spoke about crime as conflict and thus the solution to crime as encompassed by conflict resolution. He referred to instances in which the death penalty was used in African history. He stressed that, contrary to Western opinion, the death penalty in the majority of precolonial African societies was used as a last resort, in cases of extreme reoffending and danger to the community: only after banishment was not successful in keeping a community safe was an execution implemented. Adeyemi also noted that executions were used when the crime could not be dealt with rationally (as with accusations entailing the misuse of witchcraft). After providing more details on historical and contemporary issues of justice he ended by urging, "It is high time that we come back to embracing traditional justice."

Adeyemi's presentation prompted comments by the representative of the Nigerian Prison Service related to root causes of crime. He spoke about the social problems that criminalize people on a national scale and the Nigerian society on an international scale. He pointed out that capital sentences increase crime in the large divisions they cause by marginalizing, stereotyping, and demonizing entire populations of people: the prisoners he worked with every day are one of the most socially feared populations in the country. He stated that the panel needed to talk less about those stereotypes, and more about alternatives and penal abolition.

In response the police officer on the panel spoke about the fact that mediation as an alternative to penality is easier among homogeneous populations, and he thought that Nigeria has what he called 'the stranger element' with the hundreds of different ethnic groups and languages that exist. He spoke about the churches, the mosques and the chiefs interfering in the justice process and initiating out-of-court settlements. He complained about victims who want compensation for the crimes they have suffered and expect the police to provide such compensation. He continued to stress the need for deterrence in light of the high rates of violence in Nigeria, specifically associated with the trafficking of women and children, and with armed robberies. He stressed that long terms of imprisonment will have no benefit as an alternative to the death penalty in Nigeria because, unlike in Western nations, the criminal justice system's budget is not vast. These budget restrictions are clear when one assesses the court system and finds that 62.4 percent of the prison population has never been to court and may wait an indefinite number of years before being taken to court, or getting legal representation. It became clear in this discussion that the police hold a much more conservative view of the penal system than the prison officials do in Nigeria. An informal discussion after the panel revealed to me that the prison administration feels an African sense of responsibility toward the prisoners whom they have been hired to care for. In this instance African culture transcended, at least in ideology, the penal institution's attempts to westernize Africa.

Discussions were rounded off with comments from the Honourable Ibrahim Zailani of the House of Representatives. He stated that, "While Nigeria may not be ready to abolish the death penalty, this panel has made it clear that [more culturally and socially appropriate] alternatives need to be put in place of the penal system in Nigeria." He asked that PRAWA and ICOPA X assist in putting together a committee to help the House of Representatives in drafting legislation to put before the house, promoting the implementation and recognition of alternatives to imprisonment and penality. Contact information was exchanged, and communication started about forming this committee and drafting the legislation.

ICOPA X: Lagos Conference

From August 24 to August 29, 2002, ICOPA X was hosted by PRAWA at the University of Lagos. On Saturday, August 24, ICOPA participants attended the Black Heritage Festival held at CMS on Lagos Island. The festival is an annual event held in Nigeria in memory of the oppressive history of slavery and colonization, and to reinforce black pride, promote peace in Africa, recall that the abolition of such oppressive forces is possible, and stress that the African people have survived massive atrocities. The opening ceremonies of this event were held at the Race Course Stadium, a large and expensive stadium built by the British colonial government for horse-racing, an event that is not necessarily popular in Nigeria. The stadium has never been used for horse-racing. It came to represent the inappropriateness and the extravagant lifestyles of colonialists. It was later used as the venue for the independence ceremony from the British when institutionalized colonial rule was abolished in Nigeria. The opening ceremonies of the Black Heritage Festival attended by ICOPA X participants included a celebration of the abolition of institutionalized slave trading of West Africans. Dances and festive costumes from all over the country paraded before the public and the *oba* ("king") of Lagos Island.

The second day of ICOPA X, August 25, was dedicated to the memory of Dr. Ruth Morris. She was a Canadian/American, prison/peace, Quaker activist and one of the original organizers of ICOPA I, held in Montreal in 1983. Ruth was an activist volunteer in her children's schools and began to visit prisons through a Quaker programme. She also began to bail men out while they were awaiting trial, and taking them into her home for shelter and support. Throughout her life she advocated for the rights of some of the most stigmatized prisoners and ex-prisoners in society. Ruth was a leading international theorist of what she called "transformative justice." She was the author of many books and information pamphlets in the area of penal abolition and transformative justice. She led the organization of ICOPA IX in Toronto in May 2000, and sadly she died in September 2001. An optional church service in her memory was organized at Yaba Glory Worship Centre, followed by visits to the Kirikiri medium and maximum security prisons, where ICOPA X participants shared meals and music in solidarity with prisoners. About 1,000 prisoners ate and participated in song with ICOPA X participants that day. In the evening a candlelight vigil was held at the Lagoon Front in memory of Ruth. People gathered with lit candles, and spoke about her life and her work. Songs were shared after a moment of silence in her memory.

The official ICOPA X opening ceremony was held on Monday, August 26, at the University of Lagos Conference Centre. It was followed by presentations by Professor Julia Sudbury of the Department of Ethnic Studies at Mills University, California, highlighting the racist and economic elements of the US justice system, while emphasizing the importance of an international abolitionist movement that will work in unity to abolish the atrocities occurring through penal systems around the globe. Justice S. A. Brobbey from the Court of Appeal in Ghana ended with a presentation about human rights issues in relation to the criminal justice system's failures in West Africa. The theme was established early: the penal system is malfunctioning around the globe, and alternatives are desperately needed.

Presentations throughout the conference included an assessment of the psychological consequences of torture, the implementation of transformative and community justice programmes around the globe, and the successes of, and obstacles to, resistance movements. A powerful moment during one of the sessions included Chino Hardin, with the Prison Moratorium Project in New York. She discussed the problems with the US criminal justice and narrated personal experiences from her time in US youth jails. This session challenged the general stereotypes of crime and criminals that abide in Nigerian society. Hardin spoke about her years as a member of a street organization (what is referred to in mainstream society as a street gang) and the armed robberies in which she was involved. In Nigeria armed robbers are feared more than any other category of people and are viewed as the most dangerous threat to social safety. The Nigerian participants' reaction to Chino, whom they had spent time with prior to this session, was open-minded, and, upon seeing her accomplishments, hearing about her hardships in prisons, and listening to her call for abolition, many later stated that their stereotypes about armed robbers had been greatly challenged.

Tuesday, August 27, was dedicated to a focus on alternative models to the penal system, both in theory and in practice. Traditional African models of justice were presented and discussed in detail, with Professor Oko Elechi outlining the historical aspects of general African indigenous justice systems and the links of most of them to transformative justice ideology. He stressed that most contemporary justice systems are Euro- and male-centred, and are not natural to African societies in general. An understanding of these misogynistic and racist components of the dominant European forms of justice was accentuated with presentations about the Maori struggle in New Zealand and the inappropriateness of the colonial justice system in dealing with conflict in colonized ("non-European") communities.

These criticisms were followed by a plenary focusing on practical alternatives to the penal system. The peacemaking perspective was explored and accentuated with presentations by members of the Alternatives to Violence Project (AVP) in Nigeria and their work with the International Committee of the Red Cross (ICRC). The AVP presentation focused on the Nigerian situation and the role of conflict resolution within the context of communal conflicts. Iyke Chiemeka, on behalf of the AVP, emphasized the fact that violence is inevitable in every society and that the key to managing violence is the chosen approach. He gave an analysis of what he called the chaotic Nigerian society and said that how a society chooses to manage its conflicts is what constitutes its civilization. He gave examples of Nigerian issues that have led to violence and demonstrated how the AVP resolved such conflicts non-violently. His presentation was complemented by that of Ellen Flanders from the United States, one of the founders of the AVP. She shared some of her experiences with the AVP and presented examples of how it has transcended violence in many parts of the world.

PRAWA employees participated in ICOPA X, not only through organizational efforts, but also in presentations. In a paper entitled "Alternatives to Imprisonment Measures: Lessons from Africa" Saib Feyisetan, head of the Communications and Media Department at PRAWA, presented on behalf of Chukwuma Ume, a PRAWA employee in the Prison Officers Human Rights Training Programme. This presentation highlighted some parts of the Nigerian Constitution that relate to prison and punishment, and the international laws that guide the treatment of prisoners. Feyisetan also spoke about the links between present African prisons and colonization. He emphasized the fact that alternatives to imprisonment are not foreign or new concepts in Africa; rather, they are a part of the heritage and history of the continent. He gave examples of successful implementations of alternatives to imprisonment in Zimbabwe, Kenya, and Nigeria.

Moses Blokanjay Jackson[2] spoke about the immediate need for alternatives to the penal system in Liberia. He belongs to a non-governmental organization called Volunteers for the Care of Abused and Abandoned Children. He presented a contextual account of the war in Liberia, and national and international government links to the conflicts there. He spoke about the power and economic imbalances in Liberia, and highlighted the fact that sanctioned war measures only further the wealth of the rich, while driving the poor further into poverty. He explained that the situation in Liberia, promoted by political and economic motives, forces the poor to survive only by relying heavily on the rich. He gave a diverse set of examples to support these statements, from the exploited exportation of the diamonds industry to the forced prostitution of women and children in Liberia. Within such a context, he stated, a justice system promoted by the state (those in power and in control of the nation's wealth) is not only dangerous, but also futile. With this sort of context and with a better understanding of the history of the conflicts in Liberia, it became clear that a colonial penal system is not only ineffective because of the current war, but will continue to be inappropriate after the war is subdued.

Highlighting the West African transformative justice context, Justice Brobbey from Ghana spoke about the implementation and successful functioning of the Victim–Offender Mediation Model in Ghana. He started his presentation by stating that there are two recognized justice systems in Ghana: those that are formal (run by the state) and those that are informal (run by the community). He said that people often resort to the informal sector of justice mainly due to convenience, accessibility, time, and financial restraints. He highlighted the formal system's restrictions through the court processes and the flexibility of the informal system through arbitration/mediation. He gave details of the problematic nature of the formal justice system in Ghana and contrasted it with the informal processes that the majority of the people pursue.

Dr. Senghor Aboubakar from The Gambia presented a paper on behalf of Hanna Foster of the African Centre for Democracy and Human Rights. The paper outlined the Victim–Offender Mediation Model being implemented in The Gambia. He spoke about the community's open response to it. He stated that The Gambia is a small country of about 1.4 million people, and the number of people in prison is thus relatively small. He pointed out that going to court or the police in The Gambia is considered taboo because people simply cannot embrace the idea. He spoke about the African Centre for Democracy and Human Rights mediation services and stated that they have been used in resolving many forms of conflicts ranging from individual conflicts within the home to larger conflicts in society.

It was noted that, ironically, the majority of justice projects in Africa are funded by European donors. Prior to European funds, African justice models existed throughout the continent during colonization and continue to be found. European funds aid in formalizing African justice models, and this formalization creates the danger of co-optation, opening colonial avenues for the creation of a more systematized and inflexible model that might mirror the malfunctioning and culturally inappropriate colonial criminal justice systems in Africa.

In the evening of August 27, ICOPA X participants went to the new Afrika shrine in Ikeja, Lagos, for a special concert by Femi Anikulapo Kuti entitled Exposing Oppression through Musical Expression. Femi Kuti is the son of the late musician/activist Fela Anikulapo Kuti. Fela's legend in Nigeria and Africa exhibits the oppression and inhumanity of colonization and the ensuing military regimes in Nigeria. Fela's mother was murdered by the head of the military state at the time, Olusegun Obasanjo. *Despite* being a former military dictator, Obasanjo was named the first "democratically elected" president of Nigeria in 1999. *Despite* rampant corruption and the entrenched institutionalization of poverty that he reinforced for the overwhelming majority of Nigerians, he remained in that position until 2007. He was replaced by Umaru Yar'Adua in July 2007. This is telling, since Umaru Yar'Adua is Shehu Yar'Adua's younger brother. Shehu Yar'Adua was Obasanjo's vice president during Obasanjo's military dictatorship. Fela was imprisoned several times by Obasanjo and Shehu Yar'Adua for his outspoken opposition to their military regime.

Femi grew up watching the police arrest and beat his father. Fela's original Afrika shrine was destroyed twice by the government. Femi performed for ICOPA X participants as well as the Nigerian public, for whom he made admission to the rebuilt

Afrika shrine free and open to all for the night. The African drums, dances, and instrumentals were also accompanied by Femi's speeches on the history of Nigeria's oppressive states, and the present-day hardships and exploitations of the general population, due to corporate and state-initiated embezzlement of Nigeria's resources and the unequal distribution of wealth. ICOPA X participants danced, sang, and listened to Femi Kuti's saxophone and his band's accompanying instrumentals, and they enjoyed the true African hospitality of one of Nigeria's leading musicians.

Wednesday, August 28, was dedicated to remembering the abolition of official European slave-trading enterprises in West Africa. About 100 ICOPA X participants went to the National Museum in Onikan, Lagos, and saw ancient African artifacts and tools. It was noticed that many of the most precious artifacts, such as the Benin bronzes and several ivory masks, had to be represented by present-day replicas because the originals, without the consent of Nigerian authorities, are being held in British museums for what is called proper preservation. Also in the museum was a display of past military and present rulers. On display was the car in which Murtala Muhammad was assassinated. He was the head of state of Nigeria who preceded Obasanjo's military rule in 1979, and his assassination was followed by numerous military coups. The car was in a room surrounded by pictures of past military dictators and their governors/generals.

After the museum ICOPA X participants travelled to Badagary, a small town on the outskirts of Lagos State. It is located on shores where slave-trading took place. Visits in Badagary included one of the gravesites of an African chief who participated in trading slaves to Europeans. Near his grave the shackles he used to capture and enslave people were on display. Participants walked from his grave to the Gate of No Return, which marked the spot where boats loaded for departure to the Americas and Europe. Across the street from the bronze gate, with its sculptures of white men whipping West Africans who had been stripped and shackled, were the Brazilian Baracoons. These baracoons consisted of forty slave cells used to hold people as they waited for slave ships to depart. All but two of the cells have been converted into residential homes for the descendants of the chief of that village who collaborated with Europeans and their colonies in North and South America. Inside this compound participants visited men's and women's cells. Upon learning that forty people were held in each cell forty participants, mainly students and several international participants, piled in and closed the small wooden doors. The space was very tight, and air was restricted. For a brief moment confinement was experienced in the same holding cell that had imprisoned and sold millions of slaves. On the way out of the cell was a picture of the chief who owned the cells, and the gifts and clothes he was given in return for his slave-trading contributions. These gifts included glass plates and one cup, velvet robes, and a wooden trunk. The atmosphere was tense as the realities of historical oppression were confronted physically and emotionally. The materials used in exchange for Africans were minuscule and cheap; how these artifacts could be equated with human lives was beyond comprehension.

The day rounded off with poetry readings by Dr. Tony Marino, a medical doctor, published poet, and human rights activist in Ibadan, Nigeria. Poems were also read by some Nigerian youths, and music was played by several international and national participants. After the poetry reading Marino donated books for prisoners in Lagos State. An emotional day was capped off with a sense of sadness, but a glimmer of hope in notions of resistance and solidarity through poetry and song. Although the day was intense and difficult, many felt that it would impact them for a long time. An understanding of the need to fight oppressive social and penal structures had been personalized.

The last day of ICOPA X focused on the financial context of criminal justice. Gerald Onwusi, a human rights lawyer in Nigeria, presented a detailed assessment of the oil conflicts in Nigeria's delta region. He spoke about the late political activist Ken Saro-Wiwa and the many others who have lost their lives in attempts to protect their communities and their lives from the effects of oil exploitation. He spoke about the people who hide behind company names to commit crimes against the community, and stated the need for civil justice to intervene and sue those involved to ensure that they face consequences for their misdeeds. In his paper Onwusi suggested that communities that are affected should be compensated. He mentioned the example of what the US companies have come to call the "super fund," said to be created for the purpose of paying compensation to the people of Nigerian oil communities. Unfortunately Onwusi did not highlight the fact that these funds are never sufficient in the face of the damage done to the communities and to the environment, and only serve as short-term solutions to long-term problems of exploitation, environmental damage, and community breakdown. He concluded by stating that people should know their rights and exercise them through such schemes of compensation, emphasizing the need to rely on the penal system to secure financial compensation for oil-related conflicts in Nigeria.

His presentation was followed by one that directly contradicted his conclusions. Jane Hemesson, retired commandant of the Prison Training School, retired state controller of prisons, and present deputy director of PRAWA, spoke about the financial context of the criminal justice system in Nigeria. She spoke about the large sums of money being spent on the maintenance of prisons in Nigeria and mentioned that eleven new prisons are in the process of being built in the country. She supported penal abolitionism and stressed the counterproductive financial element of a justice system that does not serve the Nigerian people. She referred to the country's massive natural resources and wealth, and stated that the growing budgets of both the prison and the police in Nigeria have begun to present a drain on the national budget, and this problem is in need of direct and immediate attention.

Conference presentations were concluded with a session focusing on the brutalities of imprisonment, and included presentations of papers written by prisoners (presented on their behalf by ex-prisoners or prisoners' rights activists) and ex-prisoners. The first presentation was written by Tiyo Attalah Salah El, serving a life sentence in a US prison. His paper was presented by Professor Hal Pepinsky and included details of the injustices implemented by the US penal system within the context of power imbalances related to class, race, and gender. He spoke about the indefensibility of the penal system, and addressed issues related to the inadequacy and inappropriateness of reform when faced with the inhumane and oppressive penal structure. Following this presentation Clever Akporherhe and Felix Obi spoke about their experiences in Nigerian prisons, and Faith Nolan presented a paper on behalf of Osadolor Eribo, who was still in prison at the time.

Sam Edokwa also presented a paper during this session. He is an ex-prisoner who is a soldier in the Nigerian army. He was arrested in 1996 on a civilian matter, picked up by the police, and—without any presentation of evidence against him—put in prison. He was held in prison as an awaiting-trial prisoner for three years and in the end was never convicted of any offence. His speech was short because military personnel came with him for the presentation. He was in full military uniform during his speech and, despite the presence of his military 'superiors', managed to emphasize the lack of implementation of the UN human rights standards for the treatment of prisoners in Nigerian prisons. Edokwa had to take time off work to present at ICOPA, hence the military uniform and escorts, but he gave an accurate presentation of his time as a prisoner and his contact with the police force. Before and after his presentation, when he was not in uniform and escorted by military personnel, he became heavily involved in abolitionist discussions, promoting the ideology and advocating for implementation of alternatives to the system that are separate from the penal structure and not within state control. His presence at ICOPA X was valuable and represented a great deal of resistance to many oppressive forces.

ICOPA X: CONCLUSIONS AND REALIZATIONS

Throughout the conference there were many intense discussions among participants. Many of the Nigerian students in attendance expressed concerns about the nonchalant attitudes of Nigerian lawyers and judges toward the suffering of prisoners. The stories shared by (ex-)prisoners, and the justifications for inhumanity presented by several criminal justice practitioners (mainly laying blame for system malfunctions on criminal justice branches for which they were not working), prompted discussions among participants between presentations and over lunch breaks. One of the Nigerian lawyers present reacted by telling a large group of students that "Nigeria has just entered into democracy after thirty years of military dictatorship," and thus their expectations for their nation's development were premature and set too high. A heated debate on the politics of injustice ensued. As at other times throughout ICOPA X, a small minority of those employed by the criminal justice system were challenged or threatened by the criticisms and facts presented. It also seemed that the more students heard, the more disturbed they were by the injustices occurring in and through the Nigerian *criminal* justice system. While many did not trust the system or the state, the details presented still shocked them. These students continue to voice their concerns about *criminal* justice in Nigeria. The new generation of young adults is at odds with a minority of the older generation of criminal justice practitioners, and some of the older generation of activists and academics. This made for some really interactive sessions and debates: ICOPA X days and nights were packed with many loud, heated, and at times hostile discussions. These discussions did not break up the group dynamic at ICOPA X. In true African spirit, those who disagreed chose to spend more time in discussion, despite recognizing possibly irreconcilable differences.

It was a powerful experience, emphasizing to me that the path to peace and equality is not quiet; it is full of stories of brutality, and it is packed with disagreements. When the people repossess the power to define and resolve their own conflicts they are bound to disagree, and that disagreement is essential. I have come to understand that silence is a tool of oppression. Speaking out is a tool of resistance. Some speak through song, some speak through stories, some speak through writing,[3] some speak through research, and some speak through action. ICOPA X spoke loudly in West Africa those few days.

The stories shared during ICOPA X, and the experiences I had in Nigeria, were intense and at times violent. The (ex-) prisoners, community members, and activists I met in Nigeria struggle every day, not only to become free, but also to survive on a basic level in extremely harsh living conditions. Nigeria is a rich nation. Africa is rich in resources. What keeps one of the richest, most abundant continents poor? It became clear to me in Nigeria that globally racist and oppressive economic structures, built during racist and violent eras of colonialism and slave-trading, continue to thrive at the expense of an entire continent. While history set the stage for the current situations and oppressions in Africa, many privileged societies choose conveniently to ignore the racist and violent foundations of their comforts. The racist and oppressive penal structures of Western societies continue to be taken for granted as civil and common forms of law. Penal structures actually represent the visible reality of the *criminal* forms of justice that colonial institutions implement. Their very existence on African soil brings to light the continuation of colonial rule in Africa. Penal institutions in Africa serve as a constant reminder of the criminal acts of colonialism and slave-trading that Europeans participated in historically; they also illuminate the continued participation in such acts by descendants of colonialists, who continue to exploit Africa and work toward the implementation of a stronger penal system on African soil.

The actions and circumstances that have led up to the contemporary conditions in which Africans and people of colour all over the globe live are racist and violent. Conflict, it seems, is inevitable; violence becomes natural within a structure that is unnatural, inhumane and repressive. Resistance, I have come to learn, lies in a commitment to build solidarity among those who are oppressed, predominantly and unquestionably people who are 'not white'. Upon building a stronger community focused on fighting such conditions, communities of colour can begin to work with allies who are white, but who choose to use their privilege to destabilize it. Solidarity occurs with the implementation of a respected diversity, an understanding that differences are not only acceptable, but also essential for the human social condition. Within the spirit of such diversity lies the understanding that institutions and systems of control are too rigid, and thus structurally too oppressive, in their interactions with the people of a flexible and diverse society.

For disempowered populations these oppressions are a reality, all-encompassing and devastating. For those who are privileged, who are empowered, who do have opportunities to speak out and create possibilities for change, it is not a choice but a responsibility to work toward freedom. It is a responsibility to fight to destabilize the conditions and structures that thrive in violence and build comforts for a *minority* rich (and predominantly white) population through the bloodshed and exploitation of the *majority*. The fight for freedom from penal oppression and colonial global structures is essential at times like this. In these times of barbaric *criminal* justice the current human condition demands that the current global order transform. A revolution of the mind, body, and spirit of contemporary social, political, and economic structures must occur. In the meantime disempowered, oppressed, and silenced populations continue to fight back and resist colonialism through *criminal* justice in Africa. The experiences, facts, and analyses shared in this book illuminate such acts of resistance, and hopefully can stimulate a discussion that is not controlled by deluded propaganda. The past is not the past, racism continues to thrive today, and there are options available to change the miserable realities of this global colonized and racist condition.

NOTES

1 Meetings are held the last Friday of every month ironically, in the British Council office in Lagos. The purpose of the meetings is to gather human rights activists and non-governmental organizations in Lagos, in order to network and build a community organized enough to implement political and social changes.
2 One of the continental participants at ICOPA. A human rights activist in Liberia, Moses spoke frequently about the civil war that his country is experiencing.
3 The *Journal of Prisoners on Prisons* presents this opportunity to prisoners all over the world.

INDEX

A
Aba, 104
Abacha, General Sani, 103, 104, 109, 251
   dictatorship, 90, 91
Abashi, Chris, 44, 101, 102, 103
Abdullah, Hussaina J., 229, 344
Abeokuta prison, 59
Abinsi prison, 59
Abiola, Chief Moshood Kashimawo Olawale, 114, 251
Abiola, Kudirat, 251
Aboubakar, Dr. Senghor, 479
Abramsky, Sasha, 267, 278
Abubakar, Atiku, 29
Abubakar, General Abdulsalami, 91, 111, 251
Abuja, 110, 212, 262
   ICOPA X, 471–475
Academic Staff Union of Universities, 89
Access for Justice workshops, 208, 209, 210
Achebe, Chinua, 230, 403
Acoli, Sundita, 419
Action Group, 93
Adegbenro, Chief, 106
Ademoyega, A., 94

Adenuga, Mike, 111
Aderemi, Oba Adesoji, 106
Adeyemi, Adedokun, 255, 256, 380, 381, 383, 384, 472, 473–474
Ado-Etiki prison, 259
Africa Confidential, 111
Africa Policy, 361
African Charter on Human and Peoples' Rights, 96, 227, 386
   and mental health disabilities, 270, 271, 272, 276, 278, 279, 281, 282, 283
   Purohit case, 275, 281
African Commission, 270, 272, 277–278
   Purohit case, 275, 279, 281–282, 283
African Commission on Human Rights and Peoples' Rights, 231
African Concord, 249, 251
African Studies Association, 91
African Union (AU), 281, 283
Agodi, 59
Agomoh, Uju, 63, 66, 233, 255, 256, 380, 381
Agozino, Biko, 4, 7
   militarization of Nigeria, 69, 70, 71, 97, 99, 106

women in prison, 246, 247, 252, 257, 262
Ajayi, Professor Ade, 86, 91
Ajegunle police, 192–194
Akhigbe, Mike, 111
Akintola, S.L., 93, 94, 105, 106
Akporherhe, Clever, 484
Akumadu, Theresa, 253, 255
Algeria, 32
"Alternatives to Imprisonment Measures: Lessons from Africa," 478
Alternatives to Violence Project (AVP), 204, 477–478
Amadi, E., 409, 410, 411, 412, 413
Amafegha, Kweku, 111
America. *see* United States
American Revolution, 309
Aminu, Alhaji, 111
Amnesty International, 164–165, 218, 232
Amni International, 111
An-Na'im, Abdullahi A., 227
Anchorage Petroleum, 111
Anyanike, I., 99
Apapa, 107
Application of Native Law and Custom, 310–311
Arakan barracks, 160
Arnold, Helen, 274
Assembly of Heads of State and Government of the OAU, 283
Asumah, Seth N., 235
AU (African Union), 281, 283
Aubert, Vilhelm, 401
Auchi prison, 259
Australia, 7, 11
AVP (Alternatives to Violence Project), 204, 477–478
Awa, E.O., 396–397
Awe, Professor Muyiwa, 89, 90
Awolowo, Chief Obafemi, 106, 251

Awopetu, Professor Idowu, 88, 89
Ayieko, Odindo, 237, 238
Ayittey, G.B.N., 397, 401
Ayorinde, Esther, 255
Ayu, Iyorchi, 91
Ayua, M., 297, 301, 343
Azikiwe, Dr. Nnamdi, 92, 93

B

Babangida, General Ibrahim, 98, 109, 252
Babarinde, Dr. Kola, 90–91
Badagary, 481
Bakolori, 107
Bala Habu, Murtala III, 364
Balewa, Abubakar Tafawa, 94, 105, 106
Bamaiyi, Ishaya, 111
Bamako (city), 232
Bamako (prison), 237
Banjoko, Tiamiyu, 106
Banking Act (1961), 105
Bar Association, 208, 392
Barbeach Police Station, 132
Barkhuizen, G., 234
Barkow, Jerome H., 302, 304, 305
Baudrillard, Jean, 246
Bayelsa State, 95, 190–191
"Beast of No Nation" (Fela Kuti), 246, 356–360, 366–367
Beasts of Burden (Women's Rights Project of the CLO), 86
Beijing Women's Conference, 223, 225, 232
Bell, M.J.V., 77
Bello, Ahmadu, 92
Bello, Sani, 111
Benin, 22, 50
Benin prison, 259
Bentsi-Enchill, Kwamena, 293, 294, 296, 299, 309, 310, 311
Benue river, 28

Benue State, 208, 219
Berlin conference, 22, 23, 28, 29, 186, 250
Bernault, Florence, 230, 235
Bill of Rights (Britain), 227
Bill of Rights (Nigeria), 102
Bill of Rights (United States), 227
Bini Kingdom, 59
Biu prison, 59, 259
Black Heritage Festival, 475
Black Women's Federation of South Africa, 238
Bohannon, Paul, 312, 313, 315
Bolle prison, 233, 237
Bonger, W.A., 424, 441, 442
Bourdieu, Pierre, 35–36
Bourvier, Odette Luce, 379
Box, S., 249
Brazil, 383
Brennan, Farmer v., 276
Britain. *see also* United Kingdom
    Africa, division of, 22, 361
    American Revolution laws, 309
    colonial history, 24, 27–28, 29, 58–60, 92, 109
    economic colonialism, 60–61, 64, 109, 309
    Empire as colonizer, 34, 35, 310
    English language in Nigeria, 29, 204, 313, 364
    incarceration rate in, 4
    independence from, 294, 361
    justice, militarization, 101
    justice, modern, 64, 104, 106, 251
    juvenile justice in, 12
    laws and colonization, 58–59, 104, 229, 395, 457
    women and resistance, 295, 299, 300, 309, 310, 311, 319, 322
    legal pluralism, 309, 339
    and prisons in Nigeria, 58–60
    women and law, 246, 247–248, 257, 260
British Council, 216, 217
Brobbey, Justice S.A., 476, 479
Browne, Julie, 419, 420, 423
Buhari, General Muhammadu, 108, 109, 252
Burkina Faso, 387
Busia, Abena, 224, 225
Butegwa, Florence, 225

C
Cabral, Amilcar, 265
Cairo, 158
Calabar hospital, 276
Calabar prison, 58
Calabar Rice Scheme, 58
California, 420
Callaway, Barbara, 295, 298, 302, 303, 306, 307
Campaign for Democracy, 105, 110
Canada
    ICOPA, 467
    incarceration rate in, 4, 422
    justice, models of, 7
    juvenile justice in, 11–12
    racism, 427
Carlen, Pat, 260
Castro, Fidel, 263–264, 372
Caulfield, Susan L., 435
Cayley, David, 422
Centre for Democracy and Development (CDD), 71, 110
Centre for Law Enforcement, 86
Césaire, Aimé, 34, 35
Chabal, Patrick, 41, 48
Chamba, 94
Chambliss, William J., 431, 447
Chanock, Martin, 228
Chevron, 191

Chevron Texaco, 253
Chiapas, 324–325
Chiemeka, Iyke, 478
China, 370–372, 373
Chomsky, Noam, 30
Christianity, 27, 186, 188, 232, 258, 295, 310
Christie, Nils, 418, 421–422, 424, 426, 433, 434, 438, 439, 440, 447, 448, 451
Civil Disturbances Act (1987), 104
Civil Liberties Organization (CLO), 86, 258, 261
Civil War, 419
CLO (Civil Liberties Organization), 86, 258, 261
CMS, 425, 426
Cobra, 371
Code of Conduct Bureau, 107
Code of Conduct Tribunal, 107
Coester, Markus, 363
Cohen, Abner, 299, 305, 307
Cohen, Stanley, 433, 434, 435, 438, 451–452
Coles, Catherine, 298, 303
Collier, Jane Fishburne, 324
Colony and Protectorate of Nigeria, 28
Comaroff, John and Jean, 229, 323
Commission of Police, Obolo v., 270
Committee for the Defence of Human Rights, 90
Committee on Economic, Social, and Cultural Rights, 280
Committee on Rights of the Child, 280
Connelly, Chris, 362, 368, 370, 371
Constitution. *see* Nigerian Constitution
Convention against Torture, 272
Corrupt Practices Decree (1975), 107

Corrupt Practices Investigation Bureau, 107
Court of Appeal, Sharia, 101, 229
Court of Appeal (Nigeria), 101, 114, 154, 160, 165–166
   Chris Affor's case, 135, 136, 137, 140, 145
Court of Appeal (UK), 274
Creevey, Lucy, 295, 298, 302, 303, 306, 307
Cross River State, 72
Cuba, 370, 372–373
Cui, Jian, 370
Custom, Immigration and Prison Services Board, 61
Customary Court of Appeal, 101

D

Daggash, Al-Amin, 111
Daily Star, 112
Dajo Oil, 111
Daloz, Jean-Pascal, 41, 48
Dangerous Severe Personality Disorder [DSPD] Order, 274
Daniel, Isioma, 245, 246
Davies, Ioan, 448, 449
Davis, Angela, 248
De Haan, Willem, 427, 430
de Klerk, V., 234
Delta River region, 190–191
Delta State, 94
Democratic Alternatives Workshop on Women's Participation in Politics, 86
Denmark, 4
Department For International Development. *see* DFID
Devil on the Cross (Ngũgĩ), 18–20
DFID (Department For International Development), 99, 208
Diamond, S., 400

Dike, C.P., 407
Directorate of Public Prosecution. *see* DPP
Dirsuweit, T., 234
Division of Human Rights and Peace, UNESCO, 79
DPP (Directorate of Public Prosecution), 154
    Chris Affor's case, 133, 135–136

E

ECOMOG (Economic Community of West African States Monitoring Group), 124, 158, 159, 160, 165, 166
Economic Community of West African States (ECOWAS), 74, 124
Economic Community of West African States Monitoring Group. *see* ECOMOG
ECOWAS (Economic Community of West African States), 74, 124
Eddington, Sir Arthur, 452
Edo, 57
Edokwa, Sam, 484
Edozien, Emmanuel, 111
Egwu, Sam, 97
Ehonwa, Osaze Lanre, 249, 258, 259, 260
Ehonwal, L., 66
Ehrlich, E., 332
Elechi, O. Oko, 397, 403, 408, 410, 411, 412, 477
Elias, Oluwale Taslim, 58, 315, 317, 384, 385
Enahoro, Anthony, 92
Engel, David M., 323, 442
England/Wales, 4. *see also* Britain
English language, 29–30, 204, 313, 362, 364
Eniwari village, 190

Enmeka, 200–203
"Entrenched Military Interests and the Future of Democracy in Nigeria" (Fayemi), 110
Enugu prison, 259, 269, 275
Enugu State, 59, 72, 109, 112
Eribo, Osadolor, 484
Esho, Kayode, 102
Estelle v. Gamble, 276
Etete, Dan, 111
Ethnic and Religious Rights in Nigeria (Okoye), 97
Europe
    colonialism, modern, 171, 176, 177, 364, 428–429, 486
    penal coloniality, 18, 20, 21, 24, 33, 37
    as colonizer, 7, 24, 34, 35, 47–48
    control over wealth, 47, 61, 64, 361
    democracy in Nigeria, 71, 401
    history in Nigeria, 22, 23, 27, 29, 109, 186–187
    and human rights, 268, 270, 283
    incarceration rate in, 6
    justice, models of, 12, 377
    laws and colonization, 230, 248, 481–482, 486
    penal coloniality, 15, 17, 18, 30, 42, 43, 45
    women and resistance, 291, 294, 310, 311, 312, 319, 321, 322
    penal system, influence on, 7–8, 424, 480
    and prisons in Nigeria, 60, 249, 250, 381
European Convention on Human Rights (ECHR), 274

Evans, Linda, 5
Ewedo prison, 58
Eye Confraternity, 90
Eze, 401

F
Fadahunsi, Chief, 106
Fairlie, Freeman v., 310
Faji, 57
Falola, T., 94
Fanon, Frantz, 32
Farmer v. Brennan, 276
Farred, Grant, 20–21
Fattah, Ezzat, 432
Fatton, R., 342
Fawehinmi, Chief Gani, 160
Fayemi, Dr. Kayode, 69–71, 99, 100, 101, 110
Federal Ministry of Internal Affairs, 62
Federal Neuropsychiatric Hospital Enugu, 275
Felix, 206–207
Fellner, Jamie, 267, 278
Fernandes, Sujatha, 372, 373
Feyisetan, Saib, 478
Finland, 4
First, Ruth, 236, 237, 238
First Optional Protocol, 279
Flanders, Ellen, 478
Florence, 192–194
Foster, Hanna, 479
Foucault, Michel, 8, 250, 368, 369, 421
France, 4, 6, 34
Freeman v. Fairlie, 310
Fulani, 295
  ethnic conflict, 94
  incarceration, 57
  language, 29
  population, 25, 26
Furnivall, J.S., 17, 18

G
Gambia, The, 268, 272, 279, 281–282, 311, 479
  Lunacy Detention Act (LDA), 272, 275, 282
Gamble, Estelle v., 276
Garland, David, 298
Gaucher, Bob, 449, 450
Gboko prison, 59
GCM (General Court Martial), 159, 160, 165
Gender Action Project of the Shelter Rights Initiative, 86
Gender Specific Litigations and Protection Strategies Workshop, 86
General Court Martial (GCM), 159, 160, 165
Germany, 4, 22
Ghana, 479
Ghunna, Michael Mac Golla, 360, 361
Gilroy, Paul, 38, 44
Giuliani, Rudy, 247
Giwa, Dele, 124
Gluckman, Max, 312, 313, 317, 401
Gobir Report, 60, 381
Goerg, O., 230
Goldie, Sir George, 28
Gottschalk, Marie, 6
Government, Nigerian, 361
Gramsci, Antonio, 79, 80, 81, 360
Grande, Elisabetta, 324
Greenhouse, Carol, 319, 320, 326
Grounds, A., 274, 276
Groves, Byron W., 417
Guardian, 111
Gulliver, P.H., 314, 317
Gunn, 384
Gwoza prison, 59
Gyekye, K., 402

H

Hall, Stuart, 79, 80, 81, 248
Hardin, Chino, 477
Harlow, Barbara, 235
"Harmful Traditional Practices Affecting the Health of Women from Childhood" (Namiji), 86
Hatoum, Mona, 368
Hausa
    ethnic conflict, 28, 92, 93, 94
    influence, 26
    language, 29, 30
    nation boundaries, 22
    population, 25, 295
    women and law, 299–307, 338–339, 346, 347
Hausaland, 26, 299–308, 347
Hawaii, 325
Hecht, David, 33, 34, 47, 48, 50, 51
Hellum, Anne, 324, 340
Hemesson, Jane, 483
Her Majesty's Prison, 58
Hess, H., 427
Heyns, C., 280
High Court (federal), 101, 103, 105, 108, 154
High Court (federal capital territory), 101
High Court (state), 114
High Court (states), 101
Hill, Polly, 317
Hirschmann, A., 342
Hobbes, Thomas, 80
Hoebel, E. Adamson, 312, 313, 315, 316, 317
Hogeveen, Bryan, 11
Holloway, K., 274, 276
Hountondji, Paulin, 42–43
House of Assembly, 102
HRC (UN Human Rights Committee), 279, 280, 282
Huang, Hao, 370, 371

Hulsman, Louk, 418
Human Rights Monitor, 95, 97, 101
Human Rights Situation Report (Human Rights Monitor), 95
Human Rights Watch, 278

I

Ibadan, 91
Ibibio, 25
Ibo, 28, 384
Ibrahim, Bariya, 229
Ibrahim, Hauwa, 226
ICCPR, 269, 270, 271, 279, 281
ICOPA X, xxi, 457, 467–487
    Abuja Panel, 471–475
    Lagos Conference, 475–484
Idem, Unyierie, 69, 70, 71, 252
Idiagbon, General Tunde, 108, 109, 252, 360, 361
Idoko, Judge Alhassan, 258
Ife, 94
Ifemesia, 403
Ifon, 59
Igbo
    Afikpo, 408, 411, 412, 413
    Council of Elders, 396, 402
    ethnic conflict, 92, 93, 94
    indigenous justice system, 395–414
    influence, 26
    language, 29, 30, 396
    people and societies, 396–398
    population, 25, 295
Igbo, E.U.M., 56
Igboland, 26, 399–403, 407–414
Ige, Chief Bola, 124
Ihonvbere, J., 94
Ijaw, 25, 26, 94, 96
Ijebu-Ode, 59
Ikeja, 149, 150
Ikeja High Court, 154
Ikorodu road, 196

Ilaje, 94
Ilorin prison, 259
IMF (International Monetary Fund), 253, 263, 265
Imoudu, Michael, 92
India, 97
Instead of Prisons (Knopp et al.), 239
International Committee of the Red Cross (ICRC), 477
International Conference on New Directions in Federalism, 110
International Conference on Penal Abolition, Tenth. *see* ICOPA X
International Monetary Fund (IMF), 253, 263, 265
Ireland, 97
Iro, M., 403
Islam, 27, 99, 186, 188, 229, 245, 258
    women and law, 99, 229, 295–296, 299, 301, 343
Itsekiri, 94
Iva Valley, 109

J

Jabri, Vivienne, 368, 369
Jackson, M., 342
Jackson, Moses Blokanjay, 478–479
Jamaica, Randolph Barrett and Clyde Sutcliffe v., 280
James, C.L.R., 248
James, Joy, 226
Jarma, I.M., 57, 60
Jega, Attahiru M., 70, 76
Jesilow, Paul, 431, 433
"John," 421
Jos, 92
Journal of Prisoners on Prisons, 448, 449
Jukun, 94

K

Kaduna, 97
Kaduna State, 72, 95, 258, 303
Kafanchan prison, 59
Kafanchan riots, 97
Kagoro, 384
Kala-kuta Republic, 370–371
Kampala Declaration, 385–386
Kano, 93, 302, 304
Kano, Sarkin, 302
Kano police post, 254
Kano prison, 59
Kano State, 72, 107, 344
Kanuri, 25
Katsina State, 306
Kawashima, Takeyoshi, 444
Kazaure prison, 59
Kemi, 254
Kennedy, Baroness Helena, 216–217
Kenya, 233, 237, 238, 387, 389–390, 478
Kinesis, 239
Kirikiri prison, 1–2, 194, 216–217
    female prison, 217, 219, 259
    maximum security, 139, 164–165, 201
    medium security, 2–3, 128, 155, 259
    penal interactions, 185, 188, 200, 201, 211, 213, 214, 215
    stories from, 119–169
Knopp, Fay Honey, 239, 442, 443
Kohn, Alfie, 441
Konate, Dior, 230
Kone, Kassin, 228, 230
Kuhn, T., 452–453
Kuteb, 94
Kuti, Fela Anikulapo, 91–92, 107, 108, 246, 291, 355–375, 480
Kuti, Femi Anikulapo, 480–481

Kuzwayo, E., 234, 235
Kwale prison, 259

L

La Torre, Massimo, 326–327, 328
Lacey, N., 248
Lafiagi prison, 259
Lagos
    Ajegunle, 192–194
    armed robbery in, 184
    elections, 93
    ethnic conflicts, 94, 95
    and Fela Kuti, 364, 368
    ICOPA X, 475–484
    language, 30, 204
    life in, 174, 189, 364
    police, 127, 181, 195, 197–198
    white people privileges, 18
Lagos Blue Book, 57
Lagos Colony, 28, 58
Lagos Island, 475
Lagos State, 72, 185, 214, 258, 259, 364
Lagos State Police, 149
"Law and Authority in a Nigerian Tribe" (Meek), 384
Law Enforcement Review (Centre for Law Enforcement), 86
Law Reform Commission, 392
Lawal, Amina, 226, 229, 245
Lebanon, 97
Lee, Christopher, 365
Legal Research and Resource Development Centre (LRRDC), 84, 85
Legal Resources Foundation v. Zambia, 282
Lemgruber, Julita, 382, 383
Lenin, V.I., 78, 79
Liberia, 124, 157, 478–479
Liebling, Alison, 274
Llewellyn, Karl N., 315, 317

Locke, John, 80
LRRDC (Legal Research and Resource Development Centre), 84, 85
Lugard, Lord Frederick D., 28, 59, 384, 385
Lunacy Detention Act (LDA) of The Gambia, 272, 275, 282
Lundberg, Anita, 365, 366
Lynch, Michael J., 417

M

Maathai, Wangari, 226
Madunagu, Dr. Edwin, 86, 95–96
Maidugiri prison, 59
Maier, Karl, 364
Maine, H., 400
Maitatsaine riots, 97
Majekodunmi, Sir Moses, 106
Makhoere, Caesarina Kone, 236
Makurdi, 93, 208, 209–210
Makurdi prison, 59, 218–219
Malabo Oil, 111
Malawi, 387
Malcolm X, 246
Mali, 228–229, 230, 231, 232, 233, 237, 387
Malinowski, Bronislaw, 312, 314, 316, 317, 327
Mamdani, M., 81
Mandela, Winnie, 226, 235, 236, 249
Manji, Ambreena S., 293, 294, 336, 342, 343
Marino, Dr. Tony, 482
Maroko slum, 253
Martins, B., 107
Masaji, Chiba, 338
Mashinini, Emma, 236, 237
Mass Mobilization for Social and Economic Recovery (MAMSER), 97

Mathiesen, Thomas, 437, 442, 443, 445, 450
Mbiti, John, 227
Mbushuu, 280
Media Rights Agenda v. Nigeria, 272, 282
Meek, 384
Meer, Fatima, 235, 236, 238
Melissaris, Emmanuel, 332
Memmi, Albert, 36, 37
(1) Mental Health Review Tribunal, North and East London Region, (2) Secretary of State ex parte H, R. v., 274
Merry, Sally Engle
    colonialism, 33, 34
    law and colonization, 45, 46
    legal pluralism, 42, 43, 294, 308, 310, 312, 318, 319, 320, 321, 322, 324, 325
Mexico, 263, 324–325
Middleton, J., 236
Mikell, Gwendolyn, 263
"The Military and the Administration of Justice in Nigeria" (Abashi), 101
Mindell, Arnold, 441
Ministry of Internal Affairs, 61, 392
Ministry of Justice (Kenya), 389
Ministry of Justice (Nigeria), 154, 389, 391
Miss World contest, 245
Mkhize, Pumla, 239
Mobil, 191
Modakeke, 94
Mohammed, Adizat, 254
Mohammed, Bala, 107
Mohanty, Chandra, 225
Momoh, A., 81
Mongella, Gertrude, 225
Moore, Sally Falk, 327
Morales, Donald, 364–365
Morris, Ruth, 426, 436, 439, 449, 475–476
Motala, Z., 401
Muhammad, General Murtala, 107, 251, 481
Muiruri, Stephen, 233
Muntaquim, Jalil, 239
Murray, Rachel, 231
Musengezi, Chiedza, 233, 234
Mussolini, 80
Mutua, Makau, 227–228
Mwita, Elizabeth, 237

N

Nader, Laura, 313, 318, 319, 324, 331
Nagasawa, Richard D., 447
Nagel, Mechthild, 225, 237, 239
Namiji, A., 86
National African Company, 28
National Assembly, 69, 102
National Bank of Nigeria, 105
National Conference on Alternatives to Imprisonment, 382
National Council of Nigeria and the Cameroons (NCNC), 92, 93, 106
National Union of Bank Workers, 114
National Union of Gas and Petroleum Employees, 114
National Union of Nigerian Students, 89
Native Authority, 59, 93, 104
NCNC (National Council of Nigeria and the Cameroons), 92, 93, 106
NEPAD (New Economic Plan for African Development), 262–263
Netherlands, Winterwerp v., 270

New Economic Plan for African Development (NEPAD), 262–263
Ngũgĩ, Thiong'o Wa, 18–20, 21, 38
Nguru prison, 59, 259
Niger Coast Protectorate, 28
Niger River and delta, 26, 27, 28
Nigeria, Media Rights Agenda v., 272, 282
Nigeria, Purohit and The Gambia v., 272
Nigeria-Biafra war, 251
Nigerian Bar Association, 208, 392
Nigerian Constitution, 104, 106, 107, 108, 139, 478
    Article 7, 272
    judicial power, 101, 102
    and mentally ill, 269–270
    and religion, 96–97, 99, 229
    Suspension and Modification Decree, 102
Nigerian Government, 361
Nigerian Labour Congress, 114
Nigerian National Alliance (NNA), 93, 94
Nigerian National Democratic Party, 94
Nigerian Prison Service, 122, 211
    administrative structure, 62
    awaiting-trial prisoners, 3
    emerging issues, 64–66
    evolution, 55–67
    food and water in, 212
    functions, 62–64
Nigerian Students and the Challenge of Leadership (Committee for the Defence of Human Rights), 90
Nigerian Youth Leadership Movement, 470
Nkrumah, Kwame, 17–18, 263

NNA (Nigerian National Alliance), 93, 94
Nnoli, O., 94
Nolan, Faith, 484
North America, 199. *see also* Canada; United States
colonialism, 37, 47, 50, 321, 362
Northern Peoples Congress (NPC), 92, 93, 106
NPC-NCNC alliance, 106
NPC (Northern Peoples Congress), 92, 93, 106
Nsereko, N., 404
Nwankwo, Arthur, 108
Nwobodo, Jim, 108

O

OAU. *see* African Union
Obasanjo, General Olusegun, 100, 111, 199, 245, 251, 263, 481
    and education, 87, 88, 107
    emergency rule, 95
    and Fela Kuti, 362, 368, 480
    presidency, 25, 29, 69
Obi, 402
Obi, Felix, 484
Obolo v. Commission of Police, 270
Obonyo, Oscar, 237
Odi, 95
Odinkalu, A.C., 66
Ogbebor, V., 255, 256, 380, 381
Ogedengbe, 262
Ogoni, 26, 96
Ogoni nine, 44, 102, 104, 251
Ogundare, Ezekiel, 470
Ogunde, Oke, 362, 371
Ogunyemi, Chikwenye Okonjo, 363
Ogwashi-Uku prison, 259
Oil Rivers Protectorate, 28, 58
Okene prison, 259
Okereafoezeke, N., 402

Oko, 58
Okoedion, Felix, 151
Okorie, Uzoma, 255
Okoth-Ogendo, H.W.O., 339
Okoye, Festus, 97, 101
Okpara, Dr. Michael, 93
Oladokim, Segim, 132
Oloruntimehin, O., 262
Ondo State, 94
Oni, Dr. Ola, 87
Onipanu, 195, 196
Onwusi, Gerald, 482–483
Onyeama, Justice Daddy, 105
Oodua People's Congress, 94
Operation Fire for Fire, 127
Ortelius, Abraham, 23
Osun State, 94
Otein, Sergeant, 149, 150
Oturkpo prison, 59
Owo prison, 59, 259
Oyinlola, Colonel, 153
Ozeko Energy Resources, 111

P

Padfield, Nicola, 274
"Pagan Peoples of the Central Area of Northern Nigeria" (Gunn), 384
Pakistan, 97
Papa, 2
Parnell, Philip, 332
Parpart, J., 342
Parrinder, 410
Patterns of Abuse of Women's Rights in Employment and Police Custody in Nigeria (Akumadu), 255
Penal Reform International, 387
People's Republic of Africa, 263
People's Republic of Africa United Democratically (PRAUD), 263

Pepinsky, Harold E., 431, 433, 442–443, 472, 484
Pittin, Renee Ilene, 298, 307
Plang, D., 97
Plateau State, 72
Political Bureau, 98
Portugal, 27, 34
Pospisil, Leopold, 318, 323, 324, 327
Potiskum prison, 259
PRAWA Circle, 141. *see also* Prisoners Support Circle Programme
PRAWA (Prisoners Rehabilitation and Welfare Action), 66, 164, 167, 173, 207
at ICOPA X, 475, 478
PRC (Provisional Ruling Council), 105
Prison Decree No. 9 (1972), 60, 61, 381
Prison Industry Authority (PIA), 420
Prison Notebooks (Gramsci), 80, 360
Prison Ordinance (1884), 59
Prison Ordinance (1916), 59
Prison Regulations (1917), 59
Prison Service. *see* Nigerian Prison Service
Prisoners Rehabilitation and Welfare Action. *see* PRAWA
Prisoners Support Circle Programme, 188, 216. *see also* PRAWA Circle
Prisons and Social Control (Kinesis), 239
Privy Council, 106
Pross, Christian, 238
Protectorate of Northern Nigeria, 28, 295

Protectorate of Southern Nigeria, 28
Provisional Ruling Council (PRC), 105
Purohit and The Gambia v. Nigeria, 272, 281–282
Pyrates Confraternity, 90

Q
Quinney, Richard, 425, 435

R
R. v. (1) Mental Health Review Tribunal, North and East London Region, (2) Secretary of State ex parte H, 274
Rader, Dan, 362, 367, 368
Radio Nigeria Kaduna, 115
Ramphele, Mamphele, 235
Randolph Barrett and Clyde Sutcliffe v. Jamaica, 280
"Reflections on the Historical Foundations of the Present-Day Transformation of Penality" (Winchman), 426
Reiman, Jeffery, 31, 247, 249, 418, 432
Resolution on the Right to Recourse Procedure and Fair Trial, 282
Rewane, Pa Alfred, 124
Rio de Janeiro, 382
Rivers State, 105, 258
Robben Island, 230
Robson, Elsbeth, 299, 301, 302, 303, 305
Rodney, Walter, 116, 248
Rosenberg, Matt T., 188
Royal Niger Company, 28, 109
Ruojie, Wu, 370, 371
Rutgers University, 224

S
Sako, R., 97
Salah-El, Tiyo Attalah, 484
Saleh-Hanna, Viviane, 167, 380
Santos, B. de Sousa, 319, 320
Sapele prison, 58, 259
Saro-Wiwa, Ken, 44, 102, 104, 251, 482
SAS detention centre, 200
Sawaba, Gambo, 235, 236
Scheerer, Sebastian, 429, 433, 444
Schwendinger, Herman and Julia, 417
Senegal, 230, 387
Serote, Mongane Wally, 365
Shagari, Shehu, 252
Sharia Court of Appeal, 101, 229
Shawalu, Rima, 235, 236
Shebi, Esther, 344
Shell, 191
Sierra Leone, 124, 157
Simmons, Emmy B., 305, 306
Simone, Maliqalim, 33, 34, 47, 48, 50, 51
Sokoto, Sarduana, 92
South Africa, 230, 234, 235, 236, 249, 374, 390
  Constitution, 228
  Supreme Court, 228
South African Prisoners' Organization for Human Rights, 234
Sowemimo, Justice, 106, 108
Soweto uprising, 236
Soyinka, Professor Wole, 89
Spain, 34, 97
Special Rapporteur on Prisons and Conditions of Detention in Africa, 231
A Special Report on Nigeria (Campaign for Democracy), 110

"The State and Democratisation of Education: Obstacles and Prospects of Independent Student Unionism under Military Dictatorship" (Awopetu), 88
Status of Women in Nigerian Police (Centre for Law Enforcement), 86
Staunton, Irene, 233, 234
Steinert, H., 427
Stern, Vivien, 226, 233, 388, 389
Stories of Transformative Justice (Morris), 449
Straudt, K., 342
Structural Adjustment Programmes, 252
Sudan, 97
Sudbury, Julia, 476
Sunday Tribune, 89
Supreme Court of Nigeria, 101, 107, 137
Swaziland, 390
Switzerland, 4

T

Tafawa Balewa riots, 97
Tamanaha, Brian Z.
    colonialism, 33, 34, 47
    law and colonization, 44
    legal pluralism, 42, 308, 329, 330, 331, 332, 333, 334, 335, 347
Tanzania, 280, 317
Taraba State, 94
Tarka, Joseph, 93
Taskforce/Committee on Prison Decongestion and Reforms, 64
Taylor, Rachel, 234, 238
Tenth International Conference on Penal Abolition. *see* ICOPA X

Tesfagiorgis, Abeba, 235
Teubner, Gunther, 329, 330, 334
Theoretical Perspectives in the Analysis of Racism and Ethnicity, 79
Things Fall Apart (Achebe), 230
This Day, 245
This Week, 108
Tiananmen Square, 370
Tibatemwa-Ekirikubinza, Lilian, 232, 234
Tinubu, Governor, 213
Tiv, 25, 26, 57, 93
Tolstoy, 426
Tosh, Peter, 91
Totex Oil, 111
Toyo, Professor Eskor, 87–88, 97

U

Uche, 195
UDHR (Universal Declaration of Human Rights), 227, 281, 283
Uganda, 232, 387
Ukpo, Anthony, 111
UMBC (United Middle Belt Congress), 92, 93, 106
Ume, Chukwuma, 380, 478
Umozuriki, U.O., 413
UN (United Nations), 158, 167, 386
    and mental illness, 276, 282
    and women's rights, 230, 233
UN conference in Beijing, 223, 225, 232
UN Conference on Financing for Development, 263
UN Fact-Finding Mission to Nigeria, 104
UN Human Development, 8
UN Human Rights Committee (HRC), 279, 280, 282
UN Millennium Goals, 224

UN Principles for the Protection of Persons with Mental Illness and Improvement of Mental Care, 272, 275
UN Standard Minimum Rule for the Treatment of Prisoners (UNSMR), 277
UN Standard Minimum Rules for Non-Custodial Measures (Tokyo Rules 1990), 386
UN Working Group on Arbitrary Detention, 283
UNESCO, Division of Human Rights and Peace, 79
United Kingdom. *see also* Britain
  Department of Health, 274
  mentally disabled in, 268, 273–274, 275, 281
United Kingdom, X v., 273
United Middle Belt Congress (UMBC), 92, 93, 106
United Nations. *see* UN
United Progressive Grand Alliance (UPGA), 93, 94
United States
  abolitionism, 428, 437
  colonization, 34, 35, 322
  community service orders, 386
  Constitution, Amendment 13, 428
  democracy in Nigeria, 71
  economic colonialism, 176
  economics of penalty, 420, 421, 426
  ICOPA X on, 472, 476, 477, 484
  incarceration rate in, 4, 6, 11, 226, 255
  and penal abolition, 419, 422, 447, 448
  justice, models of, 7
  juvenile justice in, 12
  legal pluralism, 321
  and mentally ill, 267, 276, 278, 281, 283
  penal system, 3, 4, 419, 484
  prisons funding, 5, 247
  racism and sexism, 6, 37, 373, 419, 424, 427
  resistance through music, 372, 373, 374
  Supreme Court, 276
Universal Declaration of Human Rights (UDHR), 227, 281, 283
University College, Idaban, 89
University of Calabar, 87
University of Ibadan, 87, 91
University of Lagos, 86, 475, 476
UNSMR (United Nations Standard Minimum Rule for the Treatment of Prisoners), 277
UPGA (United Progressive Grand Alliance), 93, 94
US Bureau of Democracy, Human Rights, and Labor, 302
US Department of Homeland Security, 247
US Department of Justice, budget, 3–4
Usman, Y.B., 107

V

Valdes, Francisco, 321
van Swaaningen, René, 424, 425, 426, 427, 428, 441, 442, 450
Vijloen, F., 280
Voluntary Service Overseas (VSO), 167, 173

W

Wacquant, Loïc, 6, 249
Wahl, Hans, 389

Walker, Leonore, 232
Wall, Lewis L., 297, 300, 301, 304
Wamwere, Koigi wa, 235
War against Indiscipline (WAI), 108
Warri prison, 259
Weber, Max, 47, 103
Weisbrod, Carol, 320
Welch, Claude, 225
Welch, Michael, 421
Wenk-Ansohn, Mechthild, 238
Werthmann, Katja, 297, 299, 302–303, 304
West Africa Governance Team, 99
Western House of Assembly, 106
Western Nigeria, 106
WHR.net, 224
Winchmann, Clara, 424, 425, 426, 427, 441, 442
Winterwerp v. Netherlands, 270
Women, Law, and Development Centre, 85
Women Living under Muslim Laws, 226
Women Writing Africa, 224
Women's Rights Project of the Civil Liberties Organization, 86
Women's War against Colonialism in Eastern Nigeria, 109
Workshop on Comparing Experiences of Democratization in Nigeria and South Africa, 81
World Bank, 252, 263
World Conference on Women, 223, 225, 232
World Fact Book, 24, 295
Wu, Ruojie, 370, 371

X
X, Malcolm, 246
X v. United Kingdom, 273

Y
Yaba-Lagos, 159
Yar'Adua, General Shehu, 25, 251, 480
Yar'Adua, Umaru, 25, 480
Yau, Y.Z., 97–98
Yoruba
   ethnic conflict, 28, 95
   incarceration, 57
   influence, 26
   language, 29, 30, 364
   nation boundaries, 22
   population, 25, 295
   traditions, 363
Yorubaland, 26

Z
Zailani, Ibrahim, 474–475
Zambia, Legal Resources Foundation v., 282
Zamfara State, 229
Zangon Kataf, 97
Zaria prison, 59
Zaria State, 305
Zikists, 104, 108
Zimbabwe, 233, 387, 388–389, 390, 478
Zinacantan, 325

Printed and bound in Canada
by
for THE UNIVERSITY OF OTTAWA PRESS

Typeset in 9.5 on 12 Book Antiqua
by Brad Horning

Edited by Dallas Harrison
Proofread by Patrick Heenan
Indexed by François Trahan
Cover designed by Cathy Maclean

Printed by Tri-graphic Printing Ltd.
Printed on TG Eco 50 lb